Japanese Culture and Communication

Critical Cultural Analysis

Ray T. Donahue

University Press of America,® Inc.
Lanham • New York • Oxford

University Press of America,® Inc.
4501 Forbes Boulevard, Suite 200
Lanham, Maryland 20706

12 Hid's Copse Rd.
Cumnor Hill, Oxford OX2 9JJ

Printed in the United States of America
British Library Cataloging in Publication Information Available

Library of Congress Cataloging-in-Publication Data

Donahue, Ray T.
Japanese culture and communication : critical cultural analysis / Ray T. Donahue.
p. cm.
Includes index.
1. Communication and culture—Japan. 2. Communication—Cross-cultural studies. 3. Interpersonal communication—xCross-cultural studies. I. Title.
P94.65.J3D67 1998 302.2'0952—dc21 98-14195 CIP

ISBN 0-7618-1248-2 (cloth: alk. ppr.)
ISBN 0-7618-1249-0 (pbk: alk. ppr.)

™ The paper used in this publication meets the minimum requirements of American National Standard for Information Sciences—Permanence of Paper for Printed Library Materials, ANSI Z39.48—1984

To

My grandmother, Margaret Donahue Bottari,
Hisako Kushida, Ray F. Donahue, Eileen (Dolly) Donahue
and Martin Martinez, Marty and Sue Cleary, Tom O'Neill,
and as always, Noriko, Eugene, Ken, and Rene,
and the everlasting memory of my dear mother,
Stella T. Donahue

To

My grandmother, Margaret Donahue Bottari,
Hisako Kushida, Ray F. Donahue, Eileen (Dolly) Donahue
and Martin Martinez, Marty and Sue Cleary, Tom O'Neill,
and as always, Noriko, Eugene, Ken, and Rene,
and the everlasting memory of my dear mother,
Stella T. Donahue

フレン

Overleaf: The spring festival celebrated in Handa City, central Japan, is a centuries-old tradition and is highlighted by the pulling of huge wooden carts through the streets to ensure a bountiful rice harvest. The participants wear customary headbands to show their grit and determination. It is also a time of great inebriation and cups of sake are ever flowing. Sake, a colorless rice wine, is an important component of Shinto purification rites, so special potency, even wholesomeness, comes attached. Merriment arises that much easier. This distillation of the religious with enjoyment of the common everyday is but one of the many contrasts in store for the foreign observer in Japan.

Contents

Preface ix
Acknowledgments xi

Introduction: Rationale and Overview 1

1 Japan in World Perspective 11

Part I Barriers to Cross-cultural Understanding

2 Double Standards 53
3 Misattribution and the Mysterious Orient(al) Schema 71
4 Stereotypes, Cultural Elitism and Racism 89

Part II Japanese Communication Style

5 Aspects of Language and Society 119
6 Aspects of Language and Thought 161

Part III Contrastive Rhetoric Between Japanese and English

7 Rhetorical Issues and Cross-cultural Communications 193
8 A Functional Analysis 223
9 A Further Inquiry 241

Part IV Images of the Japanese in the Mass Media

10 Culture Clashes Between Japanese and North American TV Newscasters 283
11 An Ultimate Case for Japan Bashing 301

Notes 321
References 347
Index 371
About the Author 378

Preface

Japanese Culture and Communication represents my twenty years of living in Japan, more than half spent teaching intercultural communication in programs of Japanese studies there. My courses have aimed to develop critical analysis for viewing other cultures, and the study of Japan offers an ideal basis for doing so. Part of Japan's distinctiveness is that it appears both "Eastern" and "Western" but is neither. Isolated for centuries, Japan was able to develop its own traditions, even though it borrowed massively from both east and west. Because it borrowed selectively, Japan emerged as a hybrid culture—the Japanese civilization—as it is called.

This book is intended for students at any level in Japanese studies, as well as for students in communication studies or international studies. The latter fields apply because the book does not require prior training in the Japanese language or culture. The book has wide application because it addresses the process of interacting with Japanese culture, actually any foreign culture. This process involves perception: How do we perceive other cultures fairly and realistically while viewing them through the lens of our own culture? We probably cannot if that is our sole lens. Each of us interacts (or studies) via a mindset of beliefs, values, and attitudes derived largely from our own native culture. It hardly could be otherwise. We need to remove the lens of our own culture, if only momentarily, to understand other cultures. That requires, in my view, critical analysis of our own perceptions, in order to self-manage the ethnocentrism natural to all people.

The first part of the book develops an understanding of the perceptual barriers inherent to cross-cultural communications between Japan and North America. From this, the Japanese communication style is considered, as well as contrastive studies of discourse between Japanese and English. Lastly, images of the Japanese in the mass media are studied to demonstrate links between culture, media, and mind. Once cognizant of these links, students can begin to manage their own ethnocentrism, an attribute shared by all. At the same time, greater tolerance for cultural difference may develop and lessen susceptibility to culture shock.

Acknowledgments

In the course of this work, I have incurred many debts. My early work was guided by an insight gained through Clifford Hill of Columbia University, regarding the essential flexibility of discourse, as well as by John Fanselow, of the same institution, who gave me kind advisement and critical counsel in my preparation of *Japanese Non-linear Discourse Style*, published in 1990. During this period I also benefitted by the advisement from Hiroaki Yamashita, a professor of Japanese at Nagoya University, and from Yutaka Yutani, formerly of Kyoto Gaikokugo University. My wife, Noriko, helped me with translation and data collection and has continued to serve as a sounding board. My NGU colleagues Kazuo Kanzaki, Iwao Shinjo, and Miho Steinberg provided me with discussions on the Japanese language and culture.

During the same period, I also benefitted from discussions

with Nobuyuki Honna, Michael Horne, Tomoyasu Kimura, Paul LaForge, Seiya Matsumoto, Yoshihiko Ohmori, Roichi Okabe, Makoto Omi, Harumi Tanaka, and Takeshi Uemura. In regard to Japanese American and Hawaiian culture, which occurred incidentally as a topic during my studies, the following people were greatly informative: Wayne Kitagi, Cynthia Takayama, Faye Yamamoto, Dee Yamanashi, and Cheryl Yamashita.

I continued my study in the early 1990s at the University of Virginia, benefitting much from the advisement from my dissertation committee including the former Dean of International Studies there, Peter Hackett, as well as Harold Burbach, Michael H. Prosser, and Michiko Niikuni Wilson.

I wish to further acknowledge Michael Prosser for various collaborations together and our numerous discussions on intercultural and cross-cultural topics. Scholar, mentor, and friend, he has helped me much, for which I thank him.

During this later period in specific regard to Japan, I thank Michiko Niikuni Wilson, Bruce Abrams, Ray Gehani, and my NGU colleagues Ikumi Imani, Minori Itoh, Shigeki Suzuki, and Yoshikazu Yanagi for our discussions. I am also much appreciative to the following for their critical reading of the manuscript in its early or later versions: Jeffrey Blair, D. Ray Heisey, Michael L. Maynard, Michael Prosser, David Riggs, Hamid Saleem, and Michiko Wilson. I thank Noriko, my wife, for checking my Japanese. I also thank Albert Dudley for his computer advice and proofreading. Any error, omission, or other defect remains solely with me.

Last, but certainly not least, I thank NGU for the research grant in support of this work and the steadfast support received from two former NGU presidents, Professors Hisashi Kajiwara, and Hiromi Yokoi, as well as from Professors Ryôzo Sakai, Kiyoshi Shinkuma, and Nobumitsu Tsubota, who collectively were instrumental, along with my colleagues in the Faculty of Foreign Studies, for my being granted sabbatical leave to complete my doctoral studies. Although my doctoral work forms but a portion of this book, without my NGU colleagues' help this book would not have been.

Regarding copyrights, I thank the following for permission to reprint whole or in part some of my published work:

Bates L. Hoffer, Editor of *Intercultural Communication Studies,* which published "The mysterious Orient(al) schema: Images and attribution" IV:2, pp. 63-86, 1994, for use in Chapter 3;

Shirley A. Smith, Director, Copyrights and Permissions, Ablex Publishing Corp., which published "Functional versus structural approaches to discourse analysis" in Donahue, R. T. & Prosser, M. H., *Diplomatic Discourse: International Conflict at the United Nations*, 1997, for use in Chapter 8; and "Episodes in culture clash: Interactions between Japanese and North American TV newscasters," in Prosser, M. H. & Sitaram, K. S. (Eds.), *Multiculturalism and Global Understanding,* in press, for use in Chapter 10.

I also wish to thank the following for permission to reprint other copyrighted material:

Kimberley Arrington, Permissions Editor, The Washington Post, for "Hidden wall: A native son battles Japan's trade barriers," from *The Washington Post*, June 23, 1989, pp. G1, G10, for use in Chapter 11;

Staff at the Asahi Shimbun company for "Jogging for Health," from *Tensei Jingo Vox Populi Vox Dei,* vol. 37, p. 138, for use in Chapter 9;

Cecilia M. Fujii (Suzuki), a former editor of *Kokiku* magazine for permission to reprint "May Yokomoto: Japan, it's a lot of fun" from the same magazine for May 1977, p. 7, for use in Chapter 8;

Barbara Maxwell, Director, USA TODAY Library & Research Service, for "We will never stop looking for you," *USA Today,* international edition, October 23, 1990, p. 2A, for use in Chapter 5;

Robert Matthew for "The Secretary on the Shoulder," for use in Chapter 5.

Introduction: *Rationale and Overview*

Modern technology has provided unprecedented opportunities to communicate across national borders.[1] Telecommunications, travel, and personal computers offer various means of meeting people from other cultures, creating the potential for a "global village." Yet spiraling ethnic conflicts worldwide make this village seem more like a battleground, even in our own backyards, as social diversity mounts. How we handle this diversity will depend greatly on culture and communication: Both provide the "software" for personal and professional relations.[2] Culture tells us, at least in part, what to "see" and say, and how to do so. Studies on gender, for example, show that males and females are "programmed" by culture to speak and act in different ways.

The more our backgrounds differ, the more likely that we will communicate differently. Unfortunately, "perceived differences can create barriers—blind spots—trapping us with biases, misunderstanding, personal arrogance, and attributions labeled in various ways."[3] The first step toward overcoming such barriers is developing an awareness of the link between culture and communication. Such awareness has never been more important. A useful way of doing this is by studying Japanese culture and communication.

JAPAN'S "BI-CIVILIZATION"

Japan and the "West" differ in fundamental ways, largely because Japan has been "bi-civilized"[4] between east and west like no other country, creating a "hybrid culture."[5] Although Japan has shown an immense capacity to incorporate foreign elements, this incorporation has often had clear limits. Sharp distinctions are often made between Japanese and foreign things. Written Japanese, for example, uses separate written scripts for native Japanese and words of foreign origin. Thus the difference is institutionalized, and the distinction is perpetuated.

The Japanese genius for incorporation with limits has greatly advanced its culture. New technology and the associated language can be borrowed almost effortlessly because the foreign elements can be placed at a psychologically safe distance: Native identity need not be threatened. For example, when some young Japanese come to the United States and see a McDonald's restaurant, they may say, "Americans have the same things as we do!" In Japanese, the name is written in *katakana,* script used for foreign words:

マクドナルド (Makudonarudo).

Even though the original American name also appears in the Japanese locations, "McDonald's" is seen merely as a decoration, following the common use of English in Japanese commercial signs.

Japan: An Ideal Study

"The conscious Japanese effort at massive cultural borrowing," according to Edwin Reischauer, finds "no parallel" in western history.[6] In the course of this borrowing (and thus becoming bi-civilized) Japan underwent various phases of "incubation" or isolation to protect its stability. Its island position helped greatly in this regard. "Unlike many other island nations, Japan did not suffer military invasions from other countries,"[7] due to the perilous straits separating itself from the rest of Asia.[8] Except for sporadic periods of contact with China and Korea, and later the west, Japan was alone enough to adapt and integrate its cultural borrowing into a "set of characteristics more distinctive than almost any comparable unit of people in the world."[9] This distinctiveness was given further impetus by Japan's rulers in outlawing foreign contact from 1638 to 1853. About the same time, Japanese citizens were placed into a strict caste system, enforced in part, by sword-wielding *samurai*. As a result, the Japanese people developed a keen sense of social difference that may be keenest in regard to foreigners. This difference is not insurmountable; the Japanese continue to prove themselves a most hospitable people.

As a people, however they see themselves as unique, an attitude that some observers liken to a religious fervor. Although Japan may be similar in some ways to eastern or western culture, the Japanese celebrate their uniqueness and view their culture as unlike any other. Japan, then, offers an ideal basis for cross-cultural training. "For North Americans [situated] on the Pacific rim, Japan is the epitome of the 'Far East' and its seeming enigmas. Being aware of Japanese behavior will, at the very least, raise one's sensitivities when interacting with Chinese, Vietnamese, Cambodians, Polynesians, and the multitude of people in [Asia]."[10]

In addition, Japan's distinctiveness can stimulate insights about our own culture and personal views. It is no accident that Japan is frequently characterized as "paradoxical."[11] The title of a classic work, *The Chrysanthemum and the Sword*, suggests (intentionally or not) the militaristic and artistic traditions of the Japanese.[12] Every society or culture has its paradoxes, but Japan's "bi-civilization" or duality of experience, perhaps, lends itself more readily to such contradictions. The Japanese civilization offers a perceptual puzzle, for it raises in the minds of foreigners some intriguing questions: How can a nation with so few natural resources be so economically productive? How can it appear so economically powerful while sustaining a heavy national debt?[13] How can its culture be so "nature-conscious" and yet seem to have little regard for the environment? How can the society appear so orderly without obvious repression? How can many of the people profess to be atheistic and yet follow various religions? How can Japan appear so dynamic, and yet elect seemingly lackluster national politicians?[14] How can such a famously polite and considerate people appear to lack social consciousness and mannerly public behavior?

Such apparent paradoxes, however, are precisely to our

benefit. As one Italian observer stated, "if there were no Japan it would be expedient to invent one."[15] Winston Davis commented, "Contemporary Japan poses an intellectual challenge rarely encountered in area [cultural] studies."[16] The Japanese culture challenges our fundamental assumptions about life, society, and our ways of living, for which the anthropologist Robert A. Levine calls the "Japan problem."[17] "Japan presents [us] with a problem by presenting ... an alternative cultural pattern which clearly works well without conforming to what we believe to be 'normal, necessary, and adaptive.'"[18]

The State of Japanese Studies

The field of Japanese studies has been growing at an unprecedented rate along with increased attention to Japan, its people, and its culture. This attention is a direct result of Japan's increased importance in world affairs. This growth sparked a compilation by Harumi Befu and Josef Kreiner of reports from specialists in Japanese studies worldwide.[19] Befu and Kreiner were motivated by more than a desire for information; they made the valid assumption that the object of study would be viewed differently by various observers around the world. In area studies, no pair of cultures—that of the observer and the observed—is exactly the same.

Another factor motivating Befu and Kriener's work is that Japanese studies is undergoing a paradigm shift. The formerly dominant "group model" has had to make room for a modified, if not eclectic view. The group model "seeks to explain nearly all aspects of Japanese life in terms of 1. the value system [of principally harmony and conformity], 2. the homogeneity of the Japanese people, 3. the uniqueness of their culture, 4. the existence of a modal personality [statistically, the most frequently occurring type] based on ego-repression and dependent collectivism, and above all 5. the tendency to do nearly everything in groups."[20] Harumi Befu probably did more than anyone to engender debate about this model with an article of his published decades ago.[21] Others have since continued the debate. This shift in opinion is a natural outcome of developmental change both in Japan and in the field of Japanese studies. The shift does not negate the group model; rather, it seeks a more flexible view of Japan in light of the complexity involved. Given this dynamism, there is no better time to begin a study of Japan than the present.

JAPANESE CULTURE AND COMMUNICATION

Viewing Japan as a perceptual puzzle, I attempt here to offer a primer on cross-cultural training. Such training recognizes that learning usually involves both cognition and affect. Academic subjects may be studied in isolation, but the learner still may have mental associations involving attitudes, feelings, and even physiology. Study of a second language can induce stress because of the differences of foreign sounds, grammar, or vocabulary. Similarly, the study of foreign culture cannot begin with a "clean slate": We likely possess prior images, beliefs, and feelings about other cultures. The word *foreign* has certain connotations; some of these are negative: *strange, alien, outlandish, unfamiliar.*[22] One's native culture involves an innate belief in its superiority. How could it be otherwise? We simply prefer our own way of life—which represents our family, our collective. We feel most at home in our own culture. Consequently, encounters with foreign cultures involve not only the intellect but also attitudes, feelings, and emotions.

Cultural Difference: The Lack of Shared Scripts

Cultural difference, however slight, can trigger inappropriate attitudinal or emotional responses beyond our control. Just as familiar music may elicit instantaneous feelings, cultural differences may have an immediate effect. Humor, for example, is an area of difference between North Americans and Japanese. Both peoples enjoy humor, but they may use it differently. In the following exchange, two American teachers at a Japanese school pass each other in a hallway on their way to their respective duty as test proctors:

A: Ah, would you like to proctor a test?
B: Ah, how gracious of you to ask!
A: Well, that's what friends are for! [Both laugh.]

Although A and B felt positive about this conversation,[23] their Japanese colleagues did not. The Japanese could not understand that such exchanges can energize Americans in their work. As a result, each set of people thought less well of the other.

The difference is not that the Japanese are humorless; rather, the Americans were following an American cultural script or routine. Otherwise B would have taken A's question seriously; nor could they have synchronized their speech and emotions so quickly. The Japanese simply do not have this same script, especially for the "*sensei* on duty." Their script calls for "seriousness"—a solemn facial and bodily display. Yet the Japanese can become highly animated under different circumstances. It is a naive observer who does not understand this and stereotypes the Japanese as humorless.

A Principle of Cross-Cultural Training

This case of misunderstood humor illustrates a basic principle in cross-cultural training: "The greater the cultural or behavioral difference [between people], the greater is the potential for negative evaluations of the difference."[24] Such bias may lead to distortion in the form of exaggerated or stereotyped images because the basic ethic of culture is the belief that its own values and ways are superior. The problem of cross-cultural contact can be stated as involving an observer's misunderstanding of a foreign person, object, or event due to differences in worldviews. The term *worldview* refers to "a distinctive set of attitudes, beliefs, and values...[of] particular individuals or social groups."[25] Worldviews act as perceptual filters through which we experience the world around us. Misunderstandings may arise, for example, over gesture, silence, intonation, facial expression, spatial distance, or conversational routine.

A Preview

To encourage insights into Japan's culture and communication, and into our own, Chapter 1 lays the groundwork by locating Japanese culture among world cultures and by describing diversity within Japan itself. The rest of the book consists of four major parts:

- Barriers to Cross-Cultural Understanding (Chapters 2 to 4)
- Japanese Communication Style (Chapters 5 and 6)
- Contrastive Rhetoric Between Japanese and English (Chapters 7 to 9)
- Images of the Japanese in the Mass Media (Chapters 10 and 11)

Chapters 2 to 4 discuss the perceptual barriers to cross-cultural understanding in the form of double standards, social schemas, stereotypes, racism, and related issues. Chapters 5 and 6 examine aspects of the Japanese communication style, especially in regard to speech. For written communication, Chapters 7 to 9 explore an area of research known as contrastive rhetoric. This study is rather technical but deserves attention because it is closely related to logic or thought, a common area of cross-cultural misunderstanding. The final chapters involve mass media images of the Japanese and cross-cultural conflict. The mass media are important because they may be, for many people, the main way of learning about Japan. Chapter 10 includes a study of actual culture clashes between North American and Japanese telecasters during associated world-wide broadcasts, and the ethnocentric behaviors that ensue. Chapter 11 shows how stereotypes become the basis for an ultimate case for Japan bashing in the print media. These two chapters, along with Chapter 3, provide much cause for casting the mass media in critical view.

As a special feature, several short essays by foreign residents in Japan are included for added perspectives on the culture, as well as a Japanese science fiction story translated by Robert Matthew and an essay by Michiko Niikuni Wilson. The attempt is made to provide illustrative examples throughout. The illustration of Japanese behavior is a major objective here; if I achieve no more than that, the labor involved in this work will have proved worthwhile. Beyond that, I hope to stimulate in the reader a critical stance for exploring culture. "Knowing something" involves not just knowing what that something is. It also involves knowing what that something is not. Without the latter, "knowledge" becomes blindly applied.

Conventions Adopted

Terms. I follow such works as *Culture and Self*[26] (edited by Anthony J. Marsella, George DeVos, and Francis L. K. Hsu) by not capitalizing the terms for the *west* and the *east.* This practice may be a reminder that neither are monolithic; both are heterogeneous. Lack of capitalization also may help us detach ourselves from these categories.

Generally, *intercultural* and *cross-cultural* are treated synonymously here. *Logic* will be given in its informal or popular sense as involving consistency rather than mental ability. The plural form *logics,* as in *cultural logics,* may help maintain this sense and refers to preferred patterns or ways of reasoning. *Logics* is similar to *thought patterns* or *thinking styles* as used by others.

Japanese names. For the sake of readers, I give the names of Japanese according to English convention, family name last, except for literary figures whose names are already known by the regular Japanese order.

Japanese pronunciation. Vowels in Japanese differ according to dialect and range from three in the Yonaguni dialect of Okinawa to eight vowels in the Nagoya dialect.[27] Standard Japanese has five vowels; these are roughly equivalent to English sounds, as follows:

a (as in f**a**ther)
e (as in b**e**t)
i (as in **ea**t)
o (as in h**o**pe)
u (as in b**oo**t)

These are only approximations.[28] Depending on one's reference points—the particular dialect of English and of Japanese—the sound for [e] in Japanese falls between the English vowel sounds in *bet* and *bait.* The sound for [u] falls between the English vowel sounds in *boot* and *bull.*

Single consonants in Japanese attach themselves to the following vowel sound. Elongated consonants are shown by duplicated letters (e.g., *matte*), both of which are pronounced (e.g., *mat•te*). The consonant stop sound is also found in English as with *white tape* and *black kite.*[29] Vowel lengthening is shown by double vowels instead of a macron. Note that the lengthening of the vowel [o] is a matter of confusion because it typically occurs in Japanese script as [う], which at other times is pronounced [u]. Geographical names are given here in their common English spellings, which usually ignore vowel lengthening (e.g., *Tokyo* for *Tookyoo* とうきょう).

Confidentiality. Informants who are to remain anonymous are given assumed names and are marked by an asterisk.

Ethnicity. In many cases ethnicity (or nationality) of an individual may be pertinent to report. Where it concerns a non-Japanese and his or her ethnicity goes unreported however, it can be assumed to be American. One purpose of reporting the nationality or ethnicity is to indicate that the principles and concepts developed in this book can relate broadly to various peoples and not just to Americans.

Dialogues. Unless otherwise indicated, the dialogues presented are paraphrases of the actual Japanese or English.

1

Japan in World Perspective

To help place Japan in world perspective, I employ two conceptual dimensions: individualism-collectivism and high context-low context. (*Dimension* is applied here and throughout because individualism and collectivism, for example, are not just concepts but also a pair of countervailing phenomena that share a scope of relations between them.) To develop this perspective more fully, I then consider a persistent perceptual problem for westerners: how to distinguish between the Chinese and the Japanese. Then, I briefly consider Japan's internal diversity through regional and social differences, and conclude by discussing Japanese homogeneity and how it is misunderstood in cross-cultural comparison.

INDIVIDUALISM-COLLECTIVISM

"A number of researchers have argued that one of the most important factors in a culture is the relative emphasis placed on individualism and collectivism."[1] Individualist cultures emphasize the individual over the social group; collectivist cultures, the reverse. One psychologist calls these two concepts "me" and "we" thinking, respectively.[2]

Although individualism and collectivism can be found in all cultures, one generally prevails over the other. Individualism is predominant in "North America and Western Europe, and [in] countries strongly influenced by these areas, such as Australia and New Zealand"; collectivism, in most others.[3] In general, Japan and the United States are almost diametrically separated on this dimension, while European nations fall somewhere between.[4]

Individualism and collectivism, however, are not mutually exclusive;[5] both elements are present in all cultures and may exist independently in the human personality.[6] Japan is considered collectivistic but has individualistic features as well. In the Japanese company, for example, benefits may include help in finding a spouse, home loans, and liberal maternity leave; these benefits show collective values (cooperative help) while serving the needs of the individual.

Marriage, for example, has traditionally been viewed by the Japanese more as an arrangement between families than between the individuals themselves. Even today, Japanese who seek a *renai* (love marriage), as opposed to an arranged union, seek their parents' blessings. Sometimes the parents object, and the wedding takes place only through strong personal will. For some of these persons, Frank Sinatra's song "My Way," became a personal theme and was played at their wedding reception. In cases when the parents are not won over, the pair may elope to Hawaii, a popular honeymoon destination.

In the Japanese business world, transfers are a common occurrence for salaried workers. Over the years, however, upper management has found that these workers have required different reasons. During the years immediately following World War II, the rationale was "Do it for Japan." For the next generation of workers, it became "Do it for your family." More recently, however, it has increasingly been "Do it for yourself." Thus, although Japan remains collectivistic, we must not assume that its people do not think for themselves. Westerners are prone to overdraw the notion that the Japanese are highly conformist, as in this comment by a social scientist:

> In response to standard public opinion survey questions about subjective social class, fully 90 percent of the Japanese regularly identify themselves as middle class—a finding that

> seems almost incredible from a western perspective. In part, this may be one more indication of the strength of group solidarity in Japan....[7]

This view of a Japanese "subjective middle class" is widely held but wholly misinformed. The frequency of claims to membership in the "middle class" is no greater in Japan than in western societies. Consequently the Japanese response rate deserves little notice.

Nearly all Americans, despite their strong sense of individualism, consider themselves "middle class."[8] Peter Francese, president of American Demographics, Inc., states:

> In random sample surveys taken over long periods of time, 95 percent of Americans say, "I'm middle class." Almost no one admits to being upper class or not middle class. People—Americans—want to be middle class.[9]

Europeans also respond in like fashion.[10]

The contemporary American perception of being "middle class," not the Japanese perception, deserves attention because the United States "has become the most economically stratified" society in the industrialized world.[11] "Income gap between corporate presidents and average workers in Japan is around 17 to 1, in contrast to an 85 to 1 gap in the United States."[12] Japan happens to have "the most equal distribution of income among industrialized countries."[13] Thus, the Japanese have a stronger basis for assuming themselves to be "middle class" than do Americans. Although this example does not negate the characterization of Japan and the United States as respectively collectivist and individualist, it does suggest the need for care in applying such concepts.

HIGH CONTEXT-LOW CONTEXT

Whereas the dimension of individualism-collectivism involves culture in a broad and fundamental way, high context-low context concerns communication more specifically. Cultures can be distinguished by their degree of reliance on direct verbal language. High context refers to communication whose meaning derives more from previous mental knowledge and/or contextual cues than from verbal messages. In Japanese speech, in contrast to English, personal pronouns (*I, you*) are generally avoided (though not totally); this encourages a collectivistic sentiment. The omission of sentence subjects, which can be as frequent as 74 percent,[14] also requires greater use of contextual cues: Low-context communication predominates in individualistic cultures while high-context communication does so in cultures collectivistic.[15]

As a prominent psychologist remarked, "Japanese non-verbal communication has a greater degree of subtlety than elsewhere."[16] A Japanese host, for example, when placing a dining utensil or the like in front of a guest, is likely to gently flex her wrist just after setting the object down. This wrist motion is a sign of refinement and is a nonverbal correlate of "Here you are," a message most often left unspoken. Whereas American servers (especially in the home) usually declare verbally whom they are serving ("This is for you"; "Here's your milk"), Japanese generally do not. Similarly, business cards (*meishi*) and ceremonial documents are grasped not in one hand but in two. This "doubling," which indicates respect, is also observed with ceremonial bowing and even head nodding during everyday speech. Consequently one learns to be more attentive to Japanese nonverbal cues, as is necessary in a high-context culture. High-context cultures are generally thought to include (in descending order) Japanese, Chinese, Korean, and Arab; low-context cultures, also in descending order, are Swiss, German, North American, English, and French. Intermediate on this dimension are African culture and Latin culture.[17]

Although Japan shares much with its Asian neighbors, it is actually quite separate, as symbolically represented by its island status. Moreover, in recent history, it has tended to identify with the highly industrialized nations of the west. Ultimately, however, Japan remains solitary, as exemplified by its myth of uniqueness (see Chapter 4). This sense of separateness, if not uniqueness, was identified in numerous cross-cultural studies, whose respondents combined totaled 112,000 worldwide.[18] Based on this data, Japan was placed not among eastern or western countries but in an independent category.[19] This placement can be explained by Japan's bi-civilization, described in the previous chapter.

These studies were limited by the absence of mainland China but included other Chinese areas (such as Taiwan and Hong

Kong). Thus it is likely that if mainland China had been included, it too would have been placed with other east Asian cultures. Identifying such distinctiveness between Japan and China may prove helpful because the two countries are sometimes confused: A CNN news broadcast repeatedly referred to the Japanese emperor as the "Emperor of China" during his recent visit to the United States.[20] In addition, some Americans think that dog is a Japanese delicacy[21] or that the binding of women's feet was formerly a Japanese practice. Both beliefs are false stereotypes about Japan.

Ignorance about Japan is not exclusively American. When I taught in China, I was struck by the similarity of certain Chinese stereotypes of Japanese. Nor would I excuse Europeans, though they may come to Japanese studies with a relatively sophisticated view about language and culture. Cultural conflict and human misperception are universal problems; no one is completely immune from the influences of ethnocentrism. The sooner we admit this reality, the sooner we can manage our perceptions.

ASIAN DIVERSITY: CHINESE VERSUS JAPANESE CULTURE

Given the confusion about China and Japan, it is rather revealing that few books or articles distinguish between the two cultures. Many works treat the economic or political aspects, but hardly any distinguish between their cultural characteristics. My information on this matter first came from an American in Korea, born there of missionary parents and raised there, who described his view of the Koreans and the Japanese. Through this description one can perceive the Chinese, for the three countries have a triangular relationship. (The three countries are obviously close geographically, but they also have mutually influenced each other, with China and Korea having had an enormous influence on Japan in early history, which has somewhat reversed direction over the past century. Their histories are interwoven leaving complex emotions between them in the present.) My acquaintance told me (though we must take his comment with a grain of salt) that his parents and others spoke of Koreans as the "Irish of Asia,"[22] and the Japanese as the "English." He explained that Koreans were known to be outgoing and direct, an impassioned people.

Because of the Koreans' historical subjugation by the Japanese, a neighboring island people, this metaphor seems somewhat applicable. If so, would the Chinese be the "French of Asia"? After all, the Chinese have an extraordinary view of their own culture, as do the French, and Chinese culture historically has been considered "high culture" by some of its neighbors. That idea hardly applies today, however, especially in Japan. (Actually, some Japanese say that Americans would be a better parallel than the French because of their informality.) This analogy with Europe is simply a thumbnail sketch, but it gives some sense of their differences. Below, David Riggs shares his impressions of the Chinese and the Japanese:

The Chinese and the Japanese: How They Differ

David Riggs

David Riggs, an American, is currently an English-language instructor at the Kanazawa Institute of Technology in Kanazawa, Japan. Besides a master's degree in ESL (English as a second language), he has had extensive training in Japanese, including an M.A. He has held various Japanese-language positions as teacher, translator, and tour guide. In addition to living in Japan for many years, he served for a year as an instructor of English at a college in mainland China.

As someone who has taught in both China and Japan, I would say that the single greatest difference between the two peoples is how they express themselves. Even though politically China is a communist state, and some would even call it a police state, the Chinese people whom I came into contact with were very friendly and open, willing to share personal information, even if you were not necessarily a close friend. For example, a Chinese might show you pictures of his or her family without you even asking, but a Japanese would be much less likely to do so. In general, I sensed in the Japanese a certain inwardness, whereas the Chinese share more of their personal selves with others. Why does this personal difference between the two peoples exist? One reason may be that the Japanese, being an island people and having lived in densely populated conditions, have developed behavioral patterns over many years to protect their individual privacy as compensation for the relative overcrowding.

In this sense, I felt that the Chinese are similar to Americans, who are often characterized as being "open and informal." This may explain why many Chinese are attracted to Americans and the American style of life. This contrasts with the Japanese, who are from a much smaller and more highly disciplined society. Japanese, in general, are more controlled in how they interact with others outside of their immediate family or close friends. Japanese tend to be quiet and less forthright with people who are on unfamiliar grounds.

The Chinese are rather vocal and boisterous in comparison with the more reserved Japanese. I base this observation on the difference I noticed in classrooms in China and Japan. When I taught English at the Beijing Second Foreign Language Institute from August 1984 to August 1985, one of the problems I experienced in the classroom during free discussion period was actually trying to quiet my Chinese students down when the conversation became too animated! The Chinese seem to love nothing better than to express themselves. They appear more outgoing—both men and women. This contrasts sharply with Japanese students, who are notorious among English teachers for being quiet in class and not speaking out. This was not a problem in China because it took my students there very little to get them going in active conversations. In Japan, however, more effort is needed to get Japanese students to speak. Perhaps this is due to their relatively poorer command of English, but it may also be due to a social ideal for reticence. The Japanese have an expression for it—*deru kui wa utareru*—which means that "the stake that sticks out will be hammered down." This cultural belief likely puts a damper on free expression. As a result, Japanese tend to avoid standing out from others, preferring, in many cases, the security of the group. A distinctly cultural component restrains Japanese students from being more outspoken during classroom discussions.

The *ijime* (bullying) problems that have surfaced in

Japanese schools recently are a direct manifestation of the fact that the Japanese students are taught conformity in schools, particularly in junior high schools and high schools, and those students who refuse to conform and continue to stand out become the objects of scorn and contempt by their peers. I believe that the bullying problem in Japan demonstrates a lack of tolerance for those who are different. It is an indication of the high degree of homogeneity and conformity of Japanese contemporary society.

Another situation I recall is when I invited Japanese and Chinese guests, on separate occasions, to my hotel swimming pool in China. The Japanese, who were exchange students in China, were quite subdued the entire afternoon, while the Chinese, who consisted of my school colleagues, were happy and lively, joking and laughing a lot during their stay. Once again, I was made to realize the differences in national characters between the Japanese and the Chinese.

I could also see differences between the Japanese and Chinese national characters in large discussion groups or meetings. The Chinese are more individualistic in the way that they express themselves than are the Japanese. Chinese people tend to voice their opinions frankly and without reservation when they think they have something important to contribute to the discussion. Chinese meetings, therefore, often take on the atmosphere of American faculty meetings where many people strongly voice their individual opinions. This is in stark contrast with a normal Japanese meeting where a strict agenda is followed and formalities are more easily observed. For example, at the Kanazawa Institute of Technology, where I currently teach, our faculty meetings follow an agenda very closely and move along with an almost ruthless efficiency. This can also be observed at smaller faculty meetings. Japanese teachers are generally considerate of those who have the floor, and the overall exchange of opinions has a greater orderliness than is true in China. This is probably a reflection of group dynamics in Japan, where people seek a greater degree of group consensus than is the case in either China or in the United States. It is also said in Japan that major decisions are often made prior to the formal meeting. This also could explain the lack of genuine debate in Japanese meetings. In general, the Japanese people seem a lot more self-restrained than do the Chinese.

These social differences are likely rooted in the early

years of Japanese education, in kindergarten and elementary school. From what I have read, early Japanese education does not emphasize academics so much as it emphasizes cooperation between small children. Young Japanese children are taught to cooperate with their fellow students from a very young age. The children are also taught to respect the opinions of other students in their class. These attitudes undoubtedly carry over into adult life, and explain why Japanese, in general, tend to be good listeners and do not interrupt those who are speaking.

Another difference that I observed between the Chinese and the Japanese is their degree of sophistication. In general, I think that it is safe to say that the Chinese people are a much more "earthy" people than the Japanese. By "earthy" I am referring to the basic manners, mannerisms, etiquette, and personal attire of the individual. Over the years my family in the United States has hosted various guests from both China and Japan in our suburban home near Albany, New York. Once my mother remarked how much "earthier" the Chinese seemed as compared with the Japanese. Some examples of earthiness would be the informality in which many Chinese people dress and talk, even with people newly acquainted. The Chinese people, in general, are much less concerned with niceties and formalities than are the Japanese. Consequently, my mother found it easier to relate to the Chinese.

The Japanese, by comparison, seemed more reserved and polite. After reflecting on my one-year residence in China, I tend to agree. One possible explanation of the difference in national character can likely be attributed to the degree to which the countries are developed. Japan is smaller and more highly urbanized, industrialized, and ritualized as a society, whose consumers are perhaps the most sophisticated in the world in terms of their tastes and preferences. China, on the other hand, is a large continental nation now undergoing rapid industrialization, whose consumers are increasingly becoming more sophisticated in their tastes as their country becomes materially richer. In other words, as a nation becomes more economically developed and materially advanced, the tastes of the people become more sophisticated and demanding. Consequently, the more unsophisticated, or "earthy," aspects of their national character begin to slowly disappear.

Up to this point I have painted the Chinese as a more open

people than the Japanese. Paradoxically, however, during my one year in Beijing I found the Chinese people to have a secretive aspect to their character that I didn't discover in the Japanese. When I was working as an English teacher at the Beijing Second Foreign Language Institute (in Chinese, "Er Wai"), I was often asked by Chinese students and colleagues for advice about studying and living in the United States. Many of my Chinese colleagues at Er Wai had lived in the United States previously, or planned to study in the United States in the future, so I became a convenient sounding board regarding living and studying conditions in my native country. I was happy to offer whatever constructive advice I could.

I thought it curious, however, that most of the Chinese who asked for my assistance didn't want other people to know that I was helping them. They instructed me to keep silent about the fact that they were planning to study in America. I thought this interesting because I had never experienced such behavior in Japan. The Chinese do not have a free society as found in Japan and the United States. Citizens in Japan and the US can travel freely anywhere in the world as long as they have the time and money. While Chinese people can travel freely within the borders of their own country, they often faced strict visa restrictions when they wanted to travel abroad. They simply could not travel freely as can Americans and Japanese.

Restricted personal freedom and limited domestic opportunities have encouraged the Chinese people to develop certain survival instincts unnecessary in freer societies. China has made enormous economic progress since reforms were instituted by Deng Xiao Ping in the late 1970s, but its government still watches closely over its citizens. Under the watchful eyes of government, a Chinese must be careful in whom he or she confides, which explains the greater role of trust in Chinese society than in freer societies like ours. The secrecy that the Chinese sometimes insist on is, in my opinion, not so much an intrinsic part of the Chinese character as it is a reflection of the political realities there. Because opportunities for foreign travel and free expression are more limited in China, it was remarkable that motivation to study English was so strong. I found this level of motivation missing in my Japanese students, most of whom had only general purposes for studying English. The Chinese students I had, however, were specialists with specific aims. Japanese people also can travel anywhere at any time, but the Chinese cannot, and I think this explains the extraordinary awareness and effort I witnessed in my Chinese students. The opinions above represent some of my general impressions of the differences between the two peoples. I use the word *general* because I believe that there will always be exceptions to the rule. For example, not all Chinese are "individualistic" and not all Japanese are "group-oriented." My thoughts reflect general trends or tendencies that I witnessed in the Chinese and the Japanese peoples. There are also many other differences in customs, but I thought that in the realm of personal expression lay the greatest cultural gap.

Superiority-Inferiority Complex

Alex Kerr, also a student of both cultures, concurs with Riggs's description: "In my experience, a Japanese is much less likely to say or do the unexpected than a Chinese; whatever he may think, he is more likely to do what the rules tell him to do. [The subordination of one's individual being in favor of society] is psychologically what the tragic Kabuki loyalty plays are all about."[23] Chisako Hirakawa, a colleague of mine, repeated to me what she once heard from a Korean observer: This perceived difference is at least partly due to national identity. The Chinese are at home with their national identity; the Japanese, much less so.[24] As Kerr points out,

> The Chinese have published very few books endorsing the Chinese equivalent of "theories of Japaneseness".... [A]s is evident from China's very name—Chung Kuo (the Middle Kingdom)—the Chinese are firmly convinced that their country lies at the center of the earth. Until very recently, China bestowed its culture on neighbors such as Vietnam, Korea and Japan, but received very little in return.... Consequently, the Chinese take their superiority for granted. It is the air they breathe, so there is no need to prove it to themselves or others.
>
> Japan, in contrast, was always on the receiving end of cultural imports from other countries, and deep in their hearts, the Japanese are haunted by a sense of insecurity about their [national] identity. [A great deal of its development was rooted in borrowing from others—China, Korea, and later the west.]

> People [also] are constantly made aware of the relations of superiority and inferiority..., [a] thought pattern [made a] reflex.[25]

I first heard of this superiority-inferiority complex through Richard K. Beardsley, and I have found it applicable over the years: superiority toward Asia; inferiority toward the United States and the west.[26]

The depth of this feeling seems apparent with a diary entry made by a leading Japanese novelist when hearing of Japan's successful military attack on Pearl Harbor:

> [The news] entered my pitch-dark room like a shaft of light. The announcement was joyfully repeated twice. As I listened, I felt I had become a new man, as though a flower petal stirred in my breast, cooled by the sacred breath of a deity. After this morning Japan had become a new country too....
>
> It is remarkable how hostile one can feel towards people whose eyes and hair are of a different color. I want to beat them to death. This feels quite different from fighting against China. The very idea of those insensitive American savages treading on our beautiful Japanese soil is unbearable.... Oh, beautiful Japanese soldiers, please go ahead and smash them![27]

As Ian Buruma observes, "The [Japanese] war in China, brutal and apparently endless, was an embarrassment; the war against the 'Anglo-Saxon oppressors,' the 'Anglo-American devils,' was a righteous explosion of pent-up feelings of inferiority and frustration, the revenge for countless slights and humiliations, imagined or real, personal or national, or, as was usual, a combination of both."[28] These feelings were not simply a matter of the then international conflicts but were rooted since Perry's forced opening of Japan and its subsequent treatment by western powers as an underling. These feelings were further deepened by the Japanese defeat in World War II and its dependence on the United States for security if not, its full economic recovery.

Karen Ma, a Chinese author, recently made the same point:

> Japan as a hierarchical society, appears more than other nations to venerate nations perceived as being above her and disdains those perceived as being below her. Perhaps this, as well as Japan's self-imposed mission to compete with the west, is behind her dual attitude toward the world—revering the west

and disdaining the east.[29]

Such generalizations, though, do have limits. Ma also reports an observation by a Japanese writer: The Japanese, when referring to themselves in English, follow the custom in English by placing their family name last; whereas the Chinese and the Koreans do not do so, although they also place the family name first in their own languages. He explains, "While the Japanese felt the need to appease westerners, they made a deliberate distinction between themselves and Asians. This shows an inferiority complex on the one hand, and a superiority complex on the other."[30]

I disagree on this point. The Japanese accommodation to English norms when using English may have little to do with an inferiority complex; instead it seems a practical application of "When in Rome, do as the Romans do." Of course, this case involves not a place but linguistic space. If the Japanese did not accommodate, native speakers of English would likely mistake their names. The same happens in reverse when a foreigner uses Japanese: The family name is presumed to come first, so the foreigner finds that it is expedient to follow the custom. Does this mean that the foreigner has an inferiority complex? As is so often the case, we must not generalize too broadly.

The formality suggested by Riggs of the Japanese visitors to the United States may be due to several factors. One is the precariousness of Japanese national identity as mentioned above. I can imagine that some Japanese in the past may have been in awe when first visiting the United States—the source for some of Japan's industrialization. As one Japanese visitor remarked, the American lifestyle seemed, at one time, like "science fiction," with its superhighways, high-rise buildings, and large home appliances.[31] Even today, she says, it remains a "dream country" for her and for many Japanese because of the relatively comfortable lifestyle.[32]

Mannerly Restraint (*enryo*)

Another factor is *enryo*, a mannerly restraint or reserve, what non-Japanese often find is a particular problem interculturally with the Japanese.[33] According to Japanese custom, guests must show some restraint before partaking of food or drink. A host shows reserve by disparaging his or her offerings even if exquisite. This etiquette, if applied to speech with outgroup members (e.g., non-Japanese), can have ill-effects. When the Japanese Nobel prize winner for literature in 1968 was asked at a press conference in Stockholm about his winning the prize, all he said was "Well, that's a difficult question" and stared off into space. Viewers at home in Japan, however, were moved by what they thought was his great display of modesty and politeness.[34]

Restraint or reserve historically has been a Japanese ideal, as the historian Mark Borthwick explains:

> The [Japanese] masses had been trained to be obedient and work hard during the centuries of feudal rule. Lafcadio Hearn made this observation about their tradition of obedience: "The probable truth is that the strength of the government up to [the early twentieth century] has been chiefly due to the conservation of ancient methods, and to the survival of the ancient spirit of reverential submission." Hearn goes on to comment about the great sacrifices willingly made by the people and their unswerving obedience "as regards the imperial order to acquire western knowledge, to learn western languages, to imitate western ways."
>
> Undeniably the Japanese have always been a well-disciplined, industrious, and energetic people; and unlike people living in extremely impoverished countries, hard work enabled them to survive. These qualities should not, however, be considered as having given the Japanese an edge over the Chinese because the latter were also extremely diligent and industrious. Nevertheless, it is true that the Chinese were probably less regimented than the Japanese because they were not ruled by a sword-bearing military class that was ready to cut down any commoner who stepped out of line. The virtues of hard work, thrift, self-discipline, obedience, and selfless service had been instilled in the Japanese people by the edge of the sword.[35]

Japanese observers make similar interpretations as illustrated by the title of a book recently published by two Japanese scholars: *Tokugawa Japan: The Social and Economic Antecedents of Modern Japan*.[36] The Tokugawa period (1604-1868) was known for its caste system, in which the classes were ranked in the order of warrior, peasant, artisan, and merchant; Borthwick calls this period "a feudal version of the modern police state."[37]

Though such conditions in Japan have long since passed, certain habits die hard. For example, politeness is a characteristic of the Japanese noted by early and present-day visitors. (Arthur Basnayake, a Nagoya Gakuin University colleague of mine and a former Sri Lankan ambassador to Japan, confirmed this point, based on his many diplomatic posts throughout the world.) Bowing, a practice distinctively Japanese among the major nations now that China has given it up, is likely to have gained its impetus in a caste system such as that of the Tokugawa period. Habits formed in such a system also may speak to the famed Japanese diligence and social order:

> The one area in the world where, like no other, the Japanese can be compared to other ethnic groups is Hawaii. Japanese [American] achievements compare well with those of the other twelve ethnic groups in the islands. Japanese [Americans] comprise only 27 percent of the population. Yet the government [has been] largely Japanese [American] with … [as much as] 75 percent of the state legislature being [ethnic] Japanese. Also 90 percent of all schoolteachers and 60 percent of all plant managers [were or still are] Japanese [American]. They are at the bottom among the ethnic groups in the divorce rate, in juvenile delinquency, and in families on welfare.[38]

The Samurai *Metaphor*

The Japanese offer a *samurai* metaphor that they themselves voice as an explanation. They sometimes explain employer-employee relations through this metaphor—the lord and his vassal. The vassal gives total devotion to the lord, who then may dispense benefits. Such material can be a rich source of jokes, but I have heard enough serious renditions of this theme to take it as a metaphor still pertinent to the Japanese.

I have a video clip of a Japanese sports announcer, for a college all-star football game between Japan and the "United States" (actually American Ivy League schools), explaining how a certain Japanese player's toughness had displayed *samurai-izumu* ("*samurai-ism*"). Perhaps because this game was associated with some of America's leading educational institutions, the announcer invented an erudite-sounding term for his Japanese audience. His term was an obvious historical metaphor for explaining present behavior; an American might use a cowboy metaphor in similar fashion. American sports figures, for example, are seen as "gunslingers" coming for a "shoot-out." Because "Cowboys" is the official name of an established team, sports commentators may be less likely to use the metaphor, so it may be found more in spheres outside of sports. In politics, for example, some American presidents have been likened to a cowboy, such as Ronald Reagan or George Bush.[39]

Another example of the cowboy metaphor comes from a TV program titled *Great Country Inns,* during a visit to the Woodstock Resort (Vermont), said to be located in a "fairy tale New England village." The host Susan Hunt, while sitting down for breakfast there, says to the audience, "I'm a hungry cowgirl."[40] Her statement is particularly interesting because this "fairy tale village," or former colonial settlement, could not be more remote from an Old West setting. It also shows how the cowboy metaphor can be gender neutral.

Samurai, however, is probably less extensive in Japanese discourse than what cowboy is in English. The *samurai* metaphor, though available, is not ever present in the Japanese mind. The fact that the Japanese football announcer may have coined *samurai-izumu* suggests a built-in limitation, namely newness. Its use may be associated most often with themes drawing contrasts with foreigners. Senko K. Maynard corroborates the idea that the *samurai* metaphor "still lives on" in contemporary Japan, but she illustrates this point with a Japanese TV commercial that happens to be based on a contrastive foreign theme.[41] A question arises as to what extent this metaphor operates in Japanese discourse and under what circumstances. The metaphor would have less relevance if it were evoked mainly by the presence of foreigners, foreign themes or contrasts. Although the *samurai* metaphor may be applicable at the level of individual, it may be limited to Japanese males. A metaphor with potentially wider application is the *iemoto.*

The **Iemoto** *Metaphor*[42]

Iemoto refers to a hierarchical order based on devotion to a venerated leader or founder. *Iemoto* also refers to such a leader; as a written word, it consists of the Japanese ideographic characters for "house" (*ie*) and "beginning" (*moto*): "start of the lineage." Thus, the leader is not merely a leader but the source for the whole organization, past and present. *Iemoto*, as an organizational style, has gained its fullest expression in schools for traditional arts such as tea ceremony, flower arranging (*ikebana*), calligraphy, and music (e.g., *koto*, a traditional string instrument). Each school has its own method for the practice of these arts, which are carried on and taught by associated *iemoto* and their licensed teachers. Students can earn a series of certificates of training, and, perhaps, even a license to teach. The training, however, requires years, considerable financial investment by the student, and an unswerving willingness to practice the art precisely in keeping with the *iemoto's* dictates.

Such training is popular because of the *gakureki shakai* "diploma society" in which certificated accomplishments of many kinds attest to one's character (or alternatively said, a diploma has more value than one's "real ability").[43] This is especially true among females seeking arranged marriages (*omiai*). Accomplishment in the traditional arts suggests personal discipline and refinement of character, as well as the potential for financial stability. Refinement and discipline, of course, are traditional ideals for the female. Also, if she is a licensed teacher of the traditional arts, she can teach from her own home, producing additional income for her *ie* (household). Demand for instruction is such that teaching would be a realistic prospect. Today, although arranged marriages account for only one-fourth of all new marriages,[44] the traditional arts are still much in favor and offer their followers potential financial rewards.

The significance of the *iemoto* is that the organizational network is built on the leader's authority, which parallels the basic infrastructure of Japanese society, according to the anthropologist, Francis L. K. Hsu.[45] The *iemoto* network could involve thousands of persons through licensed arrangements, as well as devotion to the master's way. In the larger society, pride and persistence for a skilled craft or service are greatly respected. Take, for example, a Japanese cook who operates a small corner Chinese restaurant in Nagoya City that appears to be a "greasy spoon," though it is widely known for its good food. His restaurant consists of a counter surrounding a small grill. Once when a Japanese customer told the cook and proprietor to go lightly with the salt in preparing his food, the cook took that request as an insult and refused him service. In a similar vein, a coffee shop in the same city operated under the peculiar name of *Stubborn*, which could be understood as "stubborn for quality." Similarly, a restaurant currently operates under the name of *Ganko Tei* ("stubborn house"). At school, *kibishii* ("strict"), in reference to teachers, usually has positive connotations. The Japanese show an expectation, even a willingness for arduous training; that is how they believe people develop their character. Thus the master, the teacher, the *sensei*, the company president receive great respect.

Although corporal punishment is illegal in Japan, I once saw a high school basketball coach pull several players from a private game (held behind closed doors) and slap each of their faces, right on the sideline. Or in a TV documentary on management training by an entrepreneur, the master resorted to slapping a trainee's face for insubordination. Further, an American teacher of English to preschoolers was told by a little girl's father, on the first day, to slap her if need be. (His intent was probably more symbolic than literal.) Such cases seem out of character for the Japanese because they generally avoid public displays of negative emotion. Yet such cases occur because of the great respect given authority figures. However, my own children, who attend Japanese public schools, say that they have seen only one such case. My wife says that she had never seen it as a student. Also, few of my college students have seen this behavior in their previous schooling beyond one or two instances. Unfortunately, comparative data appear not to exist about this issue. The Japanese, however, would probably accept such behavior by a teacher or employer more than would Americans, if the Japanese teacher or employer had a good reputation. Such acceptance is made more likely by the potential benefits of being under the master's tutelage. In other words, acceptance is not followed blindly, as long as certain advantages accrue. Within these boundaries, *iemoto* thinking has helped the Japanese to create a highly orderly and productive society.

Shyness

A personal ideal of the *samurai* was personal reserve. This still may be viable for some, according to research by Philip G. Zimbardo. Zimbardo, a pioneer in the study of shyness, found that it was more prevalent among Japanese than among other

Asians, and all other cultures he tested.[46] (Zimbardo, however, did not test the Finnish, people also known to be particularly shy.) Unlike members of other cultures, some Japanese (though not all) viewed shyness as a desirable quality. Among the mainland Chinese, in contrast, shyness appeared to be much less frequent. Unlike Japanese, Taiwanese, or other Asian groups, the Chinese had "been able to effectively prevent the devastating effects of shyness."[47] Zimbardo explained that in China "individual potential is not suppressed by group domination, but enhanced by sharing in the pride and common achievements of the group.... 'Friendship first, competition second' [is a common motto there]."[48] Perhaps more significantly, failure in that country is thought to be due more to "bad social conditions and external conditions" than to "defects in the individual."[49]

When I was in mainland China, I soon noticed that the Chinese tended to come closer physically and to engage in more touching than the Japanese. Staff members, even the women, stood or sat with me to the point of touching, when giving information. At other times, I had conversations in which the Chinese touched my arms for emphasis. I never had experienced such closeness or touching from Japanese in similar situations. In one scene from an old movie on TV about the Chinese revolution, male soldiers held each other in a jubilant moment and looked deeply into each other's eyes. Then they rubbed their faces cheek to cheek and embraced each other again. It would be hard to find a comparable scene in a Japanese movie.

Although Zimbardo did not directly survey mainland Chinese, anecdotal reports led him to conclude that shyness would not be prevalent there. It remains to be seen, however, if mainland Chinese collectivism can prevent the negative effects on social integration due to heavy industrialization and increasing urbanization. Japan followed a breakneck schedule in trying to achieve western levels of technology and development; it is hard to imagine that this high-powered economic drive had no effect on the culture's system of social rewards and penalties. With higher expectations for economic growth, individuals might be held to higher expectations from others. In this regard, one might be held more personally responsible than under traditional Chinese beliefs. Future mainland Chinese could find themselves not much better off than their Taiwanese and Japanese counterparts in preventing the growth of debilitating shyness.

Clannishness

Another factor related to shyness that particularly pertains to the Japanese is clannishness. "Until [the Japanese] feel that they have joined as 'ingroup' members, many feel communicatively inhibited; they remain silent, however much their hosts may try to 'make them speak."[50] At various times, for example, at the open house at my children's kindergarten, in Nagoya, the fathers often sat together in complete silence while their wives were busy helping with school activities. These fathers were unacquainted with each other and largely remained that way. Compared to North Americans, Japanese receive far less practice in meeting and becoming acquainted with strangers. Japanese families only rarely, if at all, entertain guests at home, so children get little experience in socializing with strangers that way. When they become adolescents, they are more discouraged than encouraged to date members of the opposite sex. Given the astounding statistic that "95 percent of Japanese highschoolers test at a level achieved only by [America's] top 5 percent,"[51] Japanese schoolchildren obviously must pay a price, most likely with their free time. With fewer opportunities to socialize, a cultural ideal for restraint, and group clannishness, it is not surprising that shyness would be especially prevalent among the Japanese.

Pragmatism

Whereas Japanese culture traditionally placed less emphasis on verbal communication, it gave more to action—especially pragmatic action. Japanese pragmatism was evident in their alteration of the Chinese Confucian hierarchy: The warrior or *samurai* class was placed at the top of the Japanese social order, a reversal of the Confucian order.[52] The *samurai* exercised their leadership in two significant ways. One was a response to the threat of western colonialism in the nineteenth century:

> The Japanese warriors immediately recognized the need to adopt western arms and military techniques if they were to modernize and thus cope effectively with the foreign threat. They further realized that any program of modernization would depend heavily upon the adoption of western science,

> technology, and industrialization. They were even willing to adopt western political and social systems if these were deemed necessary for national survival.
>
> In striking contrast to this rather pragmatic approach on the part of the Japanese military class, the Chinese ruling class was immersed in a sense of cultural superiority and ethnocentrism. This is quite understandable when you consider that China had been the center of the Asian world—which to the Chinese was the entire world—for thousands of years. China had a civilization that could be traced back three thousand years or more, and her institutions, values, and ways had served the needs of the society for more than two thousand years. As far as the Chinese were concerned , the golden age was in the past and if disorder or troubles came about, they occurred because the people had departed from the traditional values and ways. As a result, whenever the country was faced with difficulties, and this includes the crisis in the nineteenth century, the ruling class endeavored to reform the institutions and tighten the moral standards to approximate as nearly as possible those of the golden age of the past. It did not seek to resolve the problems by introducing innovations or by adopting alien institutions and values.[53]

A British scholar noted a "parable" to contrast the "cultural hubris and claims of grandeur" held by Chinese and Vietnamese Confucianism with the pragmatism of the Japanese:[54]

> When a French steamship was sighted off the shores of Vietnam in the early nineteenth century, the local mandarin-governor, instead of going to see it, researched the phenomenon in his texts, concluded it was a dragon, and dismissed the matter. ...Such neglect [of "empirical clear-sightedness"] left much of Confucian East Asia prostrate before the great lunge of western imperialism; Japan's unflinching [pragmatism] saved it.[55]

The second way in which Japanese warriors showed leadership was in their country's industrialization: "The traditional merchant houses ... did not actually turn to industrial activities until new blood was injected into them from the former *samurai* class."[56] These *samurai* had administrative experience under their feudal lords, which ultimately seemed to facilitate the brand of collectivism followed by the Japanese. Japan's collectivism, in contrast to China's, historically was based on small groups.[57] Both countries utilized wet rice agriculture, but water was much more abundant in Japan. The Japanese did not have to organize centrally directed, large-group water projects, as did the Chinese. Local Japanese communities had their own water sources and were required to work cooperatively to conserve and distribute it. Perhaps this emphasis on the small unit or group allowed for a wider development of administrative leadership. This division into small groups also may have fostered clannishness and, perhaps, inwardness.

A key difference between Chinese and Japanese is that in earlier times, according to the anthropologist Hsu, inheritance in Japan passed solely or principally to the eldest son, whereas in China it was shared equally by all the sons. As a result, younger sons in the Japanese family eventually had to leave and form their own branch families. Consequently, in Japan, networks emerged that consisted of small related groups within a hierarchy involving the chief household (*honke*) and subordinate branches (*bunke*). The same kind of arrangement is evident in the Japanese business world, with its well-known *keiretsu* enterprises, whereby affiliated companies within and across industries form networks to distribute their collective business among themselves.

Another feature that distinguishes Japanese from Chinese family organization is that the Japanese are far more open to adopting an outsider. Adoption (*yooshi engumi*) is not philanthropic; it is practiced to perpetuate the *ie.* It is not uncommon for a marriageable male to be adopted by marrying the daughter of the *ie* and taking her surname. Such adoptions occur either because the *ie* has no son or because the existing talent is thin. Could there be a more corporate mindset than that of the *iemoto*?

Although both Chinese and Japanese societies are collectivist, the Japanese perhaps have taken collectivism a step further by extending kinship outward to embrace new talent and resources. At one time, I served as a volunteer helping displaced Vietnamese "boat people," who were housed in Japan. The Vietnamese leader of this group was exceptionally talented—an ex-army officer and trained engineer who saved the lives of the people in his group after they were stranded at sea. Before that he had survived painful years under torture and confinement by the North Vietnamese communists after the war. A local Japanese man, recognizing the qualities of this Vietnamese, invited him to marry his daughter. I do not know this Japanese family's circumstances, but it was a very unusual gesture because this Vietnamese was a refugee and knew little of the Japanese language and culture. Still, it shows the extent of Japanese pragmatism despite their general racial consciousness. In contrast to the Chinese, *iemoto* thinking gave the Japanese the "psychosocial wherewithal" to modernize rapidly and forestall western colonization.[58]

Responsibility on the Receiver

From this brief presentation, we may say that in general the Chinese may seem more expressive and more outgoing than the Japanese. Of course, much depends on the situation and the individuals involved; in some cases, Japanese will act counter to expectations. If the Japanese indeed are appreciably more indirect and more restrained than the Chinese, this difference may also be related to the condition of receiver/hearer responsibility (as respect to authority). The Japanese receiver appears to carry a heavier responsibility than the Chinese or the American:

> In Japan, communication between people is successful when the listener understands what a speaker is trying to say.[59] This emphasis on the listener's responsibilities for successful communication is quite different from the emphasis in both China and the United States. In these countries, speakers are expected to make their points clearly, and examinations of communication difficulties are more likely to focus on the speaker's errors. This cultural difference shows up in answers to the question about what children should learn in preschool. Adults in China and the United States felt that communication skills were important; 27 percent and 38 percent of the respondents, respectively, in the two countries. In Japan, only 4 percent of the adults felt that communication skills were among the most important things for children to learn.[60]

Richard Brislin explains this difference by citing greater heterogeneity among Americans and Chinese than among Japanese. Even in China, diversity is much more prevalent: Numerous languages are spoken and over 50 minority groups are officially recognized.[61] "If Chinese and Americans want to communicate with others, they cannot expect so much shared culture that listeners will understand what they want. Chinese and American speakers have the responsibility to communicate, and this is an emphasis in their education as early as the preschool level."[62]

PACE OF LIFE: INTERNATIONAL COMPARISONS

Another way of placing Japan among world nations is by considering the relative pace of life. Travellers abroad often comment how some foreign locales have a faster or slower pace than their own. Next to foreign language learning, pace of life was found to require the most cultural adjustment by a group of Peace Corps volunteers.[63] Robert V. Levine and his associates have been studying pace of life internationally for a decade or more. They have measured pace of life by taking an aggregate of several measures: speed of walking, speed in purchasing a postage stamp, and the accuracy of clocks inside banks. Based on these aggregate scores, Japan ranked as having the fourth fastest pace of life out of 31 countries studied, just after Switzerland, Ireland, and Germany.[64] The countries that ranked least were (in descending order) El Salvador, Brazil, Indonesia, and Mexico, all with hot climates. Countries that had middle-ranked scores were Taiwan, Singapore, United States, and Canada.

As Levine points out, economic growth, climate, population, and cultural values (e.g., individualism-collectivism) were strongly related to the scores. Understandably, the western industrialized countries held most of the fastest paced ranks, while the developing countries, particularly those with hot climates, held the slowest ranks. Japan's high economic growth and high population density has likely stimulated a fast pace of life, despite being collectivistic. On this point, Japan appears quite apart from the ranks of the Asian "tigers": Hong Kong (10th), Taiwan (14th), Singapore (15th), and South Korea (16th). Overall, the pace of life between Japan and some of these tigers might not differ so appreciably, as the mean speed for purchasing a postage stamp in Japan was 19 seconds and just one to three seconds more in Hong Kong, Taiwan, and Singapore. A big difference emerges, however, with such countries as China (40 seconds) and Mexico (70 seconds).

If this difference were carried across everyday life, we would probably agree with Levine that "places, like people, have their own personalities."[65] We also might appreciate how "paradoxical" the United States must appear to Japanese visitors, for the mean speed to buy postage stamps in the United States was 37 seconds, not much faster than that for countries in the developing world. Is this "slowness" a matter of inefficiency at the American post office, or is it a general feature of American life? (Consider the American expressions to be "mellow" or "laid back.") Japanese visitors often cite how "slow" service seems at American supermarkets, restaurants, and other retail stores. This "slowness" seems paradoxical in a way, for the Japanese associate speed with modernization, even westernization.

Although Americans seemed slow in dispensing their postage stamps, they sped upward in rank for walking speed, placing sixth just ahead of the Japanese at seventh. Walking was measured (randomly) for "pedestrian traffic in ... main downtown area[s]."[66] These areas may well have included the higher socioeconomic strata of the countries tested—the administrative, financial, and high fashion sectors—which suggests how the United States could have very disparate scores for the pace of life across situations in its society. The United States is likely to have a less uniform pace of life, given its ethnic diversity and the country's lesser amount of urbanization as compared to Japan's: 44 percent of the American population live in rural areas, while only 13 percent of Japan's live in theirs.[67]

Conversely, the Japanese pace of life can seem relatively slow even within mainstream society. Foreigners in Japan often complain how some banking transactions take an inordinate amount of time. If so, it is probably because Japanese banking procedures (with consumers) follow more caution (a cultural value) by having two or more employees check for correctness. The Japanese medical system typically requires patients to wait a long time before seeing a doctor because appointments are not taken, which is one of the tradeoffs for Japan's low-cost national medical system. (The Japanese per-capita expenditure on health care is less than half that for Americans, even though the Japanese average hospital stay is five times longer.[68] One reason, though certainly not the only one, is that Japanese doctors see more patents but spend less time with them than do American doctors with their patients. Explanations are given less. Hospitals may require a family's help with the nursing.) Similarly, clocks in Japanese banks, in the above international study, ranked only

6th in accuracy, even though the Japanese precision in keeping train schedules is legendary. American clocks did not do any better as their measurement ranked 20th, though its rank was higher than that for postage stamps. Overall the American pace of life ranked 16th in speed.

Japan's rank in pace of life would likely be higher if two additional measures were added: commuting time and population density (as opposed to just "population"). It is not uncommon to find students (high school or college) and company employees commuting two hours or more (each way) between their home and place of study or work. Because population density is high in big cities, especially Tokyo, competition is intense for places at schools and companies. People often must settle for their lesser preferred choices, which may mean a location far from home. Relocating is difficult, not only because housing is limited, but also because another family member may be in a choice school or job in an opposite direction. The Asian tigers have similar conditions. Consequently, the pace of life in these locales may be actually much faster than reflected above.

Cultural concepts vary in application. Although American society is highly individualistic and highly industrialized, American behavior may sometimes be more characteristic of a collectivistic, traditional society. The same can be said in reverse for Japan. Perhaps, one explanation is that all societies adhere to values that operate between individualism and collectivism, depending on context. Thus contextual knowledge is essential for applying our knowledge of other cultures. Another point to derive from this section is that modern cultures are highly segmented in socioeconomic ways. People from corresponding segments (or professions) between two countries may have more in common than with people in their own countries. Lastly, the pace of life study, if valid, suggests how a world perspective can help us gain a clearer understanding of Japan by realizing that it is not quite as extreme as popularly imagined. Nevertheless, we still can see that Japan differs from its Asian neighbors in some essential way, not to mention those in North America.

JAPANESE DIVERSITY

First, I begin with a sketch of Japanese diversity, about which I learned in my early days in Japan;[69] this can serve as a basis for a deeper understanding of Japanese culture. At the very least, it is an attempt to avoid typecasting the Japanese into a single mold.

Regional Differences

Regional differences are an outstanding feature of diversity within Japan. Because such differences are related to climate, language, industry, cuisine, rituals, and history, many Japanese have regional identities. Regions developed as the natural outcome of topographical and climatic differences. A large proportion of the country is mountainous; this terrain long ago produced many isolated village communities. In addition, the climatic differences are not unlike those of the United States. Both countries have climates ranging from frigid to tropical: Northeastern Japan has some of the severest winter weather in the world, in contrast to the subtropical areas in Japan's far western end. Weather is temperate in the middle of the main island, though summer humidity can be uncomfortable. Elevated areas provide respite. Interregional travel was restricted not only by topography and climate but also by official decree. Regional dialects were a natural outgrowth of this isolation; some of these are mutually unintelligible.[70] It is little wonder, then, that each region has its own lifestyle and identity.

The most celebrated regional rivalry in Japan is between Kansai (the west border) and Kanto (the east border), each anchored respectively by Osaka and Tokyo. As might be expected, the people native to these regions have strong regional identities. Each area has its own dialect and associated reputations. The Osaka dialect is said to be"colorful" or melodic, and has "softer accents";[71] the Tokyo variety seems "regal," serving as the "received" (model) pronunciation for speech.[72] Osaka is associated with commerce due to its once historical status as the "Manchester of the East" or "Japan's kitchen," in recognition of its role as a commercial hub and industrial center from the eighteenth to the twentieth centuries.[73] Tokyo is truly the national power center; it serves as the capital, as well as the home to the leading political, economic, and cultural institutions. Tokyo Japanese, or its facsimile, has become the standard for communication across regions.

Tokyo has provided a model for standard Japanese (*hyoo-*

jungo) from its educated middle class known as Yamanote (uptown) speech.[74] However, Tokyo also has a regional dialect known as Shitamachi (downtown) speech.[75] "Standard" Japanese is most associated with formal speech and formal writing. The more informal the situation, the more likely regional or local dialects will be used.[76]

In the last 50 years, a "common language," *kyootsuugo,* has developed through a mixture of standard Japanese and one's local dialect.[77] This common language has served to bridge dialectal differences. Why not just use the standard? Because the "standard" has not been firmly established as one, which indicates the strong regionalism in Japan. Attempts were made but the "common language" movement gained sway. The common language contains enough elements from idealized Japanese (standard) to make speech mutually intelligible.

In addition to differences in region and dialect, another Japanese distinction is whether one has a city or country background. This distinction is much stronger than the corresponding difference among Americans. The Japanese, in my view, do not have what we call a "suburban lifestyle." The cities in Japan are not surrounded by communities made up of large split-level houses with spacious surroundings, all served by nearby supermarkets, shopping malls, and schools. In Japan, many of the prized amenities are located within big cities, including the better schools and shopping areas. Outside the cities, the infrastructure is unevenly developed; sewage and natural gas lines are not as good as in the cities. For example, many homes just outside the cities must rely on propane gas, a situation that would be unusual for comparable American homes. Services from sewage systems and flush toilets are much less also: "Only 51 percent of Japanese homes are connected to sewage systems and 76 percent have flush toilets compared to 73 and 98 percent respectively in the United States."[78] Thus cities in Japan usually carry greater prestige than even the neighboring areas. Again, with few exceptions, this is the opposite of the American case.

So far I have mentioned two important Japanese regions: Kanto and Kansai. These regions along with the Chubu region (central Japan, in which Nagoya is located) occupy the middle sectors of the main island of Honshu and hold half of Japan's population.[79] Their main cities—Tokyo, Osaka, and Nagoya—are situated on the Pacific Ocean side of Japan and constitute a corridor of urbanization that extends 336 miles (560 km) from Tokyo to Osaka in the west, with Nagoya in between. (This perspective of starting with Tokyo originates from the fact that Tokyo is the capital and the gateway for many foreign air travelers to Japan.) Behind this corridor—on the Japan Sea side—lie the hinterlands, which some Japanese urbanites consider the "real Japan," for there one finds remnants and folkways of the more distant past.

Northeast of Tokyo lies the Tohoku region, the "Appalachia" of Japan—rather economically depressed but scenic. Some years ago I had a Japanese friend, a college teacher, who came from a small village in Tohoku. Kenji* seemed more traditional than other Japanese. He sometimes wore *geta* (traditional wooden thongs), and his fiancee, his high school sweetheart, acted particularly meek, as if to give him the right of way. Yet he was neither backward nor sexist. His fiancee seemed to like this behavior more than he did. Because of their strong regional identities, they apparently did not care that such behavior was conspicuous in urban Japan. Such behavior is rare today, but urban-rural differences are still important. Today such differences among Japanese youths are less obvious because of the common socializing effects of Tokyo popular culture as disseminated through the mass media.

Farther north and above Tohoku is the island of Hokkaido, Japan's "last frontier." Hokkaido contains areas of large-scale farming that seem familiar to American visitors. It is also home to the Ainu, a minority group. The Ainu, a Japanese indigenous people with Caucasoid facial features, have suffered severe discrimination. Other principal Japanese minorities are Koreans, the *burakumin* (lit. "village dwellers," a euphemism for a certain outcast group of Japanese), Okinawans, and Chinese. Until recently, works on Japan generally did not include Chinese in this category. Yoshio Sugimoto estimates conservatively that minorities constitute 4 percent of the Japanese population—a sizable amount.[80]

Japanese Homogeneity

A semantic problem occurs, however, when discussing the homogeneity of the Japanese. Saying that the Japanese are highly homogenous does not mean that each and every person in Japan is homogeneous with every other. (Similarly, if we were to say that Great Britain has a great deal of unemployment, we would not mean that all the British are unemployed.) The fact remains that Japan has a relatively high degree of homogeneity, and this attribute no doubt contributed to the "Japanese economic miracle." Homogeneity also affects cross-cultural contacts with non-Japanese. Some Japanese have what they call *gaijin konpurekkusu* (a complex about foreigners). In some extreme cases, a Japanese becomes obviously nervous and withdraws physically. A more common manifestation, if the Japanese is at a distance, is to stare at the foreigner. Face to face, a Japanese might display perplexity or surprise. A Canadian man told a common story:

> It was a Sunday afternoon and I was downtown Nagoya in the lobby of a tall skyscraper. I was waiting for an elevator behind a group of other people. Directly in front of me were two women in their thirties talking to each other. Suddenly, one of them happened to notice me and gasped out to her companion: "*Bikkuri shita!* ("What a surprise!"). I just thought, "Here, we go, again."

A rather tall American woman had a similar encounter:

> I couldn't believe what happened to me the other day. I was waiting for a bus at the corner when a different bus unloaded a group of schoolchildren. They screamed, "*Gaijin!*" ("A foreigner!") and gathered around gawking at me. I had to walk away, but they even followed me for a couple of blocks.

A male Australian student gained an insight in this case:

> Here I was sitting on a ["suburban"] train and suddenly I noticed I wasn't being stared at. I started to fantasize me shouting at them to do so, because it happens so much [off campus]. At that point, I realized that, as strange as it sounds, being stared at validated my existence.

As the Japanese become more "internationalized," such cases become fewer and fewer. In the downtown areas of the big cities, especially Tokyo and Osaka, such behavior is very rare.

Nevertheless, in many ways a foreigner may be reminded that he or she is an outsider. These reminders are subtle, are delivered unconsciously, and carry no ill intent. We would expect such reminders to be a universal experience, but not so frequent in Japan, a highly educated and well-developed country. Once I wrote to an African-American friend, an art teacher in Delaware and an international traveler herself, about such experiences. About a year later, she came to visit me and recalled what I had written: "At first I couldn't believe you, but now I'm really surprised. After all, American movies and TV programs are popular here [in Japan]. Why do they stare so much?" The reason, of course, is our physical difference. Coming from a highly ethnically diverse area, such as North America, we cannot appreciate how Japanese homogeneity has affected them until we experience it personally. My friend's travels had been confined to western countries, particularly in Europe and South America, where ethnic diversity is a matter of course. Being outgoing, gracious, and well traveled, she probably didn't give much thought to possible cultural friction in Japan. Nevertheless, she developed so many rewarding relationships with the Japanese that she extended her stay. (In fact, she was later offered an unsolicited teaching position.)

One learns to take such frictions in stride because nobody can "change" Japan. With that realization, one can begin to accept the differences and move on. In doing so, one becomes acclimated and may even learn to appreciate these differences. Along the way, however, one may forget (though this is difficult) how truly homogeneous the Japanese are. Also, as more is learned about Japan, particularly its minority groups, the image of Japanese homogeneity fades somewhat. In some ways, this is good; in others, less so. If the image fades too much, Japanese homogeneity may be disregarded as a factor in intercultural relations.

Some people argue that Japanese social hierarchy is felt so strongly by the Japanese themselves that their situation is comparable to the ethnic diversity felt by people in North America. To some extent this is true, and it may be useful in giving us a sense of Japanese social difference. The resemblance ends there, however: Regardless of the social differences, the Japanese believe that they possess a great deal of homogeneity. Physical descriptions of people are a common example: Skin color, eye color, and hair color are far more similar than among North American people. These features are usually less significant in the description of a Japanese missing person than they would be in the North American case.

Japanese people also share far more customs than North Americans. Their foremost national holiday is New Year; ours is Christmas. (These two events are more comparable than one may think: The Japanese New Year includes common religious observances.) In Japan, nearly everyone celebrates New Year—a higher percentage of the population than of Americans who celebrate Christmas. A considerable number of Americans do not observe Christmas for religious reasons; even some Christians do not exchange Christmas cards because they wish to avoid the commercialization. Their action has no parallel in Japan. (Buddhist custom in Japan, in the event of mourning a loved one, dictates that greeting cards be halted, but only for one year. Furthermore, that reason has no relation to the commercialization of New Year.)

In addition, many members of Japanese minorities—*burakumin*, Koreans, and Okinawans—are physically indistinguishable from Japanese. Some of these groups are segregated somewhat by geography: Ainu in Hokkaido; Okinawans in Okinawa; *burakumin* and Koreans concentrated more heavily near Osaka than elsewhere. Consequently, a large portion of the Japanese population lives in a condition resembling absolute homogeneity. This may explain why the Japanese view themselves as "one race," a condition that they think precludes them from being racist.

Japanese social relations certainly can involve considerable social diversity, but Japanese (cultural) homogeneity hardly suffers as a result, especially in comparison with that of foreigners. Social diversity and national homogeneity in Japan usually operate at two separate levels. Thus, when we say that the Japanese are highly homogeneous, our point of comparison is most other nations. Although it is important to appreciate diversity among the Japanese, the fact remains that they perceive themselves as highly homogeneous—as one race. That perception alone warrants attention.

CONCLUSION

A world perspective on Japan was presented here as a step toward developing what the anthropologist, Brian Moeran, calls a "cubist approach,"[81] for the various points of view needed in understanding the Japanese. Moeran points out that "any characterization of Japan will inevitably be partial."[82] His statement is realistic given the complexity of Japan's bi-civilization. *Cubist* is particularly fitting for the ambiguity that must ensue in reaching only partial characterizations and for the idea that, at times, we may be dealing more with an "art" than a science, meaning that the subject may defy absolute certainties. We saw, for example, how the concept of groupism is sometimes misapplied, as with the personal opinion surveys among the Japanese about being middle class. Such mistakes may be avoided by being cognizant of both similarities and differences between Japan and other nations, and by being mindful of Japan's internal diversity. By this knowledge we may afford ourselves the flexibility required for a cubist approach to Japan. Further steps toward this goal can be taken through the next several chapters. These chapters focus on cross-cultural barriers, many of which are self-imposed through our own biases—personal and cultural. First, however, the following Application section presents an interpretation of Japanese culture by a Pakistani scientist for added perspective—particularly Asian—as well as for the cultural analysis.

APPLICATION

"Japan Through My Eyes"

A Pakistani Scientist Speaks

Hamid Saleem

Both a physicist and a poet, Hamid Saleem is currently a post-doctoral fellow at the National Institute for Fusion Science (NIFS) in Toki City, Japan, while on leave from his position of scientist at the Pakistan Institute of Nuclear Science and Technology (PINSTECH). His career has included related work at research institutes at Ruhr University Bochum in Germany and the International Center for Theoretical Physics (ICTP) in Trieste, Italy. His skill at observing things larger than an atom was honed by an earlier stint as a journalist for the English newspaper in Pakistan The New Times, *as well as through his published poetry in Urdu, the national language of Pakistan.*

For me, Japan is distinctive for being highly industrialized, yet still having much respect and regard for the traditional values of an agricultural society. Elegant manners of Japanese formalities and casual ways of life both can be seen depending upon the situation. Therefore, this is a land of wonder for most foreigners from wherever they come. The general behavior and attitudes of a nation are the reflection of it's history, geography, traditions, culture, theology, genetic factors, etc. But in this short article, my views about present-day Japan are my impressions as a visitor rather than those of an area studies specialist.

This land is a garden having all the colorful flowers of the east and west, full of beauty and scent. But by special treatment, the Japanese have combined these flowers into a beautiful bouquet of the best from both worlds. Contradictory currents of the traditional and modern flow together in this land of islands. In my point of view a true Japanese, due to politeness, cannot be very straightforward. It is almost impossible for a Japanese to refuse. Frankness is avoided. Therefore a foreigner, especially if he or she is from Europe or the USA, is misled by the Japanese manner of indirectness in avoiding direct refusals.

Japanese are preservers of great human values. But this also creates confusion sometimes. If a formal situation, they generally do not accept a social invitation immediately at once. They do, though, like to visit foreigners at their homes and mix with them. Generally, only people of similar age and rank can become close friends. Foreign researchers find themselves in a social bind in that they often fall between the highest and lowest ranked at a research center here. So forming social relations there are very slow in coming. Europeans and Americans are much more frank and spontaneous in social discussions compared to Japanese.

The Japanese are excellent hosts. They receive you very kindly. However, traditional collectivist ways, which require an established social relationship before a cooperative task is performed, form a barrier for foreign researchers here. I come from a collectivist culture, also, but I can now see its disadvantage after my enlightenment working in a German institute. In Germany, a professional relationship was formed almost immediately with my supervising professor. A social relationship was not a required preliminary. He had me involved in collaborative work almost immediately. Here in Japan, it doesn't usually happen like that (though some exceptions exist). One needs to become part of the group before substantial professional work is undertaken. Early collaborative work is unrealistic. Instead, foreigners are given full support for their own independent work. Being Asian, I should have known better, but Japan has achieved modernization as high, if not higher than the west. Japan's historical isolation and less experience with foreign collaboration explains it.

Another noticeable aspect in the laboratory is the tight relation between Japanese professors and their graduate students. As supervisors, Japanese professors want their students to be present in the laboratories and institutes most of the time. Hard working students are appreciated very much. This seems to me an Asian style because it is very similar to the situation in India and Pakistan. European supervisors act much differently. They appreciate free thinking and believe in student independence. So students in European labs come and go as they please. The extra time that Japanese put into attending the lab does not necessarily mean any better results. The reason is that their attendance is not continual work. Furthermore, the atmosphere is far less conducive to a questioning spirit found among Europeans and Americans. The result is that the Japanese educational system produces a lesser number of highly creative scientists compared to the USA and Europe.

Japanese are by nature formal and reserved. Therefore, the frank Americans especially feel the Japanese atmosphere very differently from their own. But as I said, Japanese are fine hosts. They consider it their moral obligation to help foreign visitors. For example my Japanese hosts have guided and helped me a great deal during my two-year stay here with my family. Other foreigners say so, too. But in the beginning I felt very lonely and isolated. Perhaps Japanese do not feel the presence of another human being unless he takes some friendly initiatives for this. However, in the Japanese institutes and universities one is recognized by one's status and age. Other foreign colleagues agree. From my experience and that of others, there is much less hierarchy found in American and European academia. This situation in Japan is similar to Pakistan with a difference that Japanese professors, given their better resources, have become remarkable scientists in general.

Also notable about Japan is its basic kinship with the developing countries (though it may not always recognize that). An Asian is less a foreigner in Japan than in Europe. Ancient Japan was directly influenced by China and indirectly through Buddhism by India. However, the Japanese delicacy in art and social behavior is something very original and particular to this nation. Because Japan's borders remained closed for centuries, the recent influx of foreigners here is relatively a new phenomenon. Curiosity by the common people is quite obvious. Sometimes people in the small town or village look at foreigners as if they are a new species. But this is not unpleasant at all because they have affection and regard in their eyes. In big cities people help the foreigners everywhere. But this attitude may not last. With the large influx of foreigners comes increasing crime, including illegal workers. Partly due to sensationalized media reports, some Japanese avoid encountering a foreigner, especially near big railway stations. In some European countries, there are some groups of young people against foreigners. These Europeans think that the people from Asia and Africa are polluting their culture and taking their jobs. Occasionally violence results, and some foreigners have been murdered. Luckily such incidents are unknown in Japan, and overall, it remains a wonderful place.

The United States influence is most dominant. Ability in English is considered advantageous for a Japanese. If a Japanese cannot speak English he will say, "Sorry I cannot speak English." A German will never feel sorry, if in the same situation. Even a German who knows English very well still would prefer to speak German. The same is true for people in many other countries. But this is again Japanese politeness that they do not expect foreigners to learn their language. They also understand that it is not an easy task. But, of course, the Japanese language is a must for the student. Yet this same Japanese politeness seems absent if you are alone at the airport with an overload of baggage. The Japanese there to receive you is likely not to help in this regard. Perhaps he would think it is an interference in your private matters. But if you ask him for some help, then he may be likely to want to take the heaviest bags. One very strange thing to notice, to me anyway, is that there is little variety in the formal behavior of Japanese. It is easier in Japan than in any other country to predict the likely response of a Japanese, if one has had some experience living here. This country has a highly homogeneous population compared to other places both in living standards and in behavior.

Many young Japanese wish to visit the United States. They have romantic ideas and dreams about there and Europe as well. Perhaps they are unaware of their own country's many fine points, including a peaceful environment and a low crime rate. It seems to me that what drives them to get away is their hard work schedules and relatively cramped living quarters. Japanese are serious workers and love their work places like homes. Commuters to work may have to spend 2 to 3 hours just going back and forth. Work itself may take 10 to 12 hours.

Japanese seem to have less scope for leisure and enjoyment than I had expected. When enjoying themselves, they are very fond of cooking and eating delicious foods. About Japanese young people, they differ from their elders in their attitude toward life. In the schools, they try to follow western styles of relaxation. Pop music is very popular. But the stress from studies and worries about the future limits their enjoyment. The emphasis placed on entering only the "right" schools breeds a sense of inferiority for those who fail. Youth suicide is not unheard of. Being part of the society here takes much effort. Although movements in Europe aim to reduce the work week to 35 hours, there is no such thing in Japan.

Education and knowledge is respected here as in all developed nations. During my stay in Germany, I noticed that the German students were very much interested in world history, philosophy, politics, etc. One can discuss any subject of human interest with them from the mundane to the profound. However, the same is not true in Japan (and according to hearsay, perhaps, in the USA, also). Most of the Japanese students and researchers of the natural sciences seem only concerned with their professional studies. Neither they have time nor they are interested in other subjects. Perhaps one reason to account for the German or European apparent love of ideas is that their science first grew out of philosophy. Philosophy was an early interest of Einstein's, as it was for some other prominent scientists. It was philosophical debates that gave birth to quantum mechanics, for example. On the other hand, western science reached Japan at a stage when it more or less had already established technologies. Therefore, western science had been taken as a tool for industrial progress and national prosperity, which proved to be true.

The friendship circles of Japanese youth are often confined to the same sex. In Europe, that would be rather unheard of. Japan, like other Asian countries, views friendship in a traditional way. I am not in favor of the suppression that exists in muslim countries and other poor countries of Asia, but, on the other hand, in the west, sex seems like a kind of a religion. Japan, at present, lies between these two extremes. It is important to mention that this view is in comparison with the developed countries. It does not seem reasonable to compare Japan with poor Asian countries where the social structure is centuries old and permits little exception. The poverty and prevailing injustice in such societies have adverse effects on general morality. Frustration makes the human mind aggressive and less accommodative. Ignorance and poverty usually reside together. Therefore, new ideas have no place in such social systems.

Some traditional moral values remain untouched. That is why even the modern Japanese attitudes have some similarities with poor Asian countries like Pakistan. For example, respect for teachers, elders, regard for colleagues, care for guests and friends are a few of the things shared with the middle class of Pakistan, though just a small fraction of the national population.

Like those in the other developed nations. Japanese have very loving and caring attitudes toward children. My daughter was in kindergarten in Germany. She used to say to her mother, as how children will be children: "Mama, I like my *Lehrarin* (teacher) more than you because she loves me more." A similar regard is felt for Japanese teachers especially up to and through elementary school. My daughter and son are in grades 5 and 6, respectively. They are very happy due to the encouraging behavior of teachers and the cooperativeness of other children, which is generally less common in developing countries. Poverty, hunger and disease place a toll on the developing world. These problems give rise to exploitation, which explains child labor in those countries. Such conditions are hardly conducive to loving attitudes toward children.

1. What are the several most outstanding characteristics of the Japanese in the view of Hamid Saleem?
2. How was even he, though Asian and well traveled abroad, caught off guard by Japanese customs?
3. How might his own culture or situation have influenced his view of Japan or the Japanese?
4. Analyze how Japanese research/academic centers operate using Hamid Saleem's account and applying principles or concepts found in this chapter.

Part I

Barriers to Cross-cultural Understanding

2

Double Standards

Japan—called both a "land of enigma"[1] and a "magnet for myths"[2]—remains a mystery for many people. Unfortunately, various barriers in the form of caricature or stereotype prevent a realistic view. In this book I attempt to reduce these barriers through the notion of contextualism, with a focus on the images of Japanese culture, communication, and society. Underlying the exaggerated stereotypes, myths, and over-generalizations is an apparent disregard for the context, the situation or the "context of situation," terms that I use interchangeably here. People may apply perceived rules of culture without regard to constraints. At the same time, people tend to typecast foreign peoples as illogical, particularly those whose premises are least understood. Contextualism, then, may combat multiple blind spots in cross-cultural comparisons.

Hardly anyone would deny the importance of context; yet the American cultural ethos may make us least likely to put this idea into practice.[3] In this study, I attempt to document such practice. In doing so, I hope to encourage a greater appreciation for contextualism, both to help meet the present need for realistic images of the Japanese[4] and to overcome the "Orientalizing ethnocentrism" that can be found in scholarship on Japan even today.[5] We speak here in relative terms. Scholarship can be as much a function of time and place as of the person who produces it. Ethnocentrism is inherent in perception and probably can only be minimized at best. Perhaps with perseverance, the understanding of another culture eventually will withstand the tests of time and place.

One way of working toward this goal is by becoming aware of our personal and cultural double standards. As one observer remarked, "It is astonishing how pervasive double standards are in relation to criticisms of Japanese behavior."[6] This view is shared by others in a study of recent treatments of Japan in the mass media.[7] We explore such biases through illustrative cases of the interpersonal, intercultural, and international double standards that people use in judging others. First, we consider interpersonal and intercultural double standards within the United States as a basis for considering an international double standard toward Japan. Further barriers to understanding the Japanese are illustrated in the metaphors of description and the resignation with cultural difference ("East is East, West is West"). To avoid these barriers, "contextualizing" our understanding seems necessary and an approach is offered for doing so.

INTERPERSONAL DOUBLE STANDARD

People often judge the behavior of others according to a double standard that favors themselves. In judging their own behavior, people use the situation that they find themselves in. For others, however, people often do not use situations; they use traits that they perceive others to have. When people apply such a double standard, it is not necessarily from ill intent; rather they apply it because social anxiety interferes with their usual clear thinking and because they know their own situation better than that of others.[8] For example, when Chris is left waiting for Terry, who is now very late, Chris angrily thinks, "Terry is irresponsible." If the tables were turned, however, and if it were Chris who was late, Chris would probably explain not by citing a trait but by describing a situation: "The boss made me stay late, and when I did get out, I got caught in traffic." Also, whether intentionally or not, Chris could be relieved of some of the responsibility for the behavior by placing the blame on the related circumstances. Chris, however, is less able to do so, if a personal trait is involved. People do not always use such double standards, but it happens often enough to be called by psychologists the "fundamental error of attribution." This topic will be taken up more closely in Chapter 3.

INTERCULTURAL DOUBLE STANDARD

Another double standard favors our own ingroup over other groups. Naturally we tend to prefer members of our own group or society. This preference can operate very subtly, as in the descriptions of white and black baseball stars in a leading desk reference. Consider how the following entries[9] from the edition available to me differ in their descriptions of these star players (see Box 2.1).

Box 2.1 **Descriptions Of Baseball Heroes: How do they Differ?**

A. In 1974 [he] broke Babe Ruth's lifetime record of 714 home runs.... He set major-league ... career records for runs batted in, extra-base hits, and total bases.

B. [H]e hit 660 home runs (third-highest total) and led [his league] in home runs four times. He was twice voted most valuable player. In his last season [he led his team] to the pennant.

C. One of the finest natural hitters the game has ever known. He was the last player to bat over .400. [He also hit 521 home runs.]

D. [O]ne of the great sluggers in baseball history.... His 526 home runs [are among] the leaders.... He was named most valuable player [three times]. [He] hit a record 18 home runs in World Series play.

Even a reader unfamiliar with baseball will notice that players C and D, unlike players A and B, are described in superlatives (e.g., "one of the finest"; "one of the great"). It may not be a coincidence that A and B (Hank Aaron and Willie Mays) are African American, whereas C and D (Ted Williams and Mickey Mantle) are Euro American. It is also curious that only Ruth is described elsewhere in the book as possessing "hitting prowess," even though Aaron had hit more home runs. The different descriptions seem to favor Euro Americans, suggesting a cultural bias.

This apparent double standard appears only for baseball and not for other sports. Baseball, though less popular in recent years, is still considered the "American pastime." The double standard in this case may be an instance in which the dominant culture protects what it considers to be its own domain. This should not be surprising because mainstream professional sports formerly barred African Americans from participation. One would assume that literary people, such as editors of an encyclopedia, would be sensitive to language and racism.

That assumption seems unwarranted, however, if one considers the mounting evidence that the discourse of journalism subtly follows a mainstream view, and in doing so "reproduces racism."[10] The mass media tend to report mainstream and minority affairs differently. Certain choices of vocabulary and syntax can make the difference between a positive and a negative impression of a minority-group member. Using a passive verb form to describe a minority person's action could imply a lack of autonomy, possibly suggesting irresponsibility. Such messages often are delivered implicitly and unconsciously; even if journalists are trained to be sensitive to news bias, they still may fail to detect it. Thus, one's own culture must exert a profound influence on one's worldview.

The controversy about IQ scores is a similar case. What does it mean to claim that African Americans have less intelligence than Euro Americans because of lower IQ scores? The insidiousness of such a claim, however, was not fully realized until the 1980s, when the tables were turned in favor of Japanese IQ scores over those of white Americans. Did people then conclude that Japanese were more intelligent than whites? No; a different conclusion was drawn: The Japanese were simply better test takers. Regardless of test-taking skill, if the IQ test does indeed measure intelligence as was assumed with black (and white) IQ scores, then the Japanese IQ scores must indicate intelligence as well. The apparent reluctance to accept this interpretation suggests the presence of a double standard in favor of whites, the mainstream social group. When this kind of bias operates in favor of one's nation or culture, we call it ethnocentrism—evaluating other cultures by the standard of one's own, which usually presumes a sense of superiority.

Some degree of nationalism is probably unavoidable. Indeed, it may even be psychologically healthy. For example, the strength of my native identity was brought home to me when I went to China to lecture as a representative of Japan. I already had lived a long time in Japan and had been accepted to participate in a Japan-sponsored program in which university faculty members were sent to teach in China. At the invitation of the host institutions in China, I went to lecture, and was honored at one school at a small reception held by the school president. On the main table stood two flags side by side—one Chinese, one Japanese. Much as I like Japanese culture, I felt uneasy because I am not Japanese but American. The feeling was only momentary, but it showed me the resilience of one's own native culture. As Edward Hall noted, it is "impossible [for us] to divest [ourselves] of [our] own culture" regardless of effort.[11] This is not to say that I never feel "Japanese"; sometimes I do, but not without an "as if" quality. Secure in my own American identity, I can participate freely in a Japanese lifestyle. Such participation need not challenge my own cultural identity.

INTERNATIONAL DOUBLE STANDARD

On the other hand, if I believed that my American nationality predisposed me to be a "teacher" to the Japanese, that view would be patently ethnocentric. Some American students of business may assume an unwarranted superiority when viewing Japanese business practices. Others may assume a similar attitude in other "modern" spheres. I recall that one well-intentioned but misguided American, on becoming acquainted with a Japanese, offered to teach him golf when he learned that they shared interest in the same sport. It turned out that the Japanese was by far the better player! Other Americans have been surprised to find how highly accomplished the Japanese are in classical music or in country and western music. This kind of surprise was exploited in the opening scene of the movie *Rising Sun*, in which a Japanese man sings "Don't Fence Me In."

These examples involve Americans, but all peoples have some sense of cultural superiority. An otherwise bright student of mine, a German, had once argued unpersuasively that Japanese musicians could never quite master the great pieces of German classical music because she believed, the Japanese could not fully understand the German culture. Yet that presumed lack has not prevented some Japanese (and some Chinese) from becoming world-class performers. Further discussion made it clear that this student's observations were based largely on Japanese students in Germany who were recent arrivals in that country. She had not considered that their command of the language was probably still imperfect; thus their musical learning and performance would be affected.

Ethnocentrism knows no boundaries. Anyone may be susceptible, regardless of cultural or national background. The case of my German student is memorable precisely because she was outstanding in so many other ways. Because she happened to be naturalized as a German at an early age and was of East European extraction, she may have developed more national pride than even a native-born German. Despite her sophistication gained from being multilingual and having overcome cross-cultural challenges in her past, she made this uncharacteristic remark. Some modicum of "nationalism" may be necessary to give us a sense of who we are. If it is excessive, however, such sentiment may reduce our ability to view clearly other cultures.

The West's Historical Disregard for Japan

Awareness of double standards is especially necessary in considering Japan. A double standard has been evident in the west's historical disregard for this country. First, Japan was forcibly opened by Commodore Perry and was compelled by foreign powers to agree to unequal treaties. This unfortunate beginning was followed by the American exclusion of Japanese immigrants through the "Gentleman's Agreement" (1906-1908) and the Immigration Act (1924), and by the Anglo-American rebuff of Japanese initiatives at Versailles for a racial equality clause in the charter of the League of Nations. "The failure to include a statement on racial equality ... exposed the double standards of the western powers. The democratic rights that they so loudly claimed as their inheritance were reserved for those who they deemed fit."[12] In the middle of the twentieth century, the west viewed the Japanese sometimes derisively as "economic animals." Charles de Gaulle, the French premier, called a Japanese prime minister, a "transistor salesman."

More recently, Japan often felt pressed to follow the American lead in political and economic policies. Frictions over trade triggered a wave of Japan bashing, with an intensity that seemed reserved for Japan. This is not to say that Japan is completely blameless. Rather, the criticism seemed too one-sided. Although Germany developed similar trade imbalances with the United States (on a GNP basis), and although European firms made comparable acquisitions of American assets,[13] Europe did not receive the same treatment.

Eurocentrism Illustrated

Japan is still widely misperceived as "a recently developed nation,"[14] even though before the industrial revolution first began, Japan's development was equal to that of Europe and the rest of the world.[15] (Here "national development" ought not to be confused with "standard of living," the latter which does lag behind that of North America.[16]) Since the late nineteenth century, Japan has experienced exceptional growth, as observed by Columbia University economist James Nakamura:

> By comparing the economic growth rates of ten nations (including the United States) to Japan's, [Nakamura] found that Japanese performance has been unmatched in the last century. Except for the "take-off" period (1870-1913) and the era of the Pacific war [and its aftermath] (1938-53), progress was more rapid for Japan than the other nations. Even the proto-modern Edo era (1603-1867) saw a substantial rise in per capita production.[17]

An example of the propensity to ignore Japanese achievements, or else to view them with an Eurocentric eye, seems to underlie one eminent sociologist's treatment of the development of large cities (those with a population greater than 1 million).[18]

This treatment is faulty because although done under the heading of "world cities," it apparently considers only European history. Although the city of Edo (ancient Tokyo) in Japan "reached [a population of] 1 million in 1695, making it the largest city in the world at that time"[19] and eventually, perhaps, becoming history's first million-plus city, this sociologist seems to associate the earliest development of such large cities with Europe. Thus one might be led to view modernizing changes in culture and thought as largely European.

Table 2.1 Cities of more than a Million People in the World

1800	0
1850	2
1900	10
1950	29
1970	142
1984	225

According to the same sociologist, "modernization is associated with important changes in modes of life, organizational patterns, culture traits, and psychological attitudes. All pre-modern societies are predominantly rural; they cannot produce enough surplus food to feed a large number of non-producers."[20] Table 2.1 is then presented as showing "a spectacular increase in the size and number of metropolitan cities."[21] Yet, Edo (Tokyo) had a population of 1,200,000 as early as the 1700s, easily surpassing the population of Europe's two largest cities—London and Paris—at that time.[22] Edo maintained a million-plus population through the early nineteenth century and beyond,[23] which contradicts the zero amount given for the year of 1800 in the table.

If we assume that the two cities listed for 1850 were London and Paris, the rise of the large city could be viewed as a distinctly European phenomenon—a development linked with modernization. If one associates the million-plus city with Europe, as a sign of modernizing changes in cultural traits and psychological attitudes, one could infer that modernistic thinking is exclusively European, thus implying an exalted view from which the thought patterns of non-European cultures are to be perceived. This view is evident in the equating of Japan's modernization with westernization; and in the metaphors employed in describing Japan. One such metaphor, reported by Michiko Niikuni Wilson, is of the child, as in these American newspaper headlines: "Japan Talks Back"; "Japan Getting Assertive"; and "Japan—Rich Kid in a Candy Store."[24] Given this historical disregard for Japan, it is understandable that Japanese Prime Minister Miyazawa described discussions with President Clinton in April 1993 as "the first Japan-US talks in which the United States treated Japan as an adult."[25]

The tendency to view one's own group, culture, or nation as superior to others is likely to extend to impressions of logic or illogic. People have long tended to view the behavior of foreigners as illogical; yet the behavior makes sense once the premises become known.[26] The premises represent the situation or context; without that knowledge, we are likely to attribute the behavior of others to false motivations or traits. This general tendency to ignore context or situation interpersonally seems compounded by the cultural ethos of individualism—an ethos that ultimately views the person as independent from society, and humankind as separate from nature. In addition, *reductionism,* an emphasis on the irreducible unit, has pervaded the social sciences, thus making context or situation expendable in a certain sense. Unfortunately, if individuals tend to mistake the motivations of others, and if our social sciences tend to ignore the context or situation, it will be that much harder to understand foreign peoples.

Further difficulty arises in the case of the Japanese, a people with a reputation for being "inscrutable." Ascribing this trait to the Japanese shifts responsibility for communication solely to them. Interpersonal communication is a two-way street, however. Relinquishing one's responsibility in this way violates a principle of intercultural communication: A first step toward improving intercultural communication is "assuming the burden for making the attempt."[27] Also, "to the extent that strangers do not share underlying assumptions about the nature of communication, the threatening potential of interaction with them is exaggerated—until strangers become enemies."[28] Such assumptions must be corrected, lest the cultural divide separate us ever more. Yet few people attempt crossing that divide. Instead some people believe fatalistically that "East is East and West is West."

This expression summarizes a widespread view of Japan. It not only expresses resignation about cultural difference ("never the twain shall meet") but also implies an explanation, such as this: "The Japanese are hard to understand. Why? Because they're like that—East is East...." Explanations of behavior based solely on the other's cultural membership without concern for context are common.[29] Based on circular logic, such explanations give only the illusion of explanatory power.

Moreover, few people realize that this "East is East" explanation actually takes Kipling's oft-quoted line out of context (and misconstrues Japanese behavior as well). His ballad actually had an anticolonial intent. Consider how it ends:

> But there is neither East nor West,
> Border, nor Breed, nor Birth,
> When two strong men stand face to face, though
> they come from the ends of the earth![30]

"Kipling's ballad concludes that true ... intercultural understanding is made possible by having the strength to suspend our preconceived ideas."[31] Rather than cynical despair, the ballad elegantly expresses hope for better east-west relationships.

In an analogous way, the Japanese, like Kipling's ballad, are subjected to distorted "readings." Outside their context, the Japanese can be treated as superficially as this ballad. Unless we move beyond preconceived notions—surface realities—there is little hope for meaningful exchange. "The reason for the lack of meaningful cross-cultural ... [exchange] is that meaning itself ... is created by frames of reference unique to each cultural ... community."[32] The surest way to perpetuate this lack of cultural empathy, coupled with the above observation of "strangers becoming enemies," is by accepting the "East is East" sentiment and ultimately by elevating one's own frame of reference to the status of singular truth.

THE NEED FOR CONTEXTUALIZED UNDERSTANDING

"To understand anything well we must grasp it in its context. This is particularly evident when we try to understand cultures other than our own."[33] Too often, however, culture bearers are reduced to a composite of (perceived) traits dissociated from actual situations. The Japanese are said to be group-minded, indirect, socially polite, and so on. Though these labels are partly accurate, the Japanese (like other peoples) can exhibit quite opposite behavior, as is in the example of Japanese clothing attire. Westerners tend to picture Japanese adult males in business suits, an image of strong Japanese conformism. The effect of such a narrow view was apparent when I showed a video scene of Japanese TV sports commentators to a class of American college students. Some of the students were surprised to see the (male) commentators in casual attire. The students' apparent oversight of the situation indicated the strength of stereotypes.

To further illustrate the problem of situation, consider the concept of the *geisha* and its appropriateness in polite Japanese conversation. For some foreigners, the word has an erotic meaning. Thus, two American students in Japan, after visiting the ancient capital of Kyoto, were surprised when a Japanese asked them if they had seen the famous *maiko* (*geisha* trainees). They were confused about what to say, and even more unsure about the intentions of the Japanese who asked the question. In fact, however, *geisha* were (and still are) highly cultured women, and appreciated for their artistic talents. (For talents of another kind, Japanese males were served by *yuujo*—women of pleasure.)[34] Later the two students reported feeling uneasy about their Japanese acquaintance.

Perhaps their discomfort arose from an eroticized image of Japan, an image long held in the west.[35] Also, although unintentionally, they may have developed an unsavory notion of their Japanese acquaintance. These foreign students seemed insensitive to the actual context. They never questioned their own concept of *geisha* until we happened to talk about it. Although one hears of romantic stories about some *geisha*, the role of *geisha* was artistic, not erotic.

Critical Communication

Understanding another culture is also about understanding one's own culture and even one's self. Understanding both culture and self contributes to the making of an international mind. This combined understanding implies, in part, an awareness of a cultural double standard based on inherited cultural images and ingroup allegiance. Over the years, I have seen how "East is East" thinking and other cultural double standards can lead observers astray. If Japanese behavior is judged outside its context, then what safeguard is there from false impression? In such cases, a dialectic between the unique and the universal would seem to increase our understanding. If such a dialectic were established, it would probably include the situation or context for the behavior in question.

Cultural comparisons are not immune from value judgments. To keep comparisons fair, the observer will be helped by a dialectic in which he or she remains psychologically equidistant between the cultures. Moreover, the observer needs knowledge of the cultural context sufficient enough to understand the target-culture's point of view without relinquishing neutrality. Both empathic understanding and accounting for context contribute to such a situated view.

Empathy

Discussions of cross-cultural understanding frequently include the concept of empathy. Unfortunately this concept is often treated solely in a moral sense; its complexity is side-stepped. Thus, in the end, one learns little about empathy from the literature on intercultural communication, according to a recent report.[36] Because of the generally accepted importance of empathy, its discussion is warranted here nevertheless.

As an early step toward developing a clearer understanding of the concept, I wish to share what I have found helpful. I present this information from a background of training and work as a professional counselor. This background is relevant because the concept of empathy originated in the fields of counseling and psychotherapy.

To simplify, two types of empathy exist: the ordinary and the cultivated. Everyone has empathy; without it, meaningful communication would be impossible. Extraordinary situations require extraordinary measures, however. For example, cross-cultural contacts involve a lack of shared assumptions and requires a marshaling of one's individual faculties of knowing. Such cases may involve cultivated empathy—perhaps that sought by counselors and others in the helping professions.

"Cultivated" empathy is a process for understanding another person or culture by balancing empathy between our other faculties of knowing, including identification, sympathy, inference, and intuition. Figure 2.1 attempts to show this balance between related states along the dimension of self-other and the dimension of affect-cognition. The states depicted in the figure are

Figure 2.1 A Conceptual Model of Empathy[37]

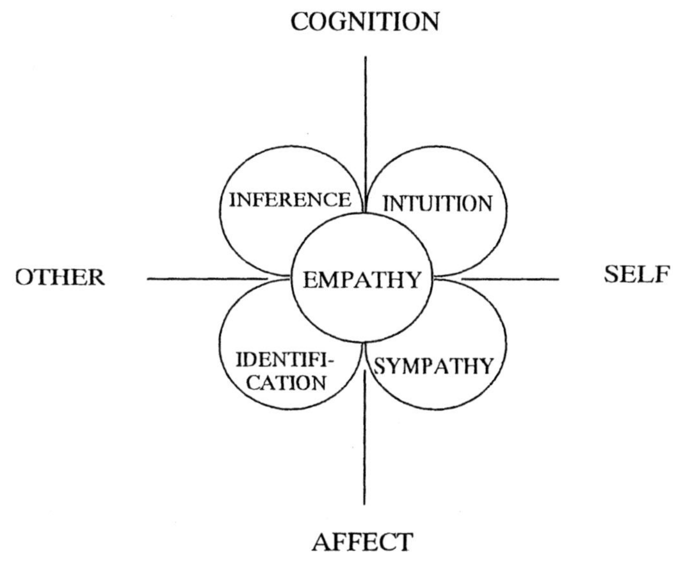

relative to each and show their essential differences. Although sympathy has altruistic intent and considers the other person, it ultimately remains focused on one's own feelings in fulfillment of social expectations. Identification, as a fixation on another person, necessarily involves a focus on the other.

The empathic state utilizes all four faculties of knowing without becoming unduly centered on either the self or the other—nor, similarly on either affect or cognition. Imagine Figure 2.1 to be a spirit level, the carpenter's tool, in which empathy is the bubble that must be moved to the centermost point. If empathy remains too long away from the center, it is no longer empathy but something else. The empathic person is "feeling" but at the same time remains detached in order to preserve self-identity while experiencing the other's frame of mind. Empathy is much more complex than often imagined; it requires cultivation through training or other means. Another point made by the model is the built-in dialectic between opposite frames of reference.

In an analogous way, a situated understanding of a foreign culture involves balancing the similarities and the differences of the cultures involved. The foreign observer identifies closely enough with the target culture to understand the particular situation while never losing sight of his or her own culture. A balance between similarities and differences helps to ensure the use of various frames of reference, rather than just that of one's own culture. This balance also is an attempt to correct the overemphasis on cultural differences, a common tendency:

> [Textbooks on intercultural communication] tend to overemphasize the differences existing between people and cultures. Admittedly some of these differences are important; however, in many ways it is our likenesses that enable us to find common ground and establish rapport.... The effective intercultural communicator is aware of these likenesses and seeks to develop them as a means of establishing a bond between him [or her]self and the rest of humanity. To know of our commonalities, and to be able to deal with them, is not a philosophical issue, but rather a practical matter.[38]

Situation is also important because of the nature of comparison. Anything can be compared, but cultural comparison involves a special purpose. Presumably the purpose of cultural comparison is to demonstrate how different the cultures are. Thus comparison must begin with similar situations to avoid confounding variables. For example, the comparison of Japanese worship at temples with American offtrack betting could not say anything significant about American religious practice unless American gambling were classifiable as religion. Nor would a comparison of a crisply written Japanese scientific article with a vague letter by an American politician to his or her constituents tell us that Americans are vague or indirect in their style of writing.

Suppose, however, that a Japanese researcher made exactly these two comparisons in claiming 1) that Americans are materialistic and 2) that Americans are illogical. Surely, constraint would be needed. Generalizations about cultures must be grounded on reasonable and fair comparisons. This fair-mindedness, however, is distorted by cultural double standards and by the observers' tendency to ignore the situation of the observed. This tendency to ignore the situation may actually be cultural in how reductionism has vied with contextualism for ascendancy in the social sciences.

Contextualism: Late Emergence in the Social Sciences

Contextualism has only recently emerged as a paradigm in the social sciences.[39] "The very commonness of the idea makes it the more striking that so little thought has been devoted to context in itself.... Neither historians nor social scientists have dealt intensively with the idea of context."[40]

One reason for this neglect is the stranglehold of positivism and, especially, reductionism on the social sciences dating back at least to the 1930s.[41]

> Modern scientists tend to foster "a militantly doctrinaire reductionism, which axiomatically prescribe[s] that all the relevant macroinformation about nature must, and eventually will, be derived completely from adding up and piecing together the microinformation about the smallest sample units. Never mind that physics had to give up that claim gradually as Bolzmann's thermodynamics, Planck's quantum theory, and Heisenberg's uncertainty principle came on the scene."[42]

A related topic is individualism, the emphasis on the person over the social group. American culture is often said to be individualistic. An example of this individualism, cited by intercultural specialists, is the popularity of psychology as a major on American college campuses. Psychology's favor seems apparent in comparison to sociology, as shown by the Graduate Record Examination (GRE) list of program codes for specialties. The GRE bulletin for one particular year listed 17 categories under the heading of psychology but only two for sociology.[43] This heavy specialization is not necessarily favorable or natural.[44]

A similar gap in popularity is found at the newsstand in a

genre of literature known as "pop psychology." One example is the magazine *Psychology Today*; no similar publication exists for sociology. Another example is the mass market for books devoted to self-knowledge, self-enhancement, and satisfaction.

Culture and a contextual view of behavior appear to be related. Low-context cultures appear less sensitive to contextual or situational explanations of behavior than do high-context cultures.[45] Whether a causal relationship exists between individualism and reductionism is unclear, but for whatever reason, American mainstream behavioral and cognitive psychology has tended to ignore social context in theories of thinking and learning.[46] These two "isms" therefore may find their fullest expression in the United States.

Ignoring social context is not limited to mainstream psychology. Even communications, a field that many would consider context-dependent, until recently took a predominantly mechanistic or reductionist view.[47] Similarly, "linguistics has also been dominated by an individualist ideology, ... the angle of reasoning [of which] has been typically from the 'language outward' rather than from the social order 'into language.'"[48] Consequently, a separate field, sociolinguistics, had to be developed not only to study actual language use (rather than abstract forms) but also the associated "context of situation." As noted above, observers of foreign people have tended to brand the observed as illogical in thought, while ignoring the underlying premises. Yet contrastive studies of discourse ought to proceed only after those premises are known: To emphasize the need for sociolinguistics, we turn to Chapter 3 for a study of western images of Japanese mysteriousness or inscrutability.

APPLICATION

1. This chapter argued that cross-cultural studies ought to maintain a balance between similarities and differences. Otherwise, cultural differences might become exaggerated such that needless psychological distance arises between peoples: The exaggerated becomes the weird and the mysterious. This attitude may even twist our commonalities or universal experiences. With this in mind, critique the following commentary on Japan from a British newspaper:

A. ***On the fascination by Japanese teenagers with children's characters in western literature:***
Peter Rabbit represents the outside world as it ought to be—cute, cuddly, naughty in a loveable way. Filling her bedroom with stuffed images of Peter, the Japanese schoolgirl may be expressing her yearning for a relationship with the outside world that poses no threat.[49]

B. ***On a tragic Japanese earthquake:***
Just as the earthquake itself strips away Japan's western veneer, revealing its Asian core and leaving it with the sort of massive death toll one would expect in a city of the Third World, so the prospect of a fatal quake exposes the unchanged, Asian contours of the Japanese soul.[50]

3

Misattribution and the Mysterious Orient(al) Schema

Recent studies of portrayals of Japan in contemporary print journalism reveal a predilection for the "weird" or the "mysteriousness" about Japanese everyday life.[1] "Journalists seem to spend much of their time laughing at the Japanese."[2] These journalists hardly seem to use critical awareness: Objects or phenomena held up as curiosities in Japan, such as "indoor resorts" or "tough working regimes" also exist in journalists' own countries (e.g., the United Kingdom in this case).[3]

> Journalistic disregard for Japan is perhaps also a reflection of the fact that it is not a country that can be easily explained in reader-friendly sound bites. Rather than going into the sort of background detail which would help the reader to understand a story, editors tend to favor articles which point out superficially how different Japan is from the west..... This translates into a simplistic 'us' and 'them' attitude which can seem implicitly

> hostile. The main justification for this would seem to be that, while Japan is a prosperous, developed nation, it retains unique traditions and customs which do not fit western perceptions of a modern society.[4]

Natural cultural differences may become exaggerated and "seen as defining characteristics of the country."[5]

The notion of Japanese mysteriousness is not a recent phenomenon. I trace this centuries-old image first in a brief historical sketch and then through analysis of a US governmental film related to the occupation of Japan in the immediate postwar era. Related imagery is also found in a contemporary children's cartoon series. These films illustrate not only the continuity of the image of Japanese mysteriousness but also the means for enculturating such images. (*Enculturation* is "the process by which individuals adapt to their culture and assimilate its values.")[6]

Japan traditionally has been viewed as part of the "mysterious Orient"; this view can be traced back to the very first European contacts with Japan in the sixteenth century.[7] "Japan is in the furthest east, indeed in the earliest [western] literature it was actually thought to be the Antipodes. [Westerners] never tired of writing that in Japan everything was antipodal, topsy-turvy and back to front."[8] As the culture was topsy-turvy, so were its people: "'Nobody can understand them.' That is the complaint that has echoed through the centuries."[9] These two notions—the mysteriousness of the culture and the inscrutability of the people—have operated in tandem ever since. Because such images of the Japanese have a long history, and for other reasons that will become apparent, I attempt to frame such phenomena in terms of a *social schema*—the "mysterious Orient(al)."

THE MYSTERIOUS ORIENT(AL) SCHEMA

A schema is a mental framework for organizing information into meaningful wholes. For example, outlines are a kind of schema used by both writers and readers to facilitate their respective tasks. "The notion of schema ... has now acquired a central position in both cognitive and social psychology. In social cognition, [schema functions] to organize our knowledge about other people and other groups and their actions."[10] Just as one might use an outline to categorize and organize notes for a lecture, one might employ a social schema when viewing people: The schema categorizes and places people into groups. Those groups may be associated with beliefs and may even include "instructions" for interacting with such people. If this process were followed blindly without concern for the uniqueness of others, we would be guilty of stereotyping. Furthermore, a social schema may be inaccurate or ill formed. Its use could lead us to view and treat others in inappropriate ways. This is what I have in mind when I refer to the "mysterious Orient(al)" schema.

The mysterious Orient(al) schema arises from a set of beliefs or group schemas[11] that forms a basis for western culture bearers' perceptions about persons of Asian origin, particularly those from China or Japan. Group schemas may tend to increase the prevalence of the fundamental attribution error. Group schemas are involved rather than just isolated attitudes because of the propensity by westerners to apply a common set of images to China, Japan, and "Asia."[12] Sheila K. Johnson finds that China and Japan, over the past century, have had to alternate in occupying favored status in the American popular imagination, and in doing so have had to trade common images as well.[13] This "seesaw correlation of American attitudes toward Japan and China—when one is up the other is down—[seems to be a reaction] to something Asian, something different from ourselves, and that the particular coloration we attach to a given country is dictated by current political considerations or events of recent past."[14]

The phenomenon of schema transfer[15] suggests why such images remain impervious to change: "Even without *any* information about a group, people may already start building an attitude about them."[16] Hence schema transfer between old and new outgroups appears to be self-reinforcing and may well sustain even the most outdated notions. In this way, various Asian groups (e.g., Chinese, Japanese, Korean, etc.) may elicit and reinforce the same central schema of "mysteriousness." Mysteriousness is not a single image but a set of images. It denotes the incomprehensible, a sense shared by other terms used in reference to the Japanese, such as *inscrutable, mindless,* and *irrational.* This connection between related images also can explain the pervasiveness of the "mysteriousness" notion over the centuries and its transferability between certain Asian groups. Thus schema possesses the property of a system or network that is usually absent from stereotypes. In sum, the mysterious Orient(al) schema involves two mental networks: mysteriousness and associated concepts, and images of Oriental or Asian peoples.

Given the historical background of this schema, I hoped to trace some of it through present-day media images. I was already aware of contemporary representations, and thus sought images that linked the present with the past. One possible source was World War II propaganda films, which were known for employing extreme caricatures. Even though these films were created in a time of war hysteria, the fact remains that stressful events are often needed to release deep-seated emotions and attitudes. Nevertheless, I was reluctant to use these films because war is such an abnormal situation. However, I learned of a film that seemed to strike a balance: a postwar US government film for training the army for the occupation of Japan. Because the war was over but still recent enough, deep-seated attitudes might have the chance to materialize. Also, because the United States occupied Germany as well, I sought and found a similar training film for occupying Germany.[17] The advantage was that the two films could be studied for their comparative images of an "Other." Would they display an excess in any direction? If they did so, it might indicate a particularly sensitive area.

Significance of the Films

Although war material has its limitations, the orientation films are an exception for several reasons. First, the war was already over. In fact, the atomic bombing of Japan induced "many Americans to feel sorrow and pity for Japan," resulting in "many of [the wartime images of the Japanese being] superseded by a new image of a mushroom-shaped cloud."[18] Second, the film scripts were a collaborative effort of numerous people, many of whom came from the American intellectual elite. Their names read like a veritable who's who of American letters and theatre, such as Lillian Hellman, William Saroyan, John Huston, John Cheever, Robert Heller, James Hilton, Ben Hecht, Irwin Shaw, Irving Wallace, Janet Flanner, and Gene Fowler.[19] The films were produced under the supervision of Frank Capra, the leading Hollywood director at the time, and were directed and co-written by none other than Dr. Seuss (Theodore Geisel), the famed author of children's books.[20] The two films, then, were not products of one person's mind but of many from among the finest in America. Furthermore, comparing the two films themselves offers us a key to America's view of two former enemies, and may open the door to deep-seated beliefs whether in war or peace. Put another way, comparing the films ought to strike a balance, so that relative inflation of national characteristics of the other, if any, may suggest a historical bias. Put still another way, if American attitudes are relatively stronger toward one over the other, then that difference might be intrinsic to American images of those cultures.

A COMPARATIVE ANALYSIS OF THE FILMS

Your Job in Germany and *Our Job in Japan*,[21] two postwar films produced for the training of American occupation forces in Germany and Japan, were examined for content. Note that this comparison seems ideal: for one, the different scripts (Germany and Japan) were produced by the same authors and filmmakers (principally Capra and "Dr. Seuss" Geisel); two, they were intended for the same audience (Army GIs); three, they served the same general purpose (orientation training); and lastly, they are from the same time frame (close of the war) and have the same objective (occupation of a former enemy nation). In this way, extraneous factors can be held in check. Analysis of the films reveals three significant features: the fundamental attribution error; a double standard in favor of Germany; and inscrutable imaging of the Japanese.

The Fundamental Error of Attribution

Attribution concerns assigning a cause to a certain behavior. As noted in Chapter 2, individuals apply situational knowledge to their own behavior that they deny in judging others.[22] However, "the tendency to underestimate situational factors when observing others is so pervasive that it has been called the 'fundamental attribution error.'"[23] Individuals tend to use a double standard in favor of themselves. From the viewpoint of the films, what causes would be given to German and Japanese warfare? These causes are presented by the films as the same problems that the American GIs had to face:

> *The German Problem*: You are up against German history. It isn't good.
>
> *The Japanese Problem*: Our problem's in the brain inside of the Japanese head....The Japanese brain bought ... exactly what the warlords wanted....That same brain today remains the problem.

The causes of the war were viewed as German history and symbolized by a history book in the related film; and the Japanese brain, symbolized by a visual of a human brain. Between the two, which is more deterministic of individual human behavior? Unquestionably, the brain.

Although historical events could influence individual human behavior, clearly the human brain does so more directly. National history is external in that we can change our national allegiance if we so desire. But not so with the brain. It follows a predetermined path of development within a certain range. Hardly anything could be more intrinsic to a person than the brain. Thus attributing war to the Japanese brain is a harsher condemnation than to a people's history. This difference follows the view held by Frank "Capra and the Pentagon, who" more readily saw individual Japanese as the enemy than in the case of individual Germans.[24]

Note that I am primarily focused on the differential imagery between German history and the Japanese brain. Both peoples were indicted as wrong for having followed evil leaders, but I am focused on the why of this blind following. I assume also that condemnation of the German people at large was necessary to ensure that GIs would keep some psychological distance from the people over whom they would be overseeing. Maintaining this distance could be especially a problem for the GIs with European ancestry, a sizable number having Germanic roots.

Some degree of "sympathy" is held toward the Germans by avoiding the ultimate step of condemnation—deducing the other's psyche to be abnormal. The act of sympathy itself is reflexive—Germany is a west European nation and therefore similar in race and culture with mainstream America. Thus the filmmakers, being of European descent, may have had some partiality toward Germany. For that reason, I have applied the principle of the fundamental error of attribution, as if the filmmakers were German (which was true in the case of "Dr. Seuss" Geisel). That partiality stopped there, however, for they also strongly condemned Nazi Germany and its people for the reason suggested.

Attributing Japan's war behavior to internal causation seems motivated because the same defect of national history could have been applied to Japan as had been to Germany. In regard to war, Japan followed a similar path from the late nineteenth century, in its surprise military attacks on China, Russia, the United States, as well as its aggression in Korea and Manchuria. Each of these attacks or aggressions could have been "chapters" producing a Japanese "history" of war as in the film on Germany. If done so, then both Germany and Japan could have been treated equally. But this would have been least on the minds of the filmmakers at the time.

The difference in treatments seems reflected in the film titles as well. *Our Job* suggests that the American elite would be working along side the GIs in Japan as opposed to what *Your Job* implies. Even if Germany had a history of "conquest disease," Japan was apparently seen as harder to deal with or, conversely, more malleable than Germany. That is, Japan, having different traditions from the west, posed the greater challenges for reform. Yet Japan also posed an opportunity for America to mold another country into its own image. In either view, American elites would be more needed in Japan, assuming significance for the difference in titles. Unfortunately, the portrayal of Japan in *Our Job in Japan* seems to echo the prewar images of Japanese mysteriousness and inscrutability. Moreover, the film on Japan need not have been so radically different from that on Germany.

Attribution of a Japanese Trait

As noted, the film on Japan states that the problem is *in the brain inside of the Japanese head*. The film emphasizes an interior metaphor: One hardly needs to be reminded of the brain's location. Yet, that message is repeated so much that the film seems to commit the same offense that it suggests the Japanese militarists committed against their own citizens—excessive drilling. The film frequently reduces the Japanese to a collective bodily organ, the brain. (Japanese *mind* is used only once; brain [or its derivative], 27 times.) By contrast, the film on Germany hardly does either: It neither "drills" the viewers (GIs), nor does it dehumanize the German people to the extent that the Japan film does. A count of the imagery (Japanese *brain* versus German *hand*) reveals that the film on Japan relied on it three times more than the film on Germany.

In brief, the film on Japan assigns the cause of the war to a Japanese trait rather than to a situation. A human trait is internal, whereas a situation is external. The Japanese brain resides inside the body; whereas the German hand outside (how these people were dehumanized in the respective films; see also the film scripts in the Appendix of this chapter). And not surprisingly, the language of the Japan film uses a container metaphor, the brain, and related spatial metaphors: *in the brain inside of the Japanese head; put inside [the brain]; hammer in; sink in; hammer out; think out of*.

Second, the brain or mind is the seat of intelligence as well as other human characteristics. Without a brain one could not act in human fashion, particularly with rationality. According to *Our Job*, Japan was a "old backward, superstitious country" whose Shinto was "a tired religion" that was "filled up ... with hokum" to lead its people to war through a lot of "mumbo jumbo." Cast in an aura of mysteriousness, the film presented the Japanese as "people trained to follow blindly wherever their leaders led them." In sum, the choice of body part (brain), spatial metaphors, and the characterization of the culture relate to a perceived trait of the Japanese—mindlessness or irrationality.

Attribution of a German Situation

In contrast, the war with Germany seems to be attributed by the film to a cause external to individual German behavior: their history. And indeed German history is later visualized as a book, an outside object. Although the film does speak of a "German conquest disease" and a "lust for conquest," these are more like states than traits. (*Disease* is defined as "any harmful condition, as of society."[25] *Condition* implies far more changeability than what *trait* does.)

Responsibility for one's actions may differ according to whether induced by a state or trait. States are more easily induced by outside forces and are relatively transitory. German history was the "outside force" inducing a state or disease for conquest. Yet, states are changeable; traits are more characteristic of one's self, permanent and immutable. And this difference between state and trait corresponds to the perceived relative difficulty of occupying the two nations as implied by the films' respective titles, a point made earlier. Consequently, Japan, having been trait attributed, carries more responsibility for war than Germany, a matter discussed next.

Responsibility for War

Regardless of however negative the image of Germans might be in the related film, compared to the Japanese, Germans seemed to have been relieved of some responsibility for the Second World War. It is almost as if the German nation could not help itself. Again, this is compared to the film about Japan, a point that must be remembered throughout this analysis. By itself, the film about Germany is extremely harsh on that nation. There is no obvious hint of sympathy. However, relative to Japan, there is a distinct difference how these matters are treated. Only by comparison would we ever think that American leadership viewed the two nations qualitatively different.

And indeed, the two films appear to arouse different conclusions as to Japan's and Germany's potential for making war again. The film on Japan emphatically states that "this is Japan's last war." But the film on Germany does not. Instead, it ambiguously seems to allow for that country to take up arms again:

> And Chapter Four [warfare] could be. It can happen again. The next war—that is why you occupy Germany. To make that next war impossible—no easy job.

On the subject of propaganda and oppression, Germany again seems to receive favor. Although the film on Germany states that propaganda in Germany "produced the worst educational crime in the entire history of the world," it is the Japanese who are shown as becoming muddleheaded. When one considers the awesome tragedy inflicted on the Jews and others in the Nazi concentration camps—all aided and abetted by German citizenry—one must wonder why the film on Germany did not wax clinic and pathologic on the German brain as was the case for the Japanese.

In brief, both countries are seen to be intrinsically warlike but for different reasons. For Japan, its warfare arises from a trait of the Japanese; for Germany, a situation of the nation. In effect, for the Japanese this means that "you can take Kenji out of the jungle, but you cannot take the jungle out of Kenji." A similar logic required placing Japanese Americans into internment camps during War World II but not ethnic Germans.[26] Germans were only dangerous in the situation of being in their German motherland; otherwise, they too would have been interned like Japanese Americans. German Americans were able to keep some respect even if they were attacked in certain communities in the United States at the time.

Compensating for the Germans in this way was a matter of course: Germany was an "old club member" of the west. And that membership bestowed certain prerogatives, including warfare. Consequently, the occupation of Japan required special attention by American elites (*Our Job* versus *Your Job)* and more determination to deter war from an upstart.

Current Trade Frictions— Reflection of the Past?

This differential treatment of the two films seems to parallel different responses to economic competition from Japan and Germany. During a period of threatened trade war in the 1980s, both countries bought up American assets and enjoyed a large trade surplus. Yet American wrath was vented almost exclusively on Japan. How can one account for this differential treatment?

Theodore White, the Pulitzer Prize author, may provide an answer. In reference to trade frictions, he tersely points out that "[t]he Germans, somehow, evoke little American bitterness because we understand their culture."[27] And White, some forty years after the war's end, echoes what was suggested above about the trait attribution of Japan. Recalling his own presence at the Japanese peace-signing in 1945, he takes up trait attribution when he writes that Americans in general viewed Japanese like "all Orientals, as errant little brown brothers who must be rebuked, but then brought into western civilization."[28] A trait attribution because it was based on an internal characteristic—biological or racial in this case.

War fever and the times contributed to such views, of course. The fact remains, however, that the Germans seemed to be treated relatively less harshly than the Japanese. No matter how one feels about the films' perspective, it is not difficult to show that the American filmmakers succumbed to subjectivity, if not irrationality, when it came to the Japanese. Qualities, in fact, they resoundingly faulted in *Our Job in Japan*. It becomes important, therefore, for Americans to recognize their own ambivalent attitudes toward Japan.

The task, then, is to be vigilant in monitoring such attitudes so as to control their related behavior. This recognition of ambivalency toward Japan, then, can lead one to a broader critique of culture and, in so doing, will underscore the value of the present research. To complete this discussion, inscrutable imaging of the Japanese will be illustrated by a contemporary example. Following that will be a short sketch (see Box 3.1) about Japanese wartime imaging of its opponents to provide some balance.

UNMASKING THE MYSTERIOUS ORIENT(AL) SCHEMA

The children's cartoon *Mask* [29] was chosen as a contemporary example of the mysterious Orient(al) schema because

> Comics, children's literature, and textbooks play an important role within the wider context of processes of socialization. They help to transmit the general cultural beliefs that have been accumulated during our colonial histories. And the media provide the more specific picture about the current ethnic situation, defining the topics of concern and the overall negative evaluation of minorities in our society.[30]

Children are vulnerable to such material because they are impressionable and naive. Thus cartoons and the like merit special attention in this regard.

Mask is a cartoon series about a team of anti-terrorist fighters and their exploits. One member of the team is a Japanese named Bruce Sato. Six episodes, approximately thirty minutes in length each, were examined to note how this Japanese was portrayed.[31] It was found that in nearly half of the situations in which Bruce Sato appears, his associates complain that he does not make sense.

Although he seems to be living in North America, Bruce Sato is identifiable as a Japanese national for these reasons:

(1) He has a foreign accent in English.
(2) Sato is a common Japanese family name comparable to Smith or Jones in English.
(3) Japan is a setting for one of the cartoons in which he states how it brings back memories of his ancestral home.

Bruce Sato speaks English correctly, yet he still miscommunicates. Indeed, this is typical behavior for him. In fact, this is made abundantly clear in his first line spoken in the series, an utterance that causes another character to say: "There he goes again ... not making any sense." Moreover, similar reactions are heard throughout the sampled cartoons. Let us consider some:

- Hey Bruce, I almost understood that. Huh, must be something wrong with me.
- What in thunder is he talking about?
- Ah gee, Bruce, can't you ever give us a break?

His problem is neither linguistic nor phonological but rather intentional: Bruce Sato simply talks in riddles—proverbs—and does not bother to explain the import of his utterances. Obviously, his character is meant to be enigmatic and echoes a long tradition of western views of Japan as discussed above.

The concern here is that *Mask* is targeted for children. Because Bruce Sato's proverbs are uncommon, likely to strike the adult as odd or foreign, their comprehension requires analysis. Children are likely to be unsophisticated about proverbs and fail to perform such analysis. Even for adults, time constraints may prevent it. Thus, Bruce Sato may seem especially circuitous in thought and thereby reinforcing the image of Japanese enigma. Thus, too, this cartoon illustrates both the continuity and substance of a North American/western culture myth about Japanese communication style being incomprehensible, circular or both. (*Circular* refers to how Japanese discourse, in form or content, is perceived as being vague or illogical. Such issues are taken up in Part 3 of this book.)

In my many years of intimacy with the Japanese, I have never met one who spoke in riddles. Yes, speech behavior in Japanese and English can be quite different, but I wonder if characterizing Japanese speech as "circular" does more harm than good. First, Japanese behavior is highly situational: One can readily see this with use of *keigo*, respect language tailored to fit perceived social differences between interactants (see Chapter 5). In other words, perceived circularity may relate to situational behavior more than inherent "Japaneseness." Second, "circular" as applied is poorly if ever defined. Third, the term is not neutral: Circular speech or thought often has a pejorative sense in English. Consequently, specialists in intercultural communication ought to rethink the utility of using a term that already possesses negative nuances. Such terms could unwittingly reinforce extreme caricature as that found in the cartoon series *Mask*.

CONCLUSION

In regard to the Japanese people, one persistent trait attributed to them is inscrutability, an image held in the west since the earliest contacts with Japan in the sixteenth century. The persistence of this image was explained through the concept of social or group schema, a system of beliefs motivated by favor of the ingroup. Group schema may tend to increase the prevalence of the fundamental error of attribution. This error in perception was identified by a comparative analysis of two training films made for the military occupation of Germany and Japan. These films differed essentially in assigning the cause of the Second World War to a German situation (history) but to a Japanese trait—mindlessness or irrationality. Having been trait-attributed in a similar way, Japanese Americans were placed in internment camps as a matter of course. If a group is already perceived as "different"—mysterious, inscrutable, or whatever—the group is likely to be discriminated against. Enculturation of the inscrutability image in contemporary North America was suggested in an analysis of a children's cartoon's portrayal of a Japanese character.

Communication specialists realize that interpersonal communication hardly ever begins with a clean slate. That the indexing of interlocutors into sociocultural categories occurs as a function of language has long been known by linguists. A host of prior images and beliefs about the other may impinge and possibly interfere even to the chagrin of the parties involved. Identifying such images and beliefs enshrined by the mysterious Orient(al) schema may be a step toward improving intercultural communication between Japanese and North Americans. It is hoped that this work will stimulate continued research into the mutual images between our cultures. After all, a landmark study by Urie Bronfenbrenner suggests that "the other group often holds very similar stereotypes, indeed they often form mirror-images."[32] Illuminating our mutual images might help remove the cultural shadows that linger from the past. Before closing this chapter, it may be useful to consider Japan's wartime propaganda images of us. We take a brief glimpse simply to show that propagandizing occurred on both sides of the Pacific (an application activity then follows). Finally, I should point out that similar work with the mass media is taken up again in Chapters 10 and 11.

Box 3.1 Japan's Wartime Propaganda

Evidence exits that Japanese print media during World War II contained racist visual imagery of Asian peoples, Americans, and others.[33] In regard to film media, the issue is uncertain. One Japanese researcher summarizes various investigations of Japanese wartime film and concludes that "the image of the 'enemy' is startlingly absent in these films."[34] Though accurate as his conclusion may be, it is also true that some known Japanese wartime film was purposely destroyed at the end of the war. "As American troops converged on Japan after the surrender, the skies of Japan were filled with the smoke of burning documents. Contributing to this haze was [at least one known propaganda film]."[35] We can suppose that the reason for this destruction was the "fear [of] reprisals from the Occupation forces."[36]

Ironically, Japanese filmmakers and propagandists found themselves in a losing struggle early on in the "film war." Their technological disadvantage, compared to western industry, may also explain why American war films so overshadow their counterparts in fury or amount.

> It is clear that the Japanese were keenly aware of the fact that the technology for [film as an] important ideological weapon belonged mainly to [the Allies]. Nothing brought this fact home more closely than the beautiful color cinematography of *Gone with the Wind*, which painfully illustrated the superiority and power of the enemy, at least as far as the 'film war' was concerned. Over and over again, Japanese writers lamented the fact that Japanese films could only be made in black and white and that production and distribution lagged far behind that of the enemy. For example, Imamura Taihei ... [wrote in 1941] "All of our motion picture cameras are American, and we do not have the means to restock any of them. This dependence on the enemy for the greatest weapon of ideological war indicates just how far behind Japan is lagging in the Greater East Asia War."[37]

American propagandists were better equipped than the Japanese to give fuller vent to war passions. That, however, does not condone the racism evident in the "Job" films discussed. Nor does it excuse it on the part of the Japanese either. We all need to work toward improved relations.

APPLICATION

Consider the following questions in relation to the film scripts in the Appendix of this chapter:

A. Undoubtedly the American military would have been concerned about its occupation soldiers becoming overly sympathetic with the people of the former enemy nation. Otherwise their duty as "guards" could be compromised.

1. Would this concern be felt equally about the Germans and Japanese? Why or why not?
2. What related strategies to deal with this concern can be found reflected in the scripts?
3. The prospect of GIs marrying women of the former

enemy, particularly Japan, was a concern (see James Michener's novel *Sayonara*). Can you find possible traces of such concern between the two scripts? (Very subtle in the case of *Our Job in Japan* but a direct reference might have been seen as potential encouragement; moreover GIs might not have been expected to become attracted to women of another "race.") What were the related social conditions in the United States at the time? What related irony is found in the script for *Our Job in Japan*?

B American idealism may have been seductive enough to make people think that the United States could mold a country into its own image. Consider the film scripts for any suggestions of this.

C How do the scripts differ in viewing Americans vis-à-vis the Germans and the Japanese?

APPENDIX

Your Job in Germany (Abridged)

1. …Germany today appears to be beaten. Hitler out. Swastikas gone. Nazi propaganda off the air. Concentration camps empty.
2. ... You are up against German history. It isn't good. This book was written chapter by chapter. Not by one man. Not by one *fuhrer*. It was written by the German people.
3. Chapter One—the *fuhrer:* Bismarck. The title: Blood and Iron. The armies: German. Under the Prussian Bismarck the German empire was built.
4. ... And Chapter Four could be. It can happen again. The next war—that is why you occupy Germany. To make that next war impossible—no easy job. …The Nazi party may be gone, but Nazi thinking, Nazi training, and Nazi trickery remain. The German lust for conquest is not dead. It's merely gone undercover. Somewhere ... are the SS guards …[and] two million ex-nazi officials.
5. [Another group to guard against is this group.] These are the most dangerous—German youth. Children, when the Nazi party came into power … [and] products of the worst educational crime in the entire history of the world….
6. Don't argue with [the Germans]. Don't try to change their point of view. Other Allied representatives will concern themselves with that. You are not being sent into Germany as educators. You are soldiers on guard. You will observe their local laws. Respect their customs and religion. And you will respect their property rights. You will not ridicule them. You will not argue with them. You will not be friendly. You will be aloof, watchful, and suspicious. …You will not associate with German men, women, or children.
7. …That is the hand that *heiled* Adolf Hitler. That is the hand that dropped the bombs…. That is the hand that murdered…. That is the hand that killed…. Don't clasp that hand. It's not the kind of hand you can clasp in friendship. "But there're millions of Germans. Some of those guys must be okay." Perhaps. But which ones?
8. …Someday the German people might be cured of their disease, the super-race disease, the world conquest disease. … Until that day, we stand guard. ... Their plan for world conquest shall stop here and now.... We are determined that the vicious German cycle of war … shall once and for all time come to an end.

Our Job in Japan (Abridged)

1. … What does a conquering army do with 70 million Japanese people? What does a conquering army do with a family of the Japanese soldier: fathers, brothers, mothers, cousins of the soldiers? ... People trained to follow blindly…. People … led into waging a war so disgusting, so revolting, so obscene that it turned the stomach of the entire civilized world.
2. … Our problem's … in the brain inside of the Japanese head. There are 70 million of these in Japan. Physically no different than any other brains in the world. Actually all made of exactly the same stuff as ours. These brains like our brains can do good things or bad things, all depending on the kind of ideas that are put inside.
3. … We had miles [and years of stinking war]. All because of one idea that was sold to the Japanese brain. That same brain today remains the problem. Our problem. It will cost us time. It will cost us patience. But we are determined that this fact will finally sink in. This is Japan's last war.
4. … [The militaristic idea had] been hammered into these people's heads. The United States Army can't hammer it out. … [The Japanese] and only they can think their way out of this stuff. Our job is to see that they do it. Our job is to watch them while they do it, to watch them for tricks, to slap down any who try to pull tricks.
5. … At the same time, [those who are honest] are looking to us to help them prove that our idea is better than the Japanese idea. These people are going to judge America and all Americans by us. That means we've got another job to do. That job is to be ourselves. By being ourselves we can prove that what we like to call the American way or democracy or just plain old, golden rule, common sense is a pretty good way to live. … We can prove that most Americans do believe in a fair break for everybody regardless of race or creed or color.
6. … And by being ourselves we can show them that though we are normally an easy going people … we know what the score is—because we do. … We're here to make it clear that the Japanese brain that we've had enough of, this bloody barbaric business, [will] last us from here on. … We're here to make it clear to the Japanese that their time has now come to make sense, modern civilized sense.

4

Stereotypes, Cultural Elitism, and Racism

In this chapter, we consider some persistent problems involving stereotypes, cultural elitism, and racism. Because the subject of these "isms" is likely to be familiar, we will move directly to applied aspects of these issues. For example, we will explore how one textbook fails to follow its own advice about stereotyping. In another case, we will see how standard material in college economics slips into ethnocentrism regarding Japan. Other topics will include issues about the accuracy of stereotypes, the usefulness of personality types, as well as the perceptual problems that the Japanese might have in viewing us. We begin with stereotypes.

STEREOTYPES

As recently argued in the psychological literature, stereotypes are not necessarily inaccurate. On the basis of an earlier idea that stereotypes possess a "kernel of truth," some researchers have legitimately challenged the notion that stereotypes must be incorrect. This issue is important for us because observers of culture typically make generalizations about other people. It is commonly said, for example, that jockeys are short, and basketball players are tall. Though stereotypes, they might prove useful for a 5-foot-tall aspiring athlete. His chances for a professional career would be far greater as a jockey than as a basketball player. This point seems sensible because it is verifiable. Physical height is readily observed, easily proving or disproving such statements. Moreover, physical data on professional athletes are typically published in printed programs and elsewhere.[1] Such examples show the accuracy of stereotypes—or do they?

What makes statements stereotypes rather than generalizations? Though I used the word *stereotypes,* I did so for present purposes. Little guidance exists on the matter, even though stereotypes have been studied in the social sciences for over 50 years. In fact, this question has emerged only recently, especially in the literature on intercultural communication. We can begin only after defining the terms. First, according to *Random House Webster's College Dictionary*, a generalization is an act, process, or result of "making a general statement, idea or principle"; "a proposition asserting something to be true either of all members of a certain class or of an indefinite part of that class." By this definition, it appears that the above statements about jockeys and basketball players are indeed generalizations.

As for *stereotype*, many definitions exist, but a consensus has not yet been reached.[2] For our purposes, a stereotype is an exaggerated image (mental, verbal, or visual) of the characteristics of a target group, which is motivated by intergroup tension or conflict. An exaggerated image typically borders on caricature and is judged negatively by or for the target group members. (*Target group* here can include any social, racial, or ethnic group.) Stereotyping is the process of imputing a stereotype to others or the treatment of others in a gross, undifferentiated manner according to some preconceived notions of the others' social or racial status.

In regard to our notion of jockeys and basketball players, unless we were to forget about individual differences, we would probably be safe in saying that these notions remain generalizations. These notions seem free from exaggeration, are not particularly negative, and do not involve caricature. In other situations, however, such cases will not be so clear cut; applying the concept will probably remain problematic. Nevertheless, we who aspire to interpret other cultures are morally compelled to be concerned. Although some stereotypes may contain a "kernel of truth," their content and use could have serious consequences.

One example involves the so-called "ethnic joke" of the type that maligns a people's intelligence or competence, such as "How many 'X' ('X' being members of a target group) does it take to screw in a light bulb?" As outrageous as it seems, I once observed a professional instructor in ESL (English as a Second Language), an American, teach his class such a joke, naming an actual ethnic group! He said that he used such jokes routinely to add humor to his classes. I also found similar ethnic jokes in two published British ESL-type textbooks. These cases, I am sure, are isolated, but they remind me that even educated people can succumb to such mindlessness.

In another example, one I have reported elsewhere, stereotyping was used unwittingly in a poster titled "Economic Growth and Competition in the Global Economy,"[3] produced to accompany an American college textbook on economics. This instructional poster was exhibited in a display case by an economics department at a state university in Michigan. From the poster I wrote down the following names of countries used in its international comparisons (see Table 4.1):

Table 4.1 Country Names from a Poster on Global Economics

Argentina	Germany	Russia
Australia	Indonesia	Saudi Arabia
Brazil	Japan, Inc.	South Africa
Canada	Mexico	South Korea
China	Poland	United States

Close inspection showed that "Japan, Inc." was not graffiti.

Table 4.1 (continued)

Even if it were, the expression merits attention. That an economics department would display it suggests its complicity. The reader may wish to pause for these questions:

1. What image is brought to mind by this name for Japan?
2. Is this name appropriate? Why or why not?
3. Is the information relevant to the place where this poster was found, concerning the academic department, the type of institution, and the geographical location? Why or why not?
4. Could this name affect the cross-cultural comparisons? Why or why not?

International understanding goes only as far as mutual respect. Recently, researchers and authors in intercultural communication have seemed to place too much emphasis on the accuracy of stereotypes. If they are truly accurate, I would question whether they were really stereotypes. A long tradition already exists, in which stereotypes are associated with inaccurate, negative notions of other people, usually those of less powerful groups. Certainly research into the accuracy of stereotypes would be fruitful, but not if that encourages us to lose our caution about stereotypes. Some stereotypes are demeaning and complicate interracial relations.

When a Textbook Does Not Follow its Own Advice

A textbook titled *An Introduction to Intercultural Communication*[4] and written by two linguists, one American and the other Japanese, disregards its own advice about stereotyping. After taking the admirable step of distinguishing stereotypes from generalizations, something rarely done by others, the authors state, "A person who maintains a stereotype believes every member of the group has that characteristic. That is, stereotypes, because of their simplistic nature, can stop us from seeing other people as individuals."[5] The authors, however, seem not to follow their own prescriptions when they report that a survey found that 25 percent of the residents of a major Japanese city, which we will presently call "City X," "avoid foreigners."[6] These residents gave various reasons for doing so, including perceived differences in language and culture. The authors then state, "What is operating here is pure stereotyping. The residents of [City X] in this survey have no real knowledge of foreigners, but feel quite strongly that foreigners cannot speak Japanese and that their personalities and customs are too different for socializing."[7] "Residents of City X"? Is that expression accurate when only 25 percent of the respondents are involved? Could it be that the authors are stereotyping the other 75 percent? And what if the original survey was not based on a randomized sample (a point not considered)?

One also might ask if the 25 percent of respondents were actually stereotyping foreigners. A problem occurs in the authors' analysis because many foreigners in Japan, many of whom are tourists or transients, are not functionally competent in Japanese. Although I do not advocate avoidance of a certain people, some Japanese may have good reason for their avoidance of foreigners. Such Japanese, for example, might include taxi drivers who had lost money on fares by serving foreigners who gave them misleading information about destinations. (Japanese courtesy may induce the taxi driver to relinquish the fare.) The same may be true of a communication gap for workers in various commercial services. More broadly, some Japanese might feel uncomfortable if English, in which they may have little fluency, became the language of communication with foreigners. Also, we do not know how far the survey respondents in question would follow their belief in the face of contradictory cases. It is possible that many of them would stop avoiding foreigners if the latter were fluent in Japanese.

I hasten to add that these authors use an overly simplistic definition of stereotypes as when someone "believes every member of the group has [a particular] characteristic." This means that hardly anyone could be accused of stereotyping because even avowed racists have been found to permit exceptional cases. It would be too easy to delude oneself by saying, "I am not stereotyping because I don't think everyone of Group X is lazy—just these over here." Or, "That Albert Einstein was a great man. It's just those others of his group in this town who are bad." This saying is the flip side of the argument known as "some of my best friends are 'X,'" which is sometimes used to deny that one has any prejudice. Consequently, the authors appear to be on weak ground for distinguishing generalizations from stereotypes.

The lack of clarity in distinguishing stereotypes from generalizations becomes problematic when the authors suggest that they can avoid stereotyping by "using words like *typically, usually,* and *most* when [they] talk about generalizations."[8] (Again, note our definition above.) Would this mean that racist language only needs such words to be "cleaned up"? The authors are at least partly right in observing that the use of such words can help. Such qualifiers, however, can help only if one is not stereotyping initially. This point is important because the authors themselves may not be clear on how to distinguish generalizations from stereotypes. Although they may use such qualifiers in *theory,* there is no guarantee that they do so in *practice.* In fact, what may be a generalization, could become stereotyping in practice. Technically, for example, these authors unwittingly stereotyped residents of City X, as seen above. These same authors similarly err in their treatment of the Kpelle of Africa, a matter discussed in Chapter 9. If these authors, while teaching how not to stereotype, slip into stereotyping themselves, then *stereotype* and *stereotyping* obviously require much more caution than previously thought.

Avoiding Stereotypes

How can we avoid stereotyping others? Unfortunately there is no easy solution. As members of the field of intercultural communication have recently realized, even our well-intentioned descriptions of others could turn out to be stereotyping. In this context, Richard Brislin, a leader of the field, makes a distinction between stereotypes and *reasonable generalizations.*[9] According to this distinction, *stereotypes* is used as if it were inherently inaccurate, which bears out our view on the subject. Indeed, this is the traditional view of stereotypes, as exemplified by the contrasting term, *sociotypes.* E. Bogardus coined this word for situations "[w]hen stereotypes involve substantially realistic assignments of traits to a group of people (i.e., are valid)."[10] Authors, however, sometimes use the term *stereotypes* when perhaps *sociotypes* or some other term might be more appropriate. Yet even if sociotypes are involved, their use could amount to stereotyping if misapplied.

Brislin essentially advises us never to forget to view others as individuals.[11] If we keep that point in mind, we are unlikely to overgeneralize information about a group to an individual person. In other words, we must treat others as human beings first, rather than as members of groups based on gender, ethnicity, religion, and so on.

When in Japan, it seems that many Japanese treat me first as a *gaijin* (foreigner) before anything else. Others, however, make me feel that they interact with me without preconceived notions of what I am or should be. This issue occurs even within one's own culture, but is more noticeable in a different culture. By recognizing such treatment, we may be more able to identify it in our own behavior toward others. Moreover, this point suggests the major reason for writing this book: Intercultural effectiveness is the result of an ongoing awareness of our perceptions and thoughts, and management of our behavior, so as to control our ethnocentric impulses and responses.

Still, a paradox remains: It may be necessary for us to be conscious of another culture's normative (or standard) behavior. Service providers, for example, must tailor their services to meet the needs of others. This tailoring process includes knowing the sociotypes—the customary behavior and interests of others. As I stated earlier, sociotypes are not the same as stereotypes, as we have defined the term. Nor are they "personality types." "As is well known, cultures do not conform to a single personality type."[12] Also, it is generally accepted that there are probably more intracultural than intercultural differences. Every culture includes members with a wide range of personality types.

Associating a culture with a certain, single personality type seems hazardous. After all, "culture" and "personality" are a bit like "fictions," as explained by Dean C. Barnlund:

> Culture has no objective existence. It is no more than a metaphor, a fiction inferred from consistency in the daily acts of individuals. It is too easy to reify this concept. Cultures are not artifacts but explanatory generalizations based on the way people make their living, compete or collaborate with one another. Consistency in behavior leads to postulating the existence of a culture to account for the similarity in Japanese or French or American behavior.

> Similarly, personalities do not have objective existence. The human personality also is a fiction, an explanatory metaphor inferred from acts over time. What differentiates one person from another—motives, needs, interests—is never directly observable but is derived from consistencies in their actions from one setting to another. Although it is convenient to talk about people as if they had a culture, neither is tangible; they are constructs rather than concretes. Their value lies in the number and importance of the behaviors they explain or predict."[13]

Description and attribution are not synonymous. Description involves the concretely observable; attribution much less so. A problem in observation occurs when attribution is treated as if it were description. What we think is the cause of another person's behavior is actually our inference: We infer causation using circumstantial information. Our accuracy is little guaranteed and even less so across cultures. In being introduced to a Japanese, for example, his or her face may appear expressionless. Our visceral response might be that this person "doesn't like me" or "doesn't like foreigners." Perhaps, but that is still an attribution: We have inferred a motive or cause. Just as likely is that the Japanese feels shy and has more positive feelings toward foreigners than we think.

The first impulse is to internalize the other's unfriendliness and defensively react by attributing this behavior to his or her assumed negative traits. Being more mindful, we hope to remember that our attributions of others are inferences and therefore fallible. (Description is also fallible but less so if kept to the concretely observable.) Recognizing this fallibility may help us to reserve judgment about traits and search for some situational reasons to explain the person's manner, such as the environmental conditions, the person's age, or his or her current activity. With more experience in Japan, we will learn that shy behaviors are more acceptable there, and an expressionless demeanor of a Japanese may have nothing to do with us or our foreignness.

A similar problem but one at a different level is the assigning of personality types to cultures:

> It is essentially impossible to describe human beings and their behavior without making some statements having to do with individual psychology; and when one characterizes the behaviors of a number of informants, deliberately or inadvertently, individ-

> ual characterizations become group typifications at some level. Human behavior is at once sociocultural and psychological, always existing on two levels.[14]

Describing people according to "types" is part of everyday life. V. Lynn Tyler of Brigham Young University, an early leader in the field, suggested that we can use the concept of "cultural personality," as long as we remain flexible enough to deal with others as individuals.[15] This advice is sound and has proved helpful. Along with that proviso and the control of our attributions of others, I suggest that we exchange the idea of "cultural personality" for "mindsets."

Mindsets

Mindsets, a term of Glen Fisher's,[16] refers to fixed ways of viewing the world as a result of experience—learning, both formal and informal. Compared to personality, mindsets are a function of *cognition* and *past learning*, and imply the possibility for change (however difficult that may be). In contrast, personality is much more deep-seated—perhaps even linked to our genes—and strongly resists change. Moreover, psychologists debate about the role of psychology in human behavior and culture. The concept of mindsets seems to involve human behavior less broadly than either "personality" or "self," and thus may allow more flexibility in viewing others.

Reality, like beauty, is in the eye of the beholder. Social situations often are perceived and understood in as many different ways as there are people. Everyone has experienced differences of opinion; most such disputes derive from the simple fact that each person is unique and is "programmed" to view things differently from others. Ethnic conflicts arise from fundamental differences in values and beliefs. These differences are not a matter of *personality* but of *perception*. Because each group contains many different kinds of individuals, too varied to be limited to one strict "type," we ought to avoid linking personality types to cultures and instead should apply the concept of mindsets. In this way, a clear break can be made with the notion of cultural personality. The latter will always have appeal, but probably it is best left in the domain of clinical theory.

In determining the mindset for a particular culture, consider the questions that follow. First, what historical or past events between their nation or culture and ours may be a sensitive issue—or, if not sensitive, remembered nonetheless? This question probably applies more often at the national than at the individual level. Still, even diplomatic matters can affect intercultural relations.

When a French politician referred to the Japanese as living in "rabbit hutches," an uproar arose in Japan. About two years after that incident, when I boarded the bullet train (*shinkansen*) in Tokyo, I took a seat in front of three Japanese men in business attire. As soon as I sat down, the three began to speak English to each other in mock ridicule so that I could hear: "Do you know that Japanese live in 'rabbit hutches'?" "No, I can't believe it." "Well, just look out there. Look at those people with the big ears going into that house...." Their voices were absent of any mirth. Imagine if they had to conduct negotiations with foreign officials. Would they be able to prevent their private feelings from affecting their work? Perhaps or perhaps not. This example also shows how the Japanese may lump westerners together, just as the reverse case may happen.

On sensitive issues like these, Japanese may "test" westerners in subtle or nonconscious ways, even if they do not intend to do so. At a party, for example, you may reach for a bottle of lemonade on the snack table at precisely the same moment as a Japanese. He or she might chuckle and say, while touching the bottle, "Ah, yellow like me." This would be a very rare event, but nevertheless how would you respond? Cross-cultural situations especially encourage us to emulate our foreign hosts' behavior. We are likely to laugh out of emotional contagion. It would be a mistake, however, to do so with the "lemonade" remark and is probably best ignored.

In a similar situation, a Canadian instructor of English took a survey of his students in his first class meeting at a school in Japan. On one form, a student had written: "What do you think of yellow monkey?" This teacher was naturally upset and had to be assured that he probably had done nothing to elicit that comment.[17] A Japanese newspaper, reporting on the historical racial epithets applied to the Japanese, suggested that Hitler had originated that of *yellow monkey*.[18] During World War II, the American Admiral Halsey referred to the Japanese in that way (the Japanese retaliated by calling Americans "albino monkeys").[19] In a twist on this story, a popular Japanese rock band was formed (years after the student comment above) by the name of "Yellow Monkey," apparently out of ethnic pride by "staring the demon right in the face."

I encountered a further twist in the early 1980s, when I was the program chair for an international conference of language teachers held in Japan. One of our plenary speakers was an educator from the United States, who had written an acclaimed resource book for applying techniques from the human potential movement to teaching and learning foreign languages. In a word, the book was "touchy-feely." She also was invited to speak at a local university in Nagoya. There she began by scanning the mainly Japanese audience and saying gleefully, "I feel so yellow today!" The comment doomed her presentation, which called for participation by the audience. Apparently, she meant that she was feeling energetic by making a metaphoric reference to the sun. The Japanese, however, customarily imagine the sun as red, as shown on their national flag and in the schoolchildren's drawings of the sun. This case illustrates the need to remain aware of cultural differences and the history of sensitive topics, such as racial relations, even though the Japanese very rarely ever make this an issue.

Another useful question about mindsets is what are model social and communicative behaviors in the respective cultures? Each culture has its own preferred social manners and styles of communication. In speech, they will differ as to spatial distance between the individuals, their amount and types of gesture and touch, preferred topics, conversational routines in listening, turn taking, floor management, and so on. We still have much to learn about nonverbal behavior, but in general, Anglo Americans tend to fall conversationally between that of Latin peoples and the Japanese. When Americans deal with Japanese, some restraint may be needed. For example, some Americans tend to interrupt Japanese speakers or monopolize the floor. This behavior is especially serious if the language used is English because Americans may forget themselves. Reticence on the part of Japanese is not necessarily a sign of disinterest or hostility; and it should never be taken as a lack of intelligence. Because of their mindset, formal social situations may prompt the Japanese to be ultrapolite, reticent, and cautious. In other settings and circumstances, their behavior will be quite different however. If we do not appreciate this variability in behavior, we are likely to fall prey to stereotypical thinking. Attitudes related to such thinking are likely to be sensed by others.

These two questions can take us a long way in applying the concept of mindsets. An advantage of mindsets in interpreting cultures is that mindsets are more restrictive than personality because they focus on cultural ideals and learned behavior. The fact that learning is involved suggests variability: Members of a culture may fulfill their cultural ideals in various ways. Some individuals are simply more orthodox than others. This point may help us to be flexible in our expectations of others.

In sum, it is natural for us to categorize others according to "types." A problem occurs if we view a people as having a single personality type. This view is mistaken because all cultures produce people along a range of personality types. Mindsets were suggested as a way to view others more flexibly. An added proviso is that Japanese social relations are highly situational. Whether we apply mindsets or personality types, Japanese public (*tatemae*) and private (*honne*) behaviors can be starkly different, more so than the case with North Americans. Thus we must be especially flexible when engaging the Japanese.

Socially, the Japanese place more importance on form than content (see Chapter 6 concerning Shinto), whereas North Americans believe in the opposite. Our impulse is to rush to break down the formality, and we may even resort to back-slapping behaviors to do so. That, however, would be a mistake with the Japanese because as Chapter 1 pointed out, *enryo*—personal reserve—is a Japanese ideal. That is why the Japanese Nobel laureate's withdrawal, in the example used, could be seen so positively by the Japanese audience. That is an extreme case, for not all Japanese would react as that Nobel prizewinner, but his *enryo* could be recognized nonetheless. In the case of Japanese *enryo*, it often needs to run its course, a reason why Japanese social relationships take time to develop (see Chapter 1, Hamid Saleem's work in the Japanese scientific laboratories). If we approach the Japanese while being mindful of the culture's model behavior (e.g., *enryo*) but ready to accept individual differences, we will be more effective interculturally.

NIHONJINRON

Nihonjinron ("discussions of the Japanese" or "theories of

Japaneseness"),[20] also known by *Nihon bunkaron, Nihon shakairon,* and *Nihonron*),[21] is a genre of thought in Japan that extols the uniqueness of the Japanese. "The Japanese manifest consuming interest in the question of who they are in a cultural sense, so much so that the discourse on Japanese identity may even be called a minor national pastime."[22] "*Nihonjinron* encompasses virtually all aspects of Japanese culture in the broadest sense—from 'race' and cultural origins to social structure and psyche."[23] "Essentially, the message ... is that Japan, the Japanese, and Japanese society are unique in the world—topographically, linguistically, structurally, culturally, even anatomically."[24] Therefore, we can readily agree with Harumi Befu that "*Nihonjinron* is ethnocentric: it aims to demonstrate the superiority of Japanese culture over other cultures."[25]

"This belief [in uniqueness] often leads [Japanese] to believe that foreigners will never be able to learn the Japanese language and that they will never really understand the Japanese culture."[26] Hence "the Japanese frequently use their language as a focal point of cultural identity, and thereby as a means of setting themselves apart from all other linguistic and cultural groups."[27] This belief in uniqueness is so naive that during World War II the Japanese military, at one point, transmitted messages uncoded under the delusion that the Allies would be unable to understand Japanese.[28]

The epitome of *Nihonjinron* is the theory by a Japanese researcher, Tadanobu Tsunoda, that the Japanese brain is neurologically different from that of other peoples.[29] Tsunoda's methodology has been shown to be severely flawed; yet some authors writing about Japan have accepted it. One source of the presumed support for the theory is the notion of the uniqueness of the Japanese language; one Japanese acquaintance of mine, a brain specialist, believed this theory himself. I had expected this person to give me some neurological or other technical reasons for his belief. When I asked him what made the Japanese language unique, he replied, "Its sentence order." Yet Japanese is classified as SOV (subject-object-verb), the world's most frequently occurring type.[30] Because this fact is generally unknown to many Japanese and because their second language is primarily English, they may develop the view that the Japanese language is unusual. Ironically, after a study of English, some Japanese schoolchildren assume that the metric system, which Japan follows, must be unique because English measurement is (or was) non-metrical.

One reason *Nihonjinron* endures, I believe, is its flip side, national self-deprecation. The naive view of metric measure is one example. Another is the "*shimaguni* sentiment," the view that Japan is not only an "island country" but also quite small. In the words of a Japanese linguist, "Japan is a very small island country...."[31] Or as in the words of a Japanese historian:

> Japan is a small island country lying off ... the coast of China. One does not have to be Japanese in order to know this elementry [sic] fact of geography.... There is no denying that in terms of total land area, Japan is one of the smaller nations.[32]

Yet Japan is one and a half times larger than United Kingdom.[33] In fact, Japan is larger than half of all the nations of the world.[34] Still, many Japanese persist in thinking that their country is small, perhaps because of its location on the map between such large countries as China and the former Soviet Union on one side, and Canada and the United States on the other.[35] Although such statements are nationally self-deprecating, they can become the basis for "uniqueness." Also, precisely because the *shimaguni* sentiment is self-deprecating, people falsely assume that it disproves any desire for national grandeur.

Nihonjinron has alternated between positive and negative aspects of Japaneseness over the last several centuries, depending on Japan's relation to the outside world.[36] These time cycles often involved international conflict and competition, which would explain why the idea of uniqueness held such interest for the Japanese. In the Japanese view, American gunboats under Commodore Perry helped thrust foreign, western culture onto the Japanese in the mid-nineteenth century. A foreign culture thrust itself onto Japan again during the Occupation years and during the post-World War II period. It happened yet again during the trade frictions in the last decades of the twentieth century, when the United States pressed Japan to change its economic structures—that is, its way of conducting commerce and trade.[37] Each of these foreign threats represented the notion that the west was superior to Japan in some way. The Japanese acknowledged this superiority only in technology; in compensation they could always say that their culture was still superior. And they did so—a perfectly understandable reaction.

One Japanese woman told me of waiting (in the mid-1970s) to

board a jet bound for the United States. She was startled when an elderly Japanese man, a complete stranger, turned and said to her, "All they ever had was the bomb." That statement suggests compensatory thinking and the threat of the western encroachment on Japanese shores felt by some Japanese. Today the "bomb" is represented by American popular culture, and a similar refrain is heard: "All they can make is entertainment." Japan has caught up to the west technologically; and therefore all that may be left to consume is western entertainment such as Hollywood movies, popular music, and fashion.

Americans need to be prepared for such Japanese attitudes and should not take them personally. If the situation were reversed, we would probably say these things ourselves. Also, the superpower status of the United States carries responsibilities: We must be careful not to assume superiority simply by virtue of our citizenship. We ought not even to joke about our country's status because non-Americans are likely to misconstrue such jokes. (In fact, probably far more Japanese view the United States favorably than do not.) Finally, we can be glad that others enjoy or admire aspects of American culture, but we must return this honor to our foreign counterparts. In this way we are sure to make our international visits welcome, not only for ourselves but also for other Americans who follow us.

The Problem Of Japanese Uniqueness (Homogeneity)

Because of their historical insularity, the Japanese "developed a strong sense of cultural identity based on a homogeneous people who spoke a common language and shared strong political, social, religious, and artistic traditions."[38] Let us consider how problematic Japanese "homogeneity" can be by the following case. This case was provided by Stephen Freeman,* an American teacher of English at a college in Nagoya.

An Account by Stephen Freeman*

Our department had recently conducted an entrance examination for a select group of senior high school students. This examination consisted of written essays in English and Japanese, as well as an oral interview. Each teacher was assigned to grade a number of the essays and then to interview the writers of the essays. Each student, then, received a grade for the essay and for the interview.

After participating, I realized that there was potential interviewer bias because each examiner of the essay later conducted a formal interview with the same applicant. What if a student was a member of a minority who inadvertently communicated that in his or her writing? Or, even if this was not the case, could certain opinions or activities discussed in the essay elicit bias from the grader? If such essays were graded unfairly, wouldn't that taint the interview grade? I decided to raise these issues even though the selection process had been completed. Perhaps the process could be improved for the next year.

When I shared my concern in a departmental meeting about the testing results, I found that mine was the only voice raised. The departmental head swiftly diverted my motion saying that "resources were inadequate to remedy the situation." Though surprised at this immediate dismissal, I replied that the examiners could trade students among themselves, at least to insure a different examiner for the interview. The department head responded that "testing bias can never be completely removed." With that, he closed the topic and went to the next item on the agenda.

I was left in disbelief. How could they appear so complacent? This is not to say that my view was correct. Rather, they seemed insensitive to social minorities and issues of bias in general. Perhaps this result is due to growing up in a culture that believes in its uniqueness and its having "one race."

I agree with Freeman's view except that another element could have been operative: his low status. He was young, a foreigner, and nontenured; therefore his comments may have been out of line. The department head may have been covering for himself or even another professor. Freeman might have been more successful if he had consulted with trusted colleagues well before the meeting. Nevertheless, the college's grading system seemed to lack safeguards against bias. To that extent, potential issues of discrimination seem evident.

Japanese education is much less egalitarian than generally believed. Elitism is very strong in the minds of the Japanese in how schools are perceived. Graduating from the "right" schools seems far more important in Japan than in North America. And not surprisingly, children from affluence have a decided advantage. For example, students at Tokyo University, the most prestigious university though public, came from families that averaged 30 percent more income than the national average, according to a recent report.[39] From that same report, it was found that "more than half of the parents of Tokyo University students held administrative or managerial jobs."[40] Similar statistics are likely found associated with prestigious schools in the west as well. The difference, however, is that the issue of social inequality seems less debated in Japan, and less opportunity exists for the social underclass there. Harry Oshima puts it succinctly:

> The concept of human rights exists only vaguely in Japan. Koreans, the Ainu (Japan's indigenous people), and other ethnic minorities face widespread economic and social discrimination. Overall there may be less minority discrimination in Japan than in the United States, but only because of the country's relative ethnic homogeneity.[41]

RACISM—THEIRS AND OUR OWN

According to Thomas Sowell, *race* is broadly "applied in everyday life to designate ethnic groups of various sorts—by race, religion, or nationality."[42] Sowell arrived at this definition in realization that the "dichotomy between race and ethnicity is misleading in its apparent precision. Neither race nor related concepts can be used in any scientifically precise sense to refer to the people inhabiting this planet today, after centuries of genetic intermixtures."[43] This view is also practical because *race,* in the current idiom, includes "any people united by common history, language, cultural traits, etc.: *the Dutch race.*"[44] Racism then is the belief in the superiority of certain races for presumed genotypic or cultural reasons.

Racism is a matter of degree, and probably almost everyone is racist in some way.[45] Yet, most people deny that this is possible for themselves. It seems worthwhile to discuss for the observation of other cultures, particularly Japanese, and so I will treat the topic in relation to both Japan and the United States.

Japanese Denial

Japanese commonly deny the possibility that they could be racists.[46] Kosaku Yoshino's *Cultural Nationalism in Contemporary Japan* is particularly noteworthy because the book recognizes a sentiment of "cultural nationalism" (as in *Nihonjinron*) among the Japanese, such as the equating of Japanese blood with Japanese language and culture. Yet the author seems to deny that this sentiment is racism by his preference for his term of "quasi-racism." He states correctly that *race* lacks scientific precision (because of too much overlap in physical features between the "races") and that race is more a social than a scientific concept (as in folk beliefs about others). Yet he adheres to the traditional, strictly genetic sense of *race.* This sense seems to conflict with the contemporary meaning, as noted by Sowell above. Sowell's definition recognizes that so-called racial characteristics such as color are not needed in treating others as members of "inferior races," as demonstrated by the treatment of the Jews in Europe and by the Japanese themselves in their treatment of "Koreans, Chinese, Burakumin, Ryukyuan/Okinawan, and Ainu in Japan."[47]

Whichever definition is used, Yoshino acknowledges that "the Japanese have tended to perceive themselves as a distinct 'racial' group."[48] This perception may explain, at least in part, why some Japanese visitors to the United States call Americans *gaijin* (foreigners; lit. "outsider[s]"), despite the fact that they are the real "foreigners" when abroad. Categorization by racial groups "presupposes the existence of racism, for without racism physical characteristics are devoid of social significance. It is not the presence of objective physical differences between groups that creates races, but the social recognition of such differences as socially significant or relevant."[49]

People typically view racism as a condition present only in abnormal individuals. Social scientists, however, are increasingly coming to understand that racial categories themselves can never be neutral. Racial distinctions are inherently value-laden because of their mental associations: us-them; powerful-weak; advantaged-disadvantaged. Research shows increasingly that people tend to favor their own ingroup members over others in allocating resources.

Yoshino's moderation of the racial overtone of *Nihonjinron* also may have been influenced by his discovery of various Japanese who initially equated Japanese blood with fluency in the language, but modified the notion of Japanese "blood" to "physical appearance" in light of certain well-known foreign media personalities in Japan who are fluent in Japanese. Yoshino's questioning enabled his Japanese respondents to recognize inconsistency in their thinking. It is likely, however, that instead of correcting their view, these Japanese simply may have rationalized that those foreign personalities are "exceptional cases." This rationalization is a typical defensive reaction found by workers in racial relations.[50] Yoshino ignores this possibility, and seems too ready to take their "change" at face value. Consequently, he avoids applying the term of *racial* to such notions in favor of his terms, *quasi-racial*, or *quasi-race thinking*. In a later article by Yoshino, these terms are dispensed with all together in favor of *chauvinistic,*[51] a further avoidance. Curiously, his later article appears in a volume with those from other researchers who document the presence of racial discrimination in Japan, as well as the racial sentiment of *Nihonjinron.* Given that Yoshino accepts that "race" is a "socially constructed" concept, his avoidance to view the Japanese racial identity as *racialized*, or to view extreme beliefs in Japanese uniqueness (racial distinctiveness) as *racism*, speaks precisely to my point.

American Racism

The reluctance of Japanese to see themselves as possibly racist resides, as least partly, in the view that racism is an American phenomenon. In the United States, a multi-racial "melting pot," tension between "races" may be unavoidable. "Race" is often a significant factor in American social relations;

thus it is not surprising that American social scientists may be in the vanguard of research on this topic. And in fact, Yoshino refers to an American author as one of the first to use the term *racism*.[52] Thus, in a sense, Americans have not only "created" this problem for themselves, but have also helped to "publicize" it. For the Japanese, then, members of a highly homogeneous society, it would seem easy to associate racism with a highly heterogeneous society as the United States. By extension, they could exclude themselves from this common human malaise by their belief that Japan contains only one "race."

Racism, however, need not be based entirely on perceived genetic differences, as shown by Sowell's explanation of the contemporary meaning of the term. The explosive feeling associated with "race" can be found with ethnicity; the tensions in Belfast or Tel Aviv are cases in point. Discrimination can result from differences in "race," ethnicity, religion, or nationality. *Racism* is a convenient term to cover these situations. It becomes even more widely applicable in light of the fact that "race" has its basis not in biology but in sociology.

Japanese Racism

Perhaps Yoshino avoided using the term *racism* in conjunction with *Nihonjinron* because the uniqueness theory tends to lack emotional intensity.[53] Certainly little that is heard about Japanese uniqueness can be equated with "intense racism." Sometimes, however, (though very rarely) foreigners in Japan are refused service in restaurants (or other establishments) simply because they are "foreign." Curiously, in some cases, the foreigner is refused on linguistic grounds even though he or she is fluent in the language. Such cases may become comical because the issue is explained and negotiated with the foreigner entirely in Japanese. Therefore the real reason is not linguistic, and more than a few foreigners have concluded that it is racist.

Such refusals to serve foreigners are rare, but a more serious matter arises in regard to social minorities in Japan. Consider this anecdote about Japanese discrimination, reported by a Japanese student in a course at an American university:

> The first time that I became aware of prejudice and discrimination was in the fifth grade [in Japan about 1970]. I went to an

> abacus training course after school. Some of us would eventually take a test for a national achievement award for the abacus. In the same abacus class, there were two Koreans, a brother and sister. They were very good at the abacus. However, the boy took the national test and failed. The class couldn't believe it.
>
> Our teacher overheard us talking about this and explained it this way: The boy failed because he was Korean. I could not understand why that was related with the test. The teacher went on to say that Koreans are sometimes disadvantaged in school or at work. If on a national qualifying test a Korean were tied with a Japanese, the Japanese would be chosen ahead of any foreigners. Never having heard of such things before, I felt very, very strange and in disbelief. Those Korean friends of mine looked exactly the same as us and were nice children. We used to play together a lot in those days. I don't think that kind of thing is allowed officially. But it seems that it still could happen.[54]

Two independent authors (one Dutch, the other American) make the same observation: Despite Japanese rhetoric about Hiroshima as a universal peace symbol, a memorial for Korean victims of the atomic blast was excluded from the grounds of the Peace Park there.[55] This memorial remains (unless it has been moved recently) on the outside edge of the park.

On the other hand, "Hiroshima public schools ... regularly bus [their pupils] to Kyoto to [visit a Korean memorial for victims of Japanese atrocities committed in an invasion of Korea 400 years ago] and ponder the suffering that Japan has inflicted on its neighbors."[56] Thus the Japanese are not completely insensitive to the issue. Nevertheless, the Japanese collective consciousness seems to include a void about Japan's colonial past. For example, a class of Japanese college students majoring in English were studying a speech address delivered at the United Nations by Roh Tae Woo, former president of South Korea. Roh stated, "In my country the end of the Second World War gave rise to overwhelming jubilation ... as the Korean people were liberated from the yoke of colonial rule and recovered [their] land...." When I asked the class who the colonial power was, I found that half had no idea, while the other half thought it was the United States!

This amnesia about Japan's wartime history is reflected in an NHK survey in which 69 percent of the Japanese respondents stated that history is insufficiently taught to the young.[57] According to the journalist Yumi Kikuchi, this history is taught only superficially in Japan because it is "taboo."[58] Kikuchi had to learn about Japanese wartime atrocities on her own because they were not previously taught in school.[59]

Japanese suffer a similar lack of awareness about Japanese minorities. Because minorities often are victims of discrimination in Japanese society, it would seem naive to rule out racism as a factor in the *Nihonjinron* phenomenon. A national ethos that promotes the belief in Japanese racial purity cannot avoid implication. Edwin Reischauer, an apologist for Japan (according to Masao Miyoshi),[60] as well as the former US Ambassador and Harvard scholar, observed that "race looms large in the self-image of the Japanese, who pride themselves on the 'purity' of their blood.... We often think of racial prejudice as being a special problem of the white race in relations with other races, but it actually pervades the world."[61] Reischauer adds that it is especially prevalent in Japan and elsewhere in East Asia.[62] This point is partially supported by evidence that Asian Americans, "many of whom were born in East Asia, ... were generally more racially prejudiced than whites against other US minorities...."[63] This quote shows that Asians are no more immune from racism than anyone else.

Our purpose here is not to judge the Japanese. Certainly, racial discrimination exists in the United States and elsewhere. Japan, however, seems "peculiar ... in its lack of recognition and admission that it has such problems."[64] Indeed, "until 1995 Japan was among the few nations [that] had not ratified the International Convention on the Elimination of All Forms of Racial Discrimination, which the United Nations brought into effect in 1969. Even after ratification, the Ministry of Foreign Affairs does not consider [discrimination against the *buraku* minority group in Japan a matter] covered by this UN convention on the grounds that it is not a racial issue."[65] This lack of support for such a human rights convention is hardly a good sign for a nation that needs and wishes to internationalize itself.

Related Ironies

Moreover, the lack of support for the convention contains two glaring ironies. First, "it now seems clear that the Japanese population stems from several ancient and distinct waves of immigration, ... [and is,] like all other modern peoples, a 'mixed race.'"[66] Second, Japanese researchers themselves show that the ancient Japanese aristocracy, perhaps even the imperial family, derived partially from Chinese or Korean ancestry.[67] We would not wish to parade this information in front of the Japanese. Nevertheless, as Tomoko Koyama believes, "the myth of Japan's ethnic homogeneity" lends itself to racial discrimination by the Japanese.[68] We hope that the Japanese people eventually will face this issue, as we must in our society.

Although consciousness raising about racial conflicts has been widespread in the United States (and the need continues), this has not been the case for Japan. It is easy to assume that the Japanese are a "pure race," although they are not. The idea of Japanese homogeneity can blind even foreign scholars: "International academic scrutiny of the notion of 'Japaneseness' has been rare."[69] Perhaps, this discussion may contribute to further exploration.

Before closing this section on internationalization, I hasten to add that conversely some Japanese have a keen interest in intercultural matters. For example, the Japanese hosted one of the first conferences in the academic field of intercultural communication, which was held in Japan in the early 1970s. Michael H. Prosser documented this conference in his seminal work, *The Cultural Dialogue,* through a journal on the encounter group experiences he had there between the Japanese and the foreign participants.[70] His journal, besides giving us insight to the process of communicating interculturally, reminds us of the heighten awareness that some Japanese have long had for internationalization. We must be careful not to think every Japanese is insensitive interculturally, for some Japanese have developed as high a capacity for intercultural relations as anyone else.

APPLICATION: JAPANESE UNIQUENESS

Donald Keene, a renowned scholar of Japanese literature, recounts an experience he had early after the Second World War, concerning the "mysterious Japan" and Japanese uniqueness. While visiting a family in Kyoto, he recalls,

> I was standing in the garden admiring the moon one night when the grandmother of the family approached me and asked, "Have you a moon in America too?" [Such remarks] typify the

> conviction that Japan is unlike any other country in the world. … Many Japanese who had never actually seen a western person, were ready to believe that they were quite dissimilar, perhaps not even human beings.[71]

The sense of Japanese uniqueness is prevalent among the Japanese. Usually, however, it does not manifest itself as strongly as in Keene's story, especially today. We also must remember that not all Japanese subscribe to ideas of cultural uniqueness; thus, not every Japanese views us as if we were a member of another species. A foreigner by definition is necessarily apart from the society into which he or she enters. Cultural frictions are inevitable. Even so, cross-cultural communication is particularly an issue for the Japanese, given their apparent homogeneity and their historical isolation.

Having said that, I wish to reconsider the Japanese woman's statement about the moon, from a different perspective. The anecdote is probably correct in all its details, but reexamination may be worthwhile. I wonder whether the woman's question was really asking if we had the *same* moon. That is, did our moon appear to be the same as the moon seen by Japanese?

Cross-cultural psychologists are familiar with the full-moon illusion, by which different peoples may "see" the full moon differently. "When seen or pictured near the horizon, the full moon seems much larger to many observers than it does when it is viewed overhead in the sky."[72] Could the compactness of Japanese urban or rural surroundings produce a similar effect by which the skyline could appear near to the moon? One American student in Japan remarked how extraordinarily large the full moon sometimes appeared there. Or was it this individual's own personal illusion? Mention of this illusion is speculative and probably does not apply. The point, rather, is that some of life's basic experiences differ across cultures and that these differences must be considered. Keene may have been correct in saying that the woman actually believed that Japan had a unique moon; such a belief calls to mind the Japanese uniqueness myth. On the other hand, she might not have intended to suggest that the United States lacked a moon but that Americans had a different vision of it. In Japanese traditional thought, the moon was held in reverence as with "moon-viewing parties" (*otsukimi*). Whether *otsukimi,* the full-moon illusion, or both are involved, awareness of such phenomena may allow us to consider other possibilities, which ultimately may strengthen our cross-cultural analysis.

FURTHER APPLICATION

A member of the Chinese ethnic minority in Japan presents his view of the Japanese, from which we can gain further insight into the situation of minorities there, as well as making distinctions between the Chinese and the Japanese peoples.

Japanese Intercultural Relations: From a Chinese Minority Perspective

Ming Shi Huang

Ming Shi Huang, a citizen of China, is an associate professor of Chinese at Nagoya Gakuin University. He has lived in Japan for nearly 40 years since first arriving at the age of six. Most of his formal education was received in Japan, from elementary school to his graduate school training. He grew up speaking Chinese and Fujianese in his home but Japanese outside. During his years as a student in higher education, he spent 10 years living in Tokyo at a Chinese foreign student dormitory. Thereafter, he received additional graduate training in Beijing for two years of which one year was spent on research at the Chinese Social Science Institute. His specialties include Chinese classical literature and the methodology of teaching Chinese as a second language. Recently, he completed a year's sabbatical study at UCLA.

One of my earliest recollections of being an ethnic minority in Japan was when, as a child in the 1960s, we went to visit an uncle of ours, who was living in Tokyo. When we children spoke Chinese in their house, our aunt, who was Japanese, told us not to because she feared the neighbors would hear. It was her intention to keep the Chinese nationality of her husband and children secret. Their children did not know of their Chinese heritage and were not told until they reached college. Among those Chinese who become naturalized Japanese, it is said that it takes three generations to eliminate a family's foreign roots.

If foreign nationality has to be hidden, then fear of discrimination is a likely cause. For Chinese and other foreigners in Japan, that fear is real. Housing produces many cases. It is not uncommon for Chinese students in Japan to select an apartment, pay their deposit, and then to be told later that the apartment is unavailable once the landlord discovers the student's nationality. I myself was discriminated against, so I know it happens. Recently, I married a Japanese, and we found an apartment to live in. Our application was initially accepted but later I was told that due to a rule of the real estate company, the apartment could not be rented out to a foreigner. I then said that my wife could be the renter. They declined the offer because my wife was unemployed.

This attitude toward foreigners is symbolized for me by an instance that happened in the 1980s when I taught Chinese to employees in a company in Tokyo that did trade with China. Once I was at a company party where an employee begged me repeatedly to tell him that I was Japanese, not Chinese. My fluency in Japanese was too much for him to accept. In his mind, only Japanese could ever be expected to speak Japanese. To him I could not fit his stereotype of "foreigner." That is the central problem—the idea that the Japanese are so unique that only they can possess "Japaneseness."

The Japanese people, in comparison with the Chinese people, do not actively expand or deepen their relations with others. In some parts of urban Japan, there is virtually no interaction between neighbors, and hardly anyone will visit another in their home. In China, on the other hand, even in Beijing, interactions between the neighbors are common. Frequency of visits vary but neighbors will often borrow soy sauce and other items. It even may happen that a college teacher will entrust his child to a neighbor if away on a long-term assignment.

This Japanese separateness from others can be seen in how Japanese, as compared to Chinese, pay their bill when eating out with friends. In Japan, each person pays his own bill, and money is collected from each one. In China, it is done quite differently. One person treats for everyone else because the next time, it will be somebody else's turn. This custom is widely followed in China, even among students.

We see this Japanese separateness, again, on airplanes, long-distance trains, or buses. Rarely does a Japanese speak to the person he or he is sitting next to. In China, people often strike up conversations, even if strangers. In China, when leaving the bus or train, a person often will be asked by another, "Are you getting off?" To ask a Japanese that would be considered peculiar. Another behavior seen much less often in Japan is someone giving up their seat for a senior citizen or for a mother carrying a child. In China most people will give up their seat at such times.

It is not that Japanese are uncaring; rather they feel shy. The recipient of such kindness may even feel the extra attention is not worth it. He or she might even decline the offer of a seat on the bus or the train. This same fear of drawing attention leads to the Japanese reputation for being passive language learners: They do not speak out much. My wife, herself a Japanese, came to this same conclusion in comparing Japanese and Chinese students of second languages when she was a student (of Chinese) and a teacher (of Japanese) in China.

This reluctance to speak out can also be seen when Japanese are dining out. Whereas Chinese people will make various requests to a waiter, even repeatedly about preparing the food, the Japanese generally do not do so, even when the food has been made poorly. They will likely eat it without complaint. To do so might hurt the other's feelings. Another point is that the Japanese would not say, "Wait," in the event a waiter takes away an unfinished plate. In China, such hesitation is unthinkable.

The extent of this fear of attention is carried even to the rest room: Japanese rest rooms give total privacy, whereas those in China do not. Chinese rest rooms rarely have barriers or screens that obstruct the view of other occupants. In this regard, American and Japanese rest rooms are similar. There is, however, a peculiar aspect of Japanese behavior shared by neither Americans nor by Chinese. Japanese women, while on the toilet, will continually flush it to muffle any sound made from urination. Recently, some Japanese toilets have been actually made to produce electronically a flushing sound, so as to conserve water use.

In Japan, there has always been pressure to conform to the behavior of those around you. This pressure for conformity likely reinforces Japanese feelings of uniqueness or separateness from others, especially non-Japanese. Paradoxically, Japanese belief in uniqueness breeds sameness. If one departs from being "Japanese," one threatens the Japanese identity of others, so the pressure for conformity is activated. My point is made only in general; not all Japanese are so inward. There always have been some Japanese who have intermingled with foreigners and have accepted their cultural differences. But on the whole, internationalization remains a challenge for the Japanese. Fortunately, Japanese are becoming more culturally aware. Japanese interest in Asia and Asian languages seems on the rise. Now, one is beginning to be able to speak a foreign language (e.g., Chinese) anywhere without concern. Bilingual and multilingual Japanese are in high demand, and it may be the case that the society is beginning to value multifaceted individuals. If so, there is hope for better intercultural relations in Japan and better improvement in status for its minority group members.

1. How do you perceive attitudes toward a foreign language being spoken in your own hometown as compared to Ming Shi Huang's experience in Japan? Would the attitudes be different toward different languages? Why or why not?
2. Analyze this data for average TOEFL (Test of English as a Foreign Language) scores and try to explain Japan's ranking (consider both cultural and non-cultural factors):[73]

Singapore	560	Korea	520	Japan	490
China	540	Indonesia	500	Thailand	480
Hong Kong	520	Taiwan	500		

The TOEFL has no passing grade but North American colleges typically require a score of 550 for entrance, which is roughly at the 70 percentile for all test takers. Nearly all scores are between 340 and 680. A score of 580 is roughly at the 80 percentile mark, and 480 is about at the 30 percentile level.

Part II

Japanese Communication Style

5

Japanese Communication Style: Aspects of Language and Society

Cultures differ according to their preferences in style of communication, the characteristic manner in which meaning is conveyed and interpreted in various interpersonal situations. Two major bases for distinguishing communication styles are by function and by degree of openness.

Language has two fundamental functions—informational and social. Both functions often operate in an interpersonal situation, but one usually predominates. For example, "How are you?" serves primarily a social function, but it can function informationally as well. Much depends on paralinguistic features such as tone of voice and word stress, as well as nonverbal factors such as facial expression and the social relationship involved.

Degree of openness refers to the amount of intimacy that is permitted and with whom. How rigidly prescribed is behavior with friends or strangers, and with people on different socio-economic levels? Such prescriptions involve various aspects of verbal and nonverbal communication from vocabulary to facial and bodily displays.

Carley H. Dodd provides a useful sketch of communication style across cultures:

> In Saudi Arabia interpersonal communication style is marked by flowery language, numerous compliments, and profuse thanks. Rarely does one publicly criticize fellow workers in that culture because that would smack of disloyalty and disrespect.[1] Africans tend to exhibit an extremely friendly and warm interpersonal communication style. Asians appear rule oriented and reserved because of procedural and cultural displays of respect and honor. Americans are informal and somewhat uninhibited and get down to the main point fairly quickly in a kind of linear, evidential manner. Britons seem to have a reserved subtlety, preferring understatement and control in interpersonal interaction. These examples remind us that it is crucial to understand the intercultural style of the people with whom we communicate.[2]

GENDER STYLES OF COMMUNICATION

We are probably aware that men and women tend to interact in characteristic ways. Deborah Tannen considers these ways a matter of cultural difference because males and females are socialized to behave differently, as if they were part of different "subcultures." If we can understand that the genders may differ in their communication styles, we ought to understand that the same is true of cultures.

We will first exercise our own intuition about gender-related communication in English as the basis for studying the Japanese communication style. Table 5.1 contains separate letters from a mother and father to their kidnapped son; the parents wrote them in the hope that they might reach the boy. The letters were published in *USA Today* a year after his disappearance (and abridged for present purposes). Read the letters and guess which parent wrote which letter. Then note features of the letters that made you guess as you did. Do this before continuing to read this chapter. Correct answers to authorship appear with the related discussion that follows.

Table 5.1 Exploring Gender Styles of Communication

Which parent wrote which letter to their son?[3] Note your reason(s) why for the discussion that follows (where the correct answers appear).

Dear Jacob,	**Dear Jacob,**
It's Saturday morning, Carmen is at gymnastics, Trevor's ... in the living room watching ... cartoons. ...I am sitting on the lower bunk in your and Trevor's room. As I look in your closet, I see your gold sweater ... you wore for your school picture ... that millions of people ... have seen on your posters, billboards, banners, newspapers and TV newscasts. Aaron is visiting his cousin in the Cities this weekend. He's disappointed ...he didn't play quarterback this year. By the way your soccer team finished second...again. Jake, this has been a very difficult year. We know what it has been for us, but we can only imagine what it has been for you. Jake, I don't care what has been done to you. I don't care what you have been forced to do. I love you—we love you. That you can always count on forever. Keep on your guard ... do what you have to.... We will never stop looking for you, that's a promise. **Love, (A)**	It's been almost a year since you were taken from us and I still miss you so very much. Some things have changed. Cinnamon is no longer a puppy—she's as big as Marcus. Trevor misses you terribly, he's so often looking for someone to play with and he lost... enthusiasm for sports. Remember how frustrated you were last fall because ... you thought you couldn't skate on regular skates? I found out ... that those skates hadn't been sharpened right and it wasn't your fault you couldn't skate on them.... You've done nothing wrong and we love you. Remember how I always believed in you—whatever you wanted to do—whatever dream you had you could do it? I still do, Jake.... We'll never stop looking for you and we'll never stop aching until we can throw our arms around you and cry and laugh and plan and strive for a better life for all of us. Hang on, Jake. **Love, (B)**

Analysis of the Letters

Deborah Tannen, in various popular and scholarly works, has described how males and females in the United States seem to talk differently.[4] Males tend to prefer what she calls "report talk"; females, "rapport talk." In other words, males tend to be informationally oriented; females, socially oriented. This difference seems to parallel the classic image of the analytical male and the nurturing female. We know that males can be nurturing and that females can be analytical. In general, however, their styles of talk appear to parallel these images, as Tannen's research indicates. This difference is borne out by the letters quoted in Table 5.1 (the author of A being the father and B, the mother). Both letters serve both informational and social purposes, but each appears to emphasize one over the other, at least early in the letters

The father begins by describing his then-present situation and that of the rest of the family. This first part is essentially an informational report. In contrast, the mother begins with an emphasis on feelings about her relationship with the son—their physical separation and her affirmation of love. The fact of separation is well known and therefore does not function as "information," but rather as an affective expression of longing to be reunited. If you were abducted, what would you want most to hear? Probably how much you were missed. The mother appears to address this need by expressing her love for her son and telling him how others also miss him. The father also expresses his love explicitly, but does so, much later in his letter. This different focus between informational and social also seems apparent in how the father and mother begin their other paragraphs. This difference in focus does not necessarily reflect the parents' actual love for their son; it relates more directly to different societal roles and different communication styles.

Traditional Gender Roles

The traditional male/father role, especially in time of crisis, is to be reserved and calm. An informational mode would help most in controlling the situation. Moreover, the father may wish as much as possible to avoid alarming the boy—that is, to help relieve him of any unnecessary worry by seeming to be calm.

Again, this approach would follow an informational, cognitive, executive mode of action. Finally, the father may have tried to offset the expected emotion on the mother's part, or simply to be "different," a value in North America. North American culture often requires speakers to be "distinctive" with language. For example, a person who is one of several dinner guests would avoid using the same words as the others in complimenting the host.[5] If one guest says, "The dinner was delicious," the next guest would not say exactly the same thing. At least he or she would change the statement somehow as in "Yes, the dinner *was* delicious." Other cultures, such as in Japan, do not require their members to be so "distinctive." There, all guests can properly compliment the host in the same words. Again, following North American ideals, the mother and the father composed separate letters. That practice is not likely to be the same across cultures.

Gender Norms

In any case, we are probably correct in saying that the two letters followed cultural practices in some ways, as well as gender norms. For example, the mother's choice of words may have been gender-related, such as the intensifiers in "I miss you so very much" or in "Trevor misses you terribly." Also, in keeping with her role of providing nurture and care for others, the mother uses *you* and *we* far more often than the father (in the original letters), suggesting an increased focus on the boy. She also uses emotionally expressive words about him ("miss you"; "[you were] frustrated"; "wasn't your fault"; "throw our arms around you," etc.), as found in the *original* letters. These patterns of gender and culture support our analysis of the first part of the letters: that the father's approach was informational, while the mother's was social (that is, relational).

The letters, however, also seem to include contradictory cues, if we are trying to guess their authorship. Some readers might be led astray by the mother's talk about sports because they viewed sports as largely a male domain. Others might view the father's talk about schedules and activity ("Carmen is at gymnastics," Aaron is visiting his cousin") as part of the middle-class mom's role. In this role, the mother is often seen as managing the family's affairs by driving children to their various daily activities, running the household, and the like. In the same vein, one might visualize the father not at home on Saturday but at the golf course or at the office, nor as writing nostalgically about the child's sweater or photo (as he does). Such conflicting cues may have prevented some readers from guessing the correct authorship of the letters. Guessing wrong is not to be taken too seriously, however. The important point is our increased awareness for gender and cultural patterns in communication.

The conflicting features also reveal that many communications have multiple purposes and involve both informational and social aspects. In most cases, one aspect will predominate; we found this in the two letters. Although the father's orientation is chiefly informational, he is also nurturing and socially oriented as well; the reverse is true of the mother.

CULTURAL STYLES OF COMMUNICATION

Scholars note that different cultural styles of communication must be acknowledged if we are to function effectively across cultures. These stylistic variations are the basis for both real and imagined differences and have "much to do with the formation of ethnic stereotypes."[6] "When people who are identified as culturally different have different conversational styles, their ways of speaking become the basis for negative stereotyping. Anti-Semites classically attribute loudness, aggressiveness, and 'pushiness' to Jewish speakers."[7] Interestingly, the stereotype for blacks appears to be strikingly similar: "inconsiderate, overbearing, and loud."[8] "It is clear that [such evaluation] as loud and pushy simply blames the minority group for the effect of the interaction of differing styles."[9] An inherent bias is at work, in that the communication style of the mainstream or dominant group is held up as the measuring stick. Differences are likely to be exaggerated or embellished, if not invented. (This is not to deny, however, that real differences exist).

JAPANESE STYLE OF COMMUNICATION

The respective communication styles of North Americans and Japanese appear to be nearly opposite, according to Dean C.

Barnlund.[10] The Japanese commonly characterize their own communication style as "wet," and that of North Americans as "dry." These terms seem to imply a bias: They connote that the former style is steeped in feelings and the latter is not, although the reverse is also likely from the North American point of view. Nevertheless, we gain a sense that the two styles are radically different, given each culture's impressionistic images of the other: "Japanese are overly accommodating and inscrutable[;] Americans are inattentive and selfish."[11] Haru Yamada describes these images in connection with international business:

> The different ways of voicing support among Americans and among Japanese lead to a mismatch of expectations in cross-cultural business conversations; the end product, as [variously] point[ed] out,[12] is often negative judgments. Americans who expect to "get down to business" frequently find Japanese support behavior overly accommodating. "Why do they keep agreeing when they don't really mean it? They just keep saying yes and that's because they are going to pull a sly move. Japanese are inscrutable." On the other hand, Japanese, who expect an overt expression of support[,] perceive Americans as inattentive. "Why are they so indifferent? They don't listen to what you say, and that's because all they do is think about themselves. Americans are *katte* (selfish)."[13]

North Americans and Japanese, especially in international business, can be viewed in general as favoring informational and social styles respectively. It is nearly a cliche that North American businesspeople are quick to "get down to business." In contrast, the Japanese spend a long time on the preliminaries, particularly on developing social relations between the prospective participants. Many of the important business transactions in Japan involve mutual connections and introductions; the "cold call" and self-introduction by letter are used far less there than in the United States. Business relations are viewed as properly begun only after developing some commonality through social ties. As a result, written contracts are given far less importance than in North America. Employment contracts, except for foreigners, are all but nonexistent; the social ties behind the relations count more than the "words written on paper." Some positions may require a guarantor who would be held responsible for the actions of the person employed. Many other positions derive from a recommendation by someone known to the company or firm, who could lose face if the employee acted negligently. Employees, then, must view their actions as having implications beyond themselves.

Key Aspects of the Japanese Style

Key aspects of the Japanese communication style include interdependence (*amae*), respectfulness, gender factors, language honorifics, relational identities, and back-channeling (*aizuchi*). These contribute to the social orientation in Japanese communication, especially speech. Social orientation has less to do with being "sociable" than it does with other-directedness and engendering close affective ties. *Sociable* is defined in the dictionary as "inclined to associate with or be in the company of others; friendly or agreeable in company; companionable."[14] Some overlap occurs, but social orientation involves social relationships more broadly and deeply than does sociability. The latter seems to be concerned primarily with making an atmosphere agreeable or pleasant, or keeping the lines of communication open. Sociability involves social niceties or courtesies; it relates largely to phatic communication (e.g., greetings) and small talk, whereas communication styles, as used here, involve communication more broadly.

Social orientation, like most other concepts, may well be bounded by culture. A social orientation in Japanese communication does not necessarily involve affective displays or self disclosures, elements that we North Americans might assume. For this reason, explanation is needed. The key aspects mentioned above make Japanese spoken communication rather socially oriented. And the element common to these aspects is attention to social status.

Interdependence (Amae)

Amae is typically translated as a *presuming upon* or a *dependency* on another, often a parent figure or mentor. Members of the collectivistic Japanese culture seem to depend a great deal on one another and to take mutual responsibility seriously. In contrast to individualism where a person is "on one's own," dependence on others is the norm in Japan. This dependence, however, is exercised so that it usually does not become overdependence in the western psychological sense. For this reason, I treat *amae* as *interdependence* rather than what is generally regarded as dependence. Haru Yamada, is of similar mind, for she calls *amae*, "sweet interdependence."[15] That captures this difficult concept quite well. The "sweet" corresponds to the desire, usually of an innocent quality, to fall into a dependency on someone. What makes it interdependent is mutuality between the parties involved.

Although Americans may experience social *amae* as "overpowering and infringing on their privacy,"[16] their reaction is as much a reflection of their own culture as of Japan's. Just as it takes two to tango, Japanese *amae* can function only between consenting parties. This point is reflected in the language as pointed out by Haru Yamada:

1. *Amayakashisugi*/Too sweet: The nurturer is overindulgent and spoils the babied.
2. *Wagamama*/Spoilt: The nurtured overindulges and exhibits spoilt behavior.
3. *Tsumetai*/Cold: The nurturer is underindulgent and does not adequately look after the babied.
4. *Katte*/Selfish: The nurtured underindulges and does whatever he or she wants.[17]

Amae can be seen readily in various spheres of Japanese life. Arranged marriage, though much less common today, provides individuals with the "service" of mate selection by relatives, close friends, or even one's employer. Potential suitors are presented without the obligation to accept. Similarly, passengers on public transportation often receive public service reminders about not forgetting one's belongings and observing caution in moving about. These messages are delivered so frequently that North Americans in Japan commonly find them overbearing. Similar announcements are virtually absent in North America.

In merchandising, customer service is practiced at a high level rarely seen elsewhere. It is not uncommon for store clerks to run about in serving a customer. Packages are often wrapped meticulously. Public service providers from elevator operators and taxi drivers to airline pilots wear white gloves, which symbolically convey respect and care for the customer. Added to this message are the frequent displays of deep respect expressed by bowing to the customer and addressing him or her as "honorable customer" (*okyakusan*).

When strangers are introduced, including students to teachers, a commonly heard expression is *yoroshiku* ("be kind to me"; "I leave it up to you"). This expression also is used to send regards to a third party ("Tell so-and-so I said, 'hello'"). In daily conversation, people's names are frequently followed with *san,* a sign of respect. Furthermore, *I* and *you* are used far less in Japanese than in English; some observers interpret this as creating social inclusion or connectivity. Displays of negative emotion are greatly restrained in public out of courtesy for others. Strangers are often called by fictive kinship terms: an old man may be called by *ojiisan* (grandfather); a middle-aged man, *ojisan* (uncle); a middle-aged woman, *obasan* (aunt); a waitress, *oneesan* (older sister) or *imooto* (younger sister). The effect of this and other practices is to create a psychological village atmosphere in which everyone is respected and is part of the community. In essence the Japanese make obvious their bonds of interdependence. With added affectivity ("sweetness") and mutuality, you come close to the meaning of *amae.*

However, perhaps to control unrestricted *amae,* Japanese society contains various checks and balances. For example, one must return something in kind for nearly any gift or favor received. Moreover, verbal appreciation must be given in the next meeting (*kono aida arigatoo* "thanks for the other day"). In addition, the Japanese abhor incurring an obligation, so they wish to save others the trouble. Thus visitors to one's home may be reluctant to accept food or drink, and may even feel overwhelmed by the American host's questions about preferences for beverage and other servings. The Japanese host, in the traditional manner, serves without giving the guest a choice.

In public, people seem slow to help a person in minor distress. My international students have repeatedly observed, for example, how Japanese on public transportation seem to turn a blind eye to elderly passengers who have difficulties. As one authority on Japanese psychology notes, "[Japanese out in public] push and pull others ferociously, and they pay little attention to those with special needs or concerns (handicapped, pregnant women, people with baggage, etc.)."[18] (An exception is the obviously "lost" foreigner at a main subway station, who always seems to attract attention and help.) Nor are some courtesies, such as opening doors for a mother with a baby carriage, found as frequently in Japan as in the United States. My wife, who is Japanese, learned this by direct experience based on living in both Manhattan and Nagoya in the mid-1980s. The Japanese seem to have a different code of public behavior than private behavior; this view is widely shared by foreigners in Japan.[19]

As compact and crowded as urban Japan is, it is no surprise that physical contact in crowded areas is generally more tolerated and often goes unacknowledged far more often than in North America. A second feature, which seems to follow, is that the Japanese appear to lack the concept of "looking out for the other guy" (strangers in public). If one ought to ignore minor physical contact, it follows that people will be less likely to look out for others. This does not mean that the Japanese are necessarily rude. Interestingly, however, Japanese public service campaigns for courteous driving often use the English loan word *manaa* ("manner"). Thus the Japanese, at some level, recognize that their public manners may be different—perhaps, even deficient.

The concept of *uchi-soto* (inside-outside) is relevant here. *Uchi*, also meaning one's home, house, or family, is associated with the ingroup or an inbred feeling or thinking. As mentioned above, Japanese simply are not raised to interact with strangers. Children generally are sheltered from such contact. Japanese families rarely hold large social gatherings, such as parties, at their homes. More often than not, visitors of some acquaintance who arrive "on short business" are not invited into the home; their business is conducted at the gate, on the doorstep, or in the vestibule. In contrast, Americans nearly always invite such people inside (to sit down), even if only as a perfunctory gesture.

The traditional Japanese house can be seen as consisting of a series of concentric circles, from the outside gate to the front door, the vestibule, the inner step-up level, the receiving room, and the more centrally positioned rooms.[20] These concentric spaces act as social buffers; penetration to successive circles is associated with the degree of intimacy or association. Even intimates, when visiting, ring a bell on the outside gate and wait for an answer from the householder over an intercom before proceeding in through the garden to the front door. How far one goes into the home depends on the social relationship and the purpose for visiting. American custom, in contrast, does not typically involve such a series of social buffer zones. The strong distinction between ingroup and outgroup in Japan may help explain why the Japanese are viewed as humorless and stiff. Foreign observers often fall into the outsider category, which engenders formal restraint, even "inscrutability," from the Japanese.

Strangers are viewed differently in the two countries, as observed by many of my Japanese students who have studied abroad. Japanese students who stay in the United States are struck by the way strangers often greet them on the street. Some of them are puzzled because it is so rare to greet strangers in Japan, even on school campuses. (For that matter, "Good morning" is said far less frequently in Japanese than in American families.[21] Also, expressions such as "I love you" apparently are found far more often among Americans than Japanese.) Similarly, a customer at a store in Japan does not say "thank you" (or anything) at the register after making a purchase. Japanese store clerks find *arigatoo* ("thank you") by the customer, a bit peculiar. Perhaps, people in Japan are assumed so secure in their social ingroups that verbal reminders are needed far less than in the United States. (The exception is between Japanese workers; their relations are considered important to "nurse.") Thus the remembrance of favors received, the general aloofness toward strangers in public, the reluctance to incur obligation, and the relative infrequency of verbalized greetings may be ways to counter *amae*—the tendency to seek indulgence from others.

Respectfulness

The basic difference between North Americans and Japanese seems to be that "friendliness" is to North Americans what "respectfulness" is to the Japanese. In an immigrant country such as the United States, its people came from all over the world. Many of these people did not share the same background. Moreover, these people had to "forge a new nation out of a wilderness." Undoubtedly these conditions contributed to Americans becoming characteristically friendly: Some signs of goodwill were probably an immediate necessity to have for others, if diverse peoples were to function together.

On the other hand, the Japanese population is one of the most homogeneous in the world. For them the major issue is not connectedness but relative social status. In the feudal era, most Japanese were bound by a rigid class system that strongly regulated their daily affairs and even their attire. Some faint remnants of inequality still remain, especially in the language. At nearly every turn, people are reminded of their respective stations in life. Job or social title often replaces a person's name in personal reference.

Distinction by age is made throughout the society. Rather than speaking simply of one's brother or sister, the Japanese distinguish by age, saying "older" or "younger" brother or sister. Older siblings have the privilege of calling younger ones by their personal name, but not the reverse; traditionally, younger siblings had to refer to older siblings by rank ("older brother/older sister"). Invariably the ages of persons appearing on TV, as interviewees or as contestants on game shows, are flashed on the screen along with their names. Until recently, age was primarily a basis on which white-collar employees progressed through their careers in the company. Older individuals, especially those of higher rank, require respect that is reflected even in grammatical features in the language.

This emphasis on respect accounts for a common cross-cultural misunderstanding: Foreigners sometimes receive an apology when they expect a thanks.[22] This does not suggest a lack of appreciativeness, but rather a concern about troubling others. These points, however, are made in general because Japanese vary as to how closely they follow the norms of etiquette.

Masculinity

Japanese masculinity is a related factor. Just as Americans hold up the "silent type" as a traditional male ideal, "seriousness" is an important attribute of the Japanese male. In the Japanese workplace, the so-called "sunny personality" is far less desirable in males than it would be in an American setting. To be sure, Japanese male workers are civil. The outgoing, effusive male, however, if he exists, is far less appreciated than an American might expect. This does not mean that Japanese males are unfriendly; the difference is that their friendliness is a bit muted as compared with their American counterparts.

The "sunny personality" is viewed more properly as a female

ideal in Japan. One way to explain this is by pitch or intonation of speech.[23] First, Japanese males are far less likely to use high pitched sounds than their American counterparts. Second, the use of high pitched sounds is far more distinguished by gender in Japan than in the United States. Traditional Japanese masculinity, as manifested by "seriousness" and expressive restraint, is likely to be misunderstood in an international context:

> Japanese expectations of sexual and social role[s] are much more rigid than those prescribed by English norms. In formal circumstances in which there is social equality between male speakers, ... Japanese males take a low profile linguistically, understating, being terse, presenting an unemotional, self-restrained exterior. ... Consider also Seward's comments that "Japanese men emphasize the masculinity of their speech by adopting a deep-voiced, guttural mode of speaking which is often accompanied by stern faces and stiff postures." This "controlled" profile, it is suggested here, is reflected in the low pitch level of Japanese males in relation to English males of generally equivalent phonational limits.[24]

The guttural tone mentioned here, however, is far from the popular image of the deep, grunt-like speech of *samurai* characters in Japanese period films. The latter is a theatrical device and has no parallel in normal, everyday speech. Yet some people (perhaps even many) in North America, and probably throughout the world, have a highly distorted image of the language, which verges on the uncouth. A case in point is the comic portrayal of a *samurai* made popular by the late comedian John Belushi. Still seen in TV reruns and videos, Belushi's "incoherent *samurai*" has been mimicked by young people for the benefit of some of our Japanese students on campuses abroad.

In Hofstede's cross-cultural study, which stands "unrivaled" "in terms of global coverage,"[25] the Japanese scored the highest among the nations tested in degree of masculinity. Here masculinity is not to be equated with machismo but rather with attention to task[26] or with differentiated sex roles.[27] "People from highly masculine cultures ... tend to have little contact with members of the opposite sex when they are growing up. They tend to see same-sex relationships as more intimate than opposite-sex relationships."[28] Consequently two outstanding features can be observed in Japanese society: Japanese males tend to lack the same ease as many western males in interacting with females, and Japanese married couples generally are strongly differentiated in role.

The former point can be observed in nearly any male group of university students or young company employees at a social function with unacquainted females of a similar age. Some of these individuals probably attended same-sex schools, in junior or senior high school or perhaps even elementary school. The sex segregation might even have continued into college, if the individual was in a high-technology field. As to the latter point, among married couples in Japan, it is a well-known tradition that the male assumes the role of breadwinner. Because of his devotion to his company, he has little time to spend with his family, even for bringing up the children. Wives perform that task exclusively. Until recently it was rare to see a father taking care of an infant. If given a baby to hold, fathers often became visibly uncomfortable. Lately, however, fathers have shared increasingly in such responsibilities.

Women's Language

It should come as no surprise that the Japanese have both a "men's" and a "women's" language: "[T]he Japanese language makes distinct syntactic and lexical distinctions between male and female language; honorific speech is also associated with femininity if not a marker of it."[29] Women, however, are not locked into a separate language. The female features of Japanese tend to be most prevalent when females "let their hair down." That is,

> sex-specific features appear only when the speaker is relaxing, talking with family members, intimate friends or acquaintances known for a long time. ...[T]here is little difference in speech between male and female speakers at formal settings like the Diet, the court, the city council meeting, the faculty meeting, etc. Even when talking privately, if both participants are not well acquainted, the conversation will show few sex-specific features.[30]

Thus, although a women's language exists in Japan, both sexes also use neutral language as well. Moreover, both sexes have engaged in linguistic crossover. Some young females, though not many, now occasionally use male-specific terms such as *boku* (I) for self-identification.[31] Such crossover actually may enhance a sense of femininity by the obvious contrast, like wearing oversized male clothing. This practice, however, does not preclude sexual discrimination.

The mere use of gender-specific language does not necessarily imply hierarchical status. Rather than being motivated by subservience, a persistent western stereotype about Japanese females, the use of Japanese women's language may be related to a female's own desire to project her femininity. "Moreover, among younger males there has been a distinct move to a politer style that is considered as 'feminine' by the conservatively-minded. It should also be noted that Japanese males also use forms associated with females when expressing empathy or gentleness and particularly when talking to children or the infirm."[32]

Language Honorifics

When Dodd discussed Asian communication style, he mentioned that "Asians appear rule oriented." This attribute, for Japanese and several other Asian cultures, certainly derives in part from language honorifics. Language honorifics embody "a special set of grammatical contrasts, in which different levels of politeness or respect are expressed, according to the mutual status of the participants."[33] Asian languages, particularly Japanese, have complex means for doing this. Japanese honorifics include several separate systems including terms denoting superior/inferior social status, respectful terms of address, and "beautification" terms for certain objects.

Verbs are the core of Japanese honorifics. Verbs can be constructed at four different levels: plain, courteous, exalted, and humble. Exalted forms raise the other person above oneself; the humble forms accomplish the same by lowering oneself. Consider these verbs:[34]

	Plain	Courteous	Exalted	Humble
to say	*iu*	*iimasu*	*osshaimasu*	*mooshimasu*
to go	*iku*	*ikimasu*	*irasshaimasu*	*mairimasu*
to read	*yomu*	*yomimasu*	*oyomi ni narimasu*	*yomasete itadakimasu*

The variants of these verbs exemplify a universal feature: The more polite language is, the longer or more complex the form. In Japanese, when a person introduces himself or herself by name, the verb *say* is used: *Watashi wa Donahue to iimasu* (literally "As for me, 'Donahue' is said," but translated as "I go by 'Donahue'" or "My name is 'Donahue'"). Between one student and another of the same age, the plain form is used. If spoken in class for the sake of the teacher, the courteous form is used. College teachers tend to use the courteous form in class, but not always. At the elementary school level, usage depends on whether one speaks to the class or to solely an individual: Between each other, teachers and students tend to use the plain form, but both switch to the courteous form if addressing the class at large.[35] As children mature into adults they eventually gain competence with the forms of deference. If a Japanese were introducing himself or herself at an *omiai*, a meeting for arranged marriage, it is likely the humble form *mooshimasu* would be used. "Exalted" is the term[36] for what some call "honorific" or "deferential." This change in term was necessitated because the overall system is often called "honorifics."

The use of four or more different verbs to say the same thing suggests a complex system. Japanese, however, does not have perfect tenses, as does English, nor so many irregular verbs. Each language poses special challenges. Foreign students learn Japanese in manageable steps. Typically, they learn the courteous and plain forms early on. A great deal can be accomplished in that way. For more complete acquisition, they learn the other forms later, depending on their objectives.

A complete survey is well beyond the scope of this book. Instead, I have selected certain features to give a basic sense of the language, and to address likely points of confusion for non-Japanese. I continue next with a world perspective to show that a number of other languages also use honorific systems.

Honorifics: A Cross-Cultural Perspective

Japanese honorifics are quite complex and pose a greater challenge than in most other languages. Table 5.2 is a rough, impressionistic sketch of the relative complexity of selected languages.

Japanese, Tibetan, Korean, and Javanese are well known

honorific languages because of the degree of politeness and respect reflected in their grammar and usage. Thai has an elaborate system of personal pronoun usage according to the speakers' relative social status. Modern Czech, French, and German have only moderate degrees of honorific structure; English, the least, but not absolutely so (as shown by the dot marks in the table). This table shows that the Asian reputation for politeness has some basis in language itself. A notable exception is modern Chinese (Mandarin), which has much fewer honorifics than most other Asian languages and is closer to the West European languages in this regard.

Table 5.2 Degree of Honorifics for Selected Languages[37]

	Javanese					French	
...	Japanese	Korean	Hindi	Thai	Czech	German	English ...
	Tibetan					Chinese	

High <<——————————————————>> Low

Degree

Terms Of Address

Many people worldwide know, because of the martial arts craze, that *sensei* ("teacher") is a term of great respect. Though it is used for schoolteachers and karate masters, it also can be applied to virtually any senior person of special accomplishment or standing. *Sensei* functions like a Japanese job title in that it can be used separately in place of someone else's name or can be attached to the other person's family name. For foreign teachers in Japanese schools, *sensei* is very useful if they forget or do not know a colleague's name.

Another well-known aspect of the Japanese system of address is the affix *-san* (Mr./Mrs./Ms.). *San* is used with job titles in the Japanese company (e.g., *shachoo-san* "president"; *kachoo-san* "manager"). In fact, superiors expect to be addressed in this way by their subordinates. Besides *sensei* and *san,* various other terms exist as well.

Leo Loveday has done an excellent job in simplifying a most complex system into a very usable flow chart about Japanese terms of address. His chart is not reproduced here, but Table 5.3 gives the essential information. The table shows a basic range of Japanese suffixes that are attached to a person's surname.

Only two options here (*-san;* -Ø) have equivalents commonly used in English. As Loveday notes, various social factors are associated with language use. An interesting affix is *-kun,* which is associated with masculinity. As mentioned previously, Japan had the highest degree of

Table 5.3 Japanese Name Suffixes for Address *

	ultrapolite	normal	intimate
Three basic options:	***-sama***	***-san***	**-Ø**
Additional options		***-kun*** (male)	***-chan*** (gender neutral)

*An adaption of Loveday (1986)

masculinity (i.e., distinction by sex) among the nations tested. A strictly corresponding term for females does not exist in Japanese. *Kun,* however, should not be regarded in a "macho" sense. *Kun* originates in a boy's early childhood in how he is addressed by his elders and is similar in that regard to the aristocratic use of *master* for a boy in English. *Kun* like *-chan,* can be used between equals (i.e., friends).

Recently, I found three female students at Nagoya Gakuin University who referred to each other by the use of *-kun* (family name with *kun* affixed). They treated this use as their own invention and employed it as a sign of affection and the exclusivity of their friendship. Since that time, however, I have learned that a similar practice may be followed when young women are "working with men in a company."[38] In the case of the NGU students, their use of *-kun* seemed to me as an accent on femininity.

Even if *-kun* and *-chan* were intended for "inferiors," they are used as terms of affection. In a sense, they are associated with *kawaiimono* ("cute things"); accordingly they are used for the youngest siblings in a family. The effect is similar to using "Jimmy" or "Jim-boy" for someone named "Jim." Classifying *-kun* and *-chan* as strictly "inferior" terms completely misses an important aspect of Japanese affectivity and intimacy. For example, *-kun* might be applied to young male workers by their senior. Does this mean that they are being "inferiorized" or made to be subservient? Not at all.

Once a young nontenured Japanese instructor taught at my university in Japan. Naturally he was concerned about his status because Japanese teachers in Japan almost always receive immediate tenure. This man, however, was hired on a temporary basis though he taught full time. I was encouraged to learn that his direct superior, a senior professor, was using the *-kun* term for him, as if treating him as "part of the family." That is, he was taking responsibility as his mentor and advocate. It may be that such language could stimulate supportive feelings in the senior. Thus, it may not be a coincidence that the instructor now has tenure.

Similarly, Laura Miller demonstrates how *-kun,* in a business setting, seems to indicate camaraderie and close relations between superior and subordinate, though she acknowledges that the term also can have the opposite connotation.[39] Consequently, a superior-inferior relationship in a Japanese group may mean far more than westerners believe. It is this case with *kun:* Foreigners tend to emphasize its non-reciprocity (never reciprocated from subordinate to superior). Its use by a superior, however, may also connote a caring, paternalistic feeling.

Relational Identities

One of the key features of Japanese culture is that the Japanese have a relational identity. That is, reference to oneself in speech depends on with whom one speaks. In English, both speaker and hearer can use the same terms: *I* and *you.* In Japanese, however, multiple terms exist and depend on factors such as the setting and one's age, gender, and organizational rank. Tazuko Ajiro Monane, a native Japanese and a college professor in the United States, told of her experience in meeting other Japanese nationals abroad. She confessed that invariably, her husband (presumably not a native Japanese) had to do most of the talking for her because, as she stated,

> In [the] Japanese language, one's *identity* and one's *self* are not established without another's identity being made clear. In these awkward situations that I have cited, "I" *as a person* did not exist precisely because the identity of the stranger was not known to me. Before we Japanese find out the other's identity, we have difficulty in engaging ourselves in *any* conversation with that person.[40]

This is largely true, but the courteous level of honorifics can act as a neutral medium though it might not satisfy all Japanese.

The Japanese may not be the only ones facing such difficulty. I once heard a story about the outback of India, where Chadwick, an Englishman, had been living. The area was so isolated that one could expect not to see a foreigner for years. One day, as Chadwick was buying some supplies at an outpost, he came across a fellow Englishman, who was sitting under a nearby tree. Chadwick eagerly said, "Hello," to which the other man replied, "Have we been properly introduced?"

If this story is true, I cannot imagine a Japanese acting in the same way. Indeed, the unusual isolation would probably melt his or her inhibitions. On the other hand, in more convenient surroundings abroad, Japanese would have much less need to interact with fellow Japanese. Thus the complications of hierarchial thinking would remain. This point explains an observed difference between Japanese and North American tourists. Between airline flights, North Americans appear "group oriented" in that they often form small conversational groups even with strangers. Japanese, on the other hand, rarely engage other Japanese whom they do not know. Evidently this difference originates with the Japanese relational identities.

The model for Japanese social interaction is the family, which is age-based. As we saw above, seniors may treat their juniors as though they were younger brothers or sisters. The roles, in addition to the parents, include older brother and older sister, and younger brother and younger sister. Typically the brother or sister is always distinguished as older or younger than the speaker. Equality in terms of reference does not exist between them. Traditionally, the younger siblings address the older in terms of rank, e.g., "big brother." Only the younger ones are addressed by their personal names or by personal pronouns (a practice mirrored in work relations as seen above). Because this distinction is made in the formative years, it is no wonder that social status is important in Japanese interpersonal life.

Some Japanese families, however, no longer follow this unequal system of address. One possible reason is practicality. In one certain Japanese family, there are three daughters. The eldest is always addressed by the second eldest as *oneesan* (older sister). The youngest, however, never uses this term because it would be confusing to address both sisters by the same name (role title). She uses their personal names instead. It can also be the case that a child with only one elder sibling refuses to address that sibling by anything other than a personal name. In still other cases, the parents may wish their children to use personal names rather than terms of respect, for "modernistic" reasons. Such cases remain the exception, however.

Personal Pronouns

Personal pronouns in Japanese are a Catch-22: They exist (depending on definition) but are avoided. *Anata,* commonly learned by foreign students as equivalent to *you,* also means the affectionate *dear* used by wives for their husbands. Although *anata* is said to be polite, it is inappropriate for addressing social superiors. Other words for *you* exist but, because of emotional nuances, are usually unfit for formal interactions. Thus, Japanese is said not to possess a completely neutral word for *you.* A grown daughter, when speaking to her mother, would still use the rank or status term *mother,* as in "I love/hate mother." The Japanese mother, conversely, would most likely use the daughter's personal name.[41] Here English has a clear social advantage in its flexibility of address, indicating less inhibition about social interaction.

When Japanese strangers meet, they feel insecure unless they know each other's "organizational identity" or relative rank in life; without this knowledge, meaningful conversations cannot begin.[42] The Japanese have been so thoroughly conditioned in this way of thinking that the habit is too strong to ignore. Once their relative ranks are known, they can speak.

To show how this relativity of social identities operates, Table 5.4 depicts the relative use of personal pronouns by members of a private dinner party. This depiction is part of my analysis of a hypothetical case presented by Akira Y. Yamamoto for a similar purpose.[43] He asked a middle-aged married couple to write a conversational dialogue and had it verified as natural by six other couples (all presumably native Japanese).

The "conversation" took place at dinner in the home of a doctor and his wife, who were joined by a friend of the doctor's (a schoolteacher) and his wife. The doctor was imagined to be in his fifties, his wife in her forties, and both guests in their thirties. The topic was about poetry and the four speakers' compositions. The dialogue, however, was purposely made short, and consisted of only 10 exchanges between the participants. Yet even this brief dialogue was enough to show that the speakers' language reflected differences in their social status, especially with the use of personal pronouns and verb forms.

Japanese has multiple word choices for saying *I* and *you*. Different choices by speakers often relate to their relative social ranks. Except for the pairing of the teacher and the doctor's wife, all other pairings used personal pronouns indicative of relative

Table 5.4 Personal Pronoun Use by Paired Japanese Speakers at Two Social Levels at the Same Dinner Party

Formal Level	D		DW
	• T	T • DW	•TW
Intimate Level	D	T	
	•DW	•TW	

D=doctor; DW=doctor's wife; T=teacher; TW=teacher's wife

rank. These rank differences are depicted in the table by placement of the individual on an upper or lower plane. Why were personal pronouns used anyway? As was stated above, Japanese tend to avoid personal pronouns. In the original Japanese and in Yamamoto's English translation, my count revealed that the Japanese versions used first-person pronouns less than half as often as the English versions and used second-person 6 times less often. Still, some pronouns were used in Japanese because the topic called for making clear whom the speakers were talking about.

At the formal level of conversation, the doctor's own first-person pronoun was less formal than that used by the other speakers for themselves. That is, his *I* was more casual than that used by the others. This difference was due to the doctor's higher occupational and age status. He was clearly polite but slightly less so than his two guests.

On the other hand, the doctor's wife used a first-person pronoun with the guests at the same level of respectfulness as she received. Perhaps she did so to honor the teacher as a friend of the doctor's. This use also reflected her central role as the matron of the household and thus the person in charge of household affairs. She showed less formality toward her husband, however, in keeping with their relationship. Overall the doctor was the only one who used the same first-person pronoun toward everyone; the others changed theirs among themselves.

In case of verbs, however, even the doctor switched levels of formality: moderately polite toward the guests but casual toward his wife. Although the schoolteacher used a more formal *I* than the doctor, they used verbs with each other at the same level of respect. The verb forms used for each other by the doctor and his wife were at the same level, that being casual.

If Table 5.4 also charted verb usage, T (teacher) would rank higher than DW (doctor's wife) in their paired conversation. She had raised the politeness level of her verb forms with the teacher to a higher level than what he had used with her. As the matron, she probably wanted to honor him as a guest and as a friend of her husband's, even though she was much older. She also accorded the same high degree of politeness to the teacher's wife.

The teacher's wife even expressed the same high level of politeness with her own husband; no doubt, she had the most psychological distance from the others. She was probably the youngest and was new to both the doctor and his wife. In this setting, in which she was a visitor to the home of a high-status person, she showed the most politeness overall.

One aspect of the dialogue that even Yamamoto apparently missed is that the dialogue included no exchanges between the doctor and the teacher's wife—theoretically, the highest and the lowest ranks. Probably their speech levels would have followed the lines already established. Thus the setting may establish the ceiling for appropriate honorifics. The fact that the teacher's wife had the "lowest" rank does not necessarily mean that the doctor would show her the least regard. It would have been interesting, however, to see how Yamamoto's associates would have handled this question.

We should view this case a traditional ideal. Some Japanese would expect less formality between the participants; some, perhaps more. Still, Yamamoto's case rings true as to the speakers' changing of speech levels to fit the differences in their social relations. Finally, young married couples of today tend to use more equal terms of address than those depicted in Yamamoto's dialogue.

Relational Terms at the Retail Store

Although it is sometimes said that the Japanese domestic economy is supplier-oriented rather than consumer-oriented, the customer is clearly treated as the social superior, in terms of interpersonal relations between store clerks and their customers. For example, a customer would never address a sales clerk using the highly respectful suffix *-sama,* although the reverse is possible. Aoi Tsuda studied actual speech between store clerks and customers in Japan and in the United States. Her findings show that the Japanese language is far richer in address forms than English, and reveals a general avoidance of pronouns in speech (see Table 5.5). These address forms are used where a simple *you* would suffice in English. They also show how social role and rank are reinforced powerfully in Japanese society.

Honorifics: Etiquette Rather Than Subservience

Japanese honorifics "function as an index of asymmetrical [social] relationships.... While honorifics are primarily a public symbol of respect, they do not necessarily indicate a 'real attitude' of respect."[44] Foreigners, however, are likely to exaggerate the inherent social inequalities. For present-day use, Japanese honorifics are probably seen more accurately as a system of etiquette: People simply wish to appear civil and refined. This wish seems to be reflected in a survey conducted by

Table 5.5 Address Forms Used Between Salespeople and Customers from the General Public[45]

By Clerk When Customer's Name Is Unknown

1. Role of visitor (*okyaku-sama/san* "honorable guest")
2. Spacial position (*sochira-sama/san* "honorable there")
3. Familial position (*otaku-sama/san* "honorable home/ family of yours") (*danna-sama/san* "honorable family head") (*okusama/san* "honorable housewife") (*ojo-sama/san* "honorable daughter")

By Clerk When Customer's Name is Known

4 Family name (family name *-sama/san*)

By Customers to Clerks

otaku-san, "name-of-store"*-san;* "name-of-company" *-san,*" "kind-of-store"*-san* (e.g. *honya-san,* "Mr./Ms. Bookstore); family name*-san**

* Tsuda includes *anata* among those used by customers at the initial stage of encounters but this use may be too infrequent to include here. Moreover, *anata* is generally avoided in use, especially by the store clerks.

Nihon Hoso Kyokai (NHK), the Japanese national broadcasting company. "Over 90 percent of the respondents felt that [honorific] language was needed in spoken Japanese, and 71 percent said that it helped in their relationships with people."[46] Assuming a random sample, we can suppose that the Japanese hold favorable attitudes toward honorific language. Indeed, "it is said to give Japanese a 'lyrical quality, expressive of feelings,'... and without it, it is felt that Japanese would lose its 'charm.'"[47]

Yet, some "feudalistic" vestiges remain[48] in the honorifics. For example, expressions of goodbye in some companies may make a distinction between superior or subordinate:

From superior to subordinate, *gokuroosama deshita;*
From subordinate to superior, *otsukaresama deshita.*[49]

Both terms functionally mean "goodbye" but more literally mean thanks for one's cooperation or work. Not all Japanese are clear about the distinction between these two expressions. Former Japanese Prime Minister Nakasone, in the 1980s, was once criticized for a faux pas in saying *gokuroosama deshita* to the then emperor (Hirohito) instead of *otsukaresama deshita*, though the latter would still not have been deferential enough.[50] Nakasone's mistake was a bit ironic because he staunchly supported commemorating some of the wartime nationalist symbols.[51] His mistake also illustrates the tension associated with age or status differences in Japanese society.

Although such differential greetings may grate on western sensibilities, social differences are inherent in human society. Also, if a Japanese "overuses" honorifics, he or she risks alienating others.[52] Women who do so are sometimes ridiculed for being a *zaamasu fujin* ("uppity lady").[53] Some calibration is needed for each communicative situation, so that one's speech fits the occasion and relationship. At issue are two aspects that we may fail to keep in mind. One is that the honorifics or speech levels (*keigo*) are not used exclusively to show deference but also for politeness. The latter purpose corresponds largely to politeness for politeness' sake. The other aspect often overlooked is the potential for subordinates to "turn the tables" on their superiors—that is, to use deference to attain their aims.

Consider the sales technique employed by an exclusive Japanese department store some 50 years ago: It addressed elderly women not with the expected *obaasan* ("honorable grandmother") but by *okusama* ("very honorable wife"). The latter term suggested that the woman was not only of high status but also much younger than she actually was.[54] (*Okusan* is used to address a middle-aged woman, usually the wife of another man.) In a similar but less obvious way, it is easy to imagine that deferential language could be used instrumentally by subordinates seeking favors or positive regard from their superiors.[55] Additional reasons for using honorifics other than social rank are related to topic, setting, social identity, and rhetorical purposes.[56] A switch to honorifics, for example, can help avoid sensitive topics or protect the ego without confrontational language. In short, Japanese honorifics function neither solely for etiquette nor solely to humble people; both potentials exist.

In considering the latter "humbling" function, however, much depends on one's point of view. In the Japanese mind, deference to deserving others is a sign of refinement. Only the "well-educated" are able to execute the etiquette flawlessly. Thus Japanese companies instruct their employees carefully in the correct use of honorifics, especially with the public. In general, honorifics have an inverse relation to intimacy: The more intimate the relationship, the less likely that honorifics will be used. Therefore honorific language is generally used with people other than one's immediate family and close friends.

Also, it appears that those who live in small rural communities make relatively little use of honorifics.[57] Rather, the skillful use of honorifics is a necessity for entry into the power circles of Japanese society.[58] Finally, the Japanese language, as recently as the early 1960s, had "lost much of the vocabulary that distinguished between social ranks and between sexes,"[59] a development generally ignored in treatments of honorifics. Even though extreme honorifics may seem archaic to us (and to some Japanese, too), the difference in use between today and the time before World War II must be considerable. Compared with the recent past, contemporary Japanese are living in liberated times.

Recently, I sensed some of this liberation when listening to a disc jockey on an FM rock music radio station in Nagoya. After encouraging his listeners to send in postcards for a promotion, he ended by saying cheerfully, *omachi shite orimasu* (I will be waiting). He could have said *matsu* or *machimasu;* his choice, the exalted form for *wait,* is typically used by service providers. (Here again we see an instance of the general principle that politeness tends to correlate with lengthier forms.) Although technically the disc jockey was placing the listeners above himself, the phrase had no significance other than indicating some politeness. That is, there was no real sense that he was lower socially than his listeners. He simply wanted to do his job conscientiously. He uttered the expression rhythmically, in time with the up-tempo beat of the background music and his commercial message. The lyrical quality made me feel good. Isn't that how we often hope to affect others?

For a more fully detailed account of honorifics, please consult a reference book on Japanese grammar. We proceed now to an even more distinctive feature of Japanese communication style—back-channeling.

Back-Channeling (*aizuchi*)

Back-channeling refers to verbal, vocal, or nonverbal responses by the listener to show his or her attention and to encourage the speaker to continue. Common back-channeling cues in English are *hm hmm*, *uh uh, really,* and so on. Japanese conversational speech is highly fragmented in that short utterances are "packaged" or "wrapped" with pauses and/or grammatical particles to elicit back-channeling cues from the listener. Frequent back-channeling is required of the listener, as is evident in Japanese telephone calls: Restrict the back-channeling cues and immediately the other person will say, *moshi, moshi* ("Are you there?"). The overall effect of this frequent fragmentation and back-channeling is not only a fast pulsating rhythm but also high conversational involvement: "The listener's constant participation creates a more intensely cooperative interaction than is typical of conversation in American English. ...Some English speakers addressing Japanese listeners may find themselves reduced to paralyzed silence by the barrage of verbal response and nodding which greet their words and seems to indicate that they have already been understood when they have scarcely begun to speak."[60]

One cannot be silent for any appreciable time in a Japanese conversation. One could go without speaking a word, but not without any vocalizations such as "oh," "ah," "hmm," and so on. The closest American counterpart is found in the responses of a counselor or therapist during a counseling session. (In the counseling profession, back-channeling is considered an essential skill.) This frequent back-channeling produces an effect almost like that of "hanging on every word," which is somewhat out of place in the usual American social conversation. Thus, any transfer of Japanese back-channeling to American conversations, especially by and for males, would probably fail. As individualists, we find intense back-channeling a threat to our social space or self-image. In a normal, casual situation, we may be made to feel as if we were dimwitted. David Riggs shares a similar consequence when he unconsciously transferred habits of *aizuchi* from Japanese into his English with a close family relative: "My grandmother in Albany once got so frustrated with my constant *aizuchi* that she finally said 'Will you stop that.'"[61] I can well understand that his intention was to encourage the speaker, yet it had an opposite effect.

Let us clarify some points about silence. One must vocalize continually in Japanese conversation, but in other ways, silence appears to be more tolerated in Japan than in North America. This is a finding of a major study of American and Japanese small-group business meetings.[62] Yet although the Japanese appear to have a greater tolerance for silence, this study is flawed. The two groups studied were structured differently, and thus were not comparable: The American group followed a written agenda, while the Japanese did not.[63] Periods of silence seem more likely to occur in formal meetings that have no written agenda. Also, meetings without written agendas probably will include more "nontask" talking. As the same researcher reflects later: "Given this fundamental difference [between the two groups], it is not surprising to find that the American strategy [in conversations] for opening topics is vastly different from the Japanese."[64] This is precisely my point, and it shows why little is gained by the use of noncomparable groups for study. Still, while we await confirmation by more rigorous studies, we can tentatively assume that the Japanese are more tolerant of silence.

Another point is that silence may function as a way to avoid social confrontation. For example, a Japanese speaker can decide not to make an assertion, and allow his or her voice to trail off. Thus a long pause may be created, which could be interpreted as a shift in topic.

Prolonged silence, in some situations, also appears to be more acceptable to the Japanese. If the other interactants in Japanese are silent, one may be silent as well. The vocalizing required from the listener need not be verbal. Thus the listener need not say anything substantive as long as he or she continues to show signs of involvement. This does not mean that a "contentless" performance is desirable, but that vocalizations indicating involvement play a large role in Japanese conversations.

Again, silence is far more acceptable than in North America, but exceptions exist. One exception was noted above. Another occurs in meeting a new acquaintance, especially in socializing with the opposite sex. At such times the Japanese, with few exceptions, find silence awkward. If, they are intimates, however, the situation changes. I am reminded of a young European male who was eager to socialize with Japanese females and derided the Japanese males for what may be a distinctive practice: In coffee shops, young couples may be seen reading magazines (usually *manga*, "comic books") together in complete silence. This occurs so widely that it could be called a custom. The European man, perhaps because of loneliness in a foreign country, seemed to envy the Japanese men in such situations. He seemed to suggest that they treated the young women poorly. Yet he did not know what these couples did before or after they visited the coffee shop. Nor could he have possibly known their degree of intimacy or the women's preferences.

In Japan, newspapers and comic books (for nearly all ages) have enormous circulations. The latter, which are largely serialized, are often available for reading in the coffee shop. Thus the coffee shop is not just for refreshment or conversation. When these couples are not reading, they can be animated conversationalists. It is simply wrong to think that the Japanese run counter to the lively, the high-spirited, the expressive. On the contrary, in their informal social situations, they can be animated as North Americans. Their society is strongly context-dependent. Certain contexts require rigid restraint; others, nearly the opposite. Unless foreign observers experience a wide range of Japanese social situations, they are likely to observe only the formal, "the proper" side that their hosts, usually elites, choose to show them.

To return to our discussion, "Japanese utterances tend to be short. [Japanese] speak for a length of approximately twenty syllables and then wait for their interlocutor to give a signal to proceed."[65] (Recall my observation about back-channeling on the telephone.) Japanese casual, informal speech contains about four words per grammatical sentence, or about 2 1/2 words per PPU (pause-bounded phrasal unit).[66] Here *word* refers to content words, conjunctions, or pronouns plus associated particles (preposition-type words).[67]

A useful strategy when listening to a Japanese speaker is to back-channel at his or her pause points between utterances. (*Pause point* refers here to the junctures between ideational units or phrases). Head nodding ("I hear you") is another back-channeling cue and is performed far more often than in the usual American conversation. When these various vocal, verbal, and nonverbal cues are activated in the tempo of the conversation, a finely tuned synchrony develops between the interactants. The speaker, in part, elicits cues from the listener, who in turn spurs the speaker on. A listener who does not provide back-channeling essentially kills the conversation. In regard to this point, Japanese conversation is quintessentially social. North Americans also must be careful to avoid monopolizing a conversation. This is likely to happen because the Japanese pause longer than North Americans at topic shifts or changes in "floor" management.[68]

JAPANESE SOCIAL ORIENTATION

Although much is still unknown, it seems safe to say that the Japanese emphasize the social mode far more strongly than North Americans. For example, it is almost mandatory for Japanese personal letters to begin with a reference to the season (as opposed to "getting down to business"). When Japanese strangers meet, especially businesspeople, they immediately exchange personal business cards to help them understand how to speak to one another. The cards indicate their relative social positions, showing who has the superior rank. Various speech routines, by which strong emotions are restrained, are followed to avoid impoliteness; some non-Japanese find the result "spiceless." The Japanese system appears exceedingly complex in contrast to our "directness." Yet to the Japanese, their own communication patterns seem "wet"; ours, "dry." Overall they regard their system as providing, figuratively speaking, *sukinshippu* ("skin-ship"), a psychological bonding, togetherness. Again, to non-Japanese, it may seem excessive.

For example, the Japanese have a drinking custom whereby people continually pour drinks for each other. Most people find this custom appealing, but it has its limits. Once I sat down with an American acquaintance who had been born and raised in Japan and was working as an interpreter for a Japanese business. When we were served our beer, I made a motion to pour him a drink, which he quickly rebuffed. Almost scowling, he insisted on pouring his own. Certainly he would never have done that in a Japanese business setting. Probably he had to engage in the custom so often that he was tired of it. Moreover, he probably wanted to follow American custom as much as he could, given his background. Japanese "skin-ship" is so intense that even some Japanese find it burdensome.

A Japanese relative of mine, upon earning his BA in engineering, realized that he was not cut out for the social drinking (*tsukiai*) expected of company personnel. He could have landed a job with a big company such as Toyota or Mitsubishi, if he had wished. Company employees, however, are expected to socialize frequently with much after-hours drinking, though not all company personnel follow this custom so closely. It is thought to develop cohesion between co-workers, and provides opportunities to air any differences. My relative expressed his concerns to his professor, who then secured him a graduate assistantship at the same university. Apparently my relative was deserving, for eventually he became the first in his field in Japan to solve a certain problem in engineering. He went on to obtain his PhD, the youngest in his class, and is now a college professor. I was struck not only by the paternalism shown by his senior professor, but also by the young man's grounds for entering academia. It was not the work in the Japanese company but the social demands that drove him away.

As an additional example, I have borrowed a case from Junko Yagasaki's study of the identity of foreigners living in Japan. Mr. Q.,* an American, appeared to be deeply immersed in Japanese culture. Yagasaki's remarks about Mr. Q.'s view of working in a Japanese company, as well as her own comments are relevant here:

> [After seven years of work with a Japanese company and acquiring native-like language and behavior, Mr. Q.'s co-workers expected him to comply with after-hours company routines.] He then realized that it had gone too far, particularly after his son was born. Although he wanted to spend more time with his son, the company demanded his loyalty. He had to devote 100 [percent] of himself to the company. He says that he realized it too late. He had been "burnt out" by the Japanese interpersonal relationships within the company, just as many Japanese salaried men are. ...Mr. Q. thinks it was not the company that bound him to his work. It was rather [he] who bound himself. ...In this sense, he was like a Japanese. He suppressed his own feelings and drove himself to the point of being "burnt out."...
>
> Now he works for a foreign company, where he can have more time to spend with his son at home. ... However, he still prefers the Japanese way of interacting with one another, because [it suits him, but] ... he considers that the Japanese themselves must sometimes feel pain in following all those

> rules and in being put under such restraint. I think that this is very true. What he does not like about Japanese ways is also most likely to be disliked by the Japanese. In terms of the Japanese obligation to follow small rules, he does not want to become a Japanese. He just follows the rules voluntarily, not because he is obliged to. Probably that is what he wants to believe himself to be doing.[69]

The case of Mr. Q. shows how intense Japanese (institutional) group life can be. The "village feeling" can be double-edged, providing "skinship" but causing hardship as well. Nevertheless, Mr. Q. found some inherent pleasure in the Japanese communication style, possibly because of the back-channeling, the intense involvement, and the high degree of ritualism of Japanese interaction in general. By high ritualism I mean that certain interactional routines that are so strongly routinized that one could operate almost on "automatic pilot" and still have satisfying social encounters. As one bi-lingual Japanese remarked to me, social interaction is easier in Japanese than in English because there is less reliance on verbalization. (No doubt everyday, casual social interaction was meant here.) As suggested earlier, North American culture seems to demand that one's utterances be "distinctive," as with the example of the dinner guests' compliments to the host. One seems to be continually expected to stand out by being witty and original—an aspect of individuality.

I once overheard a joke made in a Japanese classroom, when an instructor was calling out student numbers to check the roll on the first day. When he called out "50," a hand was raised in response, which elicited a comment from another Japanese: "Not your age—your student number!" Surely, in North America, the joke would have referred to the student's supposed IQ, not to his age. North Americans are called on to distinguish themselves, which is done more easily with an IQ score than with age. In contrast, age is far more a distinctive feature for the Japanese than for North Americans.

Age differences form a basis for social hierarchy in Japan: One must show respect to one's seniors, even if only a year apart. This respect, as we have seen, is reflected in the language by terms of address and speech levels (*keigo*). Athletic teams at some Japanese schools may use age rather than skill per se in choosing seniors for games ahead of the juniors. Everyone gets treated "equally" because each one gets a turn. In a way, age allows the Japanese to avoid individual competition in favor of group cohesion. At Japanese schools, elementary and junior high, there is no "failure"; all students are promoted regardless of test scores. (However, students are tested very frequently on school subjects, which confers "failure" on some students even if they are officially promoted.) Until recently, job promotions in Japanese companies were based more on age (= seniority) than performance. Perhaps this explains why Japanese work productivity has recently lagged behind much of the industrialized free world.[70] It also explains why Japanese can buy into their social hierarchy and the perpetuation of *keigo*. In theory, nearly everyone can eventually ascend to higher positions of respect. Thus Mr. Q. and his colleagues accepted the rigors of Japanese companies because they know that with seniority, they may eventually benefit.

Whereas the emphasis in Japanese culture is to "blend in," the emphasis in North American is to stand out. These are emphases only; both cultures call for conformity and individuality at times. In regard to the use of English, distinctiveness (individuality) does not necessarily preclude the use of formulas or established patterns of linguistic expression. Even though North Americans like to view their speech as being spontaneous and creative, "much of it [for social routines] is in fact modeled on standard formulas."[71] Although Japanese social situations may call for a greater use of linguistic formulas than comparable situations in North America, that difference is of degree, not kind. Hardly can that difference support claims that one people is more linguistically creative than another.

In regard to the Japanese suppression of feelings, that social imperative is found nearly everywhere. Societies could not survive if individuals gave full rein to their emotions. Display rules for emotions differ across cultures, however. Japanese culture restricts strong emotions from public view. The media, for example, carried a report about a Japanese fisherman who returned after being lost at sea for a considerable length of time. He did not hug or kiss his wife on his return, but shook her hand. Yet sometimes even Japanese men in public cannot avoid showing deep emotion, such as crying after hearing that tragedy has struck a loved one.

Before declaring the Japanese "emotionally repressed," however, we ought to consider that the Japanese may develop a greater tolerance than North Americans for unexpressed feelings.

"Japanese [may] have learned to modify their emotional reactions so well, and from such an early age, that as adults their reaction patterns are automatic with little conscious effort."[72] David Matsumoto, who has studied Japanese emotions intensively, reached this conclusion, in part, on the basis of his finding that the Japanese experience inner emotional states similar to those of Americans and Europeans, although they make fewer outward emotional displays and report *no greater degree of emotional control.*

CONCLUSION

In this chapter we have briefly considered the concept of communication style as pertaining to language and society. We found a number of ways in which Japanese communicate far differently than Americans. Whereas the American communication style tends to be informational, the Japanese tend to emphasize the social. This difference was exemplified by the case of international business. To complicate matters, Japanese social priorities are different. Americans wish to be friendly; Japanese, to be respectful. These priorities are not mutually exclusive, but each has a basis in its related culture. Other important features of the Japanese communication style are interdependency, recognition of age and gender, honorifics, and back-channeling.

When we are aware of such features, we can understand why Japanese behave as they do. At the same time, they may become less "inscrutable" to us. This is the value of studying cross-cultural images such as the schema of the mysterious Orient(al) as discussed in a previous chapter. If we are conscious of such exaggerated notions, we may be able to identify valid differences more accurately and to minimize our ethnocentric biases.

APPLICATION

A Japanese science fiction story follows that satirizes Japanese social talk for its sometimes long-windedness and flattery, according to the translator, Robert Matthew.[73] Though such excesses are not uniquely Japanese, they "have refined it into an art form. Confucian society is based on respect and recognition of position and while the Chinese of the Mainland at least have dropped most of their traditional honorific expressions and practices, in Japan the tradition persists. The Japanese today are the world's ... masters in the art because most other societies do not have an equivalent need of it."[74] Fine as it goes, but in reading the story, please remember that as a satire, some exaggeration is to be expected.

THE SECRETARY ON THE SHOULDER

by Hoshi Shin'ichi[75]

Translated by Robert Matthew

Hoshi Shin'ichi is a prominent writer in the world of Japanese science fiction.

Robert Matthew, a professor of Japanese at the University of Queensland, Australia, is a leading translator of Japanese science fiction. He authored, among many published works, Japanese Science Fiction: A View of a Changing Society *(Routledge and the Nissan Institute of the University of Oxford).*

As he rolled along a road paved with plastic on his auto-skates, Mr Zaim took a look at his wristwatch.

Half past four. Just time to call in on one more house before he went back to the office. He slackened his speed, and brought his skates to a halt in front of a house.

Mr Zaim was a salesman. In his left hand he carried a large case, crammed with merchandise. And on his right shoulder he carried a macaw with beautiful wings—as, indeed, did everybody else in this age.

He pressed the bell-button by the side of the front door, and waited. Presently the door opened, and the lady of the house appeared.

"Hello," he muttered under his breath.

Following this scarcely audible sound, the macaw on his

shoulder rattled on clearly:

"I'm very sorry to trouble you at a time like this. I know you weren't expecting me and you must be very busy. I hope you don't mind."

The macaw was a robot. It possessed an elaborate electronic brain, along with tape recordings and a speaker. Its function was to rephrase in greater detail whatever its owner said, and then relay the message to the listener.

Now it was the turn of the housewife's macaw to reply.

"Thank you for coming. I hope you don't think I'm rude, but my memory is not very good, and I'm afraid I don't remember your name ..."

The macaw on Mr Zaim's shoulder inclined its head and whispered in his ear: Who are you?"

The macaw could also summarize the other party's conversation and report the gist to its owner.

"New Electro Co. Buy an electric spider," answered Zaim in the same muffled tone. The macaw continued, politely and correctly.

"As a matter of fact, I am a sales representative of the New Electro Company. As no doubt you are aware, our company is proud of its long tradition and the high public confidence which it enjoys. If it were otherwise, I would not have called on you today. I would like to show you our latest product, which has just been perfected by our Research Division. Here it is—an electric spider ..."

At this point he opened his case and took out a small metallic gadget with a golden sheen about it. It looked like a spider. The macaw prattled on:

"... this is it. Whenever your back gets itchy, you can simply slip it inside your clothes. It will locate the itch all by itself, and then scratch with its legs and give you wonderful relief. It's a very handy thing to have. A high class home like yours should not be without one. With this in mind I came round specially to bring one for you."

When Mr Zaim's macaw came to an end, the macaw on the housewife's shoulder whispered in her ear in a voice too low for them to overhear:

"He wants you to buy an automatic backscratcher."

The housewife replied,

"No."

Her macaw took it up.

"It's a wonderful gadget. Your company is always bringing out new products, isn't it? I'm afraid, however, that at our house we would not be able to afford such a superb article."

"Nix!" reported Zaim's macaw.

"Try harder," he muttered.

The macaw continued with increased enthusiasm:

"I'm sorry to hear that, but for sheer convenience there's nothing to beat it. It can scratch your back where your hand can't reach, and it can do it in company completely undetected. It eliminates tiresome effort. And the price is quite cheap."

"He says you've got to buy it."

"He's a nuisance!"

After this little huddle the housewife's macaw replied:

"When I'm making purchases I never agree to buy without consulting with my husband first. Unfortunately he's not at home right now, so I can't make any decision. We should be able to have a good talk about it this evening, so perhaps you might like to come back some other time. I like it myself, but that's no good. I'm really very sorry."

Zaim's macaw summed it up for him:

"Get lost!"

He gave up, and put the spider back in his case. As he did so, he muttered,

"So long!"

The macaw relayed a polite farewell.

"I understand. I'm really very sorry too. Please give my regards to your husband."

He left the front door and revved up his skates. Then he made his way back to the office, with the macaw still on his shoulder.

Back at his desk, he pushed the keys of his computer to tot up the day's sales.

"Hey, Zaim!"

It was the divisional chief's macaw calling.

"Oh dear. I bet it's another sermon."

His macaw relayed the comment to the chief:

"Yes Sir. I'll be in directly. I'll just straighten my desk...."

He was soon standing on the carpet before his chief's desk. The chief was blowing tobacco smoke, and through the haze his macaw prattled at Zaim in serious tones.

"Well now, Zaim. This is a crucial time when our firm must take a great jump forward. I believe you are well aware of this, but a look at your performance record gives me the impression you could do somewhat better. I must say it's very regrettable. I want you to take note of this point. I want action."

Zaim's macaw whispered,

"Raise your sales."

"Just like that?" Zaim whispered back.

The macaw address[ed] the chief in meek tones:

"I understand perfectly. I am determined to increase my sales still further. But recently our rivals have brought in new methods and new products. They are trying all sorts of things. Sales are not as easy as they were. Of course, I shall redouble my efforts, but if you could pass on to the Rescarch and Production Division the message that they need to keep coming up with new products, I should be doubly obliged to you."

A bell rang. It was time to go home. Phew! The day's work was over. But after doing the rounds on sales all day long, he was dog tired. He needed to drop in at a bar on the way home to cheer his mood.

He pushed open the door of the Bar Galaxy, a place he visited from time to time. When the bar madam spotted him, her macaw accosted him in a sleazy voice:

"Ah, Mr Zaim! Do come in. We haven't seen you here for a long time. The atmosphere here has been lonely without you ..."

These were the very words he most wanted to hear.

Commentary

The translator kept rather faithful to the original and produced a superb rendition. The story captures the potential for social nicety and obliqueness. The accent is on potential, for by no means is the housewife's speech representative. In real life, Japanese are typically straightforward with door-to-door salespeople in telling them their services are not needed, such as *kekko desu* ("That's ok" / "No, thank you").[76] Nevertheless, the speech of the housewife is not beyond the Japanese imagination. A snippet of it can be found in many spheres of Japanese life, for the Japanese emphasize ritual and social nicety. According to some informants who had read the original Japanese dialogue, they imagined the woman to have a sort of aristocratic background.

Another point is that this story was conveyed here through

English, which indicates that English, too, has similar potentiality for snobbery and so forth. The difference, though, is that in this regard, the resources are more systematic in Japanese. Systematic, in that social difference in Japanese is regularly realized through grammatical and semantic devices and set phrases. For example, in the original Japanese, the social relations between the macaws and their owners are quite different. In the original Japanese, Mr. Zaim and his macaw speak mutually to each other at the same level—a plain (nonpolite) style. But not so between the housewife and her macaw. Her macaw speaks politely, but she does not reciprocate. That is clearly indicated in Japanese by the grammar of their mutual utterances, whereas the difference is far more subtle in the English version.

Moreover, as excellent as the translation of the dialogue is, it still had to use 5 to 30 percent more words than the original—a limitation of English. This indicates that highly polite expressions are more readily available in Japanese than in English. Although the Japanese speaker feels the extra demands of politeness, it still may be less demanding to the Japanese than we think. Psycholinguistic experiments indicate that this is so for Japanese sentence processing in general.[77]

Exercise

1. Analyze "The Secretary on the Shoulder" for possible reflections of Japanese culture or thought. Identify those instances and your reasons why.

6

Japanese Communication Style: Aspects of Language and Thought

It would be helpful to identify the linguistic features of Japanese most distinctive as compared to English. Whereas Chapter 5 did so at the sociolinguistic level, the present chapter does so at the psycholinguistic level. The very act of isolating such features, however, may exaggerate them needlessly, perhaps even raising psychological barriers to new students of the language and culture. Misconceptions about Japanese have existed ever since that early missionary reported to the Pope centuries ago that Japanese was the devil's language.[1] Devil or not, learning the language is not an all-or-none proposition. Various levels of Japanese can be achieved, but much depends on the individual's objectives.

In any case, this chapter offers a framework for conceptualizing the Japanese language in comparison with English. Until JSL (Japanese as a second language) becomes more widespread, North Americans are more likely to interact with

Japanese in English than in Japanese. Some North Americans may forget the accommodation made for them. They may even forget that those with whom they speak may not be native speakers of English. To counter such tendencies, it is useful to be aware of the distinctive features of the Japanese language. In this way, we will be better prepared to deal with miscommunications, as well as studying JSL.

In this chapter I describe Japanese word order and ellipsis, which affect the form of Japanese utterances (or sentences). A review of these features, though brief, will give a basic idea of the distinctiveness of Japanese. For additional insights, we will consider the Japanese cultural ethos or thought in relation to the language and discourse of Japanese.

JAPANESE WORD ORDER

For those unfamiliar with the language, Japanese sentences (or utterances) seem to be a mirror image of those in English.[2] Japanese word order is nearly the reverse of word order in English. For example, "I put the book on the desk" is rendered as

tsukue no ue ni hon o oita
desk-of-top-on-book-{*o*}-put
(Items in horned brackets { } indicate a grammatical particle.)

The word orders of the two languages are not absolutely reversed, but the patterns differ enough to make knowledge of the reverse tendencies a useful basis for translation.

The Japanese language is classified as SOV (subject-object-verb), the type most frequently found among the world's languages.[3] Because many Japanese do not know how wide-spread the SOV type is, and because their second language is primarily English, they may assume that the Japanese language is unusual. For example, two Japanese authors, in an otherwise useful article, seem to succumb to the Japanese uniqueness myth when they write:

> The Japanese language is in a class by itself. With its origin still uncertain, it defies genealogical and morphological classification. Its typical word order is SOV, as opposed to the SVO order found in many other languages [4]

The SOV order in fact is not unusual, as stated above. Also, the origin of Japanese may be uncertain, but it is not the only language with that status. Moreover, the genetic relationship between languages (as a member of a language "family") is deceptive because it does not necessarily involve similarity.[5] Two languages classified as members of the same family may share very little that will be useful for learning a second language. The genetic connection may be attributable to ancient origins that no longer apply to the languages of today.[6] Thus the unknown origin of Japanese has little significance except as a curiosity.

Ironically, the presumed rarity of SOV sentence order is sometimes cited in support for Tsunoda's theory that the Japanese brain is neurologically different from that of other peoples. It is little wonder, then, that the Japanese made their language central to their cultural identity (Chapter 4). Non-Japanese should not be fooled by this "uniqueness." Even though the syntax is the reverse of English syntax, it is systematic. In many ways Japanese appears more "logical" than English in the regularity of its rules. With practice, nearly anyone can become accustomed to Japanese word order.

Word order apparently has consequences for other structures in a language. SVO languages tend to place devices showing linguistic relationships *before* the word or words they relate; but SOV languages place them *after*.[7] Thus English uses prepositions, while Japanese uses *postpositions*. This difference is made clear in the case of a child in a bilingual family in Japan. This child, whose parents are American and Japanese respectively, had spent equal time living in Japan and in the United States during his first few years. Because he lived initially in the United States, his first language was English. In Japan, at age 4, his favorite Japanese TV program, a *Sesame Street*-type show, was titled

okaasan to issho
mother-with-together

or *Together with Mother.* Note that in this example Japanese places the linguistic marker for the semantic relationship after the "head noun" *mother,* the reverse of English. According to the boy's mother, a Japanese, he always made the mistake of reversing the show's Japanese title to *issho to okaasan.* Despite repeated corrections, his mistake persisted a long time: This made his mother think it was due to the influence of English.

This mirror image of English is found not only with prepositions but also with conjunctions, relative clauses, and auxiliary verbs, among other elements.[8] The important point, however, is that Japanese is not unique in this regard. As Susumu Kuno shows, the propensity to place linguistic markers after the words they relate is a built-in feature of SOV languages.[9]

This propensity to posteriorize elements, however, may possibly be exploited more in Japanese than in other languages. The result may be to delay the focus of information. Yoko Collier-Sanuki shows how the Japanese do so as a function of politeness.[10] Relative clauses (e.g., *Mr. Sato who has been to the USA* ...) in Japanese place the name (or head noun) at the end of the clause:

USA ← *to has been*— *Mr. Sato*
Amerika e itte ita Sato-san

Placing the name posterior delays the focus of information (Who is being talked about?). (Note that Japanese does not have relative pronouns; word order functions instead.) This delay of focus in Japanese imparts politeness in the case of personal introductions. However, Japanese speakers can also choose to be more direct by not "relativizing" the personal name:

This is Mr. Sato. He has been to the United States.

Here the name *Mr. Sato* comes before the details (*has been to the United States*). The absence of relativization, according to Collier-Sanuki, can act as an "ice breaker" in certain Japanese situations.[11] Relativization in Japanese seems to foreground informational details ahead of the focus, which could help make discourse indirect. Collier-Sanuki's research suggests both the purpose and alternative linguistic strategies for such indirectness in Japanese. Much more of this type of research is needed to show how linguistic differences become manifested at the level of discourse.

In brief, the unknown origin of Japanese and its apparent reversal of English word order, among other features, sometimes have led naive observers to view Japanese as mysterious or nonsensical.[12] Although Japanese is different from European languages, it is systematic. Moreover, because of certain features of Japanese culture, beginning learners of Japanese probably can accomplish more socially with this language than they could with other languages at the same level. For example, Japanese possesses a small set of formulaic social expressions with wide applicability. One such expression, *doomo,* can mean variously *thank you, good to see you, really,* and *goodbye.* Differences in the meaning depend on the context. Of course, some preparation is required, but this feature of Japanese can be turned into an advantage in a short time.

ELLIPSIS

Compared with English, Japanese speech shows greater use of ellipsis—the omission of certain parts of a sentence. In linguistics, the term is applied to omissions whose meanings can be recovered from context. Recovery is made possible by knowledge of grammar, intuition (experience), and information shared by the speakers. These resources are less available, of course, to non-native speakers. Therefore, to that extent, Japanese may become harder to comprehend and may induce notions of inscrutability. Japanese ellipsis, however, follows certain principles. It does not involve clairvoyance. Consider the following exchange between a husband and a wife, their first exchange of the day:

Wife: (We) have some nice bread if (you) want some.

Oishii pan ga aru, hoshikattara.
delicious-bread- {*ga*} -want-have-if

She then says a moment later:

(A/the) driver was drunk.

Untenshusan ga yopparatta.
driver- {*ga*} -drunk-was

Husband: That's not good.

Sore wa yokunai ne.
that- {wa} -good-not- {ne}

Despite the cryptic quality of the message, the woman's husband understood correctly that she was informing him that the driver in Princess Diana's fatal crash was drunk. They had spoken about it the previous day, when the crash appeared in the news. Nevertheless, in English, we most surely would have said something like "The driver for Princess Diana was drunk." Because the topic was new, we would specify it more exactly.

How did the husband know that his wife was speaking about the crash? He knew because the lack of specificity cued him to search his memory for the missing information. In other words, he instantaneously would have thought something like "This is unspecified information (which driver?). Therefore we must have already shared this information. What could it be? Of course, it must be about Princess Diana's crash." The key is that lack of specificity in Japanese cues a memory search in the hearer's mind. If the information is unknown, the speaker normally would be more specific. This principle operates far more frequently in Japanese than in English. To this extent, Japanese is more context-dependent, or high-context, as was discussed in Chapter 1. We also can imagine how tightly interwoven Japanese social relations must be.

Some Japanese say that the Japanese lack of specificity may be rooted in the ancient custom of communicating by poetry.[13] This custom was especially a part of courting ritual, by which invitations were extended and responses were given. The poetry, however, contained hidden meanings and usually required some knowledge of the classics to interpret. The earlier Japanese also believed in *kotodama:* The idea that language possesses a spiritual essence. As a result, it is believed that they became cautious about words; this caution encouraged terseness and a willingness to see words as capable of multiple meanings.

This tolerance for little redundancy of information lends itself to effective innuendo. If people already are sensitized to make sense of a seeming ambiguity, innuendo can be even more serviceable for communicating delicate matters. As an example, take a low-brow fiction story titled "*Wasabi*" (horseradish) by the woman writer, Yuko Ichijo.[14] My informants tell me that this story is unrealistic, but it is valuable in giving us a sense of Japanese innuendo and a taste of their popular humor.

A young maid is doing her chores while the master of the house, an older man, says that on the next day, many uniformed people in Japan will change to lighter clothing because of spring.

Suddenly he recites a poem for her, which he always remembers at this time each year. The poem is about the coming of spring, and a certain line carries a special meaning for this story. The line reads something like "Spring emerges even in the roots of our hair."

Throughout, both the maid and even the Japanese reader are puzzled about the man's meaning. His point is not made clear until the until the end of the story and then only because it is the end. The maid (and this may amuse Americans) stands alone outside, saying that she will never forget that day's embarrassment and complains that Americans brought the custom of shaving to Japan. Some Japanese are left hanging by this remark, but one informant explains that the man was probably referring to the prospect of seeing the maid's underarm hair because the expected change to a lighter uniform involved short-sleeves.[15] (For the record, shaving that area is customary for females in Japan, but some women may choose not to do so.) Such innuendo is also comprehensible to us, if we have sufficient contextual information.

For an actual case of social innuendo, a young Japanese man worked as a waiter but was fired for some blunders.[16] He was displeased by how his manager fired him: "You have another job [as a store clerk]. It's best that you just stay with that." That is about as clear as a firing can be—no poetic metaphors to unravel here. On the other hand, the manager spoke rather coldly (if it is ever possible to fire an employee warmly!). The waiter, who did not like this "indirect" manner, was probably affected more by the manager's attitude than by the "indirectness" of the language. Is such an action properly conducted only by the words, "You are fired"?

This case suggests the difficulties involved in labeling a certain language as vague or indirect (see Chapter 9). Interestingly, this example was considered "indirect" by a Japanese. Certainly our linguistic systems differ, and spoken Japanese has a propensity for vagueness because of its ellipsis alone. Yet if we harbor the image of the highly caricatured speech of a Bruce Sato, then we may have a poor basis for approaching the people and culture of Japan.

JAPANESE CULTURAL ETHOS: THE LOVE OF NATURE

In preparation for further work with the Japanese language, it would be helpful to consider a much discussed but widely misunderstood aspect of Japanese culture—the love of nature. Though this subject may seem tangential, I am convinced that it will prove useful. At the same time, it is convenient for showing a case of cross-cultural misunderstanding due to differences in rhetorical principles.

The Japanese love of nature is actually religious or spiritual. Many readers, I am sure, have some familiarity with this topic. I hope to show that it deserves more attention than usually given. Specifically, I wish to show how this love of nature connects to contemporary Japanese living, especially the work ethic. More importantly, I wish to apply it to our continued study of the Japanese language. For this purpose I offer my interpretation of a Japanese work on the topic, titled *Setsu Getsu Ka no Kokoro* ("Mind of Snow, Moon and Flowers") in its bilingual edition.[17]

This book presents various examples of nature motifs present in Japanese art, poetry and literature, architecture and landscapes, fashion and folkways, and other forms of expression. These motifs are historical and thus may have had a reinforcing (if not a formative) effect on the culture. Three major motifs are snow, moon, and flowers (*setsu, getsu, ka*). Though they relate to nature, they symbolize much more, as pointed out by Isamu Kurita, the author. Here I add my own interpretation of Kurita: The Japanese love of nature, I believe, ought to be taken in a spiritual sense. This spirituality is based on honoring the natural course of events—the life cycle or cosmic unity. Inherent in the life cycle is process, a life force, without which there could be no life cycle or cosmic unity. All things change and eventually merge with the surrounding environment. Thus all things, including human beings themselves, are part of the same cosmic system. This underlying life force is celebrated by the motifs of snow, moon, and flowers.

Some non-Japanese believe that the so-called Japanese love of nature is a contradiction in terms. They argue that pollution at beaches and scenic sites is all too common in Japan. They also recall how Japan stood in past international conflicts over whaling, deforestation, and other issues. In short, they believe that the Japanese lack sufficient consciousness to conserve nature. I suggest that these critics may have too narrow a sense of "nature"—that is, the purely physical or surface manifestations. Moreover, a forest, at least for the ancient Japanese, did not necessarily have the positive value we might presume. Village dwellers in old Japan regarded it as a wilderness, as the source of evil.[18] In this sense, some forms of nature are viewed as "raw," with the need to be purified or refined. Thus we can understand the development of bonsai—how a tree "needs" human intervention to "refine" its shape. Similarly, the famed Japanese garden benefits by rigorous human intervention. By this obvious "refinement," nature's life force is brought to the fore.

By extension, the same logic can be applied to human character. Rigorous work or training develops character as well as honoring or celebrating nature—the life force. It is a curious aspect of Japanese culture that they have adopted baseball as a training for character. Baseball teams in Japan are operated as if the sport were *bushido* (way of the warrior) or a martial art. This context seems to allow little room for "fun," a view contrary to that of American managers. American players also undergo serious training, but they preserve some fun to counter excess tension. Japanese players must show reverence to the baseball field as if it were a living entity. In Japanese religiosity, nearly any object has the potential to be occupied by a god. Again, viewing "nature" as an abstract entity—the life force—enables us to see how even contemporary urban life in Japan can be full of "nature." (This point does not negate the Japanese interest in scenic, countryside areas.)

Finally, if baseball can be viewed as "work" and the baseball field as an "honorable site," it is not hard to imagine the same logic applied to occupations and workplaces. Through one's occupation, one may not only develop one's character but also honor nature—for example, by "refining" materials into "honorable" manufactured goods.

Certainly spirituality is not the sole factor explaining the Japanese work ethic. Other factors, economic and social, are involved as well. But spirituality is probably the element least considered and least found in the western world of work. Thus it adds to our understanding of Japanese thinking.

The treatment of life force is a form of spirituality in Japan. Many everyday objects can have religious or spiritual connotations to the Japanese. For example, Japanese families will place foodstuffs, even soft drinks, on memorial altars at home for their deceased relatives. Objects that are mundane to us can become literally food for the gods in Japan. The key to this understanding is life force. Life force is all around us—even within us—wherever we are. Thus the "Japanese love of nature" fits Japan.

A Constructed Example

The Nike shoe company has popularized its products with the advertising slogan of "Just do it!" The company uses the same slogan in Japan. Yet if the slogan were used instead to sum up a cultural ethos, as it does so well for Americans, I would argue that it would fit the Japanese better if it were simply "Just do." With that change, we immediately see a key difference: specificity.

In theory, the pronoun *it* and the corresponding Japanese ellipsis function in the same way: Both point to a referent in the immediate environment or in a prior text. That is, in normal everyday speech. Nevertheless, a difference exits in that English makes explicit what Japanese omits here. Nike could have made its slogan *Just do,* but that represents a perceptible difference for native speakers of English and is probably not grammatical.

Americans, in particular, need and thrive on specificity because theirs is largely a low-context culture. They wish to have things spelled out; as a result, they developed the marriage contract and probably other kinds of contracts as well. A nation with such a short history has fewer shared traditions and symbols than do older nations. A wealth of shared traditions and symbols enable people to communicate in "shorthand." Americans, however, emerged collectively from an immigrant past; they forged their nation out of a "wilderness" in a "grand experiment." With such a background, Americans hardly can assume as much about their compatriots as do the Japanese about theirs, or as in other high-context cultures. Thus American communication practices presume that miscommunication arises from gaps in information, which can be bridged by explicitness and directness.

Another difference between the slogans is that a certain timelessness emerges with "Just do," which is not evident in "Just do it." The latter implies a targeted task, which in turn suggests an expected completion and thereby a beginning as well. "Just do," in contrast, could be endless, for all time. Endlessness recalls not only the Japanese philosophical focus on the "void" through Zen meditation and the famed Japanese rock garden, but also their spiritual linking up of all past and future generations of Japanese people—an endless sense of Japaneseness. The soul of the deceased is believed to return to the deceased's family's home. For this reason, the family members light a ceremonial flame (*mukaebi*) on their property to assist the spirit in its return. Ancestors also are honored by memorial shrines at home and by regular visits to cemeteries. These and other activities are regarded as duties that the living family members must fulfill or forsake the family's past and future.

In this connection, consider what an American found out when he married a Japanese, as told by Willis Applebee:*

> I fell in love with a young woman, both highly educated and independent-minded. Though she planned to have a career, we both expected to have kids. Before having any, I decided that it would be better to wait a couple of years. Then we could build a strong marriage. When I told her this, she burst into tears. She took it the wrong way. She sobbed, "Who will remember me after I die?"

This remembrance of the deceased is so strongly entrenched that a remote Japanese village recently was found by a Catholic priest to be still caring for the graves of British POWs who died there during World War II:

> ...there, in front of my eyes, was a Memorial to sixteen British soldiers who had died ... at a prisoner of war camp here. Two things immediately caught my attention: one was the Roll of Honor with the soldiers' names displayed in bold print; the other was the fresh flowers that had been placed in the receptacles on either side of the monument. ...We wondered (indeed, doubted) if a village could be found in any part of the world, where, in similar circumstances, and over [fifty] years on [later], the people would display such a generous and "Christian" outlook, as [these] villagers....[19]

As another observer pointed out, this action by the villagers was not totally philanthropic: Their religious belief also led them to fear possible retribution by spirits of the war dead, spirits thought to be of the worst kind. As another possible motivation, the young people of the village had long ago moved to the cities, leaving the aged behind with the fear of being forgotten after death. That fear may have helped them to think of the British departed more sympathetically. Whatever the motivations, humanitarianism seems to be well evident. Also this case and Applebee's story show vividly how remembrance may play an important role in the lives of the Japanese.

The desire by Applebee's wife to bear children may not simply be due to the socialization of females. (See Box 6.1 and Box 6.2 for commentary on the status of Japanese women.) Her desire may have been for her own spiritual reasons. Note that she did not say "Who will take care of me when I'm old?" Rather, she was concerned with her own good afterlife.

Japanese ancestor worship is not as gloomy and dark as some Americans imagine. On the contrary, I have found that it can be as festive as a family outing. At a cemetery remembrance, our young children frolicked in waterplay while they "washed" their grandfather's and others' memorial tablets. The outing, hosted by their Japanese grandmother, was often punctuated by her glee over the children's activity. Aside from a short prayer said for the deceased, the outing seemed to be a social occasion for all the relatives. After visiting the cemetery, we all met for a leisurely lunch at a restaurant, where the social occasion continued. The occasion was typically Japanese: It was held in a reserved room with tatami mats, on which we sat and ate in traditional style. The children, when finished eating, could run around while the adults drank and talked animatedly. Celebrations for ancestors help keep families close. At the same time, bonds are formed across generations. If Applebee's wife had had the same experience, I can understand that even a young person might take special comfort in knowing that he or she would be remembered in the next generation or beyond.

The value of "Just do" is evident only in juxtaposition with "Just do it." Of course, "Just do" is my own construction and is used here merely to suggest the distinctive values of indeterminacy, spirituality, and collectivity for the Japanese. With these elements in mind, we proceed to look at an actual case in Japan.

Box 6.1 Women in Japanese Society

According to Karen Ma, "outside Japan there is a widely held belief that Japanese women are docile and subservient. This is totally inaccurate given today's financially independent, sexually liberated and assertive young Japanese women...."[20] Applebee's case, for example, suggests that the desire by some Japanese women to bear children may have motivations other than fulfilling a traditional female role, such as spiritual or personal needs. Two British authors report that Japan ranked 8th out of 130 nations in a United Nations study of sexual equality.[21] Although I am unable to confirm this study and so caution its use, I still can understand that on certain statistical indices, Japan might fare well. Also, sexual inequality is universally found and not solely a Japanese problem. For example, average earnings by Japanese women are only 62 percent of men's, though the comparative figure for Americans is not much better—71 percent.[22] Comparing these figures, say, with those for Australia (90 percent) and the United Kingdom (69 percent),[23] suggests how relative the matter is.

Western belief in the subservience of Japanese females may be because Asian silence is often misunderstood, as remarked by two interculturalists:

> Contrary to outspoken and [individualistic] western women ..., many women in eastern cultures view their silent roles as very powerful. ...There is power of control in silence and in the outward show of reticence. This power often goes unrecognized by those who value speech-as-power and by those who value assertiveness by all, equally and democratically.[24]

An interesting but beguiling aspect of Japanese organizations is that the "leader" may turn out not to be the real leader at all. It is not unusual for the outspoken, active Japanese member to be following the directives of a quiet individual in the background.

On the other hand, Japanese society is still clearly male-oriented. In contrast to women's status in other industrialized societies, the modern career woman in Japan has a more difficult situation than her counterpart in the west. Despite a

Japanese law against sexual discrimination in employment, enforcement is very weak. Career positions for females in some fields are blatantly low. Also problematic is a general lack of consciousness of women's rights, as reflected in the images projected by the Japanese mass media. For example, if male and female commentators for a TV documentary or talk show are paired, invariably the female plays the role of seeker of information from the "expert," played by the male. Although the basis for this distinction could be age, as such pairs usually consist of a young female and an older male, their roles are likely to convey the wrong message.

The crux of the problem is the overly strong distinction made between men and women. In certain Japanese business firms or industries, women workers are required to wear a company uniform but not the men. Japanese men, according to an international time budget study, spend only a fifth of the time on household chores as what American men do.[25] This difference is reflected at the Japanese workplace by the tendency for women to assume the duty of serving tea at meetings. In some Japanese public elementary schools, boys are placed ahead of the girls in assemblies. Valentine's Day is celebrated in Japan by females giving chocolates to the males, not the reverse; the subsequent "White Day" is the men's turn to do so. This sex distinction is symbolically represented at New Year's Eve by the annually televised *koohaku (*lit. red and white)—a singing contest between a "red" team of women and a "white" team of men, all from the show business world (*geinookai*).

In compensation, Japanese women have what one American feminist admiringly calls a "woman's culture," where "psychologically, Japanese women depend largely on each other."[26] This sex-segregated society may have clear health benefits. One Stanford University medical researcher reported that social involvement is associated with higher cancer survival rates, but the type of social involvement differs according to gender: For males, it is represented by marriage; for females, by relationships with other females.[27] This could explain why the Japanese have the world's highest longevity rates,[28] which probably affects Japan's rank in the sexual equality survey, if only indirectly.

Kittredge Cherry attributes this "women's culture" to

> the residue of the Japanese matriarchy [that once existed in

ancient times]. [Even though patriarchy came into ascendence], men never isolated Japanese women to the extent of the Hindu purdah, nor crippled them with anything like Chinese foot binding, nor murdered them on the mass scale of the medieval European witch burnings. This may help explain why matriarchal influence can still be glimpsed in Japan. The sun goddess continues to be revered by Shinto followers. One custom enables a family to adopt a son-in-law who assumes his wife's surname and enters her family just as a bride would normally do. Another encourages a pregnant woman to leave her husband and stay with her mother while giving birth.[29]

Some middle-class women say that they would not wish to trade places with their *sarariiman* (salaryman, white-collar worker) husbands because their work routine is so strict. Whether this is the real reason remains to be seen. Moreover, Japanese married women typically control family finances, and thus have much influence in a family's decision-making. This status in the home, as well as the "women's culture," provide Japanese women with advantages found less often by their counterparts, even in the west. Thus, Tomoko Koyama joins Karen Ma in cautioning us that the subservient image of Japanese women is outdated; she states that "Japanese men and women today maintain an egalitarian relationship, particularly in private."[30] As Nancy Brown Diggs explains, "What we see as a subservient manner [of Japanese women] may be mere form…, one of many types of behavior fostered to smooth over dealings with the 'outside' world. …Contrary to what Americans may think, it's not a lack of strength that keeps Japanese women primarily in the home, but rather a sense of practicality, as well as priorities"[31] such as an emphasis on child-rearing.

Unquestionably, Japanese women have less rights than those enjoyed by North American women. That difference, though, tends to be exaggerated. The Japanese woman is neither Madame Butterfly nor a downtrodden figure. Given the above examples of Japanese sexism, I am surprised at the power and respect that Japanese women do have. Also, the rights held by North American women were hard fought for, and only recently gained. Women's rights is a universal issue, so Japan's case ought to be judged in a wider view.

Please see Box 6.2 for further commentary.

Actual Examples Through Japanese Advertisements

Recently I noticed a Japanese advertisement by Kirin Brewing Company in the form of a T-shirt worn by any number of college students in Japan. The front of the shirt carried a slogan, and the back, information about a Kirin-sponsored tour by a Japanese rock music group. The slogan, my case in point, was written in English and was the only item on the front of the shirt. It read as follows: *Do! Lager*. The designer had at least three choices in regard to placing the exclamation point: after *Do*, after *Lager,* or not at all. Thus the actual placement seems deliberate. The actual reason is beside the point. I intend to use this beer slogan only analogously. Through further analysis I hope to arrive at some useful insights into Japanese culture and communication.

First, if we were creating this slogan for a North American audience, most probably we would substitute *drink* for *do*. *Drink,* however, may be too explicit for Japanese consumers. Though the Japanese may appear to be crass materialists (and in this respect, a mirror image of our cultures in viewing each other alike), they still hold certain traditional values. One of those values is that money is "dirty": In noncommercial situations, one hands over money wrapped in white paper (for example, in an envelope). In Japanese stores, money is transferred between a customer and a cashier by a "money dish."

In feudal Japan, merchants occupied the lowest rung on the social ladder, even though some of those on the highest rung—the *samurai*—may have become in debt to them. Unlike the practice in some parts of southeast Asia, bargaining with a merchant is almost unknown in most areas in Japan, with the possible exception of expensive items, such as cars, homes, or electronic goods. Yet, in the past, even electronics stores in Nagoya, the nation's fourth largest city, were reluctant to bargain. The merchants acted as if they would not stoop so low. Then (and things have changed since) we foreigners interpreted this attitude, rightly or wrongly, as "*samurai* spirit." Japanese commercial activities operate with much propriety.

This propriety explains contrarily why I was able to obtain a used car from a Japanese dealer without any money down or a written contract. This dealer had only my *meishi* (name card) and my spoken assurance that I would pay in full a month later. Like the *samurai*, he believed we were men of our words. The car (a compact) was hardly a lemon: It was reasonably priced and in good condition. I had it over six years with no major mechanical problems. Since then I found that this dealer must have been the last of his breed! I have tried this approach with other car dealers, and their reaction essentially was to say, "Get lost!"

Though this transaction was quite rare in Japan, I feel it would be even less likely to occur in North America. My point is that Japanese merchants and their customers enjoy an atmosphere—even if it is only a facade—of respect and courtesy. Direct comments to use a product are rather infrequent in Japanese advertisements; thus, *do* was substituted for *drink* in the Kirin beer slogan. *Do* also has a connotation of youthful activity, which leads to my next point.

Second, the exclamation point was placed after *do* to emphasize the act, process, or setting. (The specifics, *lager,* are secondary.) The circumstances—the setting or situation—are of primary importance in Japanese discourse. Here the circumstance is *doing* and all that entails for Japanese, who are experiencing a period of unprecedented wealth and personal freedom. It is hard to imagine a similar use of *do* in North America or even for *live.* The expression "Live! Life" seems incongruous.

Third, despite the incongruity, "Do! Lager" is not a random mistake. It is used purposely along the lines as suggested above. Another example is an advertisement by a branch of the Japanese Red Cross:

> Give!! Your Blood
> Aichi Red Cross Blood Center

This is the full text, which was written entirely in English. Again, this ad emphasizes the process (of giving) rather than the particulars (blood). I am told by Japanese that such advertisements are more effective if written in English. English may allow a directness that is usually avoided in Japanese-language advertising. Ironically, some of my American students in Japan thought that these ads were a bit rude because of their commanding tone.

Fourth, *suru* ("do") also can mean *make* and sometimes existential *be*, as well as performative *have* or *take*, which enables *suru* to be a "master convertor" for changing nouns, adjectives, and adverbs into verb-like forms. In essence, static entities (nouns, adjectives) are converted into a process (verbs). The title of a book by Nobuo Sato is telling: *The Magical Power of* Suru: *Japanese Verbs Made Easy.* Sato states that such *suru* conversions are so widespread that they "can virtually replace the majority of Japanese verbs, " as with these examples:[32]

memorii (memory) + *suru* > to memorize
110 *ban (emergency number)* + suru > to call the police

A commercial by the automaker Daihatsu illustrates this *do*-magic in its slogan (created in English): *We do COMPACT*.[33] Unless this means (emphatically) the compacting of trash and the like, this slogan is ungrammatical in English. It has more meaning for Japanese consumers than for English speakers. If *compact* is used as a verb, it could mean the making of compact cars. However, the *we* could just as well refer to the people shown in the commercial using the product, and others shown admiring the car. Thus, *do compact* could take on an existential meaning for a way of life, as with "We Daihatsu consumers live the hip life, the enviable life, the 'compact' life," or whatever.

"Do! Lager," by its emphasis on *do*, may also exemplify an accent on process—a way of life or a lifestyle in these cases. The widespread use of *suru* may encourage this Japanese sensibility, even when using a foreign language, such as English.

Finally, the emphasis on *do* (i.e., minus a grammatical object) seems to be connected to Japanese spiritualism in relation to time orientation and human worth. It implies present-centeredness, perhaps, of Japanese Zen—that is, to give one's all to experiencing life. Also, in contrast to *do it, do* seems to be timeless without beginning or end. In this situation, English requires a grammatical object, which seems to imply definiteness at least about a particular task. Knowing the task, in turn, suggests that a beginning and an end are involved.

This spiritualism is coupled with a belief in human goodness, especially from Japanese Shinto, the indigenous religion. In Shinto, it is expected, or at least seems that way, that following a form is all that is needed. This form often seems to consist of brief rituals. For example, one can "cleanse" one's self (soul) on entering a Shinto shrine by wetting one's hand with the water provided outside of the shrine. It is not "sin" that we must be cleansed of, but our mundane impurities—contact with blood or corpses. Because the result of cleansing is so instantaneous, the essential goodness of humans must be implied.

Japanese informants invariably tell me that Christianity seems "strict" in comparison. Imagine how much easier their lives must be as a result of avoiding "original sin" and the "guilt" that accompanies it. Even today some Americans still feel psychologically burdened about bodily functions, as a result of the past influence of Puritanism and Victorianism.

The Japanese emphasis on *do,* even if only momentary, can be an unfettered release for enjoyment. Such a release is possible only if humans are viewed as basically good: As such, they can be trusted to "do" without disturbing others. If my view is valid, we can see that "do" could have deeper meaning for the Japanese than for us. Hence the idea that circumstance or setting—manifested by process—occupies the foreground in Japanese discourse at the expense of the actors or agents. (Here I have broadened the meaning of *setting* to be synonymous with *circumstances*: "the existing conditions or state of affairs surrounding and affecting an agent.") The reverse occurs in English.

For another example of the Japanese emphasis on process, we borrow from Haru Yamada, who points out how store signs for *open* and *closed* in Japan differ from those in the United States: In Japanese, these expressions are respectively, *eigyoochuu* (in operation) and *junbichuu* (in preparation).[34] Although both the English and the Japanese versions omit a specific actor or agent, the Japanese version seems more process-oriented.

Above I mentioned that sentence subjects are omitted quite frequently in Japanese speech. The gaps often can be filled by information obtained from context and the verb forms. Certain verbs and their inflections in Japanese are associated with only certain individuals, according to their social status. Thus listeners can track participants in discourse. This difference in focus between Japanese and English on setting and agent, respectively, has been identified by at least several researchers,[35] as we discuss next.

SETTING VERSUS AGENT: A CROSS-LINGUISTIC COMPARISON

Setting focus versus agent focus corresponds to situation and person, respectively, according to the perspective introduced by Tazuko A. Monane and Lawrence W. Rogers.[36] I substituted their terms to avoid concluding that the Japanese must be necessarily more contextually sensitive or less "humanistic" than English speakers. In some ways, the Japanese do seem more contextually oriented than westerners, as indicated in previous chapters. That does not mean, however, that the Japanese are more empathic, a conclusion sometimes drawn. The related research[37] is insufficient for such conclusions. My terms are open to similar criticism, but the consequences are less serious.

Before we look at some actual examples, let us develop some background for the term, *setting*. For this background we rely heavily on Keiko Inukai Isshiki's treatment of Japanese language and culture.[38] She points out that "the Japanese seem to perceive events involving themselves and others not necessarily as the willful act of a doer [agent] but rather merely as a result of … [a spontaneous happening]."[39] In other words, humans have little control of events. Humans are part of nature, not separated from it. This view relates to the Japanese belief about the Creation, which brings us to the connection with the idea of setting focus. Christianity believes that "[humans] and nature were created by the active will of God; [the Japanese belief is that it was nature that spawned their gods]."[40] By analogy, we can view "setting," like nature, as an arena of spontaneous happenings—where events emerge. Agents in Japanese discourse hold less of the center stage and therefore often go unnamed in speech (when identifiable from context). This unnaming, as we will see, can create social friction between the Japanese themselves.

First, however, here are some examples of the focus on setting versus agent between Japanese and English. In each of these examples, the agent or person is omitted in Japanese, whereas its mention is usually mandatory in English:[41]

booshi o nakushita.	I have lost my hat.
kaze ga naru.	I hear the wind roaring.
atama ni kita.	I blew my stack.
… ki ga suru	I feel …

John Hinds, who studied Japanese face-to-face conversation extensively, comments, "Despite the fact that ellipsis is so pervasive, there is little unintended ambiguity in Japanese conversation,"[42] and there is "not an inordinate amount of unintended miscommunication."[43]

Misunderstanding might be more likely when strangers on the telephone are involved. Perhaps more so if the strangers are of different genders. By showing such instances, I hope that the distinctive features of Japanese discourse will become clearer. In the first example, a male "salaryman" called a fellow worker but his wife answered. He began by saying politely:

> This is Yamada, um, at home?
>
> *Yamada* desu kedo, irasshaimasu ka?*

Yamada did not specify whom he wanted. Although his omission is atypical, Japanese collectivity may sometimes invite such terseness. Because his message was underspecified, this woman, as a Japanese, was likely (or expected) to assume that she must know of him. Because she and her husband were the only occupants of their residence, and because she was a faithful wife, she would logically conclude that this man was a co-worker of her husband's. Furthermore, it was likely that he had called before, but she had forgotten. Still, she was annoyed by the very small amount of information provided—that is, by the apparent assumption on Yamada's part that he need not give more verbal or vocal (i.e., paralinguistic) information. He gave no explicit sign that his association was already known.

This woman once lived abroad, which partly explains her displeasure with Yamada's way of speaking. Her explanation follows. Her husband (Japanese) was once posted to the United States by his company, and she accompanied him there. Even though he worked for the same company as in Japan, the company's social gatherings included wives, unlike those in Japan. On these occasions, she found that relations between men and women were rather awkward: She felt that many of the Japanese men seemed reluctant to talk with any women other than their own wives. She believed that this reluctance stemmed from the prevalence of sex-segregated schooling in Japan, in line with my own observation and those of others. Although Yamada was polite, his terseness reminded her of the awkwardness she felt between men and women at the company parties. She may also have been reminded of the Japanese corporate mindset that the company takes precedence over the family. Thus, a company man on business might expect such family members to be accommodating, if need be. Her own personal values seemed at odds with the traditional values of Japan. Differences in values and in gender account for her displeasure with Yamada.

The next example of communicative friction gives us a further glimpse into aspects of Japanese culture and communication. A senior officer of a company, newly transferred to the Nagoya branch, phoned a junior executive named Hata* for the first time. Hata and his wife had two children, both of school age, and lived in a condominium. Hata's wife answered the phone (M = Mr. Fujimaku, the caller; W = Hata's wife):

(1) M: Is (this) Hata? [Or] Are (you) Hata? [Or] Is (that you), Hata?

Hata-san desu ka?

(2) W: Yes.

Hai.

She thinks: "Who does he want? Me, my husband, or my children?" "Who could this be?"

(3) M: Is (he, she) home? [Or] (Is it okay for me) to stop by?

Irasshaimasu ka?

Here, the woman suspects that the man is a member of the managing board for her condominium and is calling about related business. Perhaps he wanted to pay a visit.

(4) W: Yes, (we're/ I'm/ he's) home now, but ...

Hai, ima imasu kedo...

She thinks: "You want to come over here now, at this moment?"

(5) M: • • • (silence) • • •

(6) W: What can (I, we) do (for you)?

Nan deshoo ka?

(7) M: (This) is Fujimaku.*
Fujimaku desu*.

The name Fujimaku rings no bells for her. She knows no one by that name: none of her husband's or her own associates, none of her children's teachers, and none of the condominium residents. Because she knows more about those in her own direct experience—her activities, her children's schools, and her neighborhood—she decides that this man probably wants her husband.

(8) W: • • • It's my husband (you want)?
• • • *Shujin desu ka?*

(9) M: Yes, please do (me) the favor (of getting him).
Hai, onegaishimasu.

This case, like the first, shows quite clearly that communicative mishaps due to underspecificity occur in Japanese. First, Fujimaku did not identify himself at once. Second, the ellipsis of pronouns (in utterances 1, 3, and 4) contributed to the lack of clarity. Third, Fujimaku used *irrasharu* (3), a standard ultrapolite verb that means not only *be* but also *come, go,* and *call.* The ambiguity of *irrasharu* and the pronoun ellipsis combined to suggest falsely that his intention was "to stop by." The confusion may have been further increased by differences in age and gender related role expectations about social accommodation. (Who accommodates to whom?) The reader should not conclude, though, that confusion is characteristic of Japanese speech. I cited these cases solely because they highlight some of the features of Japanese discussed above.

Let us recall that John Hinds, an expert on Japanese face-to-face conversation, concluded that Japanese is not marked unduly by communicative mishaps. Telephone conversations, however, may be quite different. Because the faces of strangers on the phone are hidden, these callers may be inclined to underspecify information, when they should do the opposite. At any rate, telephone calls may make Japanese discourse susceptible to communication breakdowns. Here high technology has an opportunity to enhance human life, through video (or teleconferencing) by which people on the telephone can see each other as if they were face to face.

These cases also suggest that not all Japanese prefer the traditional communication style, as judged by the attitudes expressed by the two women in these cases. Indeed, even within Japanese culture, a "universal" mode apparently has taken root because of Japan's modernization. According to Haruo Aoki and Shigeko Okamoto, communication styles in Japan differ with age, region, and socioeconomic status, such that the younger, more urbanized, and better-educated Japanese tend to follow informational rather than social styles.[44] "It is not surprising because [such people] tend to be among less known associates.... In a word, problems of 'cross-cultural' communication exist even among various segments within Japan itself."[45]

One can see such a difference in Aoki and Okamoto's book itself: Although the preface carries both authors' initials (in authorship), the parenthetical message *Written by H.A.* follows their initials. This statement is unusual even by Anglo-American convention. The point is that a Japanese is claiming personal credit or individual responsibility, although the book is a joint enterprise. Even more telling is the last line in the preface: "If you like the book, let us know. If you do not, write a detailed critique and place it in your circular file; this way readers can save the postage and we can save the time."[46] To be kind, we will take this as an attempt at humor. Even so, it seems boorish, especially so, because the book appears to be a serious academic work. Academic writing can include humor, but not usually at the reader's expense. His statement seems to ridicule the reader for possibly taking the book seriously. Could it be the result of a mistaken view of western communicative practices? That is, the authors may assume that this kind of joke would be acceptable even in a serious work.

JAPANESE OTHER-DIRECTEDNESS

The desire for harmony or other-directedness may explain Japanese underspecificity. For example, *sumimasen* can mean either "thank you" or "I am sorry." Thus, if it is used to express thanks, it may be rather bittersweet. *Sumimasen* is practical, however, because Japanese people are expected to be very considerate of others. This other-directedness reflects a desire to avoid friction or confrontation. Japanese also hope to avoid hurting other's feelings. People everywhere wish to do this, but the desire can become extreme among the Japanese.

Because sympathy, at a certain level, can neutralize empathy, (according to a principle in counseling psychology), I hesitate to assume that Japanese other-directedness is correlated with empathy. Japanese listeners must "read between the lines" far more than their counterparts in North America. They are also more situationally focused than we are. Nevertheless, it is still an open question whether this Japanese other-directedness is related more to empathy than sympathy.

Illustrations

Sumiyo Fukaya reported a story about a Japanese business manager in correspondence with an American company that asked in a letter for a discount.[47] The Japanese replied to his translator (an American), *"Chotto muzukashii desu ne"* (lit., that's a little difficult, you know). The translator replied by letter or telex that "it was difficult." The American company then asked again; the Japanese replied, *"Chotto muzukashii to omoimasu."* The translator replied, "I think it is a little difficult." In the end, both sides grew angry, and the Japanese manager shouted at the translator, "No discount *da yo!*" ("No discount—can't [they] take a hint!"). A similar case was reported by a former Japanese businessman, who used "it's very difficult" as a euphemism for "no."[48] In the end, he had to spell it out but at a cost to the relationship.

Sumiyo Fukaya had personally found difficulty in saying "no" while staying as a guest in someone's home in the United States. When eating pancakes, she accepted syrup despite her personal dislike for it. She did not wish to decline the kind invitation. The incident convinced her that it was Japanese other-directedness at work, even though it was uncalled for.[49]

In a similar but less trivial case, a female student, Keiko Asano,* stayed in North America in the home of a young female hairdresser, who also did ear piercing. One day Asano complimented the hairdresser on her "pierced" earrings. The hairdresser then asked Asano if she wanted pierced ears too. Although Asano did not, she felt perplexed as to how to decline in view of her praise of the North American's earrings. She said "yes," but was surprised when the hairdresser then produced a piercing instrument. Asano then said, "Let me think about it a while." To her dismay, the hairdresser "waited only five minutes" and then asked if she had decided yet. At this, Asano relented and let one of her ears be pierced, though she really did not want the procedure. Then either she made clear that the other ear was not to be pierced, or the hairdresser quit.

These cases show how deeply other-directedness is ingrained in the Japanese, and the difficulty of intercultural communication. We can also understand what a compensatory function it must serve, in view of the frequency of Japanese ellipsis, the avoidance of pronouns, and the delay of informational climax. Finally, by appreciating that this other-directedness actually may immobilize some Japanese, we can understand that their indirectness or ambiguity is related less to deceit than to the desire to avoid friction.

APPLICATION

Box 6.2

JAPANESE WOMEN

Audrey Okuda

Audrey Okuda is an American married to a Japanese and has been living in Japan for twenty years. She was born in Seattle, Washington and graduated from Pacific Lutheran University. Besides being a mother and a homemaker, she teaches English and does occasional interpreting. She also sings soprano in the Nagoya Nikikai, a western opera company.

"A homemaker is nothing but a slave," wails the wife on the afternoon soap opera. Scenes of selfless women tucking their inebriated husbands in after a "hard day at the office" flood our television screens. Such scenes reflect an uncommon devotion, from a western viewpoint, of Japanese women to their roles as homemakers and wives. Hardly does this devotion equate, however, to subservience, a common misconception held abroad.

As mentioned in this chapter, a survey on sexual equality ranked Japan among the highest-scoring nations. How can this be accounted for? Right off, regardless of stereotype, we could suppose that Japan would probably at least outscore many of the developing countries and those with strong religious strictures on women, such as found in some Muslim countries. After all, Japan is a developed country, and its women are highly educated. In thinking more about the above statistic, it made sense that Japan would rank so high. Japanese women, however, are disadvantaged in some areas, especially in the business world. But in the home and in the community, women here hold a very dynamic role that is anything but subservient.

In the elementary school PTA where I am involved, the big "heavy-duty" decision-making and project work is done by the mothers. Although more participation by the fathers is encouraged, the reality of the workplace makes it next to impossible. And even if it were, many men feel uncomfortable in such a "woman-controlled" atmosphere. The Japanese PTA is an MTA ("M" for mother) and is very different from the American model. This outside responsibility for mothers is considered a problem in light of the rise in truancy and child-committed crimes, but I do not expect much change in the near future.

The woman who bows deeply while greeting her husband at the front door at his return home is virtually a thing of the past. If she does exist, it is done as a formality, rather than an honest display of devotion. Women do not seem to expect as much from their husbands in the way of romance or togetherness as a westerner might. Attending parties or community gatherings together is almost unheard of in my neighborhood. Raising the children and building a stable family is considered more important than immediate personal fulfillment. This often causes women some frustration, but most endure it, at least, until the children reach some independence.

I once attended a lecture in Japan by an American woman who was mistakenly introduced as having left her husband and children behind in the United States for two years while she did her research here. When it was discovered that she actually had no children, the audience almost felt cheated: Abandoning a husband was perfectly understandable, but the curiosity held for her lied in the belief that she had left her children. Because the "salarymen" (white collar workers) often emphasize their company ahead of their family, wives have learned not to depend on their husbands for all their emotional support.

Although Japanese married women may lack financial independence, they make up for that by holding the family's purse strings. Even if the bank account were solely in the husband's name, the wife does the transactions. I know of no woman whose husband does the family finances, and if by chance he should overspend his allowance allotted by his wife, great friction will be the result.

Japanese women also have a canny way of making their own "community" or circle of friends, separate from their husbands'. These associations are based on their personal interests; whereas the husband's revolves around the working world. The "woman's world" can continue even after the husband's retirement, when he loses his "community," which can create problems for newly retired couples. My neighbor dreads her husband's upcoming retirement, as he has no personal hobbies or interests outside of his work; whereas she has over the years developed a network of personal fulfillment for herself. His suddenly being at home all day every day will definitely cramp her style. In Japan, "retirement divorce" is a great problem, the wife bringing out the divorce papers nearly the day the husband receives his retirement check. Some large companies have begun "retirement training" for their employees, to help them ease into the retirement period, developing common interests and renewing their relationships with their wives.

So the Japanese married woman can develop emotional independence if needed, and holds a great deal more say in her family's affairs than usually imagined. Though generally discriminated at the workplace, she frequently may work at non-career jobs once all her children are in school. If not at a job, her extra time may be taken by various outside interests, cultural, educational, or otherwise, with many women friends to share them with. This is not to say that women are completely barred from career positions. Of course, there are woman doctors, company presidents, architects and so on.

But Japanese women, in this regard, have much less opportunity than their American counterparts. While the Japanese marriage style has afforded women a large role in family, school, and neighborhood affairs, giving them unusual independence, it also, in some extreme cases, creates an emotional vacuum. Strongly distinguished by role, the husband and wife can end up having shared very little over the course of their marriage. An eventual problem about the husband's final retirement is talked about enough (even joked about) for us to assume that it is indeed an outgrowth of the Japanese marriage. Fortunately for many women, they develop an active social network that can compensate. Retired husbands are far less prepared, if the case need be.

1. What points made about Japanese women in Chapter 6 confirm or disconfirm your previous ideas about them?
2. Discuss how features of Japanese linguistic structure and cultural thought or worldview reinforce the Japanese communication style?
3. Some American visitors to Japan, mindful of its low-crime rate, its orderliness, and its mass consumerism, compare Japan as "1950s America." What aspects of Japanese gender relations would fit and not fit this "50s" analogy?
4. What value is there in such analogies? What ill could there be?
5. How does Japanese collectivity pose special advantages and disadvantages for the advancement of women's rights?

Part III

Contrastive Rhetoric Between Japanese and English

7

Rhetorical Issues and Cross-cultural Communications

The term *rhetoric* has various meanings. For our purposes, it refers to the manner of making effective, spoken or written communication. At the end of Chapter 6, I cited a case of inappropriate humor by a Japanese writing for an international audience. Such incidents can occur among Japanese and non-Japanese alike. Cultural differences exist, and in this chapter, I attempt to clarify how the overall organization of communications may differ between Japanese and North Americans. Several issues make that task difficult, namely exaggerating Japanese indirectness, equating speech and writing, and underestimating the Japanese independence of mind. These issues involve false assumptions that may lead to caricatures of the Japanese. Another problem is that the related literature offers few examples of the distinctiveness of Japanese rhetoric. Toward this goal, this chapter provides some "benchmarks" for considering Japanese oral and written communications.

INDIRECTNESS

On the basis of the high incidence of shyness found among Japanese (as cited previously), we can reasonably expect that verbal indirectness may be more characteristic of Japanese than of North Americans. But not always. Sometimes Japanese can be quite forward with foreign acquaintances in asking them personal questions about age or marital status. Apart from such matters of etiquette, let us consider the following case intended to illustrate Japanese indirectness between colleagues at a Japanese college:

Box 7.1 Japanese Indirectness (Lee Henderson*)

A professor from an American university, who was visiting my school in Japan, had just finished a lecture and was about to be taken to lunch. I happened to know him, as well, if not better than the three committee members who were hosting him. Hearing that they were all going to have lunch at the faculty dining hall, I decided to go along. Aware that I was not a member of the committee, I knew I would be on my own there.

As we entered the hall, I left them and joined the cafeteria line. From the line I could see the visitor and the committee members take seats at their reserved table, which was already set and had only four chairs. They were going to have a sit-down lunch. Luckily, the table was large enough to accommodate another chair or two.

One of the committee members, a Japanese man, approached me in the cafeteria line to say that he would be having lunch with the guest. When talking with a Japanese in formal situations, one must be ready to fathom deeper meanings. However, I may have not been in gear that day because I just gave him a blank look. He then said "You know what I mean, right?" At that, I must admit, I became a bit perturbed. His last comment seemed to suggest that the fourth seat was his, or that my presence was unwanted. He probably was expecting or hoping that I would say, "*Hai, wakarimashita. Doozo, doozo ...*" (Yes, I understand. Go ahead, go ahead ...), but I didn't. Instead I waited for him to be more frank. "Don't you know?" he asked.

Of course he was making some unwarranted assumptions about me. My entrance into the cafeteria line showed that I had no intention of taking one of those four seats, though in a public place. So, I felt that the burden was on him to spell out what was on his mind. He never did, and everything was left to me.

I ended it all by telling him that I simply was going to bring over another chair. I would not have been offended if he had said frankly, "Do you mind if I take the fourth seat? I happen to be a committee member and its my job." For me, this was a clear case of Japanese indirectness, particularly because my Japanese associate appeared to be aware that his words had an ulterior meaning.

This case also demonstrates Japanese clannishness or group orientation. The Japanese man never invited Henderson to join them, probably because the luncheon was the province of his committee and no one else's. He may have felt duty bound to show everyone that he and the rest of the committee were doing their jobs adequately. Perhaps if Henderson joined them, he might have represented unnecessary competition. Also, being an American may place him at an advantage in being a host.

Henderson, however, did not agree that being American was necessarily advantageous. He added not only that this Japanese man was rather fluent in English, but also that he himself felt at a disadvantage. He said that foreign visitors are primarily there to meet the Japanese, which he understood.

Japanese and North American Indirectness Compared

We return to Tsuda's study of sales talk in Japan and in the United States. She surveyed people in both countries and found that indirectness was much more strongly favored by Japanese customers as a strategy of refusal: "Japanese customers have a tendency to refuse unwanted merchandise circuitously rather than directly. This underlying norm of other-oriented, indirect communication helps to explain why we Japanese often refer to our own culture as *sasshi no bunka,* a 'guessing culture.'"[1]

Although most American respondents (78 percent) said that they directly refuse unwanted merchandise ("I don't want this; I'm not interested"), only 37 percent of the Japanese said that they are so direct. Instead the majority of Japanese respondents (63 percent) said that they use indirect means, as compared to only 21 percent of Americans: "I will consider it later"; I will leave it to my wife/ husband"; "I am undecided"; "I'm sorry, but I'm satisfied with what I have now." Although these figures reveal a preference for indirectness by Japanese, they also show that it is not absolute: More than one-third of the Japanese respondents reported that they use direct means of refusal.

Japanese Avoidance of *No*

In popular writing, much has been said about Japanese indirectness, particularly the avoidance of the word "no" (*iie*). Avoidance occurs, as seen in Chapter 6, with social requests, but is not completely the case. In fact, *iie* is not infrequent at all, especially as a denial of factual truth, as in the following example.

A male radio disc jockey in Nagoya called a listener, a middle-aged Japanese woman, on the air. He asked her age, and she responded, "Thirty plus nine," or 39 years (*sanjuu to kyuu*). Her wit encouraged the disc jockey to pursue the subject:

DJ: When is your birthday?
Otanjoobi wa itsu desu ka?

Woman: [It] is the 23rd of next month [December].
Raigetsu no nijuusan nichi desu.

DJ: [That]'s near Christmas!
Kurisumasu ni *chikai desu ne*.

Woman: No, the emperor's birthday.
Iie, tennoo tanjoobi desu.[2]

Clearly, *no* is not avoided here, or in other simple matters. *No* is not as rare in Japanese as some popular writings would have us believe. (The current emperor's birthday is on December 23, so the woman naturally associated that event with her own birthday. Even though few Japanese are Christian, Christmas is highly commercialized in Japan; this explains why the disc jockey apparently forgot the emperor's birthday, a Japanese national holiday.)

No in English has a wider scope of meaning than *iie* in Japanese. As responses to a question, *hai* ("yes") and *iie* ("no") are used infrequently and are best regarded as meaning respectively, "That's correct" and "That's incorrect."[3] Other means exist in Japanese for expressing truth values, such as *soo* ("that's right") and *soo janai* ("that's not right").[4] Another word that can function as *no* is *nai* ("not") as in this example:

A: *Kasa ga aru?* (Do [you] have an umbrella?)
B: *Nai.* (No.)
Nai, nai. (No, no; for emphasis)

Still other means exist, depending on context. *Iie* is not the only linguistic means of expressing negative truth value.

"Avoidance" of *no* may be explained in part by the apparent relationship between these words:

iie "no"
ii "good"; "that's okay" (a refusal)
ee "yes"; "I see"
ie "no" (informal, clipped)

These four words are distinguished clearly in speech, such that confusion does not normally occur. Their similarity, however, suggests it possibly could be otherwise. I wonder if in the feudal era of the past, such similarity could have been exploited to make evasive action for the powerless social classes. This is only speculation, but it would suggest why *iie* is more restricted in meaning than the English *no.*

This restricted meaning of *iie* became clear to me by interaction between an American and some Japanese at a "petting farm" in the United States. This farm catered to tourists and attracted its share of visitors from Japan. For that reason, the farm employed a Japanese-speaking American as a guide. I happened to overhear this guide correcting two small Japanese children by saying, *iie! iie!* ("No! No!"). The children ignored her; she repeated herself and became flustered. Her mistake was to rely on a direct translation from English.

Although *iie* can mean "no," it is not used for admonishment. For that purpose, the Japanese say *dame.* Similarly, when a Japanese makes a retort to another or disagrees with another's opinion, various expressions are available, such as *chigau* ("That's wrong"). *Dame* and *chigau* often seem ignored in discussions about the Japanese avoidance of *no.* Also ignored are set expressions such as *chotto muzukashii* ("a little difficult") as in the case considered in Chapter 6. That expression conveys denial for the Japanese. And North Americans can take hints, contrary to what the Japanese manager must have thought: In the pierced ears incident, if the Japanese woman had said something like "That's okay" (with the proper intonation), the hairdresser would have gotten the message.

Implicature is complex in any culture, not just in Japan. Statements like "The Japanese avoid saying 'no,'" may be good advice for foreign businesspeople, but not if deceit is the motivation ascribed. Such indirectness, rather than a gambit to bargain, intends to save face for the other. Japanese businesses are said to quote prices more at the actual than negotiable level. Westerners, however, tend to "go high then low," allowing a cushion for bargaining. With such different assumptions about doing business, it is little wonder that Japanese "face" and indirectness have received notoriety.

Japanese: Situationally Based

Increasingly we see that the Japanese are highly situational in their speech. For example, in Japanese restaurants the word for tea is *ocha.* In a sushi shop, however, the word is *agari.* In Japan, the word for rice depends on whether the restaurant is Japanese or western; The respective words are *gohan* or *raisu.* The only difference is the serving dish used: *Gohan* is served in a bowl; *raisu,* on a plate.

Japanese indirectness is highly situational. In formal introductory social meetings, westerners would be wise to be cautious about being too "direct." At the same time, we must be careful not to misconstrue apparent Japanese agreement when they actually mean something else, such as "I hear you."

Such relationships also may involve signs of formality that remain "frozen" in time. Once relative social positions are established, one's status will often remain as it is, especially in forms of address. Once a Japanese college teacher told me that he had married the daughter of his former professor. He continued to call his father-in-law *sensei,* until his father-in-law asked him to stop several years later. Similarly, in a Japanese TV drama, a young female schoolteacher was impregnated by her student, who still called her *sensei* even when they were alone. Another example is an American woman who divorced her Japanese husband. Sometime later she visited her former husband in the hospital where she was irked to be addressed as *okusan* (honorable wife) by her former in-laws and friends.

EQUATING SPEECH AND WRITING

Despite the fact that speech and writing employ differing syntax, vocabulary, and communicative strategies,[5] researchers in contrastive rhetoric appear to treat such differences as negligible in English, and assume the same for other languages. That seems false in the case of Japanese, for its grammar can change quite appreciably depending on mode. Expository writing in Japanese, for instance, usually does not employ elaborated verb inflections from its honorific language (*keigo*), language associated with hierarchical social relations. The Japanese expect expository writing to be free of social encumbrance, and as a result, Japanese speech and writing may differ far more than their respective difference in English. Therefore, it is not necessarily the case that because Japanese speech seems "indirect" or "circular," the same must be true for its expository writing.

THE JAPANESE LACK INDEPENDENT THOUGHT?

Another western assumption, following from the image of Japanese inscrutability and its "group culture," is that the Japanese lack independent thought. This assumption is manifested in the western charge that the Japanese economic success was founded on imitation. It is true that the Japanese have used imitation, but "Japan's experience with regard to imitation was no different from that of [other nations in the west]. Hence, the [western] image … of Japan as a nation that excels in borrowing technology belongs to the distant past, [because] Japan today leads … technolog[ically] in many areas, particularly in technology-intensive industries."[6] The charge also ignores the devastation of World War II that Japan had to overcome.

In regard to written discourse, Japanese groupism is expected to discourage the independent thought inherent to exposition. As suggested above, different "grammars" are used in Japanese to deal with different social expectations, allowing a writer to be freer than what may be expected in the western imagination. Interesting support comes from comparative studies of field independence between Japanese and Americans. George A. DeVos concludes that "the Japanese on a cognitive level are actually more capable of independent perception [than North Americans], but [not] on the level of social perception."[7] Such points are important to make because the image of Japanese conformism is so strong, that some researchers assume that the Japanese are conformist in all things (i.e., they lack independent thought, the type needed for expository writing).

An Illustration

Recent remarks made by a prominent Japanologist are considered in order to illustrate questionable presumptions about the Japanese language. The relevant issues concern how Japanese is associated with Chinese, which in turn may have implications for viewing Japanese conformism and Japanese independence of mind. It is the presumed lack of independent mindedness that is sometimes linked with nonlinear patterns of expository writing.

Interviewed in an educational film about Japanese borrowing, an American Japanologist states that "the whole language [of Japanese] comes from China."[8] This remark exaggerates the Japanese borrowing of Chinese, which may reinforce the tendency of confusing Japan with China, possibly short-changing Japanese inventiveness. If what he says is really true, then Japanese would be nothing more than a dialect of Chinese. However, the two are mutually unintelligible, a criterion for the classification of separate languages.[9] Japanese and Chinese are not even classified in the same language families.[10] The difference between the two languages is such that a genealogical connection between them is not even seriously considered.[11]

What the two languages clearly share are Chinese characters (and associated concepts)—a writing system; but the Japanese have evolved different pronunciation and form for theirs.[12] Even though Chinese formed a basis of Japanese written discourse (centuries ago), "the process of incorporation often served to efface the Chinese meaning of the character, so as to replace it with a distinctive Japanese meaning."[13]

The Japanologist also ignored the fact that English and other languages (apart from Sino-Japanese) seem to be having a profound effect on Japanese. "The average Japanese speaker uses three thousand to five thousand loanwords [largely from English], which constitutes as much as 10 percent of daily vocabulary items."[14] A large segment of English vocabulary has its roots in Latin, but one never says that that is from where the whole language came.

Even amending this Japanologist's statement to only the writing system would be inaccurate. The Japanese developed their own indigenous orthography even though they had borrowed Chinese characters. Moreover, they have combined Japanese orthography with Chinese characters, producing a multiple writing system, such that "the Japanese script remains the most difficult of writing systems of all languages and historical periods."[15] For example, Japanese *kanji* (characters) often have two or more readings (pronunciations), while the characters in the Chinese language rarely do.[16] Despite Japanese having a multiple writing system, incorporating three different orthographic systems, it "does not affect the unity of the Japanese language."[17]

Perhaps, his "whole language" meant something other than "full amount." However, he also said that "half the architecture [of Japan] comes from China and Korea,"[18] suggesting that he was using "whole language" in a quantitative sense. Regardless of his intention, the real issue concerns how an audience of that educational film would take his remarks.

A maxim in communication is that "we communicate whether or not we wish to."[19] What is to prevent listeners from reinventing stereotypical views of inscrutability? (Inscrutability, here in the context of images of "Asia," is a complex of concepts including mysteriousness, paradox, irrationality, and related behavioral attributions.) Language is naturally created by all normal individuals. Stating that the whole Japanese language was borrowed gives little credit to Japanese creativity. Such an oversight is unfortunate, but perhaps such matters will lead to more care in interpreting other cultures.

Views between Chinese and Japanese ought to be made distinct (see Chapter 1). This suggestion is not meant to minimize the influence of China on Japanese history and culture. Rather, this point reflects the problem of social schema and how images of "Asia" are traded off between China and Japan in the western mind. Even if Chinese rhetoric or expository writing were found circular in style, that alone is insufficient for generalizing to Japanese.

With these preliminary remarks, it is hoped that one seeks the facts of the case for Japanese rhetorical differences before deducing as much based on fallacious assumptions about Japanese conformism, the equating of speech and writing, and the equating of Chinese and Japanese. On the other hand, Japanese may still differ rhetorically from other languages. How this difference may materialize is explored in this chapter, as well as in Chapters 8 and 9.

JAPANESE RHETORIC: A CASE OF CROSS-CULTURAL MISUNDERSTANDING

Earlier, we discussed nature and Japanese spirituality, using as a springboard, Isamu Kurita's book *Setsu Getsu Ka no Kokoro.* We will cite his book again, but now for examples of possible cross-cultural miscommunication. The author based his book on a lecture on nature for foreign employees of a Japanese enterprise. I was intrigued because his book suggested that the Japanese love of nature could be used to explain the Japanese work ethic, among other Japanese contemporary things. It seemed a challenge to explain the practical with something seemingly obscure. I found that I had to struggle with Kurita's thesis, even though his sentences were generally well constructed. Somehow I could not grasp his point. Still, I was drawn to the challenge, and the book was filled with attractive plates for illustration.

Recently, I was reminded of my difficulty when discussing a similar case presented to an associate of mine, an Indian-born management consultant living in New York. An Austrian businessman complained to him about a Japanese publication about Buddhism written for foreigners. The manner of explanation (the rhetoric) left him confused. I happened to be there, and the three of us discussed this problem of "information transfer" or rhetoric across cultures. It seemed to me that this particular Japanese author could not project himself fully into the foreigner's mind. That is, he may not have fully realized the points of cultural difference experienced by foreigners.

By *projection,* I mean that the writer must grasp intuitively what the audience can and cannot understand. To do this, the Japanese must understand the western mind (and vice-versa). Within Japan, however, the understanding of western things is rather superficial; the reverse is true in the west. Individualism and collectivism are examples. At the extreme, the Japanese visualize us as chaotic mad devils; and we, robots of them. In regard to cross-cultural communication, Roichi Okabe, a respected Japanese specialist, suggests that the problem of "information transfer" is rooted in the difference in our communication styles—perhaps, even our cognitive styles.[20]

For an example of a rhetorical difference, let us turn to Kurita's book on the Japanese love of nature. Kurita makes it clear, that the Japanese have a special interest in nature. For me, however, the difficulty was with the connection to contemporary Japanese culture and behavior. To explain the problem of the connection of ideas, consider how Kurita uses a poem. Under the heading of "Yamato Spirit," which he does not explain directly, he states that "the Japanese pass their lives in close communion with flowers, the moon and the changing seasons."[21] No problem here: He reiterates a theme already familiar to his readers.

The problem arises with Kurita's treatment of a Japanese poem. He begins by telling us something about the poet and then presenting the poem:

> Yoshida Shoin (1830-1859), a progressive thinker and revolutionary of the mid-nineteenth century who made the first attempt to establish diplomatic relations between Japan and the United States, left the following poem to posterity:
>
> Even should my body
> Decay beneath Musashi Plain,
> Forever will I keep

> The Yamato Spirit,
> The spirit of Japan.[22]

Kurita then concludes: "The poem clearly speaks of a return to nature" ("*Masa ni, shizen e no kaiki o utatteiru no desu*").[23] But does it?

The "Yamato spirit" could represent various sentiments and meanings. Kurita describes the poet Yoshida as a "revolutionary," so the point of the poem may be far from "a return to nature." It might be an everlasting love of country, a nationalistic spirit, a wish to preserve Japan despite encroachment of the (barbaric) west. Because the author does not explicitly state what "Yamato spirit" means or explain why this poem is a "return to nature," we may be left in the dark. Even if we do know that "Yamato" was an ancient term for "Japan," we would still be puzzled. (The Japanese-language version is equivalent to this and is equally sparse in information.)

Here we may be dealing with a "dot-like" or what I am calling the "connect-the-dots" discourse pattern,[24] in which

> one item after the other [follows] in a highly anecdotal or episodic vein without articulation of the conclusion. Westerners often view such a format as devoid of any particular message, and see the speaker/writer as "shallow." The Japanese, in turn, consider the "forcing" of a conclusion on the listener/reader to be quite unsophisticated and inelegantly simplistic.[25]

In other words, the North American "step-by-step" approach may appear pedantic to the Japanese. The dot-like pattern, however, is not equivalent to illogical or circular thought, a mistaken assumption sometimes made. This issue receives separate attention in later chapters dealing with contrastive rhetoric. Until then, it will be sufficient to advise caution about mistaking mere cultural difference for lack of logic.

In Kurita's book, I found no explicit discussion of how to apply his notion about the Japanese love of nature to contemporary Japanese life. He begins by telling us that his topic is "destined to assume paramount importance in conducting business on [a] global scale in the future: the special character of the Japanese and their culture."[26] Soon thereafter, he states that "an understanding of culture is indispensable to a deeper understanding of a nation's politics, economics and lifestyle."[27] Thus he couches his talk in terms of contemporary needs in international affairs and business. An international businessperson might ask how his historical survey of the Japanese love of nature relates to today's world. I believe that he never attempts to address that point. Thus the readers—foreigners and Japanese alike—are left to their own devices.

My conclusion, which I presented in Chapter 6, was the result of a struggle. Yet the material is not that complex to warrant the extra struggle I had. The crux of it was that, in my view, the author did not anticipate enough potential misunderstanding by the foreign audience. If he had explored the various meanings of *nature,* what we call "defining terms," and had attempted to make applications to the present world, he would have avoided confusion.

In addition, the book may very well be a collection of the author's lecture notes—essentially unrevised. He does state that the book was based on his lectures. More telling, however, is an interesting difference between the author's preface and the rest of the book in honorifics. For the preface, he used the plain written style (*de aru*) closely associated with academic writing that avoids honorifics while "indicat[ing] an objectivity ... result[ing] from lack of personal interaction."[28] In contrast, the rest of the book is written at the courtesy level (see Chapter 5), which would be a style likely used if presented orally. (The courtesy level is used also in expository writing but more typically for an audience of children or the general public;[29] it is usually avoided in academic writing.) Thus communication in one setting (lecture or seminar) involving an oral, small-group mode and a spoken delivery with audiovisuals is transferred to a very different medium, namely print for an unseen audience.

In a lecture, questions can usually receive immediate reply, and commentary may be accompanied by visual aids. The book was intended to bridge that gap; it contains more than 60 pictorial plates with individual commentary on each. These commentaries, however, appear in a separate appendix. More significantly, the author only once referred to a pictorial or graphic by its exhibit number. Thus a reader could remain unaware that further information is available in the appendix—information that may be needed as one reads. This lack of coordination led me to think that the text may be largely unrevised notes for an oral presentation. If this is true, it suggests the "dot-like" rhetorical pattern, whereby members of an audience are expected to draw their own conclusions.

Other aspects of the text, however, are reasonably well organized and comprehensible. For example, the text contains advance organizers or triggers by which an author informs the reader about the organization: purpose, topical content, and so on. Furthermore, the book includes no convoluted "gyres," wild digressions, or highly unorganized portions. Generally, the text is well ordered. The noteworthy feature, again, is that some deductive statements lack support or development, and no application of the thesis is attempted.

Japanese Wholistic Thought

Kurita may be perfectly correct in his thesis, but I believe (as I have attempted to show) that some links are missing. These missing links coincide with the gaps in mutual knowledge between Japanese and westerners. Without awareness of such gaps, Japanese are likely to leave westerners in the dark (or vice versa). Okabe suggests that the Japanese tend to communicate "synthetically" or "wholistically," whereas Americans do so "analytically." *Analytical thought*, in the extreme, refers to dichotomous thinking: There is no in-between, only good or bad, black or white, right or wrong.[30] Thus, it involves an insistence on determining reasons, causes, and outcomes. To do so, topics are broken down into their parts, information abstracted, relationships drawn. This analytical process is probably found in all cultures but is most appropriate for academic or technical contexts. Even Americans may say about another as being "too analytical" if this approach is misused in a social context. Nevertheless, the Japanese seem less disposed to intellectual "sparing" in social conversations than North Americans.

The non-analytic or wholistic approach is seen frequently with Japanese requests. Japanese give much background information before actually stating their wish: A wife says to her husband, "Son Taro is at his violin lesson; daughter Shinobu is at ballet practice; but I have a dental appointment; would you pick the kids up later?" This series of elements can become quite long. North Americans often tend to do the reverse by stating the requested task first. Whereas the Japanese typically organize the information leading to the request spatially or temporally, North Americans do so analytically. Stating the request first is an abstraction of the details as a "task." It cuts through the details to isolate the most important item for the listener. The Japanese request is wholistic in that little is omitted or abstracted. It follows a natural progression in space or time. Again, these patterns are only tendencies; both patterns exist in both cultures.

Another example in which a Japanese appeared to be wholistic or "nonanalytic" is found in Box 7.2.

Box 7.2 Japanese Wholistic Discourse (Grady Whitmore*)

At my school [in Japan], there was a secretary in the office, with whom I used to talk a lot. She was friendly and spoke on familiar terms with me. Once we talked about inconveniences of daily life and mentioned the Japanese telephone company, which did not itemize its billing—a certain inconvenience to its customers.

Sometime much, much later—weeks—the secretary approached me with a billing statement from the telephone company. She spoke in a familiar manner, as it was our custom. But she spoke in a matter-of-fact tone: *mite kore* ("look at this").

At first, I thought that she was asking if I had made any of the calls. I had not, of course, because I never called from there, something she must have been well aware. But that was not her purpose. Only through questioning did I discover that she wanted to point out that the Japanese long-distance carrier was finally itemizing its bills. I remembered our prior conversation, but it had occurred long before.

If the secretary were North American and if emotionless, he or she probably would have said, "Look, the phone company is itemizing its bills," or, "Look, this is what we've been waiting for."

Could it be that Japanese discourse tends to be wholistic as compared to westerners?

A further example of Japanese wholistic discourse comes from Lance Forrest*, a bilingual American employee of a Japanese company. Box 7.3 contains a segment of conversation that took place between Forrest (A) and a bilingual Japanese (J) in the same company, in which they discussed the hiring of a new office worker.

Box 7.3 Japanese Wholistic Discourse (Lance Forrest*)

A: When did you hear that Ms. Kondo [a prospective employee] declined the offer [of employment]?
J: Well, three weeks ago, Mr. Taga [in a different office] introduced Ms. Kondo as a good candidate for the job. But [last] Thursday she told me that she couldn't take the offer because she decided to go elsewhere, to be closer to her hometown.
A: So it was just two days ago that you heard she wouldn't come?
J: Yes.

This Japanese gave background information before answering the question but apparently did not realize that the information was confusing. The American was confused in hearing that the woman had declined the offer "three weeks ago," when in fact it was the previous Thursday, just two days before. According to Forrest, this Japanese showed no noticeable hesitation or pause in his speech, which might have indicated a memory aid or search. Also, the fact that the event in question had happened just two days previously made a memory lapse unlikely. Although Forrest's exasperation is evident in his second question, he reported that the Japanese was oblivious to what had happened. Forrest also said that he could not imagine that this information was socially sensitive in any way.

If Japanese discourse is less analytical than western discourse (in an informal sense), it may be because the Japanese appear to engage in much less argumentation than westerners. I refer to the discussion of opinions that westerners tend to enjoy, in which each person tries to persuade the other of the merits of one's view. Analytical thought would be involved in such talk: Issues are often divided into parts, examined, weighed, and evaluated. Such social activity may be far more acceptable in individualistic than in collectivistic societies. It is my impression that why-questioning occurs less frequently between teachers and students in classrooms in Japan than it does in North America.[31] Why-questions, according to the psychologist Robert J. Sternberg, are indicative of an analytical style (termed "judicial" by Sternberg), a style he believes is less preferred by the Japanese.[32]

Sternberg reasons that the Japanese would tend to fit an "executive" thinking style ("wholistic" in our terms), one that prefers following directives in structured situations.[33] The kind of questions compatible for the executive style is not *why* but *what, when, who,* and *how.*[34] The analytical style and the executive (wholistic) style correspond to how North American and Japanese education appear to differ: Whereas the goal in North America "is to instill creativity, to allow students to proceed from a basic knowledge of facts to an original conclusion," in Japan, it "is to teach facts that can be recalled on cue."[35] This statement is highly generalized, for both goals can be found in both cultures to some extent. The statement, however, does capture a Japanese tendency, especially for public junior and senior high schools. (Junior and senior high schools are pivotal for college entrance, which is typically determined by tests requiring the memorization of massive information. If private, the school may be in affiliation with an associated college or university, which may make such exams less crucial for admittance.)

The North American propensity to ask "why?" is part of the ideal of developing a questioning intellect. According to our cultural ideals, we have an individual responsibility to become informed citizens in order to protect democracy through reasoned voting at the polls. Debate on the issues is part of this process. An offshoot of this political culture is a criticism of mass consumerism. Young people in North America, for example, as compared to Japanese, ridicule TV commercials for their obviously extravagant claims. Indeed, some North Americans enjoy this and make it almost a game. I have very rarely seen Japanese do so, except when they laugh at comic antics in certain commercials.

Mass consumerism may have more novelty for the Japanese than for North Americans. North American society, in contrast, exports much popular culture (though Japan does also to some extent). We grew up with it and know its good and bad points. Until recently, for example, Japanese college students were generally ignorant about the health risks of overindulging in western "fast food." The excitement about modern popular culture and how it is commercially promoted probably overshadows many new consumers' critical thoughts. How much of this idea applies to the Japanese is unknown, for Japan has had a relatively advanced, literate population for centuries. Yet it is probably true that outside academic life, the Japanese engage in much less debate and social argument than do North Americans. If this is so, they may indeed be less analytical in everyday speech.

Again, I am speaking in generalities and describe only tendencies. Context or situation is especially important in considering Japanese behavior. An apt example appears in a recent discussion on Japanese rhetoric. That discussion will be useful in encouraging a critical view for cross-cultural comparison.

Japanese Rhetorical Induction

Rhetorical induction is generally discussed in relation to written academic prose. Parallel to the wholistic patterning of a spoken request, induction first presents the details and then a related generalization. The reverse is true of deduction. Both patterns are found in the prose of English and of Japanese. Americans, however, are said to favor deduction; the Japanese, induction. This may be true, but such claims often give little attention to genre. Even in Japanese, the frequency of induction is liable to differ according to the type of writing: scientific, academic, technical, journalistic, popular, and others. Little attention has been given to these distinctions, so it may be premature to say that Japanese written prose favors induction.

Also, as Japanese communication is sometimes depicted, the Japanese are made to appear slightly bizarre. A case in point is the presentation on this topic in the book *An Introduction to Intercultural Communication,* which received focus in Chapter 4. The presentation revolves around a conversation (probably imagined) between an American teacher of English and a Japanese student (see Box 7.4). The American teacher asks the Japanese student what American author he likes best. The student does not give an answer but tells a "story" about going to America that appears unrelated to the question. The teacher does not learn anything about the student's preference in authors. The authors of the book claim that this conversation exemplifies the Japanese preference for induction,[36] but, they never consider that the student, who was using a foreign language, may not have

Box 7.4 Japanese Induction: Case 1

Speech between an American teacher (T) and a Japanese student (S):

T: Mr. Suzuki, who is your favorite American author?
S: When I was twelve I went to the United States with my parents. It was my first trip there.
T: That's very interesting, but who is your favorite American author?
S: At that time, my brother was already a high school student.
T: Thank you, Mr. Suzuki.[37]

understood the question. Perhaps to avoid embarrassment in front of others (or to save his grade!), he resorted to a circumlocution. My own Japanese students assumed that the student did not understand the question. This point is interesting because if induction were the preferred style of the Japanese, they would have grasped the authors' point immediately.

If Case 1 above is accurate, the Japanese must be strange indeed if they deal so indirectly with even the simplest questions (in any language). Consider this imaginary exchange:

A: What's your favorite ice cream, Taro?
B: One day when I was young, my mother took me downtown. I saw a lot of things, including ice cream stores. One store had many flavors. Some I couldn't even say! But after eating chocolate-watermelon my clothes became a mess. Yes, those were the days. Poor mother had a hard time. For me, my favorite is vanilla.

My ice cream example illustrates indirectness more accurately than Case 1: Taro talks about ice cream in one way or another. In Case 1, Suzuki speaks not about American authors but about his trip to America; he seems completely off the subject. If Taro strikes us as odd, Suzuki is more so.

To extend this point and to illustrate the tendency to ignore the complexity of cultural comparisons, the following example appears to show how a Japanese teacher of English made a careless comparison. The teacher observed that her group of Japanese homemakers had found it difficult to interact (in English) with American homemakers at a recent social event. (I purposely spoke with her in Japanese, and she responded in kind. Furthermore, she herself chose a case involving English. I would have preferred one involving exclusively Japanese speakers, but I let her continue.) She observed that the Japanese women generally did not answer questions directly. Asked for some examples, she cited these: "What hobby do you like to do? Do you go to church?" These questions, however, appear to be "loaded." The Japanese homemakers, who were speaking in a foreign language, were probably more aware than the Americans of the way concepts may differ cross-culturally. Was "church" used generically or only as a Christian place of worship? If used as the latter, what was meant? And so on.

Furthermore, according to the teacher, these Japanese homemakers were mothers and belonged to the upper middle class. Therefore, they were also likely to be *kyooiku mama* (education moms). As harried, busy mothers, could they ever find time for a hobby? If so, what would it mean to say so in front of their fellow Japanese? Japanese society idealizes the self-sacrificing mother (see Box 6.2). Depending on their social relations, the Japanese women might or might not have been comfortable in seeming to depart from this social ideal. Consequently it is not surprising that they apparently had "trouble" in social interactions with the Americans.

Finally, the teacher ignored the important fact that English was a foreign language for the Japanese women. Circumlocution might be more related to linguistic than cultural factors. As a linguistic strategy, it can compensate for an imperfect command of a foreign language by gaining time to formulate the desired reply or to reconsider the related conversation.

After making these points, I asked the teacher to consider Japanese-Japanese interactions. She found it difficult to think of an example. She then acknowledged that it would be strange for Japanese to answer simple requests for information in an inductive manner: a "story" or reasons first, then the main point, answer, conclusion, or generalization. In fact, my Japanese students reached this conclusion after testing the idea with other Japanese. They used a simple survey in asking about personal preferences about novels, movies and so forth. Unless the respondent was uninterested in such topics, the students received direct answers about preferences.

Again, I am not denying that the Japanese may favor different communication patterns from ours, but they do not do so across the board. Also, the difference is not necessarily linear versus circular. Much more research is needed to distinguish these differences and their frequencies; otherwise we are likely to rely on stereotypes of the Japanese such as mysteriousness or inscrutability.

BENCHMARKS FOR JAPANESE RHETORIC

As mentioned above, Japanese tend to preface requests with details that follow a spatial or temporal order. For a more complete picture, a study of Japanese business correspondence by Saburo Haneda and Hirosuke Shima[38] provides a useful array of typical Japanese business letters. These letters, as I describe them, can be categorized as I do here:

TYPE 1 The main message is sandwiched between beginning and ending salutations and acknowledgments that can consist of one or several paragraphs.

TYPE 2 In addition to the usual salutations and acknowledgments, the message is prefaced by one or more paragraphs that form a chronology of secondary details, even though these are already known.

TYPE 3 Salutations and acknowledgments are completely absent, but the main message is prefaced by one or more paragraphs that form a chronology of secondary details, even though already known.

TYPE 4 The main message is unobscured and is made directly.

The authors, unfortunately, did not indicate the relative frequencies of these types. We can suppose that Type 4 is most likely based on a well-established relationship and does not involve an offer to buy or sell something.

Westerners may describe Type 1 or 2 as roundabout or circular, but there is nothing illogical about the specimens provided by Haneda and Shima. Once the writers of the letters arrive at the matter at hand, the letters contain no wild digressions or illogical progressions. The topics or propositional content may be well ordered. The difference is the heavy foregrounding with superfluous information. The writers, however, may start with a subject heading or hint at their purpose early in the letter. Again, this shows that Japanese rhetoric is not totally oblivious to informational needs of the reader.

Finally, Types 1 and 2 demonstrate how Japanese might characterize their communication as "wet," in contrast to the "dryness" of western communications. This "wetness" consists of social ritual or other-directedness by an emphasis on salutations and acknowledgements. Research is needed to determine how frequently and under what conditions such "wetness" operates in Japanese business communications, and how effective it would be if employed by non-Japanese when communicating with Japanese. In the meantime, when dealing with Japanese, it would be advisable to be alert for delay of the main point because doing so is regarded courteous. When listening, one must keep an "ear" on the evolving talk, but the other "ear" downstream to catch the eventual point or drift. If the Japanese is not forthright, then one must be ready to put two and two together. One also needs tact and a good relationship in order to confirm one's understanding. This is why cordial relations with the Japanese must be built before doing serious business with them.

In sum, we must remember to distinguish between Japanese speech and writing. Although both modes are mutually reinforcing, Japanese indirectness is most associated with speech. To what extent it also relates to Japanese academic writing remains an open question. Before considering this question in detail in Chapters 8 and 9, we turn to the following application activities, which serve to consolidate our present study.

APPLICATION

The Guessing Culture of Japan: Gain or Pain?

Michiko Niikuni Wilson

Michiko Niikuni Wilson teaches Japanese language, literature and culture at the University of Virginia, as well as serving as editor of the M.E. Sharpe series on Japanese Women Writing. *Born and raised in Japan, she has spent over twenty years living in the United States, first as an exchange student in the American Field Service to a Missouri high school, and then in college as a regular student earning a BA in English, as well as MA and PhD degrees in Comparative Literature. She has authored* The Marginal World of Oe Kenzaburo: A Study in Themes and Techniques, *and a critical work on Oba Minako titled* Gender Is Fair Game: (Re)Thinking the (Fe)Male in Oba Minako's Works *(forthcoming). In addition, she has translated book-length works such as Oe's* The Pinch Runner Memorandum, *and Oba Minako's* Birds Crying (Naku tori no).

As Aoi Tsuda indicated above, the Japanese sometimes call their culture, *sasshi no bunka,* a "guessing culture." Good guessers (*sasshi no ii hito)* are treasured both in the home and at the workplace for their ability to intuit the needs of others and to act accordingly. A Japanese dictionary (*Nihongo Daijiten*, Kodansha, 1990) gives the English word, *consideration* as one of the definitions of *sasshi.* In practice, *sasshi* is more than thoughtfulness. It is a skill Japanese are encouraged to acquire early on, a skill that is essential to be a full-pledged social being.

However, this seemingly positive aspect of the "guessing culture" allows excessive space and occasion for Japanese to manipulate each other. Given the economy of words and impregnated silence associated with this "wholistic" style, it resists clear, verbal communication. Whereas this approach in America is considered "overly diplomatic" or "down right manipulative," (consider how presidential press secretaries dodge probing questions from the press), Japanese use it routinely and take it as a natural part of social relations. So Japanese are ever alert to make guesses about what others say. Apart from a Japanese affinity for rituals evident in this communication style, *sasshi no bunka* protects Japanese from taking responsibility for what they say because no one really takes the initiative in this kind of verbal interaction.

The other side of this culture is the "prefacing" style that Japanese often employ. I suspect that Japanese have a strong need to justify themselves to get what they want, so that they can avoid being criticized later. This fear of criticism means that they do not like being questioned. Why-questions disturb them. Words and the person uttering them are so tightly bound that Japanese take almost everything personally. What you say seems to automatically reflect your personality, and vice versa. In a culture that advocates self-discipline and refinement of character, what you utter may have grave consequences. The result is often not saying what is really on your mind.

I have observed again and again in Japan that even when someone asks you "why?" (e.g. Why did you say that? why are you late for work?), the inquirer seems already to have the answer in mind and tells the "accused" what it is. This is an extreme example of the *sasshi no bunka.* Perhaps this involves confrontation when the inquirer has lost personal restraint and holds rank above the other. Such questions, then, would acquire a negative nuance and may explain observations that Japanese react uncomfortably to intellectual questioning.

Once when I was at an academic conference with a Japanese colleague, I observed him unsuccessfully engage a Japanese from Japan in discussion about the latter's presentation. My colleague had an unanswered question and approached this scholar with it. "By the way, why do think ..." went my colleague in Japanese. The instantaneous response was "*Dooshite katte ...*" or "(You) asked (me) *why*?" But this scholar's manner made it clear that he was saying, "What do you mean *why*?" Perhaps the question was unrelated to this presentation. Still, his defensiveness made me think he was not accustomed with such questioning. It is the case that Japanese academic presentations in Japan typically do not receive the kind of questioning at the end as in the United States. When this western custom is transferred to the Japanese situation, it likely will end in pained silence. It is also true that specialists of Japanese literature in the United States rarely engage in critiquing each other's scholarship even in their writings. I suspect this is a carryover of *sasshi no bunka.*

Also related is the lack of "negotiation" in Japanese everyday personal interactions. The word for negotiation in Japanese is *kooshoo* but is more restricted in meaning for formal dialogues in business or politics. There is not much of the "give and take" of arguing for argument's sake as in the west. One reason is that Japanese seem to take criticism or disagreement too personally. There seems to be no room for "We agree to disagree." Another is that "give and take" implies equality of social relations, an aspect of only recent development in Japanese society. While there is plenty of a "one up, one down" climate in American corporate culture, business or academia, *kooshoo* encounters more difficulty in a society like Japan where hierarchy plays a central role, sweeping down through the seniority of family members, siblings, professional colleagues, and so on.

Given these aspects of the "guessing culture," an indirect, "prefacing" style is the likely result. I end up using it myself, as a kind of warm-up (like an introduction in a critical work, which western scholars insist on), a subconscious desire to tell a story perhaps. Or, it provides some sort of buffer or cushion between the speaker and the listener. In other words, Japanese enjoy being dramatic: A real good part is coming, but I have to guide you in certain ways before an unveiling.

On a related issue, I often find myself talking about the subtlety of Japanese culture to American college students, as described in *The Tale of Genji, The Kagero Diary,* haiku, Kawabata Yasunari's narratives, and other cultural traditions of Japan. I have the distinct feeling that in my mind *sasshi* and subtlety are synonymous. I think that is what Japanese want to believe and are proud of about their "guessing culture." Persons less skilled at *sasshi* are, therefore, viewed as dull-witted, unsophisticated, and crude (*sasshi no warui hito).*

A question arises, however: Are Japanese in today's Japan that subtle? If another synonym for *sasshi* is "tactfulness," which I believe it is, then I have observed Americans to be extremely *sasshi no ii hito,* even in routine encounters. This may be the positive aspect of a society that takes the essence of individualism seriously. All of us, though, need to learn and adopt different communication styles according to the situation involved. That, however, is difficult unless people try to break away from the inflexible, monolithic way of viewing the world, society and people.

The mindset of *sasshi no bunka* indicates the importance placed by the Japanese on respect and politeness. In speech, indirectness is a fitting strategy and is complemented by the readiness of hearers to fill in the gaps. This readiness to cooperate with others is seen in Japan, for example, in crowded restaurants where the seated customers hurry for the sake of those still waiting. Nothing is said by restaurant personnel; rather it is part of Japanese common sense. (In contrast, Japanese seem to turn a blind eye toward strangers in crowded thoroughfares, as noted in Chapter 1.) In such subtle ways, the Japanese social order is reinforced daily.

1 Name some other ways found in this chapter by which the Japanese reenact or reinforce their social order.
2 In what situations would you imagine the Japanese to be "direct"?

FURTHER APPLICATION

A. Consider the conversation between the American teacher and Mr. Suzuki (Case 1, Box 7.4). Determine why it does or does not support the claim that the Japanese prefer an "inductive" style of communication.

B. For contrast, the authors of Case 1 offer Case 2, a dialogue between a teacher (T) and student (S), both of whom are American. Read Case 2 and the accompanying explanation by its authors, and consider the questions that follow:

Case 2

T: Mr. Smith, who is your favorite American author?

S: Mark Twain.

T: Why?

S: Because I went to Missouri when I was twelve years old with my parents. My brother was already a high school student, and he told me about Mark Twain. So when I saw where he had grown up, I became very interested.[39]

The Authors' Explanation

> The difference [between Case 1 and Case 2] is that Mr. Smith gave the answer first, and then later offered supporting details. This was not Mr. Suzuki's approach. We might imagine that Mr. Suzuki intended to say something similar to what Mr. Smith said.... [This difference in approach is a big barrier in the] communication between Japanese and Americans.... [Americans typically make their point early on; whereas, the Japanese delay theirs in favor of their reasons or supporting details.] The teacher believes that Mr. Suzuki does not understand the question, although we can now see that he understands it perfectly.[40]

Questions (B)

1. Discuss why or why not Case 1 and Case 2 can be used to support the contention that the Japanese favor induction as a rhetorical pattern.
2. What image or images of the Japanese might arise from the example of Mr. Suzuki in Case 1?
3. Imagine that a Japanese researcher asked (in Japanese) Americans on the street in an American city their favorite movie. Imagine the "conversations" that might result with people of varying degrees of fluency in Japanese. They might not produce the "main answer" until after various other verbalizations. Why couldn't their delay of the main answer support the idea that Americans favor an inductive style of communication?
4. What principle can you derive that is applicable to study of intercultural communication?

C. This chapter gave some examples of Japanese speech that were indirect, and some that were not. In an effort to achieve a broader view, we find a reasonable statement in *An English Dictionary of Japanese Ways of Thinking.* One of the merits of this statement is that it cites specific situations for Japanese indirectness:

> The Japanese language, in contrast to other languages, is often perceived as illogical. A primary reason for this false perception seems to lie not in the structure of the Japanese language but in the way the Japanese use the language to express themselves.
>
> In comparison with western people, who generally prefer to state their opinions as explicitly, logically, and objectively as possible by following a "step-by-step" approach, the Japanese favor a "roundabout" way of approach. Japanese people choose to speak and behave in a vague, ambiguous, and indirect manner when making requests, settling business deals, and so on. They are more likely to consider other people's feelings and hesitate to make "either-or" decisions or give definite "yes-no" answers. They feel more comfortable if there is a little room for compromise so that adjustments can be made when circum-stances change. Therefore, those who are too persistent in logical reasoning and clear-cut argumentation are often reproached as *rikutsuppoi* (going beyond the point of being reasonably logical) [that is, being argumentative].
>
> Too often, Japanese reluctance to be explicit and direct results in misunderstandings when the Japanese interact with foreign people in international communicative settings. In fact, it is frequently voiced that the Japanese hide their true feelings or that they are hard to understand.
>
> Japanese logic is, as noted, different from logic as understood in the western sense. Instead of a 'black and white' approach, the Japanese like to have the flexibility of settling disputes through compromise. This may be why some say jestingly that there is a right way, a wrong way, and a Japanese way.[41]

Questions (C)

1. What image of Japanese might westerners have in light of the Japanese tendency to speak indirectly?

2. How might this image have developed?

D. A researcher reported a case of Japanese indirectness. Read and consider the merits of this case:

An American asked a Japanese female, an ESL student in the United States, what she thought about American food. Her immediate reply was:

> American food? Uh ... what can I say? Y'know, I'm living with an American family now, so, my, uh host father is a very big man, but in the dinner? ...He always does not eat so much. Maybe I will, I will eat much [more] than him ...[42]

Questions (D)

1. What factor or factors of this case would likely induce an indirect answer?
2. What aspects of the case would lead us to classify it as an example of Japanese indirectness?
3. Are there any reasons why we might not classify this as a case of Japanese indirectness? Why or why not?

8

Contrastive Rhetoric Between Japanese and English: A Functional Analysis

The point of this chapter is to demonstrate the necessity of context in cross-cultural studies, especially with contrastive discourse studies between languages and cultures. Certain linguistic studies under the rubric of "contrastive rhetoric" have characterized Japanese written prose as circular in organization. As I have reported previously in 1990 and before, these studies happen to ignore important social and cultural factors in favor of language form or structure. As a result, they end up contrasting noncomparable genres, defeating their original purpose. Moreover, they give little thought to the persistent stereotyping of the Japanese as "mysterious" or "inscrutable" and the possible effects on their own research programs. Because these studies have increasingly gained attention in Japanese studies, communication studies, and related fields, they warrant review all the more. Their review also can provide a grounding for more effective cross-cultural comparisons, an activity in which almost every student of language and culture engages. Our inquiry first begins with discussion of the concept of linguistic structure, and then moves on to a reanalysis of a landmark study in contrastive rhetoric, which purports the discovery of a circular style of expository writing in Japanese.

LINGUISTIC STRUCTURE

Functional and structural views of language and discourse represent a fundamental division in linguistics.[1] Neither side monopolizes the truth, for both have their place in linguistic studies. Our present concern, however, is with extreme structuralism that would treat discourse as if it were a "super sentence." That is, a discourse would be seen as being rigidly structured as that of a sentence. Such a view may treat paragraphing as only correctly done if initiated by a topic sentence, for example. Discourse, though, defies such strictures. The multiple functions of language make it so. Accounting for those functions, as this chapter attempts to show, is an important purpose of discourse analysis, an essential tool for doing contrastive rhetoric.

The term *structure* in linguistics has "a fairly literal meaning, akin to its original sense in the sphere of building."[2] It is said that "The different parts of a window, for example, the uprights, cross-pieces, hinges, panes, and so on, must be of the correct number and of the right size and shape as well as being in the proper relative position, and together they must form a unified whole, a window: only then do they form a structure. These requirements—number of elements, type of elements, ordering of elements—are precisely those of a linguistic [sentential/ grammatical] structure."[3]

Although this kind of structure may fit the sentence, its application to discourse is another matter. The structural view of discourse assumes that language is invariant "but … this invariance is essentially a fiction":[4]

> In real communication, an element is classified not by what it is in the linguist's scheme, but by what it does, that is, by its function in the processing of the participant. A single element may have several functions, and a single function may be assigned to several elements.[5]

The sentence grammar of English has rigid requirements about what goes with what. Discourse, however, is not governed by such rigid rules as seen in this example:

A: I have two tickets to the [movies] tonight.
B: My examination is tomorrow.
A: [Too bad.][6]

What first appears as random utterances becomes immediately coherent, not by knowledge of grammar but that of semantics. Yes, structural relations contribute to understanding these utterances individually but not collectively as a discourse. The decisive element is our background knowledge of everyday affairs. Structural relations of the sentence simply do not apply.

Because "structure" does have a tightly bound sense in linguistics, like a building, some specialists[7] avoid applying the word to discourse. Nevertheless, "discourse structure" is so widely used both inside and outside of linguistics, that it is exceedingly hard to avoid. In an attempt to show why it may be prudent to do so, we will contrast a structurally based cross-linguistic study of English and Japanese from a functional perspective.

A FUNCTIONAL REANALYSIS OF A CROSS-LINGUISTIC STUDY

As background, Robert B. Kaplan proposed that cultures differ in preferred discourse styles based on his study of essays written in English by students from various foreign countries.[8] His proposed "Oriental" style of circularity was in marked contrast to his "linear" style of English and other styles. Although Japanese formed his largest sample group, he excluded it from his Oriental classification for unspecified reasons. It was left to John Hinds's 1980 study to provide the first major study in linguistics to purport that Japanese "expository" writing predominantly follows a circular style. Such characterizations require caution because of the historical tendency in the west to view the Japanese as irrational or illogical.[9] Moreover, despite evidence for a Japanese indirect speaking style, the case for written prose in Japanese appears quite different.[10] Finally, as this chapter intends to show, Hinds's study was essentially structurally based, which led him to ignore important contextual factors related to comparative research, as well as to Japanese culture.

Using a Hawaiian bilingual guide to popular entertainment, he compared how two articles with the same topic are organized in English and Japanese. The Japanese version appears to follow a non-linear pattern, which he reports is predominant in Japanese exposition. He calls this pattern *return to baseline theme* (hereafter, *baseline theme*) because it tends to touch base with a main theme before advancing to newer perspectives.

Hawaii, the locale for this study, seems well chosen because the 50th American state appears to have native speakers for both the English and the Japanese text audiences. Bilinguals of the same region may ensure that both audiences share the same knowledge about a topic, a crucial factor for a study of this kind. For example, if the audiences were in separate countries, information gaps due to different media coverage or exposure may confound results. In the Hawaiian Islands, however, such variables as native language fluency and topic familiarity are readily controlled, so that attention can be paid to finding two published articles with the same content but different organization. If found, differences in the organization of information could be clearly linked to culture. Thus Hinds's study begins with what appears to be a superb design.

As superbly designed as Hinds's study may appear, however, it fails to identify who wrote the Japanese texts and for whom they were written. Rather, the study simply mentions that the prose style studied is for "Japanese speakers."[11] This designation is insufficient in a Hawaiian context, for "Japanese speaker" is not synonymous with Japanese national. Because the texts were printed in Hawaii and no discernible attempt was made to control differences in ethnicity and topic background knowledge between Hawaiians and Japanese nationals, we must assume that Hinds is really comparing two Hawaiian groups in their respective use of English and Japanese. *Hawaiian* is adopted here in view of its dictionary definition: "any native or *inhabitant* of the Hawaiian Islands."[12]

Even if granted that the Hawaiians in question were Japanese Americans and not Korean or Chinese, generalizing from Japanese Americans to the Japanese of Japan is highly problematic for the following reasons:

(1) "Many ... [Japanese Americans] know very little about Japan and do not wish to be identified with their ancestral homeland."[13] This is understandable given the pain that they or

their forebears suffered during World War II when their allegiance to the United States was so strongly challenged (and violated). Regarding those specifically in Hawaii, Japanese Americans identify themselves as Hawaiian before anything else.[14] An "island culture," a "common lifestyle and identity," is emerging among and between the different ethnic groups in Hawaii.[15]

(2) A rather uneven competency in Japanese is found among the Japanese Americans in Hawaii: "today it is rare to find a *Sansei* or *Yonsei* [the younger generations] who speaks Japanese."[16] Even those who do speak Japanese, "most ... suffer from a serious language difficulty."[17]

(3) Comparative research surveys done by the Japanese in the 1970s (the period in which Hinds's texts were published) discovered differences to the extent that made a Japanese researcher exclaim, "Japanese Americans [in Hawaii] are not Japanese," but "we Japanese are Japanese!"[18]

(4) This difference has been found evident in the recent influx of foreigners of Japanese ancestry who have entered Japan as migrant laborers. Although they are ethnic Japanese, "they are still cultural foreigners [in Japan] and do not adapt well into local Japanese communities, nor are they satisfied in their homeland."[19] Japanese nationals find it "incredulous" that such people are unable "to speak Japanese[20] and to think and act like Japanese."[21]

(5) Being a "cultural foreigner" in Japan applies not just in specific cases but also in general to Japanese Americans. Japanese Americans still have a "harder time [than some other foreigners] because Japanese [nationals] are less tolerant of them."[22] As one resident of Hawaii has observed, "many Japanese Americans have undesirable experiences in Japan and leave the country with ill feelings."[23] Doubtless that this is at least partly due to expectations held by both sides, as well as to the special sensitivities involved. It need not be this way, for there are those who do have positive experiences.

Nevertheless, the point being presently made is that Japanese Americans and Japanese nationals are culturally different, and one cannot be used to represent the other. Hardly could one conceive of Americans representing the British or of Mexicans, the Spanish.

In essence, Hinds's Japanese speakers may be a cultural hybrid of assorted and undefined elements, speaking a variety of Japanese, if at all, quite distinct from that found in Japan.[24] Consequently, his study can be dismissed out of hand because of confounded variables.

However, suppose Hinds's "Japanese speakers" really were Japanese nationals (a possibility not considered by Hinds). In fact, my analysis later suggests that the audience may have been Japanese nationals in Japan (again, an audience ignored by Hinds). Contrary to strengthening Hinds's case, an audience in Japan actually works against it. This origin can be substantiated by how the English and Japanese texts in question differ in content, despite previous claims that the content is virtually identical. The more the textual content can be claimed as identical, of course, the more it also can be claimed that differences in textual organization are due to culture-specific rhetorical styles. Nevertheless, textual content differs far more than Hinds seems to allow.

Contrastive Elements Between the Japanese and English Texts

The bilingual texts concern May Yokomoto, a young Hawaiian (Japanese American), who became a popular singer in Japan.[25] Both language versions report May's activities in Japan (see Boxes 8.1 and 8.2). How many differences in content can you find between the English and Japanese texts? The reader ought to consider the texts before continuing our discussion.

A problem with this cross-linguistic study was the absence of a comparison of differences in content. Instead, Hinds simply assumed that they were negligible. By assuming so, the researcher then believed that contextual factors, such as purpose, topic familiarity and location of the audience, were the same for both articles being compared. If they were the same, then any differences in style could be attributed to culture.

On the contrary, the May Yokomoto articles differ considerably in content, using Hinds's own translation. These differences form two patterns: *depth of description* and *spatio-temporal rela-*

tions. These two patterns also show that the audiences were not in the same place (Hawaii) as assumed by the researcher. Instead, the Japanese audience was perceived to be in Japan, if not actually located there. Different locations, therefore, suggest that the audiences could have differed in topic familiarity by

Box 8.1 *ENGLISH* Version, *May Yokomoto*

May Yokomoto: It's a Lot of Fun[26]

(1) May Yokomoto returned to Hawaii recently to appear in the Star-Tanjo. (2) In addition, the friendly eighteen-year old was kept busy by photo sessions with Sakiko Ito. (3) They had numerous pictures taken of them on the beach for *Myojo* magazine in Japan.

(4) She is having a good time in Japan doing commercials, television, and radio work. (5) For example, she appeared on the TV game show *"Kekkonshimashoo"* (Let's Get Married), where she won two trips to Hawaii, which she is saving for future use. (6) May also appears on "*Sekai no* Circus" with her favorite actor, Masaaki Sakai. (7) On this program, May had to dress up like a clown and (8) even swung on a trapeze. (9) She also had a radio program on Radio-KANTO called "Teach Japanese to May."

(10) May has her own apartment in Tokyo, (11) but still has a hard time getting around on trains. (12) Recently, though, people have begun to recognize "May-chan" and (13) help her find her destination. (14) She says living in Japan is not easy, (15) but is fun most of the time.

(16) May's parents are pleased that her Japanese has improved so much, (17) but she says she still has a hard time understanding some of the songs.

(18) May says, "While in Hawaii, my teacher Harry Urata always explained everything to me. He made it seem easy."

(19) May has traveled all over, from Hokkaido to Kyushu. (20) In the process, she has learned all about Japanese gourmet foods.

(21) Two years ago May was the winner of the "Star Tanjo." (22) Last year, she made her debut in Japan and (23) is already a popular talent.

(24) May began studying hula at the age of five, and (25) started music lessons with Harry Urata at the age of seven. (26) She was a runner-up in the Miss Teenage Hawaii contest in 1974. (27) Her real name is Cid Akemi Yokomoto. (28) She is a graduate of Roosevelt High School.

Box 8.2 *JAPANESE* Version, *May Yokomoto*

May Yokomoto[27]

(1) "I hosted a program called 'World Circus' with Masaaki Sakai. The film of the show came from London, and I had to do things like dress-up like a clown, and fly on a trapeze in a large studio. I'm happy."

(2) The parents of May Yokomoto keep a close eye on this modern girl who speaks Japanese fluently.

(3) She is fresh as a young sweet-fish splashing on the water.

(4) When she speaks of Japan, she continually uses the word *tanoshii* (happy). (5) Some examples of her happiness are ...

(6) When she appeared twice on Sanshi Katsura's program "Let's Get Married," she was paired with two of her fans, and she ended up winning both times; and now she has two tickets for a Hawaiian vacation.

(7) She now lives in an apartment near Tokyo Metropolitan University by herself, and since she cannot read Japanese, she has difficulty with the trains. (8) However, many strangers recognize her on the street and help her.

(9) She has traveled in her work from Hokkaido to Kyushu, and has been able to sample a variety of local foods. Etc...

(10) "Well, there are bad things too, but I forget those."

(11) She is perfectly open and friendly. (12) Because of this she is loved by everyone.

(13) "However, when I don't grasp the meaning of the songs I sing it's terrible. There are lots of words that don't appear in the dictionary. At those times I think back on all the help with the language I used to get from Mr. Urata when I was in Hawaii."

(14) She began hula lessons at five, and at seven she began singing lessons with Harry Urata. (15) She began with a song called something like "The Doll with Blue Eyes."

(16) The TV programs she appears on frequently are singing shows like Star-Tanjo. (17) Last year she had a 2 1/2 hour radio program on Radio Kanto called "Teach Japanese to May." (18) The last program at the end of March was done via international telephone from Hawaii.

(19) This time she has returned home in conjunction with an appearance on Star-Tanjo in Waikiki, and for a magazine frontispiece picture session with Sakiko Itoh.

(20) May Yokomoto, who was elected two years ago as Hawaii's new star on Star-Tanjo is a lucky girl whose looks and talents were noticed, and who has been sought after for commer-

cials for leading companies, for magazines, and for TV after her debut in May of last year. (21) She has released her third record called "Anata chance yo."

(22) Her real name is Cid Akemi Yokomoto.

(23) She graduated from Roosevelt High School. (24) She is a pure Hawaiian product, and was a runner-up in the Miss Teenage Hawaii contest in 1974.

virtue of exposure to different mass media. Furthermore, because the discourse events occur between Hawaii and Japan, differences in spatio-temporal relations reverse some of the ideational content. The Japanese discourse organization is further affected by sociolinguistic factors that compel its author to seek acceptance of the Hawaiian character by the audience of Japanese nationals. Finally, these differences in audience and purpose result in different organizational patterns apart from the purported circular nature of Japanese discourse.

Depth of Description

That the audiences did differ in location appears so from the content of the articles, as Table 8.1 shows:

Table 8.1 Depth Of Description

Item	English	Japanese
May's apartment is	in Tokyo [10]	near Tokyo Metropolitan University [7]
May samples Japanese	gourmet food [20]	local food [9]
May's background is	ø	Hawaiian [24]

Note: The university mentioned is not particularly renowned and is probably familiar only to residents of Tokyo. *Gourmet food* likely refers to the standard fare found in Japanese restaurants abroad but does not recognize local specialties in Japan.

As seen in Table 8.1, the Japanese text is specific in a way that residents in Japan would appreciate. The greater detail about her apartment hardly can be significant for those without direct experience in Japan. In fact, Hinds provided more detail in his translation than does the original. Although the name of the university is Tookyoo Toritsu Daigaku (Tokyo Metropolitan University), the original Japanese article gives it merely as *Toritsu Dai* ("Metropolitan U."). Furthermore, this university is not located in the city of Tokyo but in Hachioji City, which is in Tokyo prefecture[28] or the Greater Tokyo Area. Tokyo is the name of both a "city" and a prefecture. A prefecture is somewhat similar to a county. My point for raising this technicality is twofold: The abbreviated naming of the university suggests the informal nature of the article, as well as suggesting that the Japanese article expects its audience to have cultural knowledge about Tokyo (that the English readers may not have).

Moreover, the Japanese text treats the item about food differently: It uses the concept of *local* versus that in English, *gourmet.* There is a subtle difference that only people very familiar with Japan would know: Regional cuisines can be quite different in Japan. For example, marriages between those who come from different regions are expected to have some "friction" about different tastes for *miso* soup, a staple in the Japanese diet. "White" (*shiro*) is favored in western Japan (e.g., Kyoto, Osaka); "red" (*aka*), in central Japan (e.g., Nagoya); and mixed (*awase*) in the east (e.g., Tokyo). *Gourmet* food hardly can suggest the potential regional conflict that *local* can. Thus, the English and Japanese audiences appear to be treated as though they possess unequal familiarity about Japan. One reason is that the Japanese article could have originated in Japan but later reproduced in Hawaii. The audiences may well have been in different countries, a factor left uncontrolled by Hinds.

Assuming that most Japanese Americans have yet to travel to Japan, it is unlikely that a writer knowledgeable about Japanese Americans would write "over their heads." Consequently, it seems more likely that the text was written for Japanese nationals. Whatever doubts there are seem to retreat once it is noticed how differently May's Hawaiian background is handled by the English and Japanese versions.

Residents of Hawaii, especially Japanese Americans, would not need information about the ethnicity of one of their community's popular figures; consistent with this expectation, the

English text makes no explicit mention of May's ethnicity. In contrast, the Japanese version does mention her ethnicity, raising the question of why the Japanese text seems uncharacteristic for Hawaii. The best answer seems to be that the text is not meant for Hawaiians at all, but for Japanese nationals. (As suggested earlier, Hinds's methodology does not appear sensitive to having an audience of Japanese nationals.) A question, however, would still remain as to whether those Japanese nationals are in Japan or Hawaii. The answer to this question is "in Japan," as the next section attempts to show.

Spatio-Temporal Relations

The English text begins with May's return to Hawaii; conversely, this information appears near the end of the Japanese text (sentence numbering is Hinds's):

English: May Yokomoto returned to Hawaii recently [1]
Japanese: This time she has returned home [19]

The difference is all the more striking if the Japanese readers are also Hawaiian; they would presumably share the same anticipation of May's return as evident in the English version, even more so because May is also a member of the Hawaiian (Japanese American) community. One possible explanation is that the Japanese readers are in Japan (at least psychologically) and have been aware of only May's presence, unlike the Hawaiians waiting for her return. Consequently, time frames are reversed depending on whose perspective is adopted in reference to May's coming and going.

Additional support for different spatio-temporal frameworks arises from a choice made between the temporal conjunctions *when* and *while.* These two words differ respectively in reference between a point in time and duration. Although they overlap in meaning, *while* may impart a greater emphasis on duration.[29] It is this function of duration that seems to be exploited in the English version reporting May Yokomoto's past music lessons in Hawaii:

English: ...while in Hawaii ...[18]
Japanese: ... when I was in Hawaii. [13]

The English version seems to affirm May's Hawaiian identity; the Japanese, to underplay it. (Both writers had similar linguistic options in their respective languages.) The choices made also appear consistent with spatio-temporal frameworks related to May's absence from Hawaii (for Hawaiians) and to May's presence in Japan (for Japanese nationals). If we were to agree that the Japanese text was for an audience of Japanese nationals rather than Hawaiians, we may further agree that some differences in text organization resulted from variations in spatio-temporal relations and perceived information gaps. Whereas the former accounts for a reversal in propositional orders between the Japanese and English texts, the latter, as will be shown next, anticipates a similar result.

Information Gap Between Audiences

Why did the Japanese text open with excerpts from an interview dialogue about May's regular participation on a weekly television show? To be sure, various reasons are possible. If the readers are really avid fans of hers, however, they would already know about her television appearances. It could be that the writer anticipates reader lack of familiarity here. Although the Hawaiian television station, on whose behalf the text was distributed,[30] knows its viewers' background by virtue of the station's programming, no such knowledge would necessarily exist for an audience made up of Japanese nationals. Consequently, reference to May's television show, which is not devoted to her singing, may function to bridge perceived information gaps of the average Japanese reader. He or she may be unfamiliar with May as a pop singer, but being a television viewer, know her from the television show. In contrast, the English-language counterpart is on more knowledgeable grounds, and so the opening sentences can dispense with this information about May.

The early occurrence of dissimilarity in spatio-temporal relations and topic familiarity may profoundly affect the short text's overall organization. How significant the effects could be is unknown; nevertheless, because these differences were not included in Hinds's analysis, this oversight may weaken the conclusions his study makes. His conclusions seem less than convincing because his analysis ignores possible differences in purpose between the texts.

That the Japanese text does differ in purpose from the English seems apparent from how certain content differences relate to sociolinguistic factors between Japanese Americans and Japanese nationals. Before we demonstrate how sociolinguistic factors may have prompted different purposes for the Japanese text, a brief sketch of Japanese society may prove helpful.

Sociocultural Factors

Japanese social relations display high degrees of homogeneity, hierarchy, collectivity, and conservatism. These social aspects, conditioned by the country's island status, high population density, and centuries of self-imposed isolation from the world, cause the Japanese to be overly sensitive to ethnic and physical differences. Because of this sensitivity to difference, it is virtually impossible for *gaijin* or "foreigners" ("best translated as 'outsider'"[31]) to enter into full membership in Japanese society.[32] Foreigners are so strongly associated as outsiders that some Japanese abroad may even refer to the native people there as *gaijin,* suggesting that it means more broadly *non-Japanese.* In effect, the foreigner in Japan is kept at "arm's length," and this distancing from the outsider, in turn, reinforces Japanese insularity. Although the forebears of the Japanese Americans of Hawaii came from Japan, they were mainly from the peasant class in the south of Japan[33] and therefore were probably speakers of a low-prestige dialect. Japanese sense of social class and region, even today, may make it difficult to gain social acceptance on the Japanese mainland. It is thus very likely that a Hawaiian publication would assume the role of May Yokomoto's advocate when addressing Japanese nationals about this prized "hometown girl."

Professional entertainers, of course, are regularly promoted by their agents. In May Yokomoto's case, however, it may require more than the usual promotion. Regardless of how lucrative or respectable her profession is in the west, to the traditional Japanese, May is a female engaged in less than esteemed employment. For example, the son of Akio Morita, the founder of the Sony company, is reported to have been nearly disowned by his father because he thought of marrying a popular singer.[34] In this regard, it is not uncommon for young Japanese female pop stars to retire soon after marriage.[35] Besides her "problems" of gender and occupation, May is also an offspring of Japanese emigrants. Thus the most effective promotion would most likely seek to offset May's negative status. Curiously enough, her promotion does not begin by announcing her musical achievements, but by establishing the following points:

(1) May comes from a respectable family.
(2) May comes from good stock (ethnic or national).
(3) May is young and virginal but still sophisticated.
(4) May likes Japan (a great deal).
(5) May can be trusted as a foreigner.

To establish these points tactfully and in a few paragraphs is a formidable task indeed! Bearing this in mind, let us observe how it is done.

In a society stressing collectivist social interactions, one's responsibilities to others are ever paramount. In the Japanese text, May's parents seem respectable because they adhere to their parental duty:

English: [May's] parents are pleased that her Japanese has improved so much ... [16]

Japanese: [May's parents] keep a close eye on this modern girl who speaks Japanese fluently. [2]

Such duty, being virtuous, is accorded high prominence in sentence rank. Furthermore, close parental supervision suggests that May is young and a "sweet thing" (*kawaii-mono* in Japanese), qualities consistent with a traditional female role:

Japanese: [May] is fresh as a young sweet-fish [*ayu*] ... [3]

A principle of social psychology says that we tend to like those who like us. The author of the Japanese text, as compared to the one in English, tries to use this principle in May's favor. One can discern this subtle difference in what follows:

English: [May] is having a good time in Japan doing commercials, television, and radio work. [4]

Japanese: When [May] speaks of Japan, she continually uses the word *tanoshii* (happy). [4]

The Japanese version focuses on Japan as the source of May's happiness; whereas in English, Japan's contribution seems only coincidental. The choices made by the writer in Japanese seem rather predictable, given the issue of foreignness for Japanese nationals.[36]

This last item, along with the positive moral values that parental supervision, family cohesion, and virginity convey, serves the same social function as, for example, a *meishi* (calling card) does as a means of social introduction in Japanese society. Japanese social interaction crucially depends on a *meishi,* for the card informs one about another's occupation and thus his or her place in society. This information elicits the correct behavior relative to the hierarchical status (superior or inferior) of interlocutors, and more meaningfully, it evokes the appropriate stylistic level of Japanese (*keigo*) to be used. A *meishi* then can engender respect and deference from others, important social lubricants in Japanese society. As a result, in mainstream society, social interaction between strangers only properly begins with the presentation of one's *meishi*.

The next item engenders May's trust as a foreigner by stating overtly that she is extremely well liked:

Japanese: [May] is perfectly open and friendly. Because of this she is loved by everyone. [11-12]

On the other hand, the English text ignores her many possible friends in Japan and only perfunctorily mentions her personal characteristic of friendliness:

English: the friendly eighteen-year old was kept busy by photo sessions ... [2]

Finally, the Japanese text asserts that May comes from good stock, and therefore gratifies the Japanese desire for purity[37] or a Hawaiian author's ethnic pride:

English: ø

Japanese: [May] is a pure Hawaiian product ... [24]

The last two items from the Japanese text could have been placed earlier, but they seem to function as reinforcers of the positive image of May. Moreover, tactfulness may dictate that these points be dispersed throughout the text.

The more one considers these contextual differences and realizes that both texts may have come from the "same set of notes,"[38] the more the Japanese text appears to have ulterior motives. It is almost as if the Japanese writer exhorts the reader to accept May, a change from a focus on content to a focus on the addressee. Therefore these texts differ in purpose, which makes their comparison invalid for demonstrating culture-specific rhetorical patterns.

Because audience and purpose were insufficiently treated, the very factors that most determine patterns of discourse,[39] the researcher ended up trying to match noncomparable texts. An important point was missed: "Many [texts] employ one mode to fulfill the functions of another."[40] Rather than a single type, most actual texts combine various genres.[41] This adds up to a flexibility of discourse that may be incompatible with a strict structural view.

Would it be unreasonable for the Japanese text to be nonlinear, assuming that it seeks May's social acceptance on the Japanese mainland? Who has not been tactful, indirect, or roundabout with emotional topics? The rhetoric of nearly any politician is a prime example. Moreover, the "discovery" that Japanese writing may proceed along a baseline is less momentous than thought, because a full range of straight-line to circular discourse is possible in any language.[42] Examples of baseline theme in English can be found in advertising by which a product's value is reiterated throughout. A Radio Shack electronics store had an advertisement in which each paragraph stated a separate claim about the store (e.g., service, product quality, availability, etc.), and each paragraph ended with *Nobody Compares!* This refrain reiterated a "baseline theme" of store superiority.

Another example is Governor Cuomo's speech at the Democratic Convention in 1992 endorsing Bill Clinton for president. His speech, read as written discourse the next day in major newspapers, strategically used the phrase *We need Bill Clinton* or its derivatives as a baseline theme to promote his endorsement.[43] It was reported that Cuomo endorsed Clinton "with far more spirit and passion than many had expected."[44] It was Cuomo's rhetorical baseline theme that I contend helped make the speech impassioned and neutralized anxiety about Clinton's character.

Because *baseline theme* in English discourse was ignored entirely, it hardly can be assumed unique to the Japanese. Reviewers of cross-linguistic studies also ignore these vital points.[45] They accept too uncritically research purporting that Japanese written discourse is circular in style. One explains that baseline theme in Japanese is due to the lack of "advance organizers."[46] Advance organizers, an author's early orienting statements about how the text is organized, even if rare in Japanese, are absent in the English version of the May Yokomoto article. The same reviewers[47] similarly erred in accepting later cross-linguistic studies by Hinds that had mistaken a Japanese genre of poetic prose[48] for "exposition."[49] In such a genre, advance organizers are rare, as they would be in English, as well. The lack of critical view is so evident that one of these reviewers accepted research without apparently having examined it.[50]

Of the many aspects that cast doubt on Hinds's analysis, there is one that is indisputable. This fact goes a long way in explaining the different feel in reading the May Yokomoto texts. It so happens that contrary to Hinds's presentation, the May Yokomoto texts were actually published under different titles: "Mei [May] Yokomoto" in Japanese but in English, "May Yokomoto: Japan, it's a lot of fun." Because the difference in titles went unreported by Hinds, his article gives the false impression that these texts had the same starting point. In fact, he reduced the English title to read only *May Yokomoto*.[51] The actual title in English suggests a specific perspective, whereas the Japanese is left open-ended. Although that in itself could suggest a cultural difference, it may as well be due to genre—the entertainment guide or fan magazine. Such magazines, in either language, may allow articles about personalities to be no more than a loose collection of gossip information. Hinds's disregard of the titles highlights his overemphasis on structure or form to the neglect of function—author's purpose in this case. Different purposes may engender different strategies and organization of writing rather than culture per se.

Cultural differences exist, but that fact does not lessen concern for the effects of bias on research results. Unless researchers are able to assume the frame of reference of those whom they study, and unless they attempt comprehensive discourse analysis[52] whereby form and function are linked within their context of situation, efforts in contrastive studies of discourse are likely to be inadequate. Without accounting for author intent and other factors through "rhetorical profiles"[53] or text subtypes,[54] contrastive rhetoric is likely to match noncomparable texts, as the May Yokomoto texts appear to demonstrate. Cultural differences are bound to occur because discourse consists of multiple features.[55] A serious problem emerges, however, when the matter involves logic or thinking patterns. Thus cautioned, one may avoid the potential pitfalls associated with classifying cultures according to their presumed discourse style, from linear to circular in form.

CONCLUSION

Continuing the theme of contextualism, this chapter endeavored to contrast functional versus structural approaches to language. A reanalysis of a previously published cross-linguistic study of Japanese and English revealed a confounding of variables. Moreover, a social tension between Japanese Americans and Japanese nationals was suggested to offer a more compelling account of the "structure" found in a related Japanese news article. At the same time, the value of a functional or sociolinguistic analysis over a structural one appeared manifest. In order to understand cultural logics, their premises must be ascertained and that requires understanding the related context.

APPLICATION

1. How does grammatical structure differ from discourse structure?
2. How does the issue of *discourse structure* have special importance to cross-cultural studies of discourse?
3. Why does familiarity for a topic impact a study in contrastive discourse that compares a news article written in two different languages?
4. What important variables are related to a cross-linguistic study of a news article, or actually, any writing?

9

Contrastive Rhetoric: A Further Inquiry

In the previous chapter, the insensitivity to the context of sociocultural differences between Japanese nationals and Japanese Americans appeared to ignore the primary factors of discourse organization, audience, and purpose, leading to confounded results. In making such a statement, perhaps it becomes necessary to consider other related research pertaining to the contrastive rhetoric between Japanese and English. At the same time, this line of research may also prove instructive concerning the role of context in cross-cultural comparisons. Indeed, as I attempt to demonstrate, a number of contextual factors emerge that prompt a rethinking about cross-cultural research design, as well as cautioning previous characterizations of Japanese *expository* writing as circular in organizational style.

The oversight of context seems most unfortunate, for insufficient safeguards appear to be made against the influence of the image of Japanese inscrutability. Without such safeguards, research hardly can approach social scientific standards marked by reliability and validity, possibly destining research to become nothing more than shouting matches. This is important to realize for aspects of Japanese culture may not be what they appear nor as simplistic as assumed.

Rhetoric includes multiple features from local (sentential) to global (textual) levels of discourse;[1] hence, organizational patterns like that of Kaplan's typology are but some of the many possible rhetorical differences. And his example of his Oriental type (a Korean sample) was highly convoluted. So, the mere questioning about classifying Japanese expository writing as circular does not necessarily deny that Japanese and English differ rhetorically. Rather, the major concern is with the methodology of this line of research and the implications for cross-cultural comparison and understanding.

JAPANESE NONLINEAR STYLES: AN OVERVIEW

In Chapter 8, a review was made of Hinds's study of Japanese expository writing. However, Hinds also reported[2] two other styles of Japanese expository writing: tempura and *ki-shoo-ten-ketsu*.[3] With an apparent empirical basis, his studies are widely cited in support of the contrastive rhetoric hypothesis and cognitive schema theory as well. Hence these Japanese styles have acquired much practical importance. Yet a serious examination suggests that the evidence for the existence of these "styles" yields little support. For any number of reasons, theoretical, methodological, or empirical, each of these claimed "styles," as reported appears unfounded. It should be noted that this conclusion pertains only to contrastive rhetoric and not to any of Hinds's other research, such as conversational analysis.

Regardless of intuitive appeal, however, contrastive rhetoric or any other idea must be tested and confirmed. Research given uncritical acceptance is likely to become overgeneralized. For example, a teacher of writing, associated with a prominent university in the United States, once remarked scornfully that if the editorials found in Japanese English-language newspapers were any indication, then the hypothesis of contrastive rhetoric must be correct.

Asked what was objectionable about the editorials, the teacher replied that the point or opinion was never stated until the end. Yet withholding the opinion until the end is just how editorials are organized in English.[4] Apparently, having heard of the supposed "indirection" of the Japanese, that teacher was made to "see" indirection in their written English. Perhaps those Japanese editorials were "different" for another reason; nevertheless, that individual appeared rather misinformed. A similar fate could be in store, unless one becomes more conversant with the claims of contrastive rhetoric and associated issues.

In making further inquiry into contrastive rhetoric, the present study is limited to the overall organization of Japanese expository writing. The present concern is with propositional orders or the transition of ideas beyond the paragraph level, which is in keeping with Kaplan's apparent amendments to his program.[5] As such, the present inquiry concentrates on the research in Japanese contrastive rhetoric most known to the fields of Japanese linguistics, ESL (English as a second language), and intercultural communication, namely the nonlinear styles of Japanese exposition reported by Hinds, although his research is not the only reviewed.

As was found with the reported baseline theme style, research demonstrating the other two styles appear to lack sufficient attention to situational or contextual factors. Related issues concern "pre-scientific" notions about Japanese culture and language, and of the English paragraph, and how these notions reinforce the view that Japanese expository writing follows a predominantly circular style of discourse.

Tempura Style

Hinds contended[6] that Japanese newspaper writing has a style "similar to tempura [fish fried in batter] in that the superfluous batter must be removed before the content can be known."[7] That seems to mean that Japanese professional journalism commonly is superfluous or obscure. Such claims naturally require substantive evidence. Hinds's conclusion, however, seems to rest entirely on the observation of several sample Japanese texts translated into English by Yutaka Yutani,[8] texts provided for pedagogical demonstration not scientific inquiry. In fact, Yutani never stated that tempura represents a style. Consequently, the evidence appears insufficient for proposing this so-called style.

The Tempura Metaphor: Its Interpretation

Yutani's article[9] discussed procedures for translating Japanese newspaper articles into English. He indicated that in following the inverted pyramid format (a common newspaper form), writing a summary lead[10] is of primary importance. According to Yutani, the (summary) lead is so important that once it is written, the rest of a translation comes easily. "Translation, however, requires much caution, because Japanese news articles are similar to 'tempura' fish (fish fried in batter) with a lot of wheat flour."[11] He further stated that "the flour must be removed first in order to find out the contents—fish. If the fish alone is translated, an excellent news story in English is forthcoming."[12] He then translated a three-sentence article into English, demonstrating that the lead for the English article developed largely from the final clause of the Japanese.

At this point, one may very well think that Japanese journalism appears rather superfluous, a quality disapproved of in handbooks of English writing. Yet much depends on how "a lot of wheat flour" is interpreted, for Yutani never stated explicitly its meaning. Indeed, "a lot of wheat flour" can be alternatively interpreted to mean the normal secondary details between an article's initial sentence and its conclusion, if the original article does not conform to the inverted pyramid style. In this case, one would have to sift through secondary details to find the conclusion. And Yutani did associate a story's conclusion with the lead.[13] In other words, Yutani's tempura metaphor can represent an information search (for the story's conclusion) in the case of Japanese-language newspaper articles that do not conform to the inverted pyramid style, common in news writing.

If Japanese-language news articles are superfluous to the extent that the superfluity must be removed before the content is known, then the writing is sure to be obscure from start to finish. One can bet that translation would be difficult throughout its process, not only at the beginning. The view of the tempura metaphor as an information search is further reinforced by Yutani stating that "the method of *discovering* the 'lead' is the first prerequisite in the translation of a Japanese news story, though the *detection* of same is rather difficult for beginners."[14] As an example, Yutani produced a summary lead for one article and then stated, "The Japanese news story is, as it were, straight news and easy to translate, because it is *not* camouflaged with 'wheat flour.'"[15] Yutani's tempura, then, seems to refer to the search for a story's conclusion at the start of translation rather than to a "superfluous" surface quality of Japanese newspaper writing.

How Representative Are the Data?

If some noteworthy contrastive features of Japanese are perceived in Yutani's samples, it is one thing to suggest their presence; it is quite another to insist that these differences are indicative of a style. In fact, Yutani did not see fit to publish any information about his samples: no dates, no sources, no page numbers. He even left out mention of the sampling method used. It is impossible, therefore, to deduce how representative Yutani's samples are of Japanese-language newspaper writing.

Moreover, the Japanese samples were presented without their newspaper headlines.[16] This omission looms large, especially in the case of articles not conforming to the inverted pyramid format, because newspaper headlines function to summarize an article[17] and thus orient the reader. An article without a headline is more likely to be judged incoherent than one with the headline intact. (Here "incoherent" refers to the superfluity of making content opaque.) Consequently, the absence of headlines may have biased Hinds's findings. In short, methodological flaws prevent any generalization beyond the samples themselves, and no substantiation of a tempura style (or any other) has been made.

Do Contrastive Features Inhere?

Despite the lack of support for a style, it could be argued that contrastive features do inhere in Yutani's samples. As Hinds stated, "Yutani's examples demonstrate that the lead in an English news story must appear as the first sentence. In Japanese news stories, on the other hand, the initial parts of the article often contain details, with the lead buried almost three-fourths of the way into the article."[18] Thus Hinds made at least two assumptions:

(1) English news articles must have a lead in the first sentence. (Presumably, Hinds meant that English news articles must conform to inverted pyramid style.)

(2) Japanese news articles have leads deep within the text. (Presumably, Hinds meant that Japanese news articles do not conform to inverted pyramid style.)

Hinds seemed to make a non sequitur because a lead is merely the "opening line or paragraph of a news story."[19] Technically, therefore, it would be impossible for any newspaper article to have its lead (first sentence) buried within a text as Hinds stated. The expression "to bury a lead" would make sense only from the point of view of inverted pyramid style, but Hinds did not make this distinction explicit enough. (In this style, the first sentence becomes a summary lead containing the gist of the story.) The lack of this distinction, I believe, is symptomatic of a greater failure to acknowledge other styles of newspaper writing in English.

Hinds's second assumption, if qualified with *sometimes*, appears true, because some of Yutani's Japanese samples do not conform to inverted pyramid style. Qualifying Hinds's first assumption in the same way, however, may remove the likelihood for contrastive differences, at least for the present discussion. Consequently, Hinds's use of *must* in his first assumption appears expedient because it sets a standard for English by which the Japanese-language samples can be compared. If the Japanese departs from this purported precept of English, differences must then occur. A singular problem arises, however: Hinds did not provide any evidence for the assumption that English newspaper articles must conform to inverted pyramid style.

Apparently, then, Hinds based his view of English newspaper writing on Yutani's English translations.[20] But these are writings of Yutani's and not, of course, from an English-language press (in countries where English is the mother tongue, that is). Therefore, Hinds's view seems dependent on Yutani holding the same premise that English newspaper articles must conform to inverted pyramid style. Yet Yutani based his article on an earlier study of his that reported that non-inverted style (the absence of a first-sentence summary lead) occurs in English newspaper writing, and demonstrated such occurrence with American and British press articles along with named sources.[21] The occurrence of a purposeful non-inverted pyramid style in English is corroborated elsewhere.[22]

More surprisingly, Yutani stated that inverted pyramid style (first-sentence summary lead) has actually declined in news journalism in favor of what he calls, British style.[23] This revelation, if true, would require distinguishing American and British news writing before comparison with Japanese, a task Hinds did not perform. Equating the two presses may not be a fair assumption to make. For example, the British press apparently does not enjoy as much freedom as that of the American press according to a Freedom House Survey.[24] Whether that difference of freedom would have appreciable rhetorical effects is unknown. However, such reports do suggest possible rhetorical differences unforeseen by Hinds.

Although inverted pyramid style is the standard for news reporting, the opposite style still may function to heighten the drama of an event or to replace "stale" summary leads made obsolete by the saturation of the news through telecommunications.[25] In other words, there is no *must* about first-sentence summary leads in English. They are quite frequent but not absolutely necessary. As a result, the tempura style, as Hinds presented it, proves unsupported.

The early development of modern Japanese-language newspaper writing followed strict narrative form and ornamental style (as western journalism once did); today, Japanese newspaper writing is of a style similar to that of western newspapers.[26] Corroboration[27] is also found that a summary lead frequently begins Japanese news articles.[28] Because the Japanese modern newspaper began much later than those in the west,[29] some vestiges of earlier periods may persist, a matter to be proved by verifiable and replicable evidence. Until such proof develops, claims for the so-called tempura style are best laid to rest.

Ki-Shoo-Ten-Ketsu Style

Originally, *ki-shoo-ten-ketsu* was a four-part poetic form borrowed centuries ago from China and only much later adapted to prose. Hinds defined these four parts as paraphrased below:

1. *Ki* [pronounced *key*] begins an argument.
2. *Shoo* [pronounced *shoh*] develops it.
3. *Ten* turns the (developed) argument or idea into a subtheme connected to, but not directly associated with the major theme.
4. *Ketsu* brings everything together and forms a conclusion.[30]

Of the four, Hinds designated the last two, particularly *ten,* as diverging the most from patterns of English prose organization.

To prove this contention, Hinds used the feature column *Tensei Jingo*, from *Asahi Shimbun*, a Japanese newspaper.[31] *Tensei Jingo* is not only purportedly organized according to *ki-shoo-ten-ketsu*, the column also appears in translation in the *Asahi's* English-language daily. English and Japanese versions of the *Tensei Jingo* were read by native speakers who were then tested for recall. Among the test results, paragraphs classified as *ten* were significantly better reproduced by Japanese subjects than American. Because *ten* supposedly digresses considerably from the main theme, Japanese familiarity with *ki-shoo-ten-ketsu* apparently made the difference in giving the Japanese superior recall. Or did it?

Regardless of how Hinds attested to the quality of the *Asahi Shimbun's* translations,[32] the fact remains that the texts were not translated for cross-cultural experimentation but for domestic consumption by readers in Japan. Different purposes can result in rather different methods and standards of translation. Although Hinds did verify the texts' linguistic (clausal) equivalency, he showed no sign of performing back-translation or similar procedure, a necessary step when using translations in cross-cultural research.[33]

Such a procedure helps ensure semantic fit between original and translated versions and greater reader receptiveness to a translated text. Failure to perform this procedure may produce unequal test conditions for experimental subjects and is evident in a paragraph taken from the English version of *Jogging for Health*, one of the texts used by Hinds.[34]

I chose this paragraph not only because it appears flawless on the surface, but also because it is a *ten* paragraph reproduced by the Japanese subjects in significantly better detail than by the American subjects:

> We are in such poor physical condition that when we are dragged out to play sandlot baseball and slide into second base

> at full speed, we feel as if it is the end of the world for us. Consequently, we are not qualified to talk about running, but we do know that running increases one's ability to absorb oxygen and prevents aging.[35]

Though this paragraph is coherent enough, it is doubtful whether many American college students could or would relate to playing sandlot baseball while in poor health, feeling unqualified to talk about jogging (running), and being personally concerned with aging. Moreover, some female readers may be unreceptive to this passage because of the talk of playing sandlot baseball. This problem of reader receptiveness arises from error in translation and adversely affects the English text only.

The English text had the disadvantage of possibly appearing presumptuous to the reader because it used the all-inclusive *we* in reference to matters personal to the author. Conversely, the Japanese author referred only to *hissha nado*—someone like me (that is, like the author).[36] The Japanese writer, with both options of reference at hand, chose to be restrictive for good reason. Hence the Japanese students were possibly more comfortable or less distracted with their text.

American subjects also had to confront foreign terms, nonidiomatic expressions, illogical constructions, and a lack of contextual knowledge (see Box 9.1). Even though these defects may be few in number, they likely made reading and recall that much harder for the American than for the Japanese student. Moreover, similar problems arise in most of the other texts that Hinds used.

Errors of translation and use of foreign terms may not always directly impair comprehension; they may, however, lead test subjects to devalue the text. A wealth of evidence suggests that even the slightest aspects of language use can elicit unfavorable evaluation from others.[37]

Even if a text of Hinds's were unflawed, *Tensei Jingo* articles invariably suggest their foreign (Japanese) authorship, thereby possibly raising expectations of flaws and lowering the reader's opinion of the text in the process. A native speaker is especially prone to expect flawed language, at least unconsciously, when given the task of evaluating a foreigner's English in an experiment. This point applies particularly to Hinds's study that compared value judgments by American and Japanese readers on these articles.[38]

Box 9.1 ***Jogging for Health*** [39]

Jogging is a method for maintaining health by running. In jogging you run at a leisurely pace in accordance with the condition of your body. If you get out of breath, you walk. You do not overdo it. The late President John Kennedy first proposed it, and the running method of maintaining health is now a worldwide fashion.

Immediately after arriving in Japan, President Jimmy Carter ran in the compound of the American Embassy. Leaving the United States at 2 a.m. two days before, according to Japan time, he was busy with preparations for the summit meeting during the plane trip, which took about 16 hours. Since he ran immediately after arrival, he apparently has considerable physical strength.

We are in such poor physical condition that when we are dragged out to play sandlot baseball and slide into second base at full speed, we feel as if it is the end of the world for us. Consequently, we are not qualified to talk about running, but we do know that running increases one's ability to absorb oxygen and prevents aging.

According to books, there were once races for the training of warriors. The Hagi warlord made young warriors cover a distance of 125 kilometers in one day. There were professional runners called "haya-bikyaku" (speedy couriers). It is reported that in the Edo (old name for Tokyo) period, the relay "hikyaku" ran the distance from Tokyo to Osaka in about 60 hours. Two couriers talked to each other as they ran. At night one courier carried a light. Since there were mountains and rivers along the way, they ran at quite a fast pace.

In Japan also there was the tradition of running fast. But it was for the purpose of training and for the work of "*hikyaku*." There apparently was no running at a leisurely pace for the sake of one's health. According to Mikio Oda, in the current marathon boom in Japan, there is a strong trend toward the group racing and a preference for marathon meets.

There are many people who enjoy running at a leisurely pace by themselves early in the morning or late at night, but on the other hand there are not a few people who are deeply attached to records and rankings. The competition just before the goal line is very dangerous for amateurs. Despite this, nip-and-tuck races are run, and some runners die.

Running in a group is dangerous. In Oda's warning, "Run by yourself!" there is criticism of civilization.

How adverse the test conditions were for American performance is not the point here; such problems, however, should not occur if reliable results are needed. If back-translation and other methods had been employed along with greater care in selecting the articles, these problems could have been avoided. No matter how uniform the apparent differences in performance were between Hinds's American and Japanese subjects, Hinds's related findings[40] must be declared inconclusive because of unequal testing conditions. At best, these studies remain suggestive until more rigorous research is carried out.

Ten—Linguistically Cued?

Hinds marshaled further evidence to prove the widely digressive nature of *ten* and thereby his view that *ki-shoo-ten-ketsu* diverges considerably from English written discourse, by asserting that *ten* is initiated with a linguistic cue, the Japanese topic marker, *wa*. Among its various functions, "*wa* presents a topic that has already been mentioned and hence is old information."[41] While *wa* marks old information, Japanese has another particle, *ga*, which functions to introduce new information.[42] Because *ten* favors digression, it must necessarily present new information, and so an apparent inconsistency arises. Logically, therefore, one would expect *ten* to be initiated with *ga*, not *wa* as Hinds contended. However, this inconsistency may serve to highlight *ten*, and its digressive turn as purported by Hinds. More likely than not, however, the use of *wa* this way could confuse the reader. He or she may have to backtrack for information that was never there in the first place.

Initially, what would appear a compensatory structure for the reader really seems to be a double-edged sword. Hinds apparently tried to solve this dilemma—by relying on the explanation that Japanese readers are expected to be more tolerant in matters of style,[43] but depending on circumstances, this may or may not be true. Although Hinds's notion is an alluring one, as shown later, it appears inapplicable to the *Tensei Jingo* articles.

Hinds may be perfectly correct about *wa*'s linguistic function, but only scant support was provided. Because linguistic rules hardly ever operate without qualification, the strength of *wa* as a cue for *ten* becomes an important issue in confirming Hinds's claim. Fortunately the relation between *wa* and *ten* should be especially testable, because the apparent inconsistency of the *wa* function must make the Japanese reader doubly aware of digression. To test the *wa* and *ten* relation, I made preliminary tests,[44] and the results are presented below.

An Experiment on the **Wa** *and* **Ten** *Relation*

Two articles were selected containing paragraphs designated by Hinds[45] as *ten* and reproduced in significantly more detail by his Japanese subjects than his American ones. Next, each text was de-paragraphed (indentations removed) and read by Japanese college students, who were asked to paragraph the text. Assuming that *ten* is digressive and Japanese readers define a paragraph as a unified idea,[46] the strength of *wa* as a linguistic cue for *ten* should be demonstrable by how often the participants correctly choose the original author's paragraph indentation for *ten* (initial sentence with topic marker *wa*).

As noted by Hinds, three significant *ten* paragraphs appear as paragraph three in *Jogging for Health* and paragraphs five and seven in *Throwaway Chopsticks*.[47] All three paragraphs begin with a *wa*-marked phrase. Each sentence of the text was placed evenly at the left margin, in original sentence order and sequentially numbered.

The participants totaled 70 in number for the *Jogging* article, and 40, for *Chopsticks*. Each participant read only one article, i.e. took part in only one group. Each participant "indented" the paragraphs by circling the number of the sentence. They were instructed that this circle represented an indentation, or the start of a paragraph. That this was indeed understood to mean the beginning of a paragraph is attested to by the fact that all the participants "indented" the first sentence of each text.

The most relevant results of this experiment are shown in Table 9.1. Only case C has considerable agreement between the test participants and the original author.

These results might be unremarkable had Hinds not maintained that these very paragraphs are linguistically cued. If the premises of my experiment are valid, then the function of *wa* as a linguistic cue for *ten* seems rather unclear—at least for the texts considered. It should be noted that this experiment was meant to be exploratory and has its limits. Nevertheless, the

Table 9.1 Agreement With Original Paragraphing

CASE	TEXT	PARA-GRAPH	PERCENTAGE OF AGREEMENT	N
A	Jogging	3	16%	70
B	Chopsticks	5	13%	40
C	Chopsticks	7	98%	40

mixed results do caution against rash acceptance of Hinds's view of *ki-shoo-ten-ketsu* simply on the hint of being cued by a linguistic structure.

Hinds performed additional research suggesting a correlation between *wa* and digressive (*ten*) information.[48] This additional evidence, however, is based again on *Tensei Jingo*, data shown here to be inapplicable for Hinds's purposes. Reviewers also have expressed caution, though for different reasons.[49] Before demonstrating the inapplicability of the *Tensei Jingo*, it would be instructive to consider the meaning of *digression* and how Hinds determines *ten*.

Ten *as Digression— Its Determination*

When Hinds, in the context of presenting contrastive features of Japanese, speaks of *ten* as a "turning" or an "indirect theme," he means, one may presume, a digression or a "straying from the main topic." Thus one is given the impression that digression is unacceptable in English. Yet digression is a standard device in the familiar essay[50] and a valid option in rhetoric as well.[51]

Digression can be used profitably, for example, to make an account more interesting, or to establish solidarity with the reader with the "this reminds me of" anecdote. Even in scientific or academic discourse, digression can be used to ensure reader readiness for what is to come.[52] Indeed, "parenthetical elaboration is found in all communication, albeit with differing roles across differing forms."[53] Therefore, it must be decided when a digression is acceptable and what criteria are used in its determination. The need for such criteria becomes urgent when foreign texts are involved, because cultural blind spots may make a digression seem inappropriate or incoherent. Unfortunately, Hinds did not address this issue, nor did he establish the criteria that he had used in determining the *ten* paragraphs for his texts.

Our only recourse is to rely on Hinds's explication of digression, but if *Jogging for Health* is any indication, then his notion of digression (*ten*) appears dubious. According to Hinds, in this text, "Paragraph three constitutes the first *ten*, or indirectly related information in this essay. It represents an abrupt change from the general topic of jogging with the development of that in Paragraph two concerning individual joggers, to a perspective which is introduced by talk about being in shape and playing baseball."[54] His description seems to describe a rather bizarre text (which first led to my present research).

Hinds's description, however, is misleading. He ignored the major perspective of preventive health measures (note the title) and its Japanese context, which tie together the subtopics of jogging, baseball, and physical condition. To help the reader along (as not everyone has been to Japan) the three paragraphs are summarized here from a Japanese cultural standpoint:

(1) Given the newness of jogging for health in Japan, the Japanese author defines jogging, indicates its popularizer (President Kennedy), and its popularity (a world-wide craze).

(2) Next, the second paragraph reports that President Carter immediately went jogging after a long flight to Japan, with the implication that he is vigorous and dedicated.

(3) Evidently impressed with this apparent American excellence, the Japanese author then contrasts his or her own poor physical condition by telling how hard it is even to run the bases in baseball (a common Japanese pastime). (Japanese insularity often compels them to make such contrasts with westerners.)

Hinds's claims would be borne out only when digressive *ten* can be validly determined. That determination of *ten*, I submit, has yet to be demonstrated.

Previous Findings—A Simple Explanation

If the *Tensei Jingo* articles do turn out to be inherently digressive with *ten*, there is a simple explanation for it. As Hinds reported, *Tensei Jingo* is a daily column, and a translated version appears the next day in an Asahi Shimbun-affiliated English daily.[55] Later, these articles are collected and published quarterly in book form. What Hinds neglected to report is that the original Japanese form of *Tensei Jingo* first appears in the newspaper without a title. Only in the later book collections do the Japanese versions get titled. Absence of a title is atypical for Japanese prose; hence Hinds was led astray, it seems, in insisting that *Tensei Jingo* is representative of Japanese expository writing. (In fact, he also never gave full bibliographic information for the *Tensei Jingo* in his research articles.)

As pointed out earlier, titles (newspaper headlines) have an orienting function. Their absence allows a writer one less way to prepare the reader. The importance of titles is cogently illustrated in this example:

> With locked gems financing him, our hero bravely defied all scornful laughter that tried to prevent his scheme. "Your eyes deceive," he had said. "An egg, not a table, correctly typifies this unexplored planet." Now three sturdy sisters sought proof. Forging along, sometimes through calm vastness, yet more often over turbulent peaks and valleys, days became weeks as many doubters spread fearful rumors about the edge. At last, from nowhere, welcome winged creatures appeared signifying momentous success.[56]

This text immediately becomes coherent once its thematic title, "Christopher Columbus's Discovery of America," is known. It is hard to imagine the absence of a title as anything but a disadvantage for the *Tensei Jingo*; that is, if *Tensei Jingo* is classifiable as expository writing.

It so happens that the classification of *Tensei Jingo* is unclear to those I have interviewed in Japan, including staff members of the *Asahi Shimbun*. In general, respondents are more likely to consider *Tensei Jingo* in the *zuisoo* (random thought)[57] genre, although they also recognize it has some qualities of the *zuihitsu* (a traditional literary form of random jottings akin to the diary[58]). "In the *zuihitsu*, the writer either openly or implicitly declares that s/he intends to jot down anything, just as s/he pleases and as the moment suggests."[59]

But the *Tensei Jingo* seems far more focused than the *zuisoo* or the *zuihitsu*. Newspaper staff, when pressed further, tended to call it simply a "column." Prudence, then, urges us to treat *Tensei Jingo* and the like as a separate genre (other major Japanese newspapers publish similar columns[60]). As seen in the previous chapter, the mixing of modes is common in written discourse. For example, prose can take on the functions of poetry and is termed *poetic prose*.[61] Therefore, the genre that Hinds had been tapping into may not be expository.

Absence of title also explains Hinds's recourse to his cultural typology of writer-reader responsibility, the idea that cultures differ according to how much responsibility the reader must bear in making sense of a text.[62] Without titles, authors are less restricted to stay on track; consequently, readers must assume more responsibility for orienting themselves. In the case of *Tensei Jingo*, this arises more from a matter of situation than of culture. However, I do not deny that the Japanese receivers may have relatively more responsibility than their counterparts, say, in English. That seems so about speech, as noted in Chapter 1. What I am questioning is whether responsibility on the receiver is operative so broadly as Hinds wished to apply it.

Even if it were shown that some Japanese tend to be more digressive in thought or writing, it still is not proof positive of an overall prose organization, such as Hinds's *ki-shoo-ten-ketsu*. His appears to be a classical version and not the modern one—a correlate of the western rhetorical model. Hiroaki Yamashita, a former professor of classical Japanese at Nagoya University, maintained that *ki-shoo-ten-ketsu* never achieved the dominance necessary to become "imprinted" as a Japanese rhetorical style.[63] Although this Chinese poetic style has received attention, the Japanese have had a number of indigenous forms that lessen whatever influence classical *ki-shoo-ten-ketsu* may have had. Classical *ki-shoo-ten-ketsu* does have a natural order of its own; written characters associated with it readily suggest this order; and with skillful application, this form was applied to prose.

More importantly in the modern version, *ten* can be treated as counter-argument or elements of conflict, and not necessarily as digression, a point found corroborated in related research of student writing.[64] Further confirmation comes from informants who speak of *ki-shoo-ten-ketsu* opposing digression, such as this

Japanese college teacher who says: "When I find digression [in my drafts of Japanese prose], I feel uneasy because I didn't follow *ki-shoo-ten-ketsu*." Whether home grown or western inspired, the modern form of *ki-shoo-ten-ketsu* disapproves of unwarranted digression. Hence it is not necessarily in opposition to western rhetoric, and Hinds may have tapped a distinct poetic genre, a genre related only remotely to academic writing—if at all.

On several counts then, Hinds's claims for *ki-shoo-ten-ketsu* can only be considered suggestive, but here one assumes that the poetic genre that he studied can interfere with expository writing. This interference is unlikely; communicators are not bound to only one mode or style. Moreover, for the poetic mode to be transferred, prior competence with it would first have to be demonstrated, a mastery not demonstrated by Hinds for his Japanese participants. As a result, Hinds's claims await confirmation.

In passing, some studies[65] assume that *ki-shoo-ten-ketsu* is different from English, on the sole grounds that four parts exceed the familiar three-part Aristotelian form. There is nothing sacred about three parts; four parts are also consistent with Aristotelian thought.[66] In this case, the body contains the exposition and confirmation (arguments for and against).[67] Unfortunately, the frequency with which English prose is visualized as three parts can lead to unnecessary confusion. Indeed, one trainer in public speaking skills contends that academic presentations, spoken or written, consist of four parts: introduction, body, climax, and conclusion.[68] Later, we shall see one other four-part English form in more detail. I might add also that a five-part English form has been proposed.[69]

Modern *Ki-Shoo-Ten-Ketsu*

Barbara Easton addressed the question of whether the modern *ki-shoo-ten-ketsu* interferes with English in a case-study of a Japanese graduate student writing a thesis at an American university.[70] Based on successive drafts of the thesis and the feedback received from the student's professors, Easton concluded that the refusal of a professor to completely read an earlier draft and other negative responses were due in part to *ki-shoo-ten-ketsu.* Surprisingly, she found that the problem did not stem from *ten* and *ketsu* as predicted under Hinds's view, but from *ki* and *shoo*. As she explained, *ki* and *shoo* led to an indirect style; the student's introductory section became too lengthy, thereby obscuring the thesis statement.

Whatever the problem, it did seem to occur early in the draft because a professor gave up reading it. If it is a matter of transfer, these differences should be ascertainable because Easton pinpointed when the student relinquishes her native language rhetoric in favor of an English one: between the first and second drafts. Their comparison, then, should show how different *ki-shoo-ten-ketsu* really is. Normally, a text in English has questionable reliability in this regard; however, the Japanese student confided that her first draft was organized according to *ki-shoo-ten-ketsu*, and identified these four parts for Easton. The student's claim may or may not be true, but it is still worth investigating.

Before reading Easton's study any further, I compared the differences between the two drafts. Each paragraph was reduced to a summary statement and placed in original serial order. Next, these statements were compared, and a change of order was found between two paragraph blocks. Easton reached a similar finding, but we differ in interpretation. Let us first review Easton's explanation.

According to her, the rearrangement of paragraph blocks was made within *ki* boundaries of the first draft. Combining these two blocks corresponds to the introduction in an English paper's organization. Easton seems to accept that the student's problem was indirectness caused by Japanese *ki*: Instead of announcing the thesis statement at the outset, she spent too much time in the "arousal of interest." By reversing paragraph blocks, the thesis statement was "put up front." Easton may be correct but, I believe, for the wrong reason.

An alternative explanation considers the functions of each of the paragraph blocks in question. Essentially, the student inappropriately presented the problem before the situation, using E. O. Winter's formulation of information presentation.[71] Generally, information is presented in four parts: situation, problem, response, and evaluation, or SPRE for short. If the audience, however, is well aware of the situation, a writer need not mention it and can begin immediately with the problem. If the situation is given, however, it must come before the problem in keeping with a natural sense of time progression.[72] Thus, the student may have upset the reader's sense of natural progression

Chart 9.1 Reversal of Situation-Problem Paragraph Blocks

DRAFT 1
Javanese Rural Elite: Protector of the Peasant Mass or Exploiter?

PROBLEM

1 Villages are affected by negative influences of the central government.
2 The paper focuses on how rural elites have adapted to outside influences.
3 The villages are becoming less autonomous because of national political parties, the military, and past national identities.

SITUATION

4 Rural settlement is based on autonomous and cooperative units.
5 Village units are under a headman, *lurah*.
6 Villages were traditionally autonomous and more concerned with local than national life. Kinship loyalties were stronger than the ties with national levels. Elite and peasant had a reciprocal relationship.

DRAFT 2
Democracy and the Function of *Lurah* in Rural Java

SITUATION

1 Javanese villages are autonomous agricultural units under *lurah*.
2 Social relations are based mainly on land ownership, and its scarcity led to political factions.
3 Village leaders needed villagers' support to keep power, so some democracy existed.

PROBLEM

4 Recent national politics changed functions of village leaders and have polarized much more the differences between rich and poor.
5 Changes are a matter of adaptation of leaders to different roles created by outside forces.
6 The purpose is to trace these changes in villages based on outside influences.
7 Changes are affected by the region and other factors.
8 The main changes polarized further the rich and the poor and decreased village autonomy.

from situation to problem (see Chart 9.1).

Whether *ki-shoo-ten-ketsu* actually reverses this form is an interesting question, but one that requires more investigation. Equally likely, however, is the possibility that Easton's student was incompetent with the Japanese form. In either case, additional research is required.

Finally, a more likely explanation concerns the changes in the thesis title made by this student, Yumiko. The revision process may have made her thinking more crystallized or focused, resulting in greater clarity of writing. Whether coincidental or not, she shifted from the purported Japanese organization to an English one, at the same time that a major change in title occurred with her second draft (see Table 9.2).

Easton notes that the change in title from the first to last "focuses more precisely" on the main issue of concern, a political, rather than an economic one.[73] Though Easton does recognize this major change in title, she leaves it at that without considering the influence on overall organization of the thesis.

Yumiko's apparent "angular progression," as termed by Easton, may have been due more to the student's confusion about topic or, perhaps, the complexity of handling two major perspectives (political and economic) at the same time. On the other hand, it can be argued that the preciseness of topic occurred after a change in organizational pattern from Japanese to English. Direct or linear writing, however, proceeds after one already knows his or her point. For Yumiko, only after realizing her main issue of concern was she able to effectively organize her thoughts and her next major draft, which she had had nearly six months to develop.[74]

Table 9.2 Progression Of Title Changes

Draft	Title
1	"Javanese Rural Elite: Protector of the Peasant Mass or Exploiter?"
2	"Democracy and the Function of *Lurah* in Rural Java"
3	"Trends in 'Democracy': The Cases of Javanese Villages"

In summary, several alternative explanations exist for Yumiko's incoherent writing, including student ineptness with *ki-shoo-ten-ketsu*, lack of topic clarity, and violation of a possible English (or universal) principle of presenting the situation before problem. In any case, additional research is required. Easton's assertion[75] that *ki-shoo-ten-ketsu* interferes with academic writing in English remains inconclusive.

This conclusion, of course, does not end the debate on *ki-shoo-ten-ketsu,* nor should it; but contradictions do exist between its classical and modern forms. If one finally accepts Easton's position, how can the directness of *ki* be accounted for in Hinds's classical version? To compound matters further, there are factors that may induce indirection, such as first language (*L1,* as it is called) transfer of cohesive devices;[76] Asian deference for superiors;[77] and incompetence with orienting strategies in English.[78] To these factors, I would add another: Asian perceptions that their ESL teachers are naive about Asian culture. Until such social, developmental, psychological, and grammatical variables can be sorted out, claims for the divergence of *ki-shoo-ten-ketsu* from English must remain inconclusive, no matter how indirect Japanese communications may appear.

THE JAPANESE MYTH OF UNIQUENESS

For many reasons, the Japanese language is fertile ground for comparative studies in the social sciences, so continued research can be expected in the future. Notions of nonlinear Japanese thought and rhetoric, however, often seem to spring from the supposed intuitive character of the Japanese, which causes them to be indirect, even vague with their language. For example, Hinds tried to buttress his program with quotations from a Japanese author,[79] which claim that the Japanese enjoy incoherent prose. This point suggests a dichotomy commonly heard in Japan: The "intuitive" and "feeling" Japanese versus the "cold" and "(overly) rational" westerners. Is this dichotomy really any different from wartime propaganda that depicts enemy soldiers as tight lipped and grim faced, and the good guys as warm hearted and cheerful?

The Japanese, faced with the technological superiority of the west and the tragic aftermath of World War II, learned to survive through a universal remedy: belief in the human spirit. But when it came to "accenting the positive," the Japanese chose to rally around their cultural identity. In the process, the Japanese language and culture were made mystical, resulting in a myth of Japanese uniqueness.[80] According to this myth, only the Japanese can understand their language and culture, and from this privileged status, by definition, they are superior to all.

Related beliefs include that the Japanese language is inherently defective as a means of communication. Such notions have provided easy answers to international misunderstandings, as well as a way to preserve Japanese pride. If we are told by an economic and technological giant that we are "illogical," our subordinate status may be reason enough to accept the charge. Such a label need not be derogatory, for the trait can be turned around and be seen as gratifyingly "unique" or "humanistic." In this way, notions of defective Japanese communication advance the uniqueness myth.

"Although there is a certain amount of truth in [the] image of Japan as being 'different' from the west, we have to realize that many of these ideals [of Japanese 'uniqueness'] have been *consciously created* by the leaders of Japanese society."[81] Consequently, recognition of a possible myth-making of Japanese uniqueness would raise questions about related ideals of uniqueness including characterizations of the language as "vague" and so on. I do not wish to imply that such characterizations are completely without merit. Clearly, there are cultural differences that do matter. Nevertheless I do believe that careful and repeated study may be the only safeguard against delusion. It may be instructive, then, to consider the view that Japanese communication is defective a bit further.

The Vagueness of Japanese

A common idea is that the Japanese language is "vague" or "imprecise" because of its many homonyms and frequent ellipsis. An American professor of Japanese responds by saying

> No, Japanese is not the language of the infinite. Japanese is not even vague. The people of Sony and Nissan and Toyota did not get where they are today by wafting incense back and forth.[82]

Chinese is known to have numerous homonyms like Japanese and has been similarly charged as being vague. It has been pointed out, though, that context almost always is able to disambiguate the meaning in Chinese.[83] In comparison, Japanese actually is more advantaged than Chinese in this regard. In Japanese, one not only has situational clues but also syllable stress to distinguish their homonyms.[84] And as one professional translator attests, they have not posed a problem.[85]

Granted that Japanese may be "one of the most intricate languages in the world,"[86] characterizing it as vague seems rather deceptive, as Roger Pulvers, another translator indicates:

> These are the familiar clichés about the Japanese, as if the language itself were enshrouded in a misty tenuousness and its messages were all implied. The mystique of subtlety, like the mystique of ambiguity, apparently lies in unspoken words. I don't buy this. Every language, at least the ones I know, has masses of unspoken messages and implied subtleties, Japanese no more or less than any.[87]

To believe otherwise contradicts some of the most basic principles of linguistics, namely, the arbitrariness of sound-symbol relations and the importance of communicative context.[88] Edwin Reischauer illustrates how context can induce clarity in Japanese writing:

> Japanese can be made very clear-cut .... It can be perfectly clear and Japanese scientists learned they had to make things clear in that way. Japan has developed a great science and is much appreciated in the rest of the world. The work of the Japanese scientist can be put directly into English and spread around the world....[89]

Comparing scientific articles, incidentally, would be a logical first step in contrastive rhetoric, as this genre may provide "culture-free" content. Such content may lessen the cultural bias that certainly must ensue when observations are made between low-context and high-context cultures. Moreover, scientific genre and the like are most relevant to the tasks of foreign college students, for whom the field of contrastive rhetoric first began. Yet empirical studies of these genres are disappointingly absent.[90] To ignore genres with the most promise for straight-lined discourse is to confine contrastive rhetoric to mere speculation.

Nevertheless, Japanese is still quite different from English, and foreign speakers of the language must learn native speaker rules of use. When a speech encounter affectively seems vague to a foreigner, often times the foreigner has not attended to the most significant contextual cues, assumed certain pretexts of information, or both. Impressionistically, Japanese social speech appears to use much ellipsis (omission of words), and intended vagueness does exist. Yet, native speakers, of course, apprehend the meaning. The point is that perceived vagueness is often a matter of Japanese social norms, not the language per se.[91] The Japanese can be crystal clear, if they choose to be. Vagueness is not inherent with the language. To believe otherwise invites linguistic chauvinism.

According to Shibatani, the characterization of Japanese as vague is just one of the many myths surrounding the language and is "undoubtedly a reflection of the inferiority complex on the part of Japanese intellectuals toward western civilization."[92] Perhaps with the enlarged role Japan has been playing in world affairs and the increasing numbers of western students of Japanese, more realistic images of the language may result.

Japanese Indirectness

Another relevant belief concerns the indirectness of Japanese. The Japanese do show a tendency for indirectness and is most relevant for formal social situations. My intent is not to deny that. Rather, it is to question its presumed basis for Japanese written discourse, especially academic and technical genres. First, indirectness is a questionable term, as Pulvers so eloquently puts it:

> In fact, because of the set conventions of mutually recognized formalities built into Japanese, and because of conventions used at times for convenience sake when deeper communication is unnecessary or would cause friction, one can say that the Japanese language is highly explicit. Something which is left unsaid yet is mutually understood is about as clear a signal of communication as human beings can produce. It's the kind of explicitness we strive to attain on the stage, for instance.[93]

Although the Japanese may tend to be less confrontational

and to value silence more highly than North Americans, such views have their limits. Patricia M. Clancy, for instance, states that "fear of eye-to-eye [contact] ... is common among young adults in Japan...." She bases this largely on Y. Kasahara's report on eye-contact phobia. His report, however, developed from his observations of Japanese psychiatric patients. Furthermore, a careful reading of his report reveals that this psychiatrist in his practice has personally encountered only five cases of the phobia in question![94] Five psychiatric patients are hardly sufficient to classify an entire population as Clancy unwittingly appears to do.[95]

The phobia is not as rare in the west as Kasahara or Clancy would have us believe either. According to Kasahara "the fear of eye [contact] does not exist in the [western psychiatric] literature."[96] Nevertheless, a word exists in English for the phobia—*ommetaphobia.*[97] Westerners are not immune from this fear or phobia. The condition is rather prevalent among shy Americans, for example.[98] It is quite possible that mental health professionals, other than psychiatrists, are treating this in the US and in other western countries. Finally, such treatment could subsume eye-contact fears as a component of shyness or other social dysfunctions.

Japanese indirection may not become just distorted; it may also become mystified:

> The basis of [the Japanese style of communication] is a set of cultural values which emphasize *omoiyari* 'empathy,' and are so widely shared that overt verbal communication often is not required. Thus in Japan, the ideal interaction is ... one in which each party understands and anticipates the needs of the other and fills them before any verbal communication becomes necessary.... [I]f all is going well, there should be no need for speech.[99]

Clancy translates *omoiyari* here, as *empathy*, departing from its dictionary translation as *sympathy*.[100] If the psychological literature agrees about anything, it is that sympathy and empathy are not synonymous. By making empathy, and not sympathy, the basis of *omoiyari*, the role of silence may become exaggerated, thereby possibly mystifying Japanese communication.

A better translation for *Omoiyari* is "consideration for others."[101] Empathy is rather different. Roichi Okabe seems to realize this, for he chose to transliterate empathy into *empashii*, suggesting that the term in English has special meaning.[102] His choice seems both pragmatic and realistic, considering the conceptual complexity of empathy (see Chapter 2).

Empathy, as a psychological term, referred first to a type of motor mimicry and was later changed in clinical contexts to connote a state of understanding others,[103] so elusive that counselors and psychotherapists spend lifetimes in its pursuit. If the Japanese practice something so readily that requires lifetimes for specialists in the west to attain, then it would seem the Japanese verge on being paranormal. Besides the difficulty with viewing the Japanese as paranormal, anyone would be hard pressed in distinguishing Clancy's "empathy" from "sympathy" in actual Japanese social interaction.

In regard to *silence*, though Americans seem to value it less highly than the Japanese, some specialists caution that its function in American society is "complex and profound."[104] What is professed as ideal and what is actually practiced may be two very different things. Compared to American society, the role of silence in Japanese social interaction, then, may be exaggerated. Dean C. Barnlund concurs, stating that his findings suggest that the "Japanese use of silence as a communicative strategy is more myth than reality."[105] (This point, however, does not deny that silence is more highly valued in Japan than in North America.)

Another problem with the indirect style thesis is a lack of broad sampling of communicative behavior. The behavior most observed and cited involves Japanese formal social routines and hierarchical relations. Certainly this behavior is an important facet of Japanese culture; nonetheless, it does not mean that the Japanese cannot employ varied styles of communication. Although the Japanese, for example, may refrain from direct eye-contact in certain formal situations, for informal contexts, the "exact opposite is true."[106]

Another point concerns an apparent lack of awareness by observers about eye contact in their own culture. The way North Americans sometimes talk about Japanese avoidance of eye contact seems as though North Americans typically gaze eye to eye. But that is unfounded. Consider the findings of the psychiatrist Albert Scheflen, a premier figure in interpersonal communication, who found much less eye contact between Americans than is typically assumed:

> In face to face conversations, the orientation of middle class Americans is rarely eye to eye. Each fixates his macular vision at a spot somewhere between the cheek and shoulder of the other fellow, just out of the range for eye-to-eye gazing. ... A dominant listener may look the speaker fully in the face, but more often he looks just to the speaker's left or right and he may look down if he is under criticism or look up to the ceiling, as speakers do, to indicate thoughtfulness. ... Reciprocal speakers tend to look at each other's faces in narratives. They do not, however, look in one another's eyes except in a direct, aggressive confrontation or in a sexual, courting exchange.[107]

Finally, the Japanese indirect communication style is based largely, if not entirely, on speech situations and thus has only indirect relation to Japanese expository writing. Because the Japanese are observed using *keigo* (polite and respectful language) in speech and acting deferentially to their interlocutors, it is assumed that such behavior is diametrically opposed to the intellectual confrontation found in exposition; consequently, the Japanese are expected to follow a circular style of rhetoric. Yet writing is usually performed outside of direct social contact. In fact, the author of expository writing may never actually meet his or her audience. One would expect, therefore, the absence of *keigo* in Japanese academic writing, and that is actually what is found, with few exceptions.

An interesting example of how the Japanese differentially employ *keigo* in speech and writing is found in journalistic news reporting (ignoring genre for the moment). Japanese television news broadcasts use keigo, but newspapers generally do not, paralleling a common association of *keigo* with speech.[108] Although *keigo* is commonly associated with speech, it can and does occur in certain types of writing (as is well known). Those types may include personal letters and stories. However, the genre most pertinent to my discussion, academic writing, appears free of *keigo*, and the same is true for formal essays in magazines, according to my own informal investigation. The absence of *keigo* in writing may suggest a desire to be free of social encumbrances. If so, would the absence of *keigo* also indicate that writers of academic prose are under fewer social constraints than speakers having the same purpose and audience? If so, would fewer nonlinear rhetorical patterns be found in writing than in speech?

How significant the different uses of *keigo* really are remains unknown, for "a sociology of Japanese writing has yet to be produced."[109] Few assertions can be made for either side of the issue. One thing can be said however: The Japanese indirect style of speech may not necessarily carry over to Japanese written exposition.

Reflecting Mirrors Between Japan and the West

As noted in our early chapters, the west has characteristically viewed Japan as mysterious. Brian Moeran terms this exoticized and orientalized view of Japan by the west, *Japanism*.[110] What is particularly interesting in Moeran's thinking is the potential for Japanism to become self-reinforcing by stimulating Japanese self-images of uniqueness: "[Japanism] has now been taken over by the Japanese themselves as they, for their part, attempt to set themselves apart from, restructure, and thus gain authority over, 'the West' through what is known as *Nihonjinron* ('discussions of the Japanese'). In other words, Japanism exerts a three-way force—on Japan itself, on Japanists (or 'Japanologists'), and on western consumers of Japanism."[111]

In the realm of cultural images, this three-way force may be operative, in part, how the Japanese see themselves as "uniquely unique." At one time or other, the west had viewed the Japanese as being so extraordinarily different, that *Our Job in Japan,* as seen in Chapter 3, viewed the Japanese brain as "unique" (as a problem). In this light, it is not surprising that Tsunoda has since proposed that the Japanese brain is, in fact, unique.[112] Serious consideration of his theory is beyond present scope but suffice it to point out its possible relation to the "three-way force" of cultural imaging.

Because of the tendency to view the Japanese as inscrutable and their ways as paradoxical or irrational, and the possible influence of this Japanism on *Nihonjinron* (Japanese uniqueness theories), it is especially incumbent upon the researcher in cross-cultural studies to demonstrate that his or her findings are fueled by much more than surface impressions. Otherwise, how can one be assured that the research is not an artifact of the "three-way force" of Japanism? Given the complex sociology enveloping discourse processes, anything but frequency studies[113] would seem highly inadequate for advancing the view that one culture fashions its discourse in a way already considered aberrant, especially with an aberrance having social consequences (cf. "straight" vs. "circular" thought in American culture).

The Uniqueness Belief—
Its Psychological Payoff

Of all the people who should confront pre-scientific notions about their own language, the Japanese themselves are least disposed to do so, as these notions are part and parcel of the uniqueness myth. Some Japanese may even feel comfortable with such notions, for they serve to confirm the popular wisdom that Japanese culture is beyond western comprehension.

To this day, foreigners who show special appreciation of Japanese culture are more often than not called *henna gaijin* (strange foreigner). Consequently, charges of being irrational are not taken too seriously by many Japanese. If anything, such charges may be seen as a defensive reaction of a west widely viewed in Japan as selfishly individualistic, and hence, deficient in humanistic values.

Distinguishing ourselves from others is nothing new: Note how regional, social class, ethnic, and subculture differences may be perpetuated within a society through speech variants in accent and syntax.[114] Note also that dress may perform a similar function.[115] Cast in this light, the thinking behind *henna gaijin* and extreme beliefs in Japanese uniqueness may be rooted in a similar need for group solidarity. Thus when the same Takao Suzuki who is among those spearheading the uniqueness myth[116] asserts that the Japanese like incoherent prose, one probably should take it with a grain of salt.

Suzuki's point may deserve more credit than has been given here, but all cultures, not just the Japanese, are capable of using a poetic mode in communication.[117] Whether *objets d'art* or not, products of the poetic mode can still be enjoyed even when not understood. However, the purveyors of Japanese uniqueness seem to think that this mode is the exclusive domain of the Japanese themselves. Some things Japanese may well be incomprehensible, much as an individual's internal experiences are beyond anyone else's complete understanding. In the case of the uniqueness myth, however, that truth seems to be stretched beyond reason.

STRUCTURAL VIEW OF THE PARAGRAPH[118]

Structural paragraph refers here to a "deductively" organized group of sentences "locked into place" and serving as a "self-contained unit" of discourse. This kind of paragraph, in a strict sense, is conceptualized as being as stratified as that of a sentence. Francis Christensen, a major champion of this view, explained that

> the paragraph has, or may have, a structure as definable and traceable as that of the sentence and ... can be analyzed in the same way.... I have come to see that the parallel between sentence and paragraph is much closer than I suspected, so close, indeed, ...[that] the paragraph seems to be only a macro-sentence or meta-sentence.[119]

A Foundation of Contrastive Rhetoric

The paragraph as a macro- or meta-sentence is not a new idea but a pedagogical tradition dating back to Bain, a 19th century rhetorician.[120] From this tradition, Robert B. Kaplan forged his contrastive rhetoric. That Kaplan's linear paragraphing did have such roots seems clear from his teaching paragraph patterns and syntactic patterns by nearly the same method[121] and his advocating the Christensen paragraph model.[122] Since then, however, debate has raged between structural and functional views of the paragraph culminating in accommodation and a more flexible view of the paragraph.[123] Therefore, Kaplan's original conception of linear writing may have been unrealistic and his nonlinear classifications as well. In other words, contrastive rhetoric may require a new research criterion.

With the advantage of hindsight, one should remember that ideas are as much a product of the times as the person who voices them. During the time of Kaplan's inception of contrastive rhetoric, the structuralist or formalist view of the paragraph was clearly dominant. One cannot fault Kaplan for embracing what probably seemed the most reasonable model at that time. Nevertheless, the roots of contrastive rhetoric need to be made clear for understanding the amendments Kaplan has made and the direction contrastive rhetoric is likely to take in the future.

The Platonic or Ideal Paragraph

Ultimately, it may be argued, "the fact that paragraph structure is taught shows that there is an ideal standard."[124] Perhaps, but only if educators know what is ideal to begin with. Perusal of the related literature will show that recognition of an ideal standard is far from an open-and-shut case. As Paul C. Rodgers, Jr. observed, expository paragraphs may be a function not only of logical, and formal, but also "physical, rhythmical, tonal, … and other rhetorical criteria,"[125] and he concluded that

> Paragraphs are not composed; they are discovered. To compose is to create; to indent is to interpret. Accordingly, the qualities of the paragraph can no more be grasped through normative statement than can the qualities of discourse.[126]

Another compositionist sums it up well: "One finds paragraphs with apparently more than one main idea, paragraphs with implied main ideas, multiple paragraphs that can be collapsed into one, paragraphs of one sentence and paragraphs of pages. Faced with this onslaught of qualifications and appendages, rhetoricians have begun to question, if not reject, the paragraph as a viable unit....[127]

What has been increasingly called into question is exactly the "ideal standard" invoked by Hinds. A century ago, it was pointed out that conceptions of the paragraph arose from pedagogical reasons, not empirical ones.[128] Furthermore, "there may be as many types of paragraphs as there are ways of developing an idea. Exhaustively to enumerate these types would be useless and would require an arbitrary method."[129] As a result, compositionists have settled for general principles, which is reasonable as long as some flexibility is retained.

There may be an ideal, but it has not yet been uncovered, in spite of the voluminous findings of the cognitive sciences on the subject.[130] In short, "there is no single *correct* way to make paragraphs, but only a range of *motivated* ways."[131] As a result, "most current researchers have stopped looking for a Platonic paragraph, and instead seek to identify and describe different kinds of actual paragraphs."[132]

The "ideal standard" appears more as a stop-gap measure in treating the academically unprepared than as an actual criterion of English prose. Christensen said it all when he stated, "I doubt that many of us write many paragraphs the way we require our charges to write them or that we could find many paragraphs that exemplify the methods of development or the patterns of movement."[133] Pedagogy has its own purposes, and in some ways even the paragraph-as-sentence analogy may be useful in certain cases. The objection is making the structural paragraph of pedagogy the only measuring stick for contrastive rhetorical purposes.

A Questionable Unit of Research

It may be no accident that Kaplan soon abandoned paragraphs for paragraph blocks but then even larger discourse units: "The fact remains that in order to make significant claims about the nature of written text, it will be necessary to examine rather long segments, perhaps whole books."[134] Moreover, he admits originally "having made the case [for contrastive rhetoric] too strong."[135] The general disaffection with the structural paragraph had probably influenced this turn of events.

Researchers would likely favor the smallest reducible unit for research possible. Kaplan's forecast for the study of "whole books" seems to sound the death knell for the structural paragraph as the unit of research for contrastive rhetoric. Thus, structural approaches to the paragraph may be built on shaky grounds, and their use as English paragraph models may make Japanese nonlinear discourse more apparent than real.

DIFFERENCES IN RHETORIC BETWEEN JAPANESE AND ENGLISH

The questions we ask determine much of what we will know. Asking whether rhetorical styles in English and Japanese differ is hardly sufficient without also asking how and when they do differ, and what difference it makes. Too often, it seems, impressions are taken as prima facie evidence for Japanese circularity of discourse. For instance, a Japanese states a preference for reading philosophical works in English rather than in her own native language. Does this preference indicate psychological or substantive differences? If the latter, does it qualify as a rhetorical difference? If rhetorical, does it manifest an overall organization pattern, such as Kaplan's English or Oriental styles? These are a few questions that seem rarely to be asked.

In the same vein, several other issues arise regarding the rhetorical differences of Japanese discourse. These issues pertain to lexical differences, taxonomical concerns, culture as the determinant of discourse linearity, and differences between American and British rhetorical patterns.

Lexical Differences

To hear of a preference for English over Japanese does not mean ipso facto that Japanese expository writing is circular or even indirect. Some American psychologists may prefer German to English for certain kinds of conceptual analysis.[136] Certainly, this preference for German does not qualify English as nonlinear, nor does a similar preference for English necessarily make Japanese any less linear.

In some areas one language may have a more differentiated vocabulary than another. An additional factor is a bilingual's relative ability between English and Japanese. As "an equal command in two languages ... is extremely rare,"[137] a bilingual's impression of a language's degree of linearity may sometimes be swayed by differing vocabulary held or the previous experience with a particular genre.

Finally, Japanese may simply require a larger vocabulary than some other languages: Indeed, some evidence suggests that "in order to read a text in Japanese, we have to know a considerably larger number of words than if we read a comparable text in a European language.... These statistical studies support the informal observations of many foreign learners: [E]ven after years of working with the language one has to accept that words one has never seen before will be coming up on every page of a Japanese text."[138] Impressions about English or another language being "clearer" than Japanese, therefore, may have more to do with differential vocabulary than propositional ordering per se.

Taxonomical Concerns

Beyond psychological and lexical differences, a need exists to develop a clear taxonomy of rhetorical devices and strategies. Eugene Nida made a start in that direction.[139] Rhetorical devices and strategies may or may not be related to discourse linearity. It has been said that Japanese texts appear to contain fewer topic sentences and supporting details than those written in English. Even if this were true, it would still not mean that Japanese texts can be characterized by the wildly digressive example text given by Kaplan for his Oriental category. (Kaplan, in fact, explicitly excluded Japanese discourse from his Oriental category.) Nor would it necessarily mean a nonlinearity of any kind, as much depends on other discourse features, such as implied topic sentences and the sophistication level of the audience. (High-context cultures may obviate the need to overspecify textual detail. This would mean a contrastive rhetorical difference, but not necessarily in global or overall organization patterns of discourse.) In short, written discourse involves a broad range of local and global textual features, as well as factors of audience and purpose. To say that Japanese differs rhetorically from English may mean little without also specifying which rhetorical features and under what conditions.

Culture—The Determinant of Discourse Linearity?

Central to Kaplan's thesis seem to be the assumptions that "Logic (popular), ... the basis of rhetoric, is evolved out of a culture; it is not universal"; and that English linear style derives from a "Platonic-Aristotelian sequence [of thought], descended from the philosophers of ancient Greece and shaped subsequently by Roman, Medieval European, and later western thinkers."[140] Given these premises and Kaplan's graphic depictions of various languages, it appears that he visualized the English "straight-line" pattern as the archetype of western thought or rhetoric. Culture, therefore, seems to be the determinant of rhetorical patterns. On the contrary, I wish to suggest that culture plays only a secondary role in accounting for the apparent cross-culturally different overall patterns of discourse reported by Kaplan. (With rhetorical differences other than overall patterns, culture may be more directly related.)

"The dominance of [cognitive structures characteristic of modern scientific and professional contexts] is not at all 'natural'—indeed, they were not dominant in western cultures prior to the rise of modern science...."[141] Substituting "industrialization" for "modern science" in this comment may explain English being an archetype of written discourse linearity, as the industrial revolution began in England. It may also explain why Kaplan could not include Japanese in his Oriental category. Though industrialized later than most of the First World countries, Japan has been industrialized for at least a century. If this substitution of terms were shown to be valid, then the degree of industrialization may prove more explanatory in power than culture as a factor of discourse linearity. As a result, Asian or Oriental may not be synonymous with nonlinearity of discourse. Care is needed, therefore, to avoid typecasting Asian languages as circular in rhetorical thought simply because of geographic location.

American and British Discourse—Identical Rhetorical Patterns?

Another question is whether American and British authors follow the same rhetorical patterns. So far, researchers in contrastive rhetoric seem to assume that rhetorical patterns are the same on either side of the Atlantic. But is this a safe assumption to make? Yutani, as seen before, suggested that newspaper writing styles between these two countries are employed in different frequencies. Further, a linguist has pointed out what he perceives to be a "rambling essay style not uncommon among British scholars."[142]

Some Japanese specialists of English see parallels between British and Japanese writing styles, though not necessarily as "rambling." For example, one Japanese professor of English literature in Japan, who trained in the United States, contends that if Japanese prose were to be characterized as nonlinear, this nonlinearity may be similar to how he perceives some British authors differing from Americans in style. Little more can be said for any such observations without substantial data in support. Such observations, however, do hint that English also may have its share of nonlinear discourse and that Japanese exposition may not be so far removed from "English" style (on overall or global levels).

On ESL Studies

Mention ought to be made about pedagogical studies in contrastive rhetoric, an area productive, if not substantive.[143] This area has presently not been included because of agreement with Hinds's rejection of methodology based on ESL classroom compositions.[144] Contrastive rhetoric seems most properly based on comparison between comparable native speakers in the respective countries being compared.

Moreover, the classroom researchers in ESL seem to neglect that even native speakers of English write illogically: "Anyone who has had the misfortune to deal with the written essays of [American] college freshmen will know how often they are vague, illogical, lacking in definition, unoriginal, and incapable of putting meaning into sentences."[145] Indeed, illogic, as a cover term for such complaints, is the most common fault found with written compositions in English as a first language.[146] Some composition teachers who have taught both Japanese and American college students find circular writing common to both groups.[147]

Similarly, two Canadian researchers compared Japanese learners of English and North American learners of Japanese, but failed to find support for the claims of Hinds and Kaplan.[148] Even though Japanese and other Asian students may seem to follow "circular" rhetorical patterns more than their European counterparts in ESL compositions, such a condition may be more a matter of sentence-level linguistic differences: Asian languages differ far more linguistically from English than do European languages. Contrastive rhetoric seems to have seriously ignored such linguistic differences.

Lastly, a cultural myth has existed that those of the advanced industrialized societies possess superior cognition or intellect to those of the traditional or less modern.[149] Such myth is seductive given our wealth and high technology. For example, a team of cross-cultural psychologists refer to "the long sad history of measuring the 'intelligence' of peoples of various cultures [as being] full of … biases … and impossible inferences."[150] The risk of bias is so great, that any foray into topics of culture and cognition—including logic and reasoning—must be approached with caution.

Take, for instance, how two linguists misapply research done with the Kpelle, a traditional society in West Africa. These linguists claim that "rather than answer abstract questions the way we do in the west, the Kpelle must have concrete knowledge."[151] These linguists say so because some Kpelle were found to give wrong answers to problems of syllogistic logic, such as:

All farmers eat well.
Ben is a farmer.
Does Ben eat well?

Correct answer: Yes (*indicative of abstract reasoning*)
A Kpelle answer: "I don't know Ben, so I can't answer."[152]

This Kpelle answer seems rather sophisticated given the potential suspicion possibly felt from being tested by outsiders (western researchers). This issue, however, is secondary to two serious errors of interpretation made by the linguists involved (Hinds and Iwasaki).

First, they assumed that such Kpelle error was due to culture, when, in fact, it was related to schooling: The more formally schooled the Kpelle were, the higher their scores were on the syllogism tests,[153] and, if schooled, they scored similar to those tested in the west.[154] Even if Kpelle schools may follow a "western" curriculum, their instructional methods and school operations appear rather different from those in the west.[155]

Second, Hinds and Iwasaki erred in overgeneralizing to the population at large without sufficient cause. Only a portion of the Kpelle produced "concrete" answers as "there [was] considerable diversity of performance [even] among the [non-schooled individuals]."[156] Moreover, poor performance on these particular tests does not necessarily preclude the use of abstract reasoning in other situations. Hinds and Iwasaki simply have no grounds for saying that "the Kpelle must have concrete knowledge" in order to reason.[157]

Michael Cole and Sylvia Scribner, two leading authorities on this topic, concluded that such studies as those with the Kpelle provided "no evidence for different *kinds* of reasoning processes" cross-culturally.[158] Such differences could still exist, but the Kpelle studies were too inconclusive to show that. Thus Hinds and Iwasaki misconstrued the Kpelle studies, which illustrates again a disregard of context by not seeking alternative explanations. As a result, their textbook, as noted in Chapter 4, seems to fall into stereotyping others. This disregard may also reinforce belief in the "primitive mind" of traditional peoples. Such belief, if operative, could have serious implications for studies in contrastive rhetoric.

CONCLUSION

However much one accepts cognitive schema theory or the Whorfian hypothesis,[159] characterizing Japanese written discourse as nonlinear seems unwarranted. The bulk of studies that advance this view lack rigor, subscribe to structural views of discourse, or both. It should go without saying that audience and purpose are vital determinants of discourse organization; yet these situational factors have been ignored in most of the studies surveyed. Until these situational factors are accounted for in discourse analysis, and agreement reached about the structure of English discourse, claims for characterizing Japanese expository writing as nonlinear remain unjustified.

Hinds appears to have since accommodated his previous view by proposing that Japanese and other Asian languages show a preference for a rhetorical style that he terms *quasi-inductive*.[160] Essentially, the quasi-inductive style appears to be between deduction and induction in organization. And because of that, English-speaking readers, according to Hinds, misinterpret the style as "induction" when it is not. He considers this misinterpretation a matter of "fallacious familiarity."[161] Yet it is not deduction either because the discourse does not immediately indicate its purpose. He calls this style "delayed introduction of purpose."[162] This delay reminds us of Collier-Sanuki's research noted in Chapter 6, which showed how Japanese conveys politeness by a delay of informational focus at the sentence level. To what extent delay of purpose is indeed manifested in Japanese prose remains an open question. Hinds's proposed style, however, seems more appropriate than his earlier characterizations of Japanese written exposition, as well as intuitively appealing given Collier-Sanuki's research. In either case, the critical points raised in this review of contrastive rhetoric would still apply.

As Hinds's research received the main focus of this review, it is only fair to mention that he had made admirable contributions in other areas in general linguistics and Japanese linguistics, including an extensive grammar of spoken Japanese. If the conclusions of this review are valid, readers familiar with Hinds's studies in Japanese conversational analysis may wonder how to account for the rather different results obtained between conversational analysis and contrastive rhetoric.

Conversational analyses have obtained firmer results because, in addition to not being strictly contrastive, they have been better controlled for situational variables. Some of these studies have used laboratory conditions, allowing the setting, participants, and perhaps even the conversation topic to be controlled. In fact, the mere choice by a researcher of his or her (student) participant, (campus) location, and instructions given before and during the experiment can act as sociolinguistic controls in themselves. Consequently, despite a structural approach to discourse, if that be the case, substantive results can be obtained. (Mention of a structural approach intends nothing more than the recognition that different choices in approaches inevitably lead to different research methodologies and results.) Perhaps, by adding the necessary sociolinguistic controls, future studies in contrastive rhetoric may achieve more substantial results than what seems to have previously been the case.

APPLICATION

1. Summarize the main faults of the studies reviewed in contrastive rhetoric and how Japanese is likely to differ rhetorically from English.
2. If you were planning to compare writing styles between Japanese and English, what steps would you consider necessary for doing this kind of study and why?

Part IV

Images of the Japanese in the Mass Media

10

Culture Clashes Between Japanese and North American TV Newscasters

To demonstrate how the best of us can succumb to ethnocentric behavior when interacting cross-culturally, this chapter follows various episodes of culture clashes that developed between Japanese and North American newscasters while engaged in a segment of an ABC News program broadcasted worldwide.[1] These segments, titled *Asia Business Now*, were broadcasted regularly by *ABC World News Now*, an early morning program (5:00 EST)[2] from New York in the mid-1990s. In each segment, the ABC anchor engaged his or her Japanese counterpart from NHK News in Tokyo via a live satellite hookup. These interactions had more than usual significance as Dick Schaap, veteran ABC news anchor, told it:

> One of the nice things about this program is that the so-called anchors [from NHK and ABC] have time to chat with one

> another. These brief but meaningful conversations help the viewers to get to know us as people and allow the anchors to form bonds long after the red light has gone on.[3]

This is an ideal, however, for cultural frictions frequently emerged during the two-year period that I had observed. In fact, Schaap actually was speaking sarcastically and anyone who had been a regular viewer would have understood. The truth be known, though, is that the North American side appeared often to succumb to ethnocentrism and tactlessness, if not irrational behavior.

Various incidents of abusiveness toward the Japanese are found among more than 50 airings that I had video recorded from Japanese telecasts. Because this involves news anchors, individuals skilled at communication and presumably well educated also, their behaviors are particularly noteworthy. Such behavior would likely surprise even the North Americans involved, for surely as professionals, they would not intend to offend anyone. Yet that does happen and unfortunately reinforces some ugly American stereotypes in the Japanese mind. That reason alone merits attention.

Moreover, the episodes illustrate the underlying process of why and how the related ethnocentrism materializes. And having professional communicators involved suggests that the same could befall any of us. By documenting these cross-cultural episodes, this chapter hopes to lay bare not only aspects of cultural styles of communication but also ethnocentrism, behavior normally unexpected from professional broadcasters—model communicators.

After a brief description of the method and procedure, this chapter will take representative discourses from the series to identify ethnocentrism on the part of the ABC personnel in the form of cultural insensitivity, cultural defensiveness, cultural narrow-perspective, and finally, related cultural metaphors. By doing so, this chapter hopes to make a small contribution in showing how culture clash or friction in communicative style may become manifested in ethnocentric behavior, in part due to cultural metaphors held about the Other.

METHOD

This study involves discourse analysis of video recordings of the TV news program in question for a two year period and began after observing friction develop between a North American (a Canadian) anchor and his Japanese counterpart.[4] Previously made recordings for another purpose added to the data base. This author, situated in Japan, had to rely on irregular broadcasting by NHK of the ABC News program. Although ABC broadcasts the program daily in the United States, NHK airs it irregularly in Japan because of various schedule conflicts. Availability was further reduced by Japanese national holidays because NHK newscasters were only carried live on the related ABC news segment. Further restrictions arose due to the personal resources and travel absences of this author. In all, more than 50 different programs were video recorded (though other observations were made also) over a two-year period.

Participants

Seven ABC newscasters of whom two were female were included. For NHK the total was four and divided equally in gender. NHK newscasters were all judged fluent in English. No attempt was made to compare unique pairings of the newscasters. Program availability and resource limitations obviated strongly against this inclusion. However, these newscasters are professional communicators (i.e., their living is made as a newscaster) and so can be assumed to be considered a model communicator in their respective countries and cultures. Thus grounds appear solid for considering them representative of their cultures.

Procedure

Discourse analysis was performed on non-news material of the broadcasts, namely, introduction of *Asia Business Now* and the Japanese news anchor, greetings made between the ABC and NHK anchors, and any conversation exchanged. Broadcast material that evidenced friction and those that did not were compared. Friction was evidenced by such elements as content, facial expression, and other nonverbal signs.

Observations were validated by having separate audiences of Japanese and international college students in Japan view the video material. The Japanese group numbered 30 in total; the international, 14, of whom included 7 Americans and the rest, Australian (2), Canadian (1), Chinese (1), German (1), Indonesian (1), and Malay (1). Agreement was adjudged if 60 percent or more of the group assented. In actuality, agreement was found unanimous with both groups that the ABC/NHK exchanges evidenced cultural friction. Further agreement found unanimous was that at least some of the North American behavior appeared ethnocentric. One respondent (German) went as far as describing the North American behavior overall as "derogatory," an assessment that was shared by many others. Thus the news broadcasts could be judged interculturally problematic with implications for North American ethnocentrism. The task then became to identify the ethnocentric behavior and its roots. To begin, it would be helpful to present some exchanges that characterize cultural insensitivity and/or ethnocentrism. Related evidence is based on actual video recordings, the dates for which are noted herein.[5]

DISCOURSE ANALYSIS

Cultural Insensitivity

At the outset, it should be stated that *ABC World News Now* is (or was) atypical even for American TV news programs. It purposely had a format of lightheartedness that encouraged ribbing between the ABC newscasters. Granting that nevertheless, my focus groups—international and Japanese—found that the North American behavior with their Japanese counterparts was highly inappropriate. Regardless of format, ABC lacked cultural sensitivity with the Japanese, as shown in the episodes that follow.

Within several days of the tragic Kobe Earthquake in Japan, ABC anchor Bill Greenwood reported grimly that the "earthquake [was] the deadliest to hit Japan in more than 70 years" with more than 4,000 killed.[6] Later in the same program, an NHK female anchor, Eriko Kojima, reported further that

> The city of Kobe put on a brave face today. Houses that only

> days ago were sources of pride and comfort are now only useful for the kindling they provide. ... The first day of the Diet session opened up on a somber note with a minute of silence dedicated to the victims. ... Repair costs as high as 80 billion dollars [have been estimated], 4 times as that of last year's quake in Los Angeles. That's *Asia Business Now* in Tokyo. Back to you, Bill.[7]

In what appeared to be insensitive, if not ethnocentric, the ABC anchor replies with glee while stretching up and out in his seat:

> Eriko, thank you. I'm sure that there are a lot of American companies that would be more than happy to sell you some construction equipment. On Wall Street this morning, folks, the Dow Jones Industrials opened the day ....[8]

Could there be any worse time to plug commercial interests than when a city, actually a nation, is still in deep mourning? Not surprising, the Japanese anchor remained silent and flashed a smile, one the Japanese term, *aisoo warai* (a flattering or ingratiating smile). This can be identified by the momentary reflex of the mouth without apparent movement of other facial areas, particularly around the eyes. This appears so with Eriko Kojima and especially if compared with her characteristic broad and sustained smiles seen during other programs.

Kojima's ingratiating smile and that of Greenwood's broad beaming appear in stark contrast. Her smile ought to be readily understood by westerners, for such a smile is in our social repertoire, too. However, if she were a North American anchor, she would probably have said something—anything—at least. At such times, the Japanese penchant for silence and subtly of gesture can seem beguiling. For example, a female office worker informs you of a college student's suicide. And upon your inquiry, she tells you with a smile that he committed it over a girl. Or, an elderly neighbor whose husband had recently died visits your home to say thank you for the gesture of sympathy previously sent. You meet her at the door and express something heartfelt only to have her smile at you. These smiles of enigma are well understood by the Japanese as it is their custom. Although some cultural blind spots are unavoidable, Greenwood's statement seems inexcusable. Because his statement is as likely to have been ABC's as much as it were his own, we might begin to wonder about the collective cultural sensitivity of North

America. After all, we can suppose that TV news anchors for an elite media company are appreciably skilled communicators, perhaps from among the finest of the general population.

If even in the slightest way this incident shows a collective insensitivity toward the Japanese, we ought not to be too surprised if ABC anchors were found to experience communicative friction with their Japanese counterparts. And indeed they do. Although much of the friction is simply a function of communicating across cultures, ABC personnel become so frustrated that they engage in ridicule of two of the Japanese anchors. North Americans in the face of cultural discomfort will typically resort to humor[9] but increasingly to irony and sarcasm if unrelieved.

For example, Japanese and North Americans differ somewhat regarding the sense of personal privacy. Whereas it is taboo for North Americans to ask adult acquaintances their age, for the Japanese this is usually not the case. If so asked, North Americans would likely take it as an affront. Sarcastic answers might be resorted to in hope that the questioner takes a hint. But a Japanese, often as not, does not understand and becomes puzzled by the perceived anger. In the end, the cultural gulf may become enlarged because neither really catches on.

Although fluent in English, the NHK anchors follow a behavioral "script" foreign to their North American colleagues. Their behavior is judged solely through North American eyes, which leads to unrealistic expectations of the Japanese. When these expectations are unmet, ABC personnel act in ways many would or should find regrettable. At least this is expressed by Americans, Japanese, and others after viewing video tapes of the actual ABC-NHK broadcasts.

After failed attempts to "chat" with his Japanese counterpart, Kevin Newman, Canadian and of ABC, seems to lose patience (first names are used in reference):

Kevin: Do ya have a fun weekend planned, or ?

Okito: Well, I am afraid I'll be working part of the time at least. But uh

Kevin: Oh so you have another job? [*ABC Co-anchor chuckles*]

Okito: Yes, well, it's the same job.

Kevin: Oh. I don't plan to be here. Are you gonna be here, Jim?

Jim: No.
Kevin: No, not a chance. Okay, Okito. Thanks a lot. See ya.
Jim: I just have one job.
Kevin: Absolutely. um, Here's the Dow Jones Industrials...[10]

What begins with apparently good intentions ends with aggressive one-upmanship by the ABC anchors. (Note how Kevin cuts into the middle of Okito's first words to give the "joke.") But it doesn't end there, for the ABC personnel become progressively more aggressive and rude in their exchanges. For instance, in one episode, ABC introduces *Asia Business Now* by a singing accordion player in front of a movie marquee of flashing lights that surround the face of the Japanese news anchor. He sings,

ABC: Who's the wackiest guy that you ever did know? Okito! Okito! Whose riotous antics brighten our show? Okito! Okito! A cutup, a smartie, the life of the party; he always brings good cheer. Get ready for lots of fun 'cause Okito is here. Toyoda! Take it away, Tokyo.
Okito: Lots of fun. Well, good morning. Tokyo stocks ... [11]

Though this brings laughter from my international respondents, they recognize that it is at Okito's expense. Okito, visibly annoyed, manages to stay calm and even dishes out some sarcasm of his own. The lyrics of the song are satirical—not literally intended—as judged from the reaction of my international respondents and Okito himself. In effect, the lyrics ridicule Okito, a matter my Japanese respondents found insulting.

Some weeks later, Okito gets a substitute at NHK in Hiro Sakamaki, who is even more taciturn. Within days of his "debut" on ABC, he is given the serenade treatment and humor a bit juvenile in content:

ABC: The business day in Tokyo is over. I have a question for Japan. How come your anchors never stay? Who's the new guy at NHK? Did you ever know that you're our hero? Hiro Sakamaki is your name. Although you're not our pal, Okito, here's *Asia Business,* just the same. Take it away, Hiro.[12]

At that the Japanese appeared crushed: After a long pause, Hiro says glumly, "Good morning," and then kept his head down for some length while reporting the news, an uncharacteristic action for him. His most humiliating moment, however, was still to come in a later broadcast.

Hiro Sakamaki proved to have thick skin. Even after various slights received, he never seemed to alter his style of performance, one marked by solemnness and stiffness of manner. These attributes are manifested by complete absence of smile, head movements made forward but hardly ever latcrally, and rather monotone in voice. This ultra seriousness did not apparently permit personal conversations with others on the air. It could be countered that the stimulus offered by ABC for personal exchanges was a bit oppressive.

It should be noted also that the other male Japanese, Okito Toyoda, had a performance appreciably different. He was not unknown to laugh, smile, or to share personal conversation. Also, he showed more variety in facial expressions and tone of voice. But these aspects were still muted relative to North Americans, so he still drew their ire. In effect, Okito still cast a seriousness that the North Americans probably found uncomfortable (or capable of poking fun at).

After six months of having Hiro's ultra-seriousness, ABC flashed on the television screen a name title for him that said, "Not a robot."[13] By doing so, it implied the opposite. And that interpretation fits with the ridicule made of him many times before. Even ABC would have to admit that Hiro, at least, was tough for having withstood the onslaught. If Hiro had ever come close to becoming unhinged, it had occurred previously as shown in the next episode.

Alexander Johnson, an ABC anchor, was making his debut, and he was to introduce the Asian business segment. His performance was so substandard that it seemed staged to fit in with a gag played on Hiro:

Alexander: Well, my first half-hour anchoring [the news] is almost over. Fortunately, I'll have the weekend to recover. But, of course, the weekend has already arrived uh, uh, in Japan.

Co-Anchor: Ya did great. You're doing really well.

Alexander: Yeah, I think so. I think so. That means its's time for uh time to turn to news uh to world news uh a veteran uh his name is uh what? Hiro Sakama—ki

	ya think?
Co-Anchor:	Hiro Sakamaki.
Alexander:	Hiro, ya there? Uh for more news uh
Hiro:	Good morning
Alexander:	For more uh business news uh from um Asia. Good morning, Hiro.
Hiro:	Good morning, Alexander.
Alexander:	Any advice, any advice for a newcomer?
Hiro:	Uhh u okay um anyway, Tokyo stocks ended ... [*Alexander dips his head down in apparent laughter; Hiro, his in apparent embarrassment.*][14]

Elements here that suggest the staging of this event are 1) Alexander's disfluent speech; 2) his unfamiliarity with Hiro's name; 3) his laughter; and 4) a title with Hiro's name is flashed on the screen that says: "one word—'PLASTICS'." This title is flashed precisely when Alexander asks for advice. This expression was popularized by the movie *The Graduate* as the advice given to the character played by Dustin Hoffman, the graduating student. This advice then became a gag phrase in American conversation as evidenced here. The precise insertion of this title strongly suggests how preplanned everything may have been—even Alexander's "poor" performance. This "advice" also seems derisive because it is foolishly out of date.

This elaborate staging to make fun of the Japanese anchors, if not to belittle them, occurs enough to suggest something beyond the desire for TV ratings. If the ABC personnel were entirely motivated by ratings, then it must be wondered why the female NHK anchors were not also made a mockery. The NHK females accommodated more in fulfilling North American expectations of social conversations, particularly related to informality. When the Japanese males were either unable or unwilling to follow in suit, the clash of cultures became most evident. If ever a case would be needed for showing the need for intercultural training, this seems it.

Cultural Defensiveness

The clash in cultural differences not only appeared to elicit the anger of ABC personnel but also defensiveness about their own culture. Because the (male) Japanese anchors did not accommodate to North American conversational ideals (as if they should), the ABC personnel may have viewed this (at least unconsciously) as a rejection of their culture. This psychology seems to underlie the introduction to *Asia Business Now* by Thalia Assuras (also Canadian), ABC anchor:

> In Japanese restaurants, the food is carefully presented. It is we are told, the custom in Japan to prepare each taste delicately for the palate, and each morsel carefully for the eye. This morning here at [ABC] we had macaroni and cheese scooped from a big plastic chafing dish and plopped on paper plates. Okito Toyoda was hiding in Tokyo, but you should have been here, Okito.[15]

Her talk both acknowledges a Japanese masterfulness in aesthetics and rejects it at the same time in favor of North American informality. This seems apparent particularly by her voice tone: low-toned for talk of Japanese food; high-toned, for that of North America. She seems to say "Japanese culture may have some exquisite cuisine but give us North American anytime." So this irrelevance of content and differential tone suggest an ulterior motive. That motive possibly was to shore up cultural pride after frequent rebuffs by the Japanese to engage in social conversations.

A similar dynamic appeared to be at play in a broadcast much earlier. Recall the bantering of Okito for working on weekends, which also suggested that he was a moonlighter. Given Okito's formality of dress and manner, the image of Japanese workaholics came into play. Various times Okito was suggested as overworking. In one such broadcast, the ABC anchors did not appear—only their life-size posters and pre-recorded voices. Here Kevin Newman's voice recording introduces *Asia Business Now*:

> *Kevin:* ... And now I am enjoying a little bit of fishing with my son. Sorry about that Okito, but uh just think as soon as you tell us what happened today in the Tokyo markets, you can leave, too.
>
> *Okito:* Right. Well, good morning uh images of Kevin.[16]

Note Okito's skillful reply as he is made to interact not with a real person—but a poster. The hidden message of Kevin's seems clear: "We North Americans have it better." Here is another case of one-upmanship by the North Americans, and one requiring elaborate planning by ABC. In other words, not only one or two individuals are involved but many. Because such an elite media as ABC is involved, solid ground exists for generalizing to the wider culture at large—North America. (Some ABC anchors are Canadian as surmised from comments made on their broadcasts. Identifying their nationality as such intends nothing more than to lay grounds for terming the ABC broadcasts as *North American.*)

Cultural Narrow-Perspective

How wide a cultural perspective that ABC permitted itself can speak much in regard to the cultural friction found. The more narrow the view, the more friction we might expect. To begin, consider the problem about the perspective of time as brought by telecommunications technology. People from different time zones can be brought "face-to-face" in teleconferencing. If it is morning and one switches on the computer to teleconference with a Japanese in Tokyo where it is evening, do you say "Good morning," or "Good evening"? In the case of ABC personnel, they largely took their own perspective in using the former expression with their NHK counterparts. Conversely, NHK completely accommodated to the other in greeting the North Americans with "Good morning." Could this difference in perspective-taking be symbolic of the friction that they had experienced?

The lack of perspective by ABC on Japanese culture can be found more directly in their suggestions

(1) that Hiro normally celebrates St. Patrick's Day in Japan;[17]
(2) that he does Christmas shopping as North Americans do;[18] and
(3) that Asians were eagerly following the news for the Georgia (Republican) Primary results.[19]

This projection of one's own cultural values onto the other became particularly clear on a July 4th broadcast. On that day, *Asia Business Now* was introduced by the ABC anchor (an American) by saying, "Amazingly, although the Fourth of July is nearly over in Japan, I hear NHK's Hiro Sakamaki has yet to do any picnicking or parading. He's been at work all day…."[20] Then, Sakamaki was greeted with a question by anchor Mark Mullen as paraphrased below:

Mark: Will you be doing any fireworks later?
Hiro: [*Asks quizzically*] Fireworks? [*pauses*] Tokyo stocks...[21]

Perhaps recognizing the apparent tension in their exchanges, ABC attempted at various times to follow the "Japanese way" in hopes of repair. Dick Schaap did so but laughed at the attempt:

Dick: [Working on a morning show], I [often] have to say, "Good morning," "Good morning," "Good morning." Now, it's a treat to talk to someone in Tokyo. It's nighttime there. They're done with trading. They're ready to give us the evening's business news. So, we turn to NHK's Hiro Sakamaki. I change my line: Good evening, Hiro.
Hiro: Good morning, Dick. [*A deep belly laugh is heard from Schaap*].[22]

Thereafter, ABC reverted back to using, "Good morning." Apparently to ABC, therefore, the expressions "Good morning" and "Good evening" appear too incongruous to occur simultaneously.

Thalia Assuras also wished to repair the relationship with the Japanese but by a different way. She tried by the use of her business card:

> Well, we were recently told that in Japan as in the United States it's a tradition to present someone your business card before you talk business with them. Of course, in Japan the cards are presented with a bow. We've been talking business with our NHK anchors all this time, all this time for two years—whatever. Without observing this. So we are making amends this morning. So, Hiro Sakamaki, here is my business card. It is an honor to talk business with you. [*Thalia bows her head.*] What can you tell us this morning?[23]

If ABC was so seriously concerned about the Japanese perspective, such actions would have been taken long before. Actually, this cavalier showing of a business card on the air seemed a bit bizarre because it is simply not done in Japan. Because it is so bizarre, North Americans might find it amusing.

In a more obvious attempt to make amends and again on a separate occasion, these ABC anchors wished to send a gift to

NHK:

Sheila: ... Okito, to thank you and Hiro, who are on the air with us, we are sending you a gift.
Thalia: These mugs—[ABC] mugs, Okito. Also for your producers.... We really appreciate all your help. Just wanted to say "Thanks," and we found some mugs.
Sheila: And we may need to get new ones now. [*Thalia seems to squeeze her lips to restrain her laughter.*][24]

While Americans pride themselves in being "spontaneous," they may find it hard to see its misuse (or abuse). Sheila's comment illustrates just how some foreigners can come to view Americans as irrational. To the Japanese, wrappings, whether material or immaterial, may be more important than the gift itself. Even Thalia recognizes that as seen by her reaction.

Cultural Metaphors

Given the frequent cultural frictions and insensitivities found, the next step was to identify the possible metaphors underlying the ABC view. Metaphors are the basis of thought,[25] as well as language.[26] Introductions by ABC, salutations, and captioned titles given to the Japanese were collected and analyzed. Because of the ease of working with titles and their potential as summarizing statements, they were first considered. All the known titles were put into common groupings. Analysis of these groups reveals four main metaphors, which I have termed: 1) Vaudeville Manager (ABC); 2) Poor Man; 3) Dull Guy; and 4) Mysterious Japanese. Metaphors 1 and 3 are superordinate to metaphors 2 and 4, respectively. Metaphors 1 and 2 relate to the roles of guest employee and guest foreigner that the Japanese news reporters have. Metaphor 3 "dull guy" is borrowed from the title of a training video for international educators titled "The Dull Guys" (produced by Elena Granate and distributed by NAFSA), concerned with the related stereotyping of certain foreigners on American campuses. The naming of metaphor 4 relates to a historical western view about the Japanese that continues until this day.[27] The titles follow under their related metaphor (see Table 10.1). Some titles could reasonably be categorized more than one way, in which case the more dominant association was used.

Table 10.1 Cultural Metaphors

Vaudeville Manager [28]
You asked for him now you got him
He's not Okito but he is all we've got

Poor Man

< Misfortune >[29]
My watch is broken
Suit at the cleaners
Saving jacket for the weekend
Okito has [Hiro's] coat
Never had a dinner

< The Guest Employee >[30]
Who writes this stuff?
What happened to Alexander?
Hey, what have you done with Thalia?
How am I doin?
Would rather have the cash

< The Guest Foreigner >[31]
It's all Greek to me
Leap what? [February 29]
Erin go what? [St. Patrick's Day]
What is she talking about?
What did she say?

Dull Guy [32]
Mr. Excitement
Mr. Perfect
The Animal
King of the Ad-libs
Doesn't have time for this
"One word—'Plastics'"
Work, work, work!

Mysterious Japanese [33]
Too polite to tell us what he's thinking
Watch my blinking eyes
Feeling extremely festive
Laughing on the inside
Can you say "tsunami"?
Not a Robot

Vaudeville Manager. The metaphor of the vaudeville manager, a person in charge of a rather humble theatre of stage acts, emerges in that the two related titles suggest an inferior (stage) attraction of some kind. Such "announcements" to an audience are unimaginable in contemporary stage, theatre, or TV. Rather they seem to be throwbacks to an earlier age of popular (unsophisticated) entertainment. Such announcements suggest a very small theatre—perhaps even a barroom—by which a manager could or would take requests from the audience. The entertainment would be rather amateurish by today's standard. ABC says so in jest, of course, but in doing so, it assumes a role of superiority—the manager —even if only in fun.

A subtle message is that the Japanese males are inadequate. Thus some superiority accrues to ABC as a result. How much so could be a root cause for its own intercultural discomfort. A first step toward improving intercultural communication is "assuming the burden for making the attempt."[34] This involves accommodation. However, as already seen, ABC showed little accommodation to the cultural difference of the Japanese. For instance, ABC almost always greeted the Japanese with "Good morning," despite that the time in Japan was evening.

Poor Man. Cast as an inferior "entertainment" by the "vaudeville manager," the Japanese were naturally imagined inferior in other ways, too: Employment, status, and intelligence. "Poor man" refers as much to being unfortunate as it does in an economic sense. Recall that the image of the Japanese workaholic loomed large in a number of the ABC broadcasts. This is exemplified by the title "Never had a dinner," which refers to a comic allusion made on the same show that the Japanese anchor was tied to his news desk in overwork. Other titles refer more directly to the element of misfortune from having a broken watch to having to share a suit of clothing. The latter allusion was made because the Japanese male anchors were said to have adopted the ABC "dress code" of shirtsleeves on Fridays. Still other titles relate to the "guest employee," but one having inferior status.

This inferiority is carried over to the status of foreigner for the lack of knowledge of the target culture (North American). Note, however, that this is even enlarged to include general knowledge or intelligence: The title "leap what?" suggests that the Japanese anchor lacks the concept of leap year. This progression of perceived inferiority from job status to cultural knowledge and then to intelligence mirrors how people can and do view immigrants and other foreigners in the real world. "Foreigner" status may forever keep minorities outside of mainstream society, thus creating a vicious cycle, reinforcing an "enduring image of Asians as being foreign."[35] For example, some Asian Americans report being complimented by Euro Americans for speaking English "like an American," even though native born, as this ethnic Asian indicates:

> The issue for Asian Americans is that we are considered

> foreign. I am a fifth-generation American and often when I meet white people, they say, "You're more American than I am." And I want to say, "Well, thank you, but that's not really news to me."[36]

Dull Guy. For one reason or another, Asians are stereotyped as "dull," that is, the opposite of lively or interesting. A slang equivalent is "nerd," which originated in the 1960s[37] for the high achieving and non-sociable person: "one who is not with it."[38] Such a person dresses and acts conservatively and, if an adolescent, is likely to be unpopular at school. Immersed in study, a nerd "doesn't have time for" fun. Being serious-minded, he might be perceived as "Mr. Perfect," and the one to pursue serious advice ("one word—'plastics'"). Consequently, he may become less skilled at social small talk ("Mr. Excitement"; "King of the Ad-libs") or athletic pursuits ("The Animal"). Once labeled "dull," it may prove to be a self-fulfilling prophesy for intercultural relations with Asians.

Mysterious Japanese. Japan has characteristically been viewed as the "mysterious Orient" (see Chapter 3). The significance of this and related metaphors or schemas pertains to schema transfer[39] and how they may frame subsequent social interaction. Once a person is seen as mysterious or inscrutable, he or she may be given responsibility for frictions in communication. Placing this responsibility onto others may be further encouraged by superiority seemingly held by the ABC personnel either because of their membership in a personally esteemed company, culture, or both. On this basis, culture clashes in communicative styles are less likely to be resolved and may reinforce stereotypes (caricatures) of the cultures involved.

CONCLUSION

The ABC/NHK interactions demonstrate typical reactions by North Americans to stressful intercultural contacts: resorting to humor but increasingly to irony and sarcasm. What was stressful for the ABC personnel was the cultural difference in communicative style on the part of the Japanese—a traditional style characterized by emotionless facial and vocal expressions, reticence, serious demeanor, and an unremitting sameness of routine. Where the North Americans sought casualness, the

Japanese sought formality. Where the North Americans sought spontaneity, the Japanese sought consistency. Where the North Americans sought variety, the Japanese sought routine. These differences were most epitomized by their expressions of greeting and leave-taking. The Japanese anchors rarely departed from set phrases, whereas the North Americans individualized much of theirs. Moreover, the two Japanese males were wont to avoid "small talk" with their North American counterparts. In fact, their facial expression appeared as "frozen in neutral," which a Korean scholar on Japan, O-Young Lee,[40] likens to the Noh drama mask, known for its blankness of expression. This kind of expression is advantageous in hierarchical social situations for preserving social harmony. Both sides can interpret the expression to their own liking! Or that sometimes seems so.

Lest we create a stereotypical image of the Japanese, Lee's characterization pertains largely to certain formal situations. For example, a number of Japanese who have viewed these programs comment that the Japanese male newscasters follow the NHK News style. "The gravity of the news presented on NHK [in general] is accentuated by the staid delivery of the conservatively dressed announcers, who rarely smile or comment on the news they read,"[41] a description echoed by others.[42] However, other Japanese broadcast companies have "adopted an American-style 'happy news' format."[43] Even NHK seems to aim for that (or similar) format, by some of their news reporting on its domestic satellite channel in recent years. Recognition of a "style" by my Japanese informants suggests that different styles of newscasting do exist in Japan. This applies also on the interpersonal level, for Japanese authentic smiles occur more than they seem otherwise. The difference is largely situational.

The ABC/NHK interactions show concretely how cultures can clash communicatively. The fact that model communicators were involved suggests that no one is immune to ethnocentric or irrational behavior. This realization is important because people are just as likely to assume the opposite. In stressful intercultural contacts, individuals are likely to construct "comforting cognitions" in order to preserve one's ego.[44] These cognitions (or cultural metaphors) work to displace the discomfort onto the Other as the cause. This reaction becomes self-defeating because it not only may create negative stereotypes (e.g., the ugly American; the mysterious Japanese) in the minds of others, but it also may blind us from seeing what it really is—ethnocentrism.

Seeing that in model communicators may help fortify us to face our own. Finally, the ABC/NHK episodes show how the mass media can become the subject for natural observations in researching intercultural or international communication. Whether print or non-print, the mass media offer various ways in illustrating or developing important concepts and principles in communication studies.

APPLICATION

1. How did the respective newscasting manifest different communicative styles?
2. If someone were to say that the North Americans were being humorous rather than ethnocentric, how would you respond? How are ethnic jokes related?
3. Why can we say that the North American newscasters acted in collusion with their broadcast company and that a connection exists to the wider culture?
4. What makes these episodes more than just "isolated incidents"?
5. How may have these episodes been impacted by cultural values and international conflicts; and what implications arise for multiculturalism and global understanding?

11

An Ultimate Case for Japan Bashing

"Scholars o[n] Japan are divided as to whether Japan Inc. … actually exists."[1] "Japan Inc." refers to the alleged collusion between Japanese government and businesses to keep foreigners out of their market. Early in the post-war years, Japan did have a well protected market to help it recover. Over the past two decades it has done much to dismantle those barriers. Japanese are often heard to agree that their economy must be "deregulated"; however, that is not the same as agreeing about a de facto "Japan Inc." arrangement. Rather it is the recognition that their economy is much too regulated and that such regulation makes it hard for any newcomer—whether Japanese or foreign. On the other hand, Japanese psychology, based on its historical isolation, may not be quite attuned to having a market completely open to foreigners. Such a market, though, probably does not exist anywhere. All countries follow some protectionism however small. Solving this quandary is not the purpose of this chapter. Rather, it is to show how "Japan bashing" in the mass media may ignore certain facts to the detriment of cross-cultural understanding. This appears particularly so with a news article that can be described as the "ultimate case" for Japan bashing. Thus this chapter necessarily concentrates on American shortcomings, simply to expose information that the Japan bashing ignores. Neither side is solely to blame. The trade issue is far too complex to blame any one party, and bashing each other is hardly the solution.

Discussion begins with a brief look how the mass media may help incite trade conflict and the popular view of Japanese trade practice as unfair and why this is oversimplified. A case of Japan bashing is then taken up to show the weakness of this type of journalism. Discourse analysis of the newspaper article reveals that the article is heavy on persuasion but short on evidence for its views.

THE MASS MEDIA—PROVOCATEURS?

Japan and the United States have frequently engaged each other in an "emotional war of words" over trade. This bashing, in part, has been instigated by "adversarial-style" news reporting that has "heightened tensions between the two countries," according to a significant number of journalists from both countries surveyed by the East-West Center in Honolulu.[2] For example, certain American newspapers, by ignoring the context of a Japanese remark about Americans, turned it into slander, thus enlarging the rift between the two countries.[3] "We have entered an era of attack journalism," an era marked by a lowering of journalistic standards that allows the media "to print things and to air things that are unsubstantiated, that are essentially gossip and rumor without substantial evidence to back them up."[4] This seems so with the case of Japan bashing considered here, by which stereotypes substitute for journalistic evidence. By unveiling this lack of evidence, this case shows how bias can motivate distorted cultural views.

THE VIEW OF JAPAN AS UNFAIR

Japanese have been typically viewed by Americans as having "beaten [American] manufacturers by underhand means";[5] yet the Japanese have had superb products and marketing strategies, and their trade barriers have not been greatly unlike those found in the west.[6] A World Bank study found that, contrary to the popular image, Japan actually had fewer non-tariff barriers than the US and the then-EEC.[7]

What may be a surprise also is that Japan's exporting is not as extensive as popularly believed: Among twenty-three westernized industrialized nations, Japan was surpassed by all but the United States for exports as a percentage of GDP (gross domestic product) in 1988,[8] the period most relevant to the case of Japan bashing considered here. Japan, however, does have an "export" division of its economy,[9] which is highly concentrated both in the number of companies and the kinds of products produced for export.[10] And it is their heavily concentrated exporting into certain product markets overseas that has hastened the trade frictions.

Peter Drucker, "often called the father of modern management," views the trade deficit with Japan a "mirage," for as he states, "it is the result of the [long term] worldwide depression in raw materials and food prices."[11] Another generally less-known explanation is the "twin-deficits" hypothesis. This hypothesis, held by a number of "well respected economists both in Japan and the U.S," considers the trade deficit a function of the large US government deficit and the relatively low rate of American savings.[12] Furthermore, as of the relevant time period, the late 1980s, the Japanese outspent Americans on a per capita basis nearly two to one on goods produced by the other.[13] This observation was based on data from US Customs and findings from McKinsey & Company. Lastly, penetration by the two countries in each other's market is "practically identical," a conclusion based on the fact that American companies *producing in Japan* sell to the Japanese over $40 billion worth of goods, a figure nearly four times more than that done conversely by Japanese companies in the United States, figures excluded from calculations of the trade deficit.[14]

> The statistics [on trade] do not take into account the fact that an increasingly larger fraction of the goods manufactured abroad by subsidiaries of US businesses erroneously appear on the "imports" side of the balance sheet, and not as part of US business operations. Those goods are actually not from "them" but from "us." ... Thus, the classical tools of analyzing

> international business by trade statistics don't work. [For as Kenichi Ohmae points out,] if American Toyotas and Japanese IBM computers are factored in, there is no real trade imbalance between [Japan and the United States].[15]

Unfortunately, such information appears unknown to the general public and includes some of our leading media journalists, such as Ted Koppel, who confessed that he arrived at some of this knowledge only accidently and only of late at that:

> What we do not hear ..., and what many of you do not know and what I must confess I did not know until this morning, is that Japan buys more products from the United States than any other country in the world except Canada. You heard right. Japan is our second largest trading partner in the world.[16]

Another point is that the United States is far from innocent in free-trade disputes. According to one news report, the United States "violates some of the same trade principles it wants others to follow," and its "trade barriers to foreign products cost Americans as much as 70 billion dollars a year, raising questions of just who is being protected."[17]

The automobile industry has been a linchpin for some of the most heated trade disputes. For that reason, the following remark by an American executive in that industry seems rather telling. Asked to explain why Detroit has been slow in adapting to the Japanese automobile market, a GM executive in Japan replied on a Japanese televised newscast:

> The Japanese cars are getting larger [in Japan]. So forget [about Americans] bringing in larger vehicles. The fact is the Japanese car has grown over the last two decades, and certainly if you look at the Lexus and the Infinity. Our colleagues—our competitors on the other side—have certainly grown up in terms of size of the vehicles. So don't think that [the case of large-sized American cars] is appropriate at all. The fact is that what you try to do is provide vehicles that the consumer would want.[18]

Although one might ignore the apparent ethnocentrism of viewing the Japanese as becoming "grown-up," it is hard to overlook how this statement seems to skirt the issue. His statement seems symptomatic of the long reluctance of American automobile makers not only to downsize their models for the

Japanese market but also to switch the steering column to right-hand drive (for driving on the left side of the road there).

Such reluctance appears to be part of an American "[un]willingness to cater their products to the Asian market,"[19] according to a Malaysian news journalist. "Indeed, some have argued that the Big Three [American producers] have no real interest in penetrating the Japanese market—that the actual goal of these complaints is to justify protection at home."[20] It is only recently—after decades of disputes—that the American car industry has begun to produce right-hand drive automobiles for the Japanese market.[21] Understandably, Japanese indicate that their own car industry never had this problem when they entered the US car market. Bruce Stokes appears justified, therefore, in attributing the difference to American arrogance, especially if one also notes that American manufacturers, as of the early 1990s lagged behind the Japanese in producing cars with quality, reliability, and fuel efficiency according to the Economic Strategy Institute.[22]

Nevertheless, some American trade negotiators had argued that the issue over automobile steering was moot because many European automobiles are sold unmodified to Japanese, who seem to buy for that very reason. The purchase of such luxury vehicles, however, can have an obvious social motivation. The opposite steering can accentuate for the driver (and others) the specialness of the vehicle. Much less clear is how American mass-produced automobiles could be so easily equated with those of the European limited-production upscale variety. And this attitude seems to belie statements made by automobile executives that Detroit has had the Japanese consumer truly in mind.

In short, American companies might not be such the grieved party as assumed in the rhetoric of Japan bashing.

> [In the late 1980s], Japan took important measures to open its markets, although the beneficiaries were more likely to be the Asian NICs than American exporters. Japan's trade greatly deepened with Korea, Taiwan, Thailand, and other Asian states; in the period 1985—89 Japan's manufactured imports from Asia more than doubled. ... Increasingly nations in the West Pacific (comprising East Asia, the ASEAN region, and Australia) trade more with each other than with the west. ... Instead of gearing up to compete in this dynamic region Americans are more likely to complain about trade restrictions that other nations manage to get around.[23]

Detroit has sometimes complained about the difficulty of setting up dealerships in Japan, but "Germany's BMW has a network of 135 showrooms in Japan"[24] for example. As *The Economist* saw it, "America's arguments in its trade quarrel with Japan range[d] from the limp to the ludicrous."[25]

Nevertheless, according to Leonard J. Schoppa, there is still something "odd" about Japanese trade practices. He reported that "the most obvious indicator suggesting that something odd is going on in [Japan's] trading patterns is the *nai-gai* price differential: the difference in prices for an item purchased inside Japan compared to the price for the same item purchased abroad."[26] One of the items he pointed out is color film, reporting that it "costs 47 percent more in Tokyo than in New York," yet in a chart on his next page, the Tokyo price is still cheaper than in both London and Paris! In fact, Tokyo prices beat those of either London or Paris on more than half of the consumer items listed in his chart. Most of these are manufactured goods, which puts a damper to the *nai-gai* argument.

Prices in Japan on average are nearly twice those in the United States.[27] But that is not necessarily due to having a closed market. Because I often complain about Japanese prices myself, I became particularly intrigued with the idea that Japanese goods are sold more cheaply outside than inside of Japan. So, when I returned from Japan to live in the United States in the early 1990s, I was keen to compare prices. I was especially interested in electronic equipment because I had to equip a new household. Regarding TVs and VCRs, I found comparison was impossible. Most American stores simply did not stock the high quality of Japanese equipment I had in Japan. My overall impression was that the electronic goods in the stores in my college town (and other locales) appeared of cheap quality. Some of the models may have been similar, but the American ones usually had less functions and of cheaper construction. A further difficulty had been the abnormally weak dollar, which inflated the prices of Japanese consumer goods in comparison. Consequently, I could not prove that Japanese goods were cheaper outside of Japan, even though I really wanted to. I am unhappy about the prices in Japan, but I must admit that I do receive unparalleled quality and service.

A further problem with the *nai-gai* argument is that Japanese retail stores may have higher overhead costs than stores in North America. The price of a square foot of commercial real estate in

Tokyo is twice that of the price in New York City.[28] If retailer overhead costs are higher in Japan, then that would explain why Japanese goods can sell at lower retail prices abroad. The *nai-gai* argument may still be valid but requires much more development.

This is not to say that certain complaints about Japan are unjustified. Japanese commerce is heavily regulated in comparison, and its business environment makes startups costly. For example, Japanese product standards might focus more on design rather than performance, inviting protectionism against outsiders (foreign or domestic). And if it were not such bureaucratic barriers, it might be the complex Japanese distribution system that would surely try the patience of even the most steadfast of importers. Also, the Japanese are highly cohesive, which is especially encouraged by the competition with foreigners. Even without intending it, some Japanese may discriminate against foreigners. The Japanese government at one time did exactly that. But isn't that part of human nature?

Still, the consensus among foreigners in Japan is that the Japanese are prone to do so—not because of their "character" but their mindset. The Japanese see themselves as living precariously on a resource-poor island country dwarfed by huge nations on either side. They view Japan as being naturally disadvantaged, which must be compensated for by a work-hard ethic and, perhaps, extra consideration by others. For example, the cost of land in Japan, as noted above, is extremely high. From their view, they feel American complaints are unreasonable coming from such a "great and rich" country. That is why North Americans must be especially prepared for the Japanese market. Ultimately, the central issue is "fairness," a term that will likely differ across cultures. But as long as political and private agendas, such as Japan bashing, impact on trade disputes, the issue of fairness is likely to be clouded for some time to come.

To illustrate how Japan bashing can be distorted, one has but to look at "Hidden Wall: A Native Son Battles Japan's Trade Barriers,"[29] an article from the *Washington Post*. This article was selected because its headline suggested the ultimate case against Japanese trade: the thrust being that even if an American is already deeply knowledgeable of the Japanese language and culture—someone native born to Japan in this case—he or she still faces insurmountable barriers to trade, thereby substantiating charges that Japan engages in unfair trade. Rather than provide substantiation, however, the article appears to rely solely on stereotypes about the Japanese. By showing this inherent bias, the case also indicates the relativity of cultural worldviews and the need for a critical eye in such cultural conflicts.

DISCOURSE ANALYSIS

The *Hidden Wall* article appears in Box 11.1. The article reports how a Japanese businessman in an American company returned to Japan only to meet with business failure. His case suggests that Japan trades unscrupulously because, as the article reports, he had every reason to succeed there. Consequently, this article merits regard, for the light it might shed on the trade disputes, or at least I had thought. The reader ought to read the article before going on. Thereafter, the major highlights of a discourse analysis will be presented, which begins with the article's rhetorical message.

The Rhetorical Message

Analysis of *Hidden Wall* reveals a rhetorical (persuasive) message that Japan, irrational and unfair, follows exclusionary trading practices. These practices are rooted in perceived faults of Japan:

I Japanese group harmony (Paragraphs 13-14)
II A lack of free competition—"Japan Inc." (Paragraph 22)
III Postponement of buying until the foreign patent expires (Paragraphs 23-29)
IV Suspicion of foreigners (Paragraph 30
V Trust only in their own craftsmanship (Paragraph 31)
VI Japanese irrationality (Paragraph 32)

The rank placement of these practices or faults within the article appear organized in a semantic superstructure, circular in form, with each fault subordinate to its antecedents as supporting evidence. Fault I, harmony or groupism, is the point of origin and return, and is supported by Fault II and that by III, and so on. These faults are stereotypical of the Japanese.

Despite the belief that some stereotypes contain a grain of truth,[30] they like other generalized rules of culture have constraints. Although such stereotypical behavior may be operative in the case of *Hidden Wall*, the journalist appears to ignore a more powerful explanation. That explanation is social/situational rather than cultural: Relinquishing one's native identity/citizenship is likely to raise social barriers with those of the former national/social group.

Box 11.1

Hidden Wall: A Native Son Battles Japan's Trade Barriers[31]

Fred Hiatt

1 It seems, at first, a familiar story. American businessman comes to Japan with great hopes, works his heart out and, four years later, retreats to New Jersey, a beaten man.

2 Ryusuke Hasegawa had heard such tales, but thought he was immune. Hasegawa, a naturalized American, was born in Japan 49 years ago, attended college here [in Japan] and didn't leave until he was 24, Japanese master's degree in hand. No one could complain that he didn't know the language or customs.

3 He came, moreover, with a high-tech product to sell, a $12 billion corporation, Allied-Signal Inc., to back him up and a partnership with some blue-chip Japanese companies.

4 Yet this month Hasegawa, like hundreds of less-prepared businessmen before him, will indeed retreat, somewhat bitterly, to New Jersey. He has spent much of his time defending Allied's invention against patent challenges by Japanese competitors and meeting and drinking with potential customers who never seemed quite ready to buy. At the same time, the Japanese government was funding research to catch and surpass Allied-Signal.

5 "I feel bad for American companies," Hasegawa said in a recent interview. "We do a lot of basic research, and when we are about to be successful, a Japanese company comes in and gets the business."

6 Hasegawa's disappointment may help explain one side of the $50 billion US trade deficit with Japan that is frustrating policy-makers and inflaming anger on both sides of the Pacific. Like many foreigners before him, Hasegawa ran into invisible cultural trade barriers, a Japanese instinct, official and unofficial, to protect its industry from foreign competition and the willingness of cash-rich Japanese firms to invest hugely in research rather than cede any ground to competitors.

7 And while Allied's failure so far cannot be blamed solely on Japan, the company appears to have avoided many pitfalls to which Japanese often attribute American business failures here, such as lack of cultural and linguistic understanding or an expectation of instant results in this difficult market.

8 With Hasegawa's departure, Allied-Signal will not give up its efforts to sell the amorphous metal products it developed in its New Jersey laboratory. Hasegawa, who will visit frequently, still thinks Allied's joint venture here will succeed.

9 Moreover, Allied-Signal has other subsidiaries, joint ventures and affiliates, some of which have been here [in Japan] more than 50 years, together generating sales of $700 million a year.

10 Altogether, US exports to Japan totaled $42 billion in 1988, up from $31.5 billion the previous year.

11 But Hasegawa, in a recent interview, acknowledged that he is frustrated by the meager fruits of his four years' labor. Nippon Amorphous Metals Co. Ltd., as the joint venture between Allied and the Mitsui group is called, is still earning only $2 million a year, half its operating expenses.

12 "I thought, 'This is ridiculous. I speak the language, I understand the customs, this isn't going to happen to me,'" Hasegawa said. "And then things didn't go as I expected.

13 "The Japanese like harmony," he continued. "You say, 'Buy ours, it's cheaper,' and they won't. And you say, 'Why not?' And they say, 'Because we're happy. You're destroying our harmony. Everything was harmonious until you came along.'"

14 "We buy Japanese cars because they're good. Well, we have a high-tech product that is good—and they're not listening to us."

15 Hasegawa wears the navy suit of a businessman but, with his shy manner and hair falling just above his eyes, has the look of a scientist. In fact, he is both, an engineering PhD from the California Institute of Technology as well as vice president of Nippon Amorphous Metals Co.

16 He left Japan in the 1960s to get the best science education possible. Like many Japanese scientists—including Susumu Tonegawa, Japan's Nobel Laureate who did his prize-winning research in Switzerland and now works at the Massachusetts Institute of Technology—Hasegawa was attracted by an openness in US labs that encouraged creative thinking.

17 "In Japan, you can't speak your mind," he said. "The professor is all-powerful. You can do improvement over certain technology, but if you want to do something drastically different, it is very difficult."

18 So Hasegawa chose to stay, working first for International Business Machines Corp. and, for the past 14 years, at Allied-Signal. There, in the 1970s, he was part of a laboratory team, along with Indian-born David Marasimhan, that discovered how to make "amorphous metals."

19 Such metals are heated until molten, and then suddenly cooled—from 1,000 degrees centigrade to room temperature in a millisecond—so that they retain the crystal structure of a liquid. With the process Allied developed, components of computers and other electronics can be made smaller and electric transformers in utility poles can be made more energy efficient.

20 "Japan has no oil," Hasegawa said, so he believed utilities here would welcome the product. Enough utility-pole transformers are replaced here annually to offer a $65 million market, he said. Several utilities in the United States, including Virginia Power Co., have begun replacing old transformers manufactured by Westinghouse or General Electric Co., with those that use Allied's amorphous metal.

21 They are more expensive to buy than traditional steel transformers, according to the Electric Power Research Institute, but save money in the long run by minimizing energy loss.

22 But after four years, Hasegawa was unable to interest a single electric company here in Allied's product. The utilities never said no, but always they needed more time, more tests, more study. Allied's efforts challenged two of Japan's most powerful corporations, Nippon Steel and Kawasaki Steel, which make the silicon steel now used in transformers. Hasegawa said giant firms use their muscle to keep competitors out, threatening to cut off supplies if the system is disrupted.

23 Hasegawa noted that Allied's Japanese patents on amorphous metals expire in the mid-1990s. "The utilities say they're interested, but not now," he said. "They may be waiting for our patents to expire."

24 Indeed, a Nippon Steel spokesman said his company is developing its own capability to make amorphous metal, aided by more than $11 million from the government's New Technology Development Corp. since 1981. But the spokesman, who asked not to be named, denied that Nippon Steel pressured utilities to stay away from Allied. "We are just proceeding with our own effort," he

said.
25 A spokesman for Tokyo Electric Power Co. declined to comment.
26 Meanwhile, another corporate giant, Hitachi Metals Co., challenged Allied's patents and filed its own. The time spent in patent court troubled Hasegawa most, since he believes that Hitachi changed Allied's process slightly and claimed it as a new invention.
27 "If you invent a knife of a different shape, in Japan you can patent that," Hasegawa said. "In the United States, it's still a knife." A Hitachi official disagreed, arguing that Hitachi independently invented a way to make amorphous metal. Hitachi has won one legal battle against Allied, allowing it to sell some products in the United States, while most Japanese battles remain unresolved.
28 Whatever the merits of this case, Allied's complaints are not unusual, according to a US Commerce Department official.
29 "Many practitioners in the United States believe that Japanese courts have been less than friendly in providing a fair measure of protection to patented inventions," Michael Kirk, assistant commissioner for external affairs, told a Senate subcommittee in February.
30 In all, Hasegawa said, he came to feel that Japanese companies regard his venture with suspicion because it is foreign, despite his Japanese partners and his own Japanese heritage.
31 "The Japanese have this strange custom," he said. "They have to do everything themselves. Why do they have to make scotch whiskey? Why do they have to make wine? They don't even have a grape suited to wine.
32 I was born in Japan, I was brought up in Japan, but I still don't understand it."

The Social Situation

The expression *native son* in the United States, a land of immigrants, connotes idealistically the wishful thinking that a native son is always welcomed in his ancestral land. Common sense tells us that if we break ties with one social group to join another, the original group may never accept us again. When such groups are nations at war, change in allegiance results in our being branded a traitor and can result in our peril. Of all people, a native son or former emigrant may have the least chance of being accepted in their homeland.

As noted in Chapter 8, Japanese Americans may meet with

difficulty in Japan because of unrealistic expectations, perhaps on both sides, but especially with Japanese nationals. As for Hasegawa, the "native son" in the article, it could be argued that his experiences in Japan might even be found more undesirable than the average Japanese American's because he willfully gave up Japanese citizenship in favor of an American one. Moreover, he returned to Japan after living in the United States for twenty years, a period nearly as much as the time he had previously lived in Japan.

"[T]he better one does at L2 [a second] language and culture the more likely that person will undergo L1 [first language] loss."[32] Although such L1 loss appears an unrecognized idea in general, the possibility is hardly unknown to those experienced with life abroad or their intimates. For example, Americans, after a long-term stay abroad, are sometimes perceived to sound "British" in their speaking, perhaps due to their past habit of enunciating for non-native speakers. Although total loss of L1 is rather rare, the possibility still exists. After the breakup of the former Soviet Union, the press reported the case of a former American GI who had defected to Russia in the 1960s, and on his return to the US decades later, he had to use an interpreter because his loss of English had been so profound.

Even if Hasegawa's fluency in Japanese remains completely intact, he still may unconsciously reveal to Japanese nationals that he no longer owes allegiance to *Nippon*. "When people of Japanese descent visit Japan as successful citizens of their new countries, it is all too clear to both themselves and the Japanese that they are not 'insider' Japanese but 'outsider' foreigners."[33] As a result of Hasegawa's apparent rejection of Japanese ingroup membership, by virtue of having become American, Japanese nationals may naturally feel suspicious toward him. This suspicion particularly will become intensified in competitive contexts such as international business, not to mention an era of threatened trade war. The idea that Hasegawa could pass himself off as any other Japanese national is rather naive. Thus the newspaper journalist seems misled in building a case for Japan's unfair trading based on Hasegawa's experience.

Although this social difficulty might be particularly acute in a collectivist culture like Japan's, nevertheless, if the situation were reversed, it is not hard to imagine an American experiencing social difficulties in American business circles after having become a naturalized Japanese. It must be remembered also that those business circles would be rather conservative (public utilities) and might involve millions of dollars. In other words, a great deal of trust would be required, far different from say, selling novelties or sundry items.

Perhaps doing business in the United States would still be easier. Nevertheless, that is insufficient for concluding unfair practices in Japan. Rather than the Japanese cultural traits presumed by the article, which would lead to concluding Japanese unfair trade practices, the social situation seems a more accurate explanation. And my interpretation is bolstered by the finding that among my international students in Japan: Americans seem least likely to perceive the situational factors of the article as compared with European and Asian students, the latter (e.g., Chinese, Thai) using situational explanations the most. This American performance was probably due, at least partly, to overexposure of the trade issue in the US.

Despite the United States having a highly diverse population, Americans, in general, are monolingual with limited experience using foreign or second languages by world standards, a fact that prompted US Congressman Paul Simon to call his fellow citizens "tongue-tied."[34] This state of affairs is explainable, in part, by the fortune or misfortune of having a mother tongue that has become a lingua franca. Thus Americans have less imperatives to speak other tongues as compared to others from non-English speaking countries.

Two other factors are prominent in explanation. One is an isolationist sentiment, stimulated by the "pioneer spirit" needed to settle its vast wilderness, by the abundance of natural resources, and by a large interior far from contiguous national states. The second factor is a melting pot ethic that emphasized assimilation of a unifying language and culture. Monolingualism seems, then, to have been a foregone result. Because of the historical need for a unified language and culture, Americans may develop less cultural sensitivity than what might be otherwise, even though the country is so ethnically diverse. Hence some truth inheres in the image of the naive American abroad, a literary image of Henry James's, and one applied by a work[35] on the Japanese and American trade frictions.

Influence of Worldview

Regardless of whether "Japan, Inc" had conspired against his company, Nippon Amorphous Metals, the company had had $8 million total sales (in four years) in Japan (Paragraph 11), so it is not that Japan is completely closed. Furthermore, the suggestion that the Japanese have tried to infringe on the company's patents was undercut somewhat by an American court ruling against its claim (Paragraph 27). Investigation of these two aspects—sales and legal issues—appear important but were left unexplored: Why did some Japanese customers buy and others not? Why did the American court rule unfavorably against the company? If one, however, were convinced that the Japanese traded unfairly and were too irrational even for themselves, one might be less likely to seek alternative explanations. Consequently, reliance upon stereotypes might seem sufficient in accounting for Hasegawa's business results in Japan. It also might explain the rhetorical features of the article. One feature was already mentioned—the arrangement of the stereotypes. The stereotypes were hierarchically ranked in mutual support, which seemed to obviate the need for other evidence. If not so arranged, the journalist might have been more disposed to seek alternative explanations.

Other Rhetorical Links with Worldview

Other possible rhetorical links to the journalist's own worldview range from the global to local textual levels: from a proverbial story frame and two possible American literary icons to word choices at the sentence level. The first paragraph frames or organizes the entire article by talk of a mythological American businessman. Mythological because *American businessman* is unmodified by a grammatical article (a/the). In that form, the related sentence takes on the quality of a proverb (e.g., "He who goes to Japan fails"). And whether a proverb or not, it is a *familiar story* (Paragraph 1), thus possibly revealing the journalist's own bias or cultural worldview.

Crafting the story in a proverbial frame may elicit various mental associations. One, literary, is that of the "beaten man," an image that may strike a chord in many hearts of Americans made sensitive by Arthur Miller's powerful characterization of Willy Loman, the dejected salesman. It is not that the journalist necessarily has Willy Loman in mind. Rather, Willy Loman is so well established in American culture that the character represents an icon in the American collective consciousness, the extent of which is suggested by how the media apply it to our politicians, as was done during a recent Presidential campaign:

> TED KOPPLE: Chris Bury mentioned to me before the program that there is sort of a Willy Lomanesque quality about Newt Gingrich [US Speaker of the House] these days. I know you all know what I mean but let me raise that with you when we come back [after a commercial break]. And we're back once again with Susan Yoachum [and others]. Arthur Miller's great play, *Death of a Salesman*. The central character, the salesman Willy Loman—sort of a sad figure trying desperately to get respect late in life. Susan, does that ring any kind of bell with the way [Newt Gingrich] has been stumping for votes in … California?
>
> SUSAN YOACHUM: You know, Willy Loman has also been used as the comparison with Bob Dole [the soon-to-be-defeated Republican candidate for President]. So I think that particularly this year ... we see a Newt Gingrich, who is casting about trying to figure out [why he and his fellow Republicans fell out of grace with the American public after launching a much herald "revolution" in government].[36]

In another example, Haynes Johnson, a political analyst, in a discussion about political speechmaking, comments about Paul Tsongas, a former presidential candidate: He had a "Willy Loman frame … and an Elmer Fudd delivery."[37] Note that no explanation about Willy Loman was given, as Johnson probably assumed that his use needed none. Moreover, Willy Loman is used in the same breath with Elmer Fudd, a famous cartoon character from the popular culture.

The Willy Loman character is established enough to be considered an icon and may be evoked in people's minds, consciously or unconsciously, simply by associated images. That is the power and value of icons: They serve as "mental shorthand" for some established meanings or even ideologies at times. (An excellent example is a nation's flag.) Given Willy Loman's place as an icon, it is hard to imagine that any literary craftsman would not be reminded of it by the image of a defeated businessman.

(Here, businessman is used in the sense of one having a sales function, a reasonable assumption to make considering the content of *Hidden Wall*.)

While on the topic of American icons, another literary characterization that may apply is Henry James's naive American characters who fail in dealing with foreign cultures abroad. This icon seems applicable given the country's historical isolationism and melting pot ethic, as made mentioned above. The Jamesian icon together with the Willy Loman icon may form two complementary frames, one cognitive, the other, affective, in which Hasegawa's account is understood and appreciated. The Jamesian icon may serve cognitively by knowledge of the situation of a foreigner abroad; whereas the Willy Loman icon may do so affectively by the imagery of a defeated saleman. These icons, as shared aspects of American culture, are already in place in American consciousness. Thus, a writer or journalist need not make direct references to put them into play. All that may be needed are associated images. If that is the case, then it is all the more reason for a close and critical reading of the *Hidden Wall.*

IMPLICATIONS

An unwary reader may nod his or her head in approval upon reading Hasegawa's account, especially since he is "Japanese." Even some foreign students in Japan, who are probably better informed and more magnanimous in thought about Japan than citizens back in their home countries, tend to sympathize with Hasegawa and assign the cause of his lack of success to Japanese culture. On the contrary, as I have attempted to show, Hasegawa and the journalist's implied claims appear without much evidence.

Certainly, cultural differences exist, but the article does not substantiate any of its implied claims. To make Japanese culture the cause for a native son's setback does not at all imply ill-will; but, it may indicate, perhaps unavoidably so, perceptual distortion or cultural bias. And recognizing possible cultural bias has been a major endeavor of this book.

One must wonder about perceptual distortions and bias when only two American companies bother to translate their literature into Japanese out of more than fifty companies participating in a trade fair in Tokyo specifically to help American businesses.[38]

Another case involved the American firm, ABC Consulting (a fictionalized name), in their campaign to attract Japanese retailers as clients.

A Japanese grocery store, not much bigger than the average American's living room, received a letter written in English from ABC about the firm's services. The storekeeper, ignorant of its contents, showed me the letter. To give the reader a gist of the letter, I paraphrase its opening contents:

> Dear Sir or Madam:
>
> ABC has a deal for you! ABC is able to revamp your marketting program to become cost-effective and a real bell ringer. ABC GUARANTEES ...

It is hard to believe that this company actually expected to attract Japanese clients this way. The letter not only was in English but used colloquialisms likely to be unfamiliar even to the most proficient among Japanese users of English. Doing business in Japan typically requires establishing prior relations of some kind. This requirement especially relates to foreign firms. Foreign firms quite naturally have more to prove than those of domestic origin.

One cannot generalize about American business based on only one or two such cases, but they do indicate that some individuals lack cross-cultural awareness and skill. Yet, the mass media hardly ever consider such factors in reporting about American charges of unfair Japanese practices. For instance, ABC Consulting could complain that the Japanese market is not open enough, but most Americans would be ignorant of the fact that the ABC campaign appeared so poorly conducted. I do not wish to suggest that Japan has a de facto open market; however, the trade dispute is far more complex than what is generally believed.

The Japanese seem to think that American business firms collectively do not do enough to break into their market. Of course, there are exceptions. However, the Japanese compare how hard they had to work to master foreign languages, learn the tastes of foreign consumers, adjust to exotic ways, and overcome the once shoddy image of Japanese goods. The Japanese quite naturally expect the same kind of efforts made in return. Surely, without evidence of such efforts, there is no reason for them to support fair trade. It is in such a situation that hidden trade barriers are likely to be encouraged.

CONCLUSION

This chapter presented a discourse analysis of a newspaper article from a genre that could be called "Japan bashing." It was selected because it seemed to report on the ultimate case showing unfair Japanese trade practices. On the contrary, the article seemed to ignore situational factors that would explain the businessman's failure in Japan. More specifically, the article naively assumed that a Japanese, naturalized as an American and after having lived in the United States for over twenty years as an adult, could later pass in Japan as a fellow Japanese. If my analysis and observation of international student reactions to the article are valid, then this article seems to illustrate well the need for greater critical awareness when comparing cultures.

At the same time, I am reminded of the many calls for respect for diversity and internationalization in the United States and elsewhere. "Internationalization" seems a buzzword, for few people seem to reflect upon its meaning. To me, at least part of what it means for a person to become "internationalized" is the awareness of one's own personal and cultural biases or stereotypes of foreign cultures. No one can be completely free of such biases, but I hope that through the critical analysis this book has attempted to develop, more effective intercultural relations and cross-cultural studies can result.

APPLICATION

1. Discuss the case of Hasegawa and his Nippon Amorphous Metals Company as to why or why not it supported the view that Japan engages in unfair trading practices.
2. Rhetorically speaking, how does the first paragraph of *Hidden Wall* function?
3. How would you characterize the view of the author of *Hidden Wall*? Support your characterization with related details from the article.
4. Identify the author's strategies or elements of persuasion.

Notes

INTRODUCTION

1 Inspiration for this first paragraph came from Prosser 1989.
2 Hofstede 1991, among others, also uses a computer metaphor for the mind.
3 Dodd 1991, p. 5.
4 This term is borrowed from Edwin Reischauer.
5 Yoshida, Tanaka & Sesoko 1984.
6 Reischauer 1977, p. 44.
7 Hume 1995, p. xi.
8 Reischauer 1988.
9 Reischauer 1988, p. 32.
10 Harris & Moran 1979, p. 292.
11 Mouer & Sugimoto 1986.
12 Benedict 1946; Mouer & Sugimoto 1986.
13 *Japan 1998;* Kennedy 1997.
14 This view is commonly found among the Japanese. See Cooper-Chen 1997.
15 Maraini 1973, cited by Eisenstadt 1996, p. 5.
16 Davis 1992, p, 1.
17 Cited by Tobin 1983.
18 Tobin 1983, p. 6.
19 Befu & Krciner 1992.
20 Davis 1992, p. 38.
21 Befu 1980.

22 *Random House Webster's* 1991; *Roget's International Thesaurus* 1977.
23 Conversations presented by this author in this book, whether in English or in Japanese, are paraphrases of actual speech, unless otherwise noted.
24 Berry, Poortinga, Segall, & Dasen 1992, p. 9.
25 O'Sullivan, Hartley, Saunders, Montgomery, & Fiske 1994, p. 333.
26 Marsella, DeVos, & Hsu 1985.
27 Shibatani 1990a.
28 See Tsujimura 1996.
29 Example from Tsujimura 1996.

CHAPTER 1

1 Brislin 1993, p. 47, who cites Hofstede 1980; Triandis 1990; and Triandis, Brislin, & Hui 1988.
2 Myers 1994.
3 Brislin 1993, p. 48.
4 Lipset 1994.
5 Berry, Poortinga, Segall, & Dasen 1992.
6 Berry, Poortinga, Segall, & Dasen 1992.
7 Inglehart 1990, p. 168; emphasis added.
8 Francese 1995; Sirevåg 1991.
9 Francese 1995.
10 Lipset 1994
11 Bradsher 1995.
12 Kerbo & McKinstry 1995, p. 7.
13 Oshima 1998, p. 196.
14 Martin 1975 as cited by White 1989.
15 Gudykunst & Nishida 1994, p. 28, who cite Gudykunst & Ting-Toomey 1988.
16 Argyle 1981 as quoted by Holden 1983, p. 157.
17 These classifications are based on Dodd 1991 and Samovar & Porter 1995.
18 Anderson 1997.
19 Ronen & Shenkar 1985 as cited by Anderson 1997.
20 "Chugoku" 1994.
21 Clarkson 1997.
22 Chesanow 1985 also uses this analogy.
23 Kerr 1996, p. 99.
24 Chisako Hirakawa, personal communication 1997.
25 Kerr 1996, pp. 105-106.
26 Beardsley 1965.

(Chapter 1)

27 Dazai Osamu as quoted by Buruma 1996, pp. 195-196.
28 Buruma 1996, p. 196.
29 Ma 1996, p. 27.
30 Tonedachi 1992 as cited and quoted by Ma 1996, p. 28.
31 Kobayakawa 1994.
32 Kobayakawa 1994.
33 See, for example, Gudykunst & Nishida 1994; Ishii 1984.
34 This example comes from Ishii 1984, p. 50.
35 Borthwick 1992, pp. 157-158.
36 Nakane & Ooishi 1990.
37 Borthwick 1992, p. 49.
38 Ruch 1984, p. 21, who cites Kelley 1981.
39 See Sternberg 1997.
40 Hunt 1998.
41 Maynard 1997.
42 This section has its basis in Hsu 1985.
43 *Kenkyusha's* 1987.
44 Iino 1991.
45 Hsu 1985.
46 Zimbardo 1977.
47 Zimbardo 1977, p. 214.
48 Zimbardo 1977, pp. 214-216.
49 Zimbardo 1977, p. 216.
50 Neustupný 1987, p. 75.
51 White 1993, p. 6.
52 Burks 1991.
53 Borthwick 1992, p. 157.
54 Williams 1996, pp. 10-11.
55 Williams 1996, pp. 9-10.
56 Borthwick 1992, p. 158.
57 Kerbo & McKinstry 1995, who cite Reischauer 1988.
58 Hsu 1985.
59 Lebra 1976 as cited by Brislin 1993, p. 156.
60 Brislin 1993, pp. 156-157.
61 Brislin 1993.
62 Brislin 1993, p. 157.
63 Spradley & Phillips 1972 as cited by Levine 1998.
64 These rankings and others in this section are taken from Levine (1998), who cites the work of Levine & Norenzayan (1996).
65 Levine 1998, p. 30.
66 Levine 1998, p. 31.
67 White 1993.

68 *Japan 1998.*
69 This sketch finds support from these principal sources: Burks 1991; Reischauer 1988; and Sugimoto 1997.
70 Shibatani 1990a.
71 "Foreign Students" 1994, p. 5.
72 Backhouse 1993.
73 Moriya 1985.
74 Neustupný 1987.
75 Neustupný 1987.
76 Neustupný 1987.
77 Shibatani 1990a.
78 Horioka 1998, p. 6.
79 Based on *Teikoku's Atlas* 1985.
80 Sugimoto 1997.
81 Moeran 1990b.
82 Moeran 1990b, p. 6.

CHAPTER 2

1 Eisenstadt 1996, van Wolferen 1989.
2 Emmott 1989.
3 Ross & Nisbett 1991.
4 Neustupný 1987.
5 Befu 1992a.
6 Ben-Ami 1997, p. 15.
7 Hammond 1997a.
8 Brislin 1981, 1993.
9 These entries are taken from Levey & Greenhall 1983.
10 Lemert 1989; van Dijk 1991.
11 Hall 1966, pp. 188-189, as quoted by Prosser, 1989, p. 125.
12 Owens 1997, p. 38.
13 Yamada 1990.
14 Umesao 1990.
15 Perrin 1988; Reischauer 1981; Ruch 1984.
16 See Horioka 1998.
17 Burks 1991, p. 127, who cites Nakamura & Shimbo 1988.
18 Caplow 1991.
19 *Kodansha* 1983, vol. 8, p. 61.
20 Caplow 1991, p. 24.
21 Caplow 1991, p. 24.
22 M. Yoshida 1986.
23 *Kodansha* 1983, vol. 2, p. 169.
24 Michiko Niikuni Wilson, personal communication 1993.
25 "Top Leaders" 1993.

26 Steinberg 1982.
27 Dodd 1991, p. 17.
28 Darnell 1985, p. 61.
29 Gudykunst & Kim 1992.
30 *Collected Works* 1970, p. 217.
31 Shaner & Duval 1990, p. 156.
32 Shaner & Duval 1990, p. 158.
33 Scharfstein 1989, p. xii.
34 Dalby et al. 1984, p. 194.
35 Wilkinson 1983.
36 I heard this at the conference, Intercultural Communication: The Last 25 Years and the Next, Rochester Institute of Technology, New York, July 1995.
37 Donahue 1986.
38 Samovar, Porter, & Jain 1981, p. 210.
39 Georgoudi & Rosnow 1985; Jaeger & Rosnow 1988; Morris 1988; Rosnow & Georgoudi 1986; Scharfstein 1989.
40 Scharfstein 1989, p. 4.
41 Morris 1988.
42 Weiss 1971, p. 19 as quoted by Alford 1978, p. 493.
43 *GRE* 1992.
44 Magnusson 1988.
45 Gudykunst & Kim 1992.
46 Bredo 1992.
47 Georgoudi & Rosnow 1985.
48 Horowitz 1987, p. 121.
49 From *Independent,* July 25, 1995 as cited by Hammond & Stirner 1997, p. 89.
50 From *Independent,* January 18, 1995 as cited by Hammond & Stirner 1997, p. 102.

CHAPTER 3

1 Hammond 1997a
2 Hammond & Stirner 1997, p. 100.
3 Hammond & Stirner 1997.
4 Mayes & Rowling 1997, p. 130.
5 Mayes & Rowling 1997, p. 132.
6 *Random House Webster's* 1991.
7 Wilkinson 1981, 1983.
8 Wilkinson 1981, p. 23. Antipodes in this quote refers not to an actual place (i.e., the islands off of New Zealand) but to an entity considered diametrically opposite in the western imagination. Some British authors capitalize this term as Wilkinson does here.

9 Statler 1984, p. 12.
10 van Dijk 1987, p. 184.
11 van Dijk 1984.
12 Cobb 1990; Johnson 1988; Wilkinson 1983.
13 Johnson 1988.
14 Johnson 1988, p. 12.
15 van Dijk 1984.
16 van Dijk 1984, p. 24; author's emphasis.
17 I first found these films separately at the University of Viriginia, but they are now available on one video tape from International Historic Films, Box 29035, Chicago, IL 60629, tel. 312-927-2900.
18 Garten 1992, pp. 68-69.
19 McBride 1992.
20 MacDonald 1988; McBride 1992.
21 United States Army Pictorial Service 1945, 1946.
22 Brislin 1981.
23 Ross 1977, as quoted by Brislin 1981, p. 93.
24 Hammond 1997b, p. xi.
25 *Random House Webster's* 1991.
26 No causal link is being made, of course, between the *Our Job* film and the internment of Japanese Americans because the film came much later. Rather the concern here is with an apparent logic common to both—misattribution of Japanese ethnic traits.
27 White 1985, p. 38.
28 White 1985, p. 20.
29 DIC Enterprises 1985.
30 Quoted by van Dijk 1984, p. 10, who cites Katz 1976 and Husband 1982.
31 *Mask* was originally co-produced in Canada and France and was aired on American television. The six episodes of this study appear in Volumes 1, 2, and 4 of the video series and were chosen solely because of availability.
32 Argyle 1992, p. 173; Bronfenbrenner 1961.
33 Borthwick 1992; Dower 1993.
34 Ueno 1994.
35 Abé 1994, p. 235.
36 Abé 1994, p. 238.
37 Ueno 1994, p. 74-75.

CHAPTER 4

1 This information, however, may not always be accurate. Some athletes or their teams may wish to "fudge" their measurements

(Chapter 4)

for image purposes. Nevertheless, we can assume that if it is done, it must be negligible or the measurements would become too incredible for belief.

2 A. Miller 1982. See Sitaram 1995 for a cross-cultural perspective.

3 For *Economics* (Lipsey, Courant, Purves, Steiner 1992; Tenth edition; Harper Collins College Publishers; as cited on the poster. According to the publisher (HarperCollins College Publishers), as of July 1995, the poster was already out of print, which thwarted attempt at confirmation.

4 Hinds & Iwasaki 1995.

5 Hinds & Iwasaki 1995, p. 57.

6 Hinds & Iwasaki 1995, p. 58.

7 Hinds & Iwasaki 1995, p. 58.

8 Hinds & Iwasaki 1995, p. 57.

9 Brislin 1993.

10 Gudykunst & Kim 1992, p. 92.

11 Brislin 1993.

12 Draguns 1997, p. 238.

13 Barnlund 1989, p. xvi; author's emphasis.

14 Erchak 1992, p. 104.

15 V. Lynn Tyler, personal communication 1990.

16 Fisher 1988.

17 This incident occurred in April 1982, the start of the Japanese academic calendar, and a date I had to since verify because seven years later a current Japanese rock music band was formed under the name of "The Yellow Monkey." According to a recent NHK TV program (*Yellow Monkey* 1997), this band was formed on December 28, 1989, which clearly means that the student could not have been referring to the band. To my knowledge there was no other publicly known name to negate interpreting the student comment as referring to the racial epithet. At least that is how the English teacher took it.

18 Hirano 1994.

19 Meo 1968.

20 Goodman 1990, Moeran 1990b.

21 Befu 1993.

22 Befu 1993, p. 107.

23 Befu 1993, p. 109.

24 Goodman 1990, p. 60.

25 Befu 1993, p. 126.

26 Yagasaki 1990, p. 146.

27 Moeran 1988, p. 428.

(Chapter 4)

28 Edwin Reischauer.
29 Tsunoda 1978.
30 For example, Clark & Clark 1977.
31 Tsujimura 1996, p. 365.
32 Sonoda 1985.
33 Based on *The World Almanac* 1991.
34 Koyama 1985.
35 Reischauer 1988.
36 Befu 1993; Yagasaki 1990.
37 To name just one change, the Japanese repealed its size regulations governing large retail stores, which enabled the American retailer Toys R Us to build its stores in Japan. Within two years of building one in Nagoya, I have noticed that three or four toy stores have gone out of business. Because no other toy stores took their places, Toys R Us is the only retail toy store in my community. Absent of any competition, Toys R Us is now free to charge high prices. As a result, some community people wonder what real benefits have been served. Such a large store does not provide personal service or free demonstrations of the toys as the small retailers did. Moreover, motor traffic is appreciably heavier on the streets around this large store. Finally, the closure of the small stores meant disruption not only for their owners and families but for other residents who felt a loss of community.
38 Hume 1995, p. xi.
39 Oshima 1998.
40 Oshima 1998, p. 203.
41 Oshima 1998, p. 202.
42 Sowell 1994, p. xiii.
43 Sowell 1994, p. 6.
44 *Random House Webster's* 1991, p. 1110.
45 Donahue in press; Gudykunst & Kim 1992.
46 For example, Inamoto 1982.
47 Weiner 1997, p. xi. The capitalization of *Burakumin* is maintained in this quote although I do not capitalize it myself because of uncertainty about it being truly an identifying term by the *burakumin* themselves.
48 Yoshino 1992, p. 24.
49 van den Berghe 1967, p. 11 as cited by Condor 1988, p. 82.
50 For example, Gudykunst & Kim 1992, p. 100.
51 Yoshino 1997.
52 Yoshino 1992.
53 Befu 1993.

54 Kushida 1993
55 Broadbent 1991; Buruma 1995.
56 Kristof 1997.
57 *Today's Japan* 1995.
58 Kikuchi 1993.
59 Kikuchi 1993.
60 Miyoshi 1991.
61 Reischauer 1988, p. 396.
62 Reischauer 1988.
63 Sautman 1995, p. 211, who cites National Conference 1994.
64 Sugimoto 1997, p. 189.
65 Sugimoto 1997, p. 189.
66 McCormack 1996a, pp. 4-5.
67 Kato 1988 as cited by McCormack 1996b; and NHK 1997 as cited by Noriko Kushida, personal communication.
68 Koyama 1992.
69 McCormack 1996a, p. 3.
70 Prosser 1989.
71 Keene 1982, pp. 13-14.
72 Quoted by Price & Crapo 1992, p. 13, who cite Segall, Campbell, & Herskovits 1966.
73 These scores are estimated for the years 1993 to 1995 as based on information in *Japan 1998.*

CHAPTER 5

1 Harris & Moran 1991.
2 Dodd 1991, p. 33.
3 "We will never stop" 1990.
4 For example, Tannen 1990, 1994.
5 Hinds 1986b.
6 Tannen 1994, p. 192.
7 Tannen 1994, p. 71.
8 Tannen 1994, p. 72.
9 Tannen 1994, pp. 71-72.
10 Cited by Prosser 1989.
11 Yamada 1992, p. 129.
12 De Mente 1989; Graham & Sano (reported in Pfeiffer 1988); Harris & Morgan 1987; and Thian 1988.
13 Yamada 1992, p. 130.
14 *Random House Webster's* 1991.
15 Yamada 1997.
16 Yamada 1997, p. 13.

(Chapter 5)

17 Yamada 1997, p. 10.
18 Matsumoto 1996, p. 55.
19 Lehner 1996.
20 Makino 1993.
21 Aoki & Okamoto 1988.
22 Nakada 1992.
23 Loveday 1986.
24 Quoted by Loveday 1986, p. 95, who cites Barnlund 1975, Lebra 1976, and Seward 1968, p. 111.
25 Smith & Bond 1993, p. 39.
26 Smith & Bond 1993.
27 Gudykunst & Nishida 1994.
28 Gudykunst & Nishida 1994, 35.
29 Loveday 1986, p. 94.
30 Hori 1995, p. 166, note 5.
31 Yamada 1997 also notes this.
32 Loveday 1986, pp. 13-14.
33 Crystal 1987, p. 99.
34 After Kaneko 1990.
35 Cook 1996.
36 Moeran 1988.
37 Based largely on Neustupný 1978 and Hori's 1995 observance of Tsujimura 1977.
38 Wenger 1984, p. 275.
39 Miller 1988.
40 Monane 1976, p. 78; author's emphasis.
41 This example is from Monane 1976.
42 Monane 1976.
43 Yamamoto 1984.
44 Wenger 1984, p. 267.
45 An adaption of Tsuda 1984, p. 135.
46 Kaneko 1990, p. 243.
47 Bunkachoo 1974, pp. 9-10 as quoted by Hendry 1993, p. 53.
48 Aoki & Okamoto 1988.
49 Kaneko 1990.
50 Yoshikazu Yanagi, personal communication, 1998.
51 Buruma 1995; McCormack 1996a; 1996b.
52 Neustupny 1987.
53 Wenger 1984.
54 Thanks go to Hisako Kushida for this example.
55 Hendry 1993.
56 Miller 1988.

(Chapter 5)

57 Hendry 1993.
58 Hendry 1993.
59 Okuaki 1988, p. 23.
60 Clancy 1982, p. 74 as quoted by Loveday 1986, pp. 113-114.
61 David Riggs, personal communication 1998.
62 Yamada 1992.
63 This is implicit in Yamada 1992 but made explicit in Yamada 1997: "Formalized in a written agenda, the setup in the American meeting differs from the Japanese *uchiawase* (soundout) in which there was no agenda to prescribe an expected sequence of talk throughout the meeting. Given this fundamental difference, it is not surprising to find that the American strategy for opening topics is vastly different from the Japanese" (Yamada 1997, p. 74). Note that Yamada here is speaking about the same American business meeting she studied in Yamada 1992, as the dialogues are the same on page 66 in Yamada 1992 and that on pages 74-75 in Yamada 1997.
64 Yamada 1997, p. 74.
65 Akasu & Asao 1993, p. 101.
66 Maynard 1989.
67 Maynard 1989.
68 Yamada 1992.
69 Yagasaki 1990.
70 *Japan 1998,* in regard to manufacturing, which shows United Kingdom, the United States, France, Germany, Canada ahead of Japan in this order. These were the only countries listed. This rank of Japan's was similarly held in the late 1980s well before going into recession in the 90s. Moreover, there has been, in general, a steady rise in labor productivity for all these countries over these two decades. Although growth rates in GDP or GNP may be a likely factor, my source did not include long-term GDP or GNP growth rates for these countries. However, statistics on Japanese productivity may actually be inflated depending on validity of the hours reported for Japanese employees. One hears conflicting reports about Japanese working hours between the actual and the reported.

A question arises as to how to explain the rank of Japanese labor productivity when Japan's long-term economic growth rate has been "unmatched," as noted in Chapter 2. "Economic miracles," as such as Japan's, eventually emerge into a "mature" economy as it is said in economics, whereby only modest GNP growth rates obtain. Today, Japanese productivity rates will necessarily be without the benefit of the phenomenal growth of its "miracle" decades ago.

Another factor may be related to the Japanese "social contract" between Japanese management and labor. By this social contract, workers are promised relatively long-term security in exchange for their unswerving loyalty. Workers are expected to be available for work more than their western counterparts. A Swiss executive in Japan once told me that he was surprised how Japanese workers at his plant could be counted on to extend their shifts according to production demand, whereas in Switzerland, that could never be expected. He also noticed that Japanese workers are not necessarily involved in continual work, an aspect noted by Hamid Saleem about students in Japanese scientific labs. This work flexibility seems well suited for "just-in-time" production by which Japanese manufacturers produce goods to order, so that retailers or distributors need not keep heavy inventories. In return for this worker loyalty (flexibility), companies refrain from lay-offs during a recession. Thus, Japanese firms may be "over-staffed," which could help explain the Japanese rank for labor productivity in the recessionary 1990s Japan. This "over-staffing" may become ignored by economic analysis during high economic times but prove baneful during downturns. Since the early 1990s, corporate Japan has been giving much attention to "downsizing," in realization the increasing global competition leaves them little choice. To what extent the "social contract" will be amended is unclear, but the twenty-first century is likely to lead to greater "rationalizaton" in labor practices.

71 Miller 1988, p. 135.
72 Matsumoto 1996, p. 72.
73 Matthew 1989.
74 Matthew 1989, p. 156.
75 Hoshi (n.d.).
76 This latter gloss comes from Kaneko 1990.
77 Mazuka & Nagai 1995.

CHAPTER 6

1 Seward 1976.
2 Smith 1978.
3 Clark & Clark 1977.
4 Haneda & Shima 1982, p. 20.
5 Backhouse 1993.
6 Backhouse 1993.

(Chapter 6)

7 Kuno 1986.
8 Kuno 1986; Shibatani 1990b.
9 Kuno 1986.
10 Collier-Sanuki 1997.
11 Collier-Sanuki 1997.
12 Note the title of Hinds 1986c *The Mysterious Language of Japan,* which was apparently how Hinds perceived the popular image of the language.
13 Noriko Kushida and Mina Yamaji, personal communicatons 1997.
14 Ichijo 1997. I thank Naoto Mizutani for this example.
15 Noriko Kushida, personal communication 1997.
16 Naoto Mizutani, personal communication 1997.
17 Kurita 1987a.
18 Ohnuki-Tierney 1984.
19 Murphy 1988 as quoted by Knight 1997, p. 203.
20 Ma in Soares 1996, p. 3.
21 Hammond & Stirner 1997.
22 Oshima 1998.
23 "Count Cost" 1995, p. 6.
24 Ishii & Bruneau 1988, p. 311.
25 Mason & Ogawa 1998. This figure of one-fifth is actually conservative.
26 Cherry 1987.
27 NHK TV news (BS 7) broadcast December 15, 1997.
28 *Japan 1998.*
29 Cherry 1987, pp. 10-11.
30 Koyama 1992, p. 61.
31 Diggs 1998, pp. 152-153.
32 Sato 1995.
33 Aired on TV channel 35, Nagoya, September 5, 1997.
34 Yamada 1997.
35 Hinds 1986b; Monane & Rogers 1977.
36 Hinds 1986b; Monane & Rogers 1977.
37 Hinds 1986b; Monane & Rogers 1977.
38 Isshiki 1981.
39 Isshiki 1981, p. 6.
40 Isshiki 1981, p. 23.
41 These examples are from Monane & Rogers 1977.
42 Hinds 1984, p. 157.
43 Hinds 1985, p. 18.
44 Aoki & Okamoto 1988.
45 Aoki & Okamoto 1988, p. 253.

46 Aoki & Okamoto 1988, p. iv.
47 Sumiyo Fukaya, personal communication 1997.
48 Haneda & Shima 1982.
49 Sumiyo Fukaya, personal communication 1997.

CHAPTER 7

1 Tsuda 1984, p. 148.
2 Nagoya Zip FM radio, November 27, 1997.
3 Hinds 1986a.
4 Hinds 1986a.
5 Brown & Yule 1983; Chafe 1982; Tannen 1982.
6 El-Agraa 1988, p. 16.
7 De Vos 1992, p. 213, who bases this on Vaughn 1988 and his own observations.
8 From an interview in Kolker & Alvarez 1991.
9 Trudgill 1983.
10 Crystal 1987.
11 Shibatani 1990a.
12 Reischauer 1988.
13 Crump 1988, p. 140.
14 Stanlaw 1992, p. 61 and based on *Kokuritsu Kokugo Kenkyuujo* 1970-1974.
15 Neustupný 1987, p. 182.
16 Hatano, Kuhara, & Akiyama 1997.
17 Reischauer 1988, p. 382. Romanization is not included here.
18 From an interview in Kolker and Alvarez 1991.
19 Prosser 1989, p. 2.
20 Okabe 1983.
21 Kurita 1987a, p. 51.
22 Kurita 1987a, p. 51.
23 Kurita, 1987a, pp. 50-51.
24 Loveday 1986; Okabe 1983.
25 Loveday 1986, p. 116.
26 Kurita 1987a, p. 21.
27 Kurita 1987a, p. 23.
28 Hinds 1986a, p. 323.
29 Shibatani 1990a.
30 Okabe 1983. The wholistic pattern may not be uniquely Japanese but rather pan-Asian. See Scollon & Scollon 1995.
31 "'Naze?'" 1992.
32 Sternberg 1997.
33 Sternberg 1997.
34 Sternberg 1997.

35 Hinds & Iwasaki 1995, p. 74.
36 Hinds & Iwasaki 1995, p. 85.
37 Hinds & Iwasaki 1995, p. 86.
38 Haneda & Shima 1982.
39 Hinds & Iwasaki 1995, pp. 86-87.
40 Hinds & Iwasaki 1995, p. 87-88.
41 Honna & Hoffer 1989, pp. 176-178.
42 Okazaki 1993, p. 77.

CHAPTER 8

1 Schiffrin 1994.
2 Allerton 1979, p. 12.
3 Allerton 1979, p. 12.
4 Quoted by Horowitz 1987, p. 121, who cites Beaugrande 1985.
5 Beaugrande 1985, p. 49 as quoted by Horowitz 1987, p. 121.
6 Widdowson 1983 as quoted by Nunan 1993, p. 74.
7 For example, Hoey 1983, 1991.
8 Kaplan 1988/1966.
9 Donahue 1994.
10 Donahue 1990; Karatsu 1992; Kubota 1992; Ludden 1994; Uzawa & Cumming 1989.
11 Hinds 1980, p. 150.
12 *Random House Webster's* 1991, emphasis mine.
13 Kitano 1993, p. 123.
14 Ogawa 1973.
15 Ogawa 1973, p. 176. I should note also that however the ethnic composition in Hawaii may have changed in recent years is irrelevant, for Hinds's specimen texts were published in 1977 (Hinds 1980).
16 Higa 1975, p. 75.
17 Ogawa 1973, p. 11.
18 Quoted in Burks 1991, p. 167.
19 Saeki 1991.
20 Suzuki 1980, p. 363 as cited by Befu 1993, p. 116.
21 Befu 1993, p. 116, who cites Hamabata 1990 and Kondo 1990.
22 Prosser 1992.
23 Kurokawa 1987, p. 30.
24 Monane 1976. Japanese Americans in Hawaii generally speak a dialectal form of Japanese distinguishable from what is spoken in Japan.
25 I have chosen for analysis the largest of two Japanese specimen texts in Hinds's 1980 study. I also take Hinds at his word that "due to the brevity of [his other] article, it is difficult to offer any strong

(Chapter 8)

evidence for [Hinds's] analysis ..." (1980, p. 134). So my present analysis, like Hinds's, relies on the May Yokomoto text.

26 This title is of the original article in *Kokiku* (May 1977, p. 7).

27 This title is of the original article in *Kokiku* (May 1977, p. 7). This translation is Hinds's (1980) and is as presented here. Note that the name of Ito in the original English version was given by Hinds as Itoh in his translation; both spellings are correct and are maintained here. (The two spellings follow different conventions of transliteration.)

28 *Teikoku's Atlas* 1985.

29 Quirk, Greenbaum, Leech, & Svartvik 1985.

30 This information is based on the recollections of two Japanese Americans of Hawaii (in Japan), who recalled that the *Kokiku* publication was produced in conjunction with the KIKU (Hawaii) television station.

31 Jeremy & Robinson 1989, p. 29.

32 Reischauer 1988, p. 399.

33 Yoshida 1978, p. 26; originally 1909. Thanks go to Dee Yamashita, who pointed this out and provided the reference as well.

34 Buruma 1996.

35 Gundersen 1990 reported how Seiko (Matsuda), a Japanese popular female singer, after her marriage and a five-year retreat, was trying to make a comeback not in Japan but in the United States. Seiko was quoted as saying, "I stayed home for two years and did housework and had a baby.... Then I tried to come back. But Japan is very traditional. Women stay home after they are married." In her actions, Seiko, as the article noted, had "become the unwitting leader of a women's movement...."

36 Hinds also recognized the Japanese foreignness syndrome, but he ignored the apparent attempt by the Japanese (Hawaiian) text to counter this syndrome. Under Hinds's analysis, some of his "foreignness" items also appear in the English text, which means that the items may not be distinctive to Japanese culture. Consequently, the present analysis has an advantage because its foreignness items appear only in the Japanese text, suggesting distinctive Japanese cultural features.

37 Reischauer 1988.

38 Hinds 1980, p. 124.

39 Cooper & Matsuhashi 1983; Odell 1981.

40 Britton, Burgess, Martin, McLeod, & Rosen 1975, p. 5.

41 Beaugrande 1984; Nida 1984.

42 Kaplan 1987, p. 10.
43 "Address delivered by Cuomo" 1992.
44 Toner 1992, p. A1.
45 For example, Clyne 1994 and Connor 1996.
46 Clyne 1994.
47 Clyne 1994 and Connor 1996.
48 Term is from Gray 1990.
49 Donahue 1990; Kubota 1992.
50 Connor 1996, p. 41 describes a study by Hinds reportedly published in *Studies in Linguistics* (1984, Vol. 8), but it does not appear there in that year or any other year. This paper was referred to by Hinds and listed in Connor and Kaplan's 1987 edited collection as appearing in the same journal. Yet it does not exist, at least not in *Studies in Linguistics.*
51 Hinds 1980, p. 124.
52 Hill & Larsen 1983.
53 Larson 1984.
54 Grabe 1987.
55 For example, Nida 1984.

CHAPTER 9

1 Nida 1984.
2 Hinds 1983a.
3 *Ki-shoo-ten-ketsu* is an actual Japanese term for a style. At dispute is Hinds's interpretation of the term and how he supports his claims. I should note also that Hinds later proposed another style of Japanese prose. I will reserve comment on this additional style until the end of this chapter. Until then we will concentrate on the *tempura* and *ki-shoo-ten-ketsu* styles.
4 Fredrickson & Wedel 1984.
5 Kaplan 1972, 1987.
6 Hinds 1983a, 1983c.
7 Hinds 1983c.
8 Yutani 1977.
9 Yutani 1977.
10 Term by Fredrickson & Wedel 1984.
11 Yutani 1977, p. 53.
12 Yutani 1977, p. 53.
13 Yutani 1977, p. 54.
14 Yutani 1977, p. 54; emphasis mine.
15 Yutani 1977, p. 54; emphasis mine.
16 Headlines usually accompany Japanese newspaper articles as they do in western newspapers.

(Chapter 9)

17 van Dijk 1985.

18 Hinds 1983a, p. 80

19 *American Heritage Dictionary* 1975, p. 743; also Yutani 1976, p. 12. Some confusion does exist with the term "lead," because it is also used to mean "summary lead." However, a distinction must be made because newspaper leads—first sentences—vary in their degree of being summaries, while some do not function that way at all. Hence the need for the term, "summary lead." See Fredrickson & Wedel 1984.

20 Hinds 1983a, p. 80.

21 Yutani 1976.

22 Fredrickson & Wedel 1984.

23 Yutani 1976, p. 25.

24 Stephens 1991.

25 Yutani 1976.

26 Yutaka Yutani, personal communication, 1985. Nobuyuki Honna, a Japanese sociolinguist, told me much the same thing about Japanese newspaper articles having a style similar to western newspapers. He noted also that the case was quite different about fifty to sixty years ago.

27 Kabashima 1980 and Takemata 1976 as cited by Kobayashi 1984. It should be noted that Takemata is incorrectly listed as Takematsu by Kobayashi 1984, whose citation I have borrowed.

28 Kobayashi 1984, pp. 26-30 posits an inductive pattern of Japanese exposition, but she bases her assertion entirely on Hinds's treatment of Yutani's 1977 article and several pedagogical studies. However, Yutani's study proves sorely inadequate as just seen, and the several other studies are all based on ESL compositions, a methodology Hinds 1983b rightly rejects for contrastive rhetoric.

Although Kobayashi supplemented her ESL compositions with native language ones, her samples were all classroom products. (Her results supporting Japanese indirection may simply be a function of the late training that Japanese students appear to receive in composition.) For these reasons and Kobayashi's confinement to samples of "paragraph length" (p. 42), I do not give her study a full review. I do discuss the paragraph somewhat, but it is done only peripherally as it relates to Hinds's return to baseline theme style and structural views of discourse. Her study, otherwise, is well written and conceived and may have pedagogical implications worth considering.

29 Haruhara 1985.

(Chapter 9)

30 Hinds 1983a, p. 80, who cites Takemata 1976, p. 26.
31 Hinds 1983c.
32 Hinds 1983b.
33 Brislin 1976, 1980; Nida 1976.
34 Hinds 1983c.
35 Asahi Shimbun 1979, vol. 37, p. 210 (English version).
36 Asahi Shimbun 1979, vol. 37, p. 209 (Japanese version).
37 For example, Bourhis 1979, Edwards & Giles 1984, Giles 1979, Giles & Powesland 1975, Sebastian & Ryan 1985.
38 Hinds's 1983b study has the same weaknesses found with his other study using *Tensei Jingo:* absence of back-translation, translation errors (as noted by Hinds), foreign terms used exclusively by the English version, and the apparent foreign (Japanese) authorship of the English version.

Mention ought to made also about Jenkins & Hinds's 1987 study of business letter writing. Although that study does not directly relate to *ki-shoo-ten-ketsu,* it still is sometimes used as further support for the view that the organization of Japanese writing is different, even circular. Yes, I agree that Japanese business letter writing may follow different conventions than in English, as seen in Chapter 7. However, I disagree that the Jenkins & Hinds's study can be used to support classifying Japanese *written exposition* in terms of Kaplan's Oriental type. First, "because of the formal nature of [Japanese] business letters, only polite forms are used" (Jenkins & Hinds 1987, p. 339). As they pointed out, these polite forms are part of *keigo*, the honorific language (p. 338), language not generally used in Japanese expository writing. Second, Japanese business letter writers can dispense with the preliminaries by using the set expression *zenryaku* (p. 337), an option that the authors do not explore further. Also consider the TYPE 4 business letter mentioned in Chapter 7. Third, no source is given for the Japanese "example of business letter writing which is representative of this genre" (p. 330), but sources *are* given for English and French "represen tative letters" (see Appendix A to D, pp. 346-349 in Jenkins & Hinds 1987.). The reader, therefore, does not know whether the Japanese letter comes from 1) a textbook idealization; 2) actual Japanese correspondence; or 3) Hinds's own hand. Validity varies among these possibilities for representing Japanese business letter writing.

39 Asahi Shimbun 1979, vol. 37, p. 210 (English version). The original text is reprinted as is, including foreign terms that were not

(Chapter 9)

italicized.
40 Hinds 1983b, 1983c.
41 Gunji 1987, p. 166.
42 Carlson 1983, Gunji 1987, Kuno 1972, Makino 1993, Makino & Tsutsui 1986.
43 Hinds 1987a.
44 Donahue 1990.
45 Hinds 1983c.
46 Makino 1978.
47 Hinds 1983c.
48 Hinds 1987b.
49 Brockett 1989, Shibatani 1990b.
50 Holman 1978.
51 Lanham 1968.
52 For example, Young & Sullivan 1984, p. 217.
53 Goffman 1981, p. 178.
54 Hinds 1983c.
55 Hinds 1983c; 1987a.
56 Dooling & Lachman 1971 as quoted by Sanford & Garrod 1981, p. 9.
57 *Kenkyusha's* 1987. I also remind the reader that the romanization here for *zuisoo* follows that of Japanese linguistics in general by doubling the vowel to show lengthening. Although the final vowel sound is realized in the written *hiragana* script as う [u], the [u] is silent, and [o] of [so], lengthened.
58 Kurita 1987b.
59 Dalby et al. 1984, pp. 74-75.
60 I thank Makoto Omi for bringing this to my attention.
61 Gray 1990.
62 Hinds 1987a.
63 Hiroaki Yamashita, personal communication 1985.
64 For example, Easton 1982 and Yamaguchi 1967.
65 For example, Easton 1982, Hinds 1981, Makino 1978.
66 Lanham 1968.
67 Lanham 1968.
68 Reagan 1992.
69 Donahue & Prosser 1997.
70 Easton 1982.
71 Hoey 1983.
72 Jordan 1984.
73 Easton 1982, p. 72.
74 Easton 1982, p. 34.

(Chapter 9)

75 Easton 1982.
76 Easton 1982; Young 1982.
77 Young 1982.
78 Scarcella 1984.
79 Suzuki 1975.
80 For example Befu 1992b, Dale 1986, Gill 1986, Miller 1977, Moeran 1990a, Mouer & Sugimoto 1986, Shibatani 1990b.
81 Moeran 1990a, p. 10; emphasis, the original.
82 Rubin 1992, p. 15.
83 DeFrancis 1984.
84 Elliott 1991, p. 11.
85 Elliott 1991.
86 Burks 1991.
87 Pulvers 1982, p. 148.
88 Miller 1986.
89 Reischauer 1989.
90 Hinds 1980 states in a footnote that scientific and other types of writing in Japanese emulate English writing style. He, however, does not explain why the Japanese emulate English writing style and not Dutch or German, the two languages that provided the Japanese their earliest knowledge of the west and its science (Bartholomew 1989; Burks 1991). In regard to the extent of his observation, the use of topic sentences is only one of many stylistic features one would want to know about.
91 Rubin 1992.
92 Shibatani 1990b, p. 127.
93 Pulvers 1982, p. 148.
94 Kasahara 1974, p. 402.
95 Other red flags that go up in regard to Kasahara's study are as follows:

(1) Kasahara's paper is a reprint of one originally addressed to a mental health audience (p. 396f), an audience that will likely interpret his speculations differently from a non-specialist one.
(2) It has been the practice of Japanese psychiatry to subsume fear of eye-to-eye confrontation with other related phobias under the heading of fear of interpersonal relations (pp. 396-397). I suspect a similar practice occurs in the west.
(3) Although Kasahara entitles his article "Fear of eye-to eye confrontation ...," other phobias (e.g., fear of odors) are given as much attention. Therefore, eye contact phobia may not be as important to him as his title suggests.
(4) Among the cases of fear of interpersonal relations that he has

(Chapter 9)

seen, eye-to-eye confrontation cases account for only 12 percent (p. 402)! In fact, body odor concerns are more than double the frequency of eye-to-eye confrontation phobia (p. 402).

(5) The occurrence of eye-to-eye confrontation fear seems to get inflated because Kasahara combines it with odor fears when speaking of case frequency among neurotics (p. 402).

96 Kasahara 1974, p. 397.
97 *Roget's International Thesaurus* 1977.
98 Zimbardo 1977.
99 Clancy 1985, p. 495.
100 *Kenkyusha's* 1987.
101 Maynard 1989.
102 Okabe 1991.
103 Allport 1968, Stewart 1976.
104 Quoted by Barnlund 1989, p. 143.
105 Barnlund 1989, p. 143.
106 Loveday 1986, p. 109.
107 Scheflen 1973, pp. 65-67.
108 For example, Miller's 1967 treatment of *keigo* as levels of speech.
109 Loveday 1986, p. 11.
110 Moeran 1990b.
111 Moeran 1990b, p. 2.
112 Tsunoda 1978.
113 Crystal & Davy 1969.
114 Ball, Giles, & Hewstone 1985; Montgomery 1986, Ryan 1979.
115 Knapp 1978.
116 Dale 1986, Miller 1977, 1986.
117 Dale 1986.
118 This section owes much to Clifford Hill for having identified it as an issue in contrastive rhetoric. Regarding the choice of term, *structural,* here it refers broadly to an emphasis on language structure and has no other intended meaning. Although compositionists may use *formalist* instead, *structural* seems more familiar to specialists in international studies.
119 Christensen 1965, p. 144.
120 Lewis 1894.
121 Kaplan 1988, pp. 216-217.
122 Kaplan 1988, p. 221.
123 Irmscher 1979; Eden & Mitchell 1986.
124 Hinds 1980, p. 151f.

(Chapter 9)

125 Rodgers 1966, p. 6.
126 Rodgers 1966, p. 6.
127 Markels 1984, p. 42.
128 Lewis 1894.
129 Lewis 1894, p. 27.
130 Sanford & Garrod 1981.
131 Beaugrande 1984, p. 304; emphasis, the original.
132 Markels 1984, p. 43.
133 Christensen 1965, p. 144.
134 Kaplan 1987, p. 18.
135 Kaplan 1987, p. 10.
136 Stewart 1976.
137 Stern 1983, p. 15.
138 Neustupný 1987, pp. 181-182.
139 Nida 1984.
140 Kaplan 1988, pp. 208-209.
141 Coe 1988, p. 54. See also Scollon & Scollon 1995.
142 Dahl 1979, p. 199 as quoted by Odlin 1989, p. 62f.
143 See Leki 1991.
144 Hinds 1983b.
145 Halverson 1991, p. 625.
146 Beaugrande 1984.
147 Donahue 1990, Shishin 1985.
148 Uzawa & Cumming 1989, p. 179.
149 Cole 1996.
150 Berry, Poortinga, Segall, & Dasen 1992, p. 117.
151 Hinds & Iwasaki 1995, pp. 75-76.
152 This is my own constructed example based on one given by Hinds & Iwasaki 1995.
153 Cole 1996.
154 Scribner 1979.
155 See Cole 1996.
156 Scribner 1979, p. 226.
157 Hinds & Iwasaki 1995, pp. 75-76.
158 Cole & Scribner 1974, p. 170, emphasis added.
159 As is well known, the Whorfian hypothesis or linguistic determinism is generally accepted only in its qualified (weak) version (Berry, Poortinga, Segall & Dasen, 1992 Clark & Clark, 1977; Crystal, 1987; Hill, 1988; Trudgill, 1983): "Language may not determine the way we think, but it does influence the way we perceive and remember, and it affects the ease with which we perform mental tasks" (Crystal 1987, p. 15). The operative word

here is *determine,* for the word appears too strong. However, if replaced by *influence,* as with "language or perception influencing thought," linguistic determinism, in modified form, appears a reasonable explanation in some cases.

Cognitive schema theory has its roots in cross-cultural findings that peoples may hold different mental scripts for storytelling or semantic concepts. In no way can that mean that ipso facto, Hinds's versions of Japanese rhetorical styles are valid.

160 Hinds 1990.
161 Hinds 1990, p. 90.
162 Hinds 1990, p. 98.

CHAPTER 10

1 The period covered for these Asia news segments was 1994-1996 though the program lasted until March, 1997.
2 This time is approximated as based on the broadcast of the same program on September 28, 1994 when an ABC clock was visibly shown to read 5:23 toward the end of the program and subsequently confirmed by this author during a visit to New York in July, 1996.
3 ABC News, April 10, 1996.
4 This friction occurred in an airing in September, 1995.
5 The actual video recordings were shown publicly by the author in July 1996 at the conference Multiculturalism, Cultural Diversity, and Global Communication held at Rochester Institute of Technology, as well as in the Department of Professional and Technical Communication of the same institution.
6 ABC News, January 20, 1995.
7 ABC News, January 20, 1995.
8 ABC News, January 20, 1995.
9 Imahori & Cupach 1991, as cited by Gudykunst & Nishida 1994.
10 ABC News, May 19, 1995.
11 ABC News, September 21, 1995.
12 ABC News, October 11, 1995.
13 ABC News, April 10, 1996.
14 ABC News, March 1, 1996.
15 ABC News, April 15, 1996.
16 ABC News, June 22, 1995.
17 ABC News, March 15, 1996.
18 ABC News, December 18, 1995.
19 ABC News, March 5, 1996.
20 ABC News, July 4, 1996.
21 ABC News, July 4, 1996.

22 ABC News, April 12, 1996.
23 ABC News, December 20, 1995.
24 ABC News, February 9, 1996.
25 Hobbs 1979, Lakoff & Johnson 1980.
26 Holman 1978.
27 Donahue 1994.
28 ABC News, September 25, 1995; October 6, 1995.
29 ABC News, June 22, 1995; September 29, 1995; October 13, 1995; March 14, 1996; April 4, 1996.
30 ABC News, March 5, 1996; March 19, 1996; March 25, 1996; March 26, 1996; April 5, 1996.
31 ABC News, December 20, 1995; February 29, 1996; March 15, 1996; April 19, 1996; June 18, 1996.
32 ABC News, July 3, 1995; September 19, 1995; September 21,1995; February 22, 1996; March 1, 1996; March 13, 1996; April 8, 1996; April 24, 1996; some items were also repeated on different dates.
33 ABC News, October 11, 1995; December 18, 1995; March 21, 1996; April 10, 1996; April 17, 1996; April 22, 1996.
34 Dodd 1991, p. 17.
35 Narasaki 1997.
36 The News Hour, December 3, 1997. The speaker was an unidentified member of a "town meeting" held with President Bill Clinton in Akron, Ohio.
37 *Random House Webster's* 1991.
38 *Picturesque Expressions* 1985
39 van Dijk 1984.
40 Lee 1982.
41 Stronach 1989, p. 149.
42 Krauss 1996.
43 Stronach 1989.
44 Tobin 1983.

CHAPTER 11

1 Jenkins 1993, p. 168.
2 "US-Japan 'bashing'" 1991.
3 Oda 1992.
4 Sabato 1994.
5 Oppenheim 1992, p. 4.
6 Oppenheim 1992.
7 Mourdoukoutas 1993.
8 Oppenheim 1992.
9 Mourdoukoutas 1993.

(Chapter 11)

10 Garten 1992.
11 Memmott 1990.
12 Mourdoukoutas 1993.
13 Ohmae 1988.
14 Ohmae 1988. Again these figures are more relevant for the time period in question. Since then, Japanese companies have greatly expanded overseas operations, and the yen has strengthen even more in value. Nevertheless, these later developments remain irrelevant to the related time period.
15 Gehani 1991, p. 9A.
16 Koppel 1994.
17 ABC News, *World News Tonight*, March 31, 1994.
18 Bodkin 1994.
19 Hashin 1994.
20 Bergsten & Noland 1993, p. 115.
21 NHK News 1994; Stokes 1994.
22 Economic Strategy Institute 1992 as cited by Bergsten & Noland 1993.
23 Cumings 1993, p. 60.
24 *Putting a stop* 1995, p. 18.
25 *Putting a stop* 1995, p. 16.
26 Schoppa 1997, p. 55.
27 Horioka 1998.
28 Mourdoukoutas 1993. The price that I quoted for Tokyo is actually 25% lower than that found in my source cited here. I did so to add some conservatism to the current monetary exchange rates, which appear a bit inflated.
29 Hiatt 1989.
30 For example, Myers 1994.
31 Hiatt 1989.
32 Major 1993, p. 463.
33 Reischauer 1988, p. 399.
34 Simon 1980.
35 Riccomini & Rosenzweig 1985.
36 ABC News *Nightline* October 30, 1996.
37 Johnson 1997.
38 This lack of translation occurred at a Tokyo trade show in 1977, when trade disputes were just as heated as they are today.

References

ABC News. (1994-1996). *Nightline*; *World News Now; World News Tonight* [TV broadcasts].

Abé, M. N. (1994). Dawn of freedom. In M. N. Abé & Y. Fukushima (Eds.), *The Japan/America film wars: World War II: Propaganda and its cultural contexts.* Chur, Switzerland and Langhorne, PA: Harwood Academic.

Address delivered by Cuomo nominating Clinton for president. (1992, July 16). *New York Times,* p. A14.

Akasu, K., & Asao, K. (1993). Sociolinguistic factors influencing communication in Japan and the United States. In W. B. Gudykunst (Ed.), *Communication in Japan and the United States.* Albany, NY: State University of New York Press.

Alford, D. K. H. (1978). The demise of the Whorf hypothesis. *Proceedings of the fourth annual meeting of the Berkeley Linguistics Society.* Berkeley, CA: Berkeley Linguistics Society.

Allerton, D. J. (1979). *Essentials of grammatical theory.* London: Routledge & Kegan Paul.

Allport, G. W. (1968). The historical background of modern social psychology. In G. Lindzey & E. Aronson (Eds.), *The handbook of social psychology* (Vol. 1). Reading, MA: Addison-Wesley.

American heritage dictionary of the English language. (1975). New York: American Heritage Publishing Co.

Anderson, W. N. (1997, July). Cultural values and problem solving. Paper presented at the conference, Communication, Technology and Cultural Values, Rochester Institute of Technology, New York.

Aoki, H., & Okamoto, S. (1988). *Rules for conversational rituals in Japanese.* Tokyo: Taishukan.

Argyle, M. (1981). *Bodily communication.* London: Methuen.

Argyle, M. (1992). *The social psychology of everyday life.* London and New York: Routledge.

Asahi Shimbun. (1979). *Tensei jingo vox populi, vox dei.* (Vols. 37-38). Tokyo: Harashoboo.

Backhouse, A. E. (1993). *The Japanese language: An introduction.* Melbourne: Oxford University Press.

Ball, P., Giles, H., & Hewstone, M. (1985). Interpersonal accommodation and situational construals: An integrative formalization. In H. Giles & R. N. St. Clair (Eds.), *Recent advances in language, communication, and social psychology.* London: Lawrence Erlbaum.

Barnlund, D. C. (1975). *Public and private self in Japan and the United States.* Tokyo: Simul Press.

Barnlund, D. C. (1989). *Communicative styles of Japanese and Americans.* Belmont, CA: Wadsworth.

Bartholomew, J. R. (1989). *The formation of science in Japan.* New Haven: Yale University Press.

Beardsley, R. K. (1965). Personality psychology. In J. W. Hall & R. K. Beardsley (Eds.), *Twelve doors to Japan.* New York: McGraw-Hill.

Beaugrande, R. de. (1984). *Text production: Toward a science of composition.* Norwood, NJ: Ablex.

Beaugrande, R. de. (1985). Text linguistics in discourse studies. In T. A. van Dijk (Ed.), *Handbook of discourse analysis: Vol. 1, Disciplines of discourse.* New York: Academic Press.

Befu, H. (1980). The group model of Japanese society and an alternative. *Rice University Studies*, 66, 169-187.

Befu, H. (1992a). Introduction: Framework of analysis. In H. Befu & J. Kreiner (Eds.), *Othernesses of Japan.* Munich: Iudicium Verlag.

Befu, H. (1992b). Symbols of nationalism and Nihonjinron. In R. Goodman & K. Refsing (Eds.), *Ideology and practice in modern Japan.* London and New York: Routledge.

Befu, H. (1993). Nationalism and Nihonjinron. In H. Befu (Ed.), *Cultural nationalism in East Asia.* Berkeley: Institute of East Asian Studies, University of California.

Befu, H., & Kreiner, J. (Eds.). (1992). *Othernesses of Japan.* Munich: Iudicium-Verlag.

Ben-Ami, D. (1997). Is Japan different? In P. Hammond (Ed.), *Cultural difference, media memories: Anglo-American images of Japan.* London: Cassell.

Benedict, R. (1946). *The Chrysanthemum and the sword.* Boston: Houghton Mifflin.

Bergsten, C. F., & Noland, M. (1993). *Reconcilable differences? United States-Japan economic conflict.* Washington, DC: Institute for International Economics.

Berry, J. W., Poortinga, Y. H., Segall, M. H., & Dasen, P. R. (1992). *Cross-cultural psychology.* Cambridge: Cambridge University Press.

Bodkin, D. (1994, February 23). Interview with Dalton Tanonaka. *Japan Business Today* [TV broadcast]. NHK.

Borthwick, M. (1992). *Pacific century.* Boulder, CO: Westview Press.

Bourhis, R. Y. (1979). Language in ethnic interaction: A social psychological approach. In H. Giles & B. Saint-Jacques (Eds.), *Language and ethnic relations.* Oxford: Pergamon.

Bradsher, K. (1995). US gap in riches widens. *Asahi Evening News*, pp. 1-2.

Bredo, E. (1992, April). John Dewey and situated cognition, discussion of 'Situated learning: John Dewey revisited?' Paper presented at the American Educational Studies Association meetings, San Francisco.

Brislin, R. W. (1976). Introduction. In R. W. Brislin (Ed.), *Translation: Applications and research.* New York: Gardner Press.

Brislin, R. W. (1980). Translation and content analysis of oral and written material. In H. C. Triandis & J. W. Berry (Eds.), *Handbook of cross-cultural psychology* (Vol. 2). Boston: Allyn and Bacon.

Brislin, R. W. (1981). *Cross-cultural encounters.* New York: Pergamon.

Brislin, R. (1993). *Understanding culture's influence on behavior.* Fort Worth, TX: Harcourt Brace College Publishers.

Britton, J., Burgess, T., Martin, N., McLeod, A., & Rosen, H. (1975). *The Development of writing abilities 11-18.* London: Macmillan Education.

Broadbent, J. (1991, April). A question of academic freedom in Japan. *Footnotes* [American Sociological Association], 19, 4, p. 5.

Brockett, C. (1989). *Wa* marking: Is discourse all? *Journal of the Association of Teachers of Japanese,* 23, 135-146.

Bronfenbrenner, U. (1961). The mirror image in Soviet-American relations: A social psychologist's report. *Journal of Social Issues,* 17, 345-356.

Brown, G., & Yule, G. (1983). *Teaching the spoken language.* Cambridge: Cambridge University Press.

Bunkachoo (Ed.). (1974). *Kotoba shirizu: Keigo.* Tokyo: Bunkachoo.

Burks, A. W. (1991). *Japan: A postindustrial power* (3rd, rev. ed.). Boulder, CO: Westview Press.

Buruma, I. (1995). *The wages of guilt: Memories of war in Germany and Japan.* New York: Meridian.

Buruma, I. (1996). *The missionary and the libertine.* London: Faber & Faber.

Caplow, T. (1991). *American social trends.* New York: Harcourt Brace Jovanovich College Publishers.

Carlson, L. (1983). *Dialogue games: An approach to discourse analysis.* Dordrecht: D. Reidel.

Chafe, W. L. (1982). Integration and involvement in speaking, writing, and oral literature. In D. Tannen (Ed.), *Spoken and written language.* Norwood, NJ: Ablex.

Cherry, K. (1987). *Womansword.* Tokyo and New York: Kodansha International.

Chesanow, N. (1985). *The world-class executive.* New York: Rawson Associates.

Christensen, F. (1965). A generative rhetoric of the paragraph. *College Composition and Communication,* 16, 144-156.

'Chugoku no kootei' to Bei-CNN ga hoosoo. (1994, June 14). *Chunichi Shimbun* (morning ed.), p. 31.

Clancy, P. M. (1982). Written and spoken style in Japanese narratives. In D. Tannen (Ed.), *Spoken and written language.* Norwood, NJ: Ablex.

Clancy, P. M. (1985). The acquisition of Japanese. In D. I. Slobin (Ed.), *The crosslinguistic study of language acquisition* (Vol. 1). Hillsdale, NJ: Lawrence Erlbaum.

Clark, H. H., & Clark, E. V. (1977). *Psychology and language.* New York: Harcourt Brace Jovanovich.

Clarkson, B. (1997, July 23). Hey kids, Japanese don't eat dog *sushi* or burp after meals. *The Japan Times,* p. 3.

Clyne, M. (1994). *Inter-cultural communication at work.* Cambridge: Cambridge University Press.

Cobb, N. O. (1990). Behind the inscrutable half-shell: Images of mutant Japanese and *ninja* turtles. *Melus,* 16 [In combined issues 1989-1990], 487-498.

Coe, R. M. (1988). *Toward a grammar of passages.* Carbondale, IL: Southern Illinois University Press.

Cole, M. (1996). *Cultural psychology.* Cambridge, MA: Belknap Press of Harvard University Press.

Cole, M., & Scribner, S. (1974). *Culture and thought.* New York: John Wiley & Sons.

Collected works of Rudyard Kipling. (1970). New York: AMS Press.

Collier-Sanuki, Y. (1997). How to be polite using Japanese relative clauses: 'Framing' function of Japanese relative clauses. *Journal of Japanese Linguistics and Education*, 4, 1-20.

Condor, S. (1988). 'Race stereotypes' and racist discourse. *Text*, 8, 69-89.

Connor, U. (1996). *Contrastive rhetoric.* New York: Cambridge University Press.

Connor, U., & Kaplan, R. B. (Eds.). (1987). *Writing across languages: Analysis of L2 text.* Reading, MA: Addison-Wesley.

Cook, H. M. (1996). The use of addressee honorifics in Japanese elementary school classrooms. In N. Akatsuka, S. Iwasaki, & S. Strauss (Eds.), *Japanese/Korean linguistics, Vol. 5.* Stanford, CA: CSLI Publications.

Cooper, C. R., & Matsuhashi, A. (1983). A theory of the writing process. In M. Martlew (Ed.), *The Psychology of written language.* New York: John Wiley.

Cooper-Chen, A. (1997). *Mass communication in Japan.* Ames: Iowa State University Press.

Count cost of women's work. (1995, August 18). *The Guardian,* p. 6.

Crump, T. (1988). Alternative meanings of literacy in Japan and the west. *Human Organization,* 47, 138-145.

Crystal, D. (1987). *The Cambridge encyclopedia of language.* Cambridge: Cambridge University Press.

Crystal, D., & Davy, D. (1969). *Investigating English style.* London: Longman.

Cumings, B. (1993). Japan's position in the world system. In A. Gordon (Ed.), *Postwar Japan as history.* Berkeley: University of California Press.

Dahl, O. (1979). Review article of John Lyons' *Semantics. Language,* 55, 199-206.

Dalby L. et al. (Eds.). (1984). *All-Japan: The catalogue of everything Japanese.* Kent, England: Columbus Books.

Dale, P. N. (1986). *The myth of Japanese uniqueness.* New York: St Martin's.

Darnell, R. (1985). The language of power in Cree interethnic communication. In N. Wolfson & J. Manes (Eds.), *Language of inequality.* Berlin: Mouton de Gruyter.

Davis, W. (1992). *Japanese religion and society.* Albany, NY: State University of New York Press.

DeFrancis, J. (1984). *The Chinese language: Fact and fantasy.* Honolulu: University of Hawaii Press.

DeMente, B. L. (1989). *Businessman's guide to Japan: Opening doors ... and closing deals!* Tokyo: Yenbooks.

DeVos, G. A. (1992). *Social cohesion and alienation: Minorities in the United States and Japan.* Boulder, CO: Westview Press.

DIC Enterprises. (1985). *Mask* [Film].

Diggs, N. B. (1998). *Steel butterflies: Japanese women and the American experience.* Albany: State University of New York Press.

Dodd, C. H. (1991). *Dynamics of intercultural communication* (3rd. ed.). Dubuque, IA: Wm. C. Brown.

Donahue, R. T. (1986). A semantic analysis of psychological concepts related to second language acquisition. *NGU Round Table on Languages, Linguistics and Literature,* 14, 23-35.

Donahue, R. T. (1990). *Japanese non-linear discourse style.* New York: Applied Linguistics Research.

Donahue, R. T. (1994). The mysterious Orient(al) schema: Images and attribution. *Intercultural Communication Studies,* IV, 63-86.

Donahue. R. T. (in press). Critical discourse analysis: Racism and the ethos of equality. In K. S. Sitaram & M. H. Prosser (Eds.), *Multiculturalism, cultural diversity, and global communication.* Greenwich, USA & London, UK: Ablex.

Donahue, R. T., & Prosser, M. H. (1997). *Diplomatic discourse: International conflict at the United Nations.* Greenwich, USA & London, UK: Ablex.

Dooling, D. J., & Lachman, R. (1971). Effects of comprehension on retention of prose. *Journal of Experimental Psychology*, 8, 216-222.

Dower, J. W. (1993). *War without mercy: Race and power in the Pacific War* (7th printing, rev.). New York: Pantheon.

Draguns, J. G. (1997). Abnormal behavior patterns across cultures: Implications for counseling and psychotherapy. *International Journal of Intercultural Relations,* 21, 213-248.

Easton, B. (1982). Blended beginnings: Connections and the effects of editing in a case of academic 'Japanese English.' Unpublished doctoral dissertation, University of Hawaii.

Economic Strategy Institute. (1992). The case for saving the Big Three. Washington, DC: Economic Strategy Institute (mimeographed).

Eden, R., & Mitchell, R. (1986). Paragraphing for the reader. *College Composition and Communication,* 37, 416-430.

Edwards, J., & Giles, H. (1984). Applications of the social psychology of language: Sociolinguistics and education. In P. Trudgill (Ed.), *Applied sociolinguistics.* London: Academic Press.

Eisenstadt, S. N. (1996). *Japanese civilization: A comparative view.* Chicago: University of Chicago Press.

El-Agraa, A. M. (1988). *Japan's trade frictions.* London: Macmillan.

Elliott, T. I. (1991, December 13). There's more to Japanese than *kanji* characters. *The Japan Times,* p. 11.

Emmott, B. (1989). *The sun also sets.* London: Simon and Schuster.

Erchak, G. M. (1992). *The anthropology of self and behavior.* New Brunswick, NJ: Rutgers University Press.

Fisher, G. (1988). *Mindsets.* Yarmouth, ME: Intercultural Press.

Foreign students wrestle Osaka dialect. (1994, January 5). *Asahi Evening News,* p. 5.

Francese, P. (1995, January 17). Interview with P. Solman: *The MacNeill/Lehrer News Hour* [TV broadcast]. PBS.

Fredrickson, T. L., & Wedel, P. F. (1984). *English by newspaper.* Rowley, MA: Newbury House.

Garten, J. E. (1992). *A cold peace.* New York: Times Books.

Gehani, R. (1991, February 25). U.S. still no. 1 in trade. *Democrat and Chronicle* [Rochester, NY], p. 9A.

Georgoudi, M., & Rosnow, R. L. (1985). The emergence of contextualism. *Journal of Communication,* 35, 76-88.

Giles, H. (1979). Sociolinguistics and social psychology: An introductory essay. In H. Giles & R. N. St. Clair (Eds.), *Language and social psychology.* Oxford: Basil Blackwell.

Giles, H., & Powesland, P. F. (1975). *Speech style and social evaluation.* London: Academic Press.

Gill, R. (1986, January 12). Beating 'we Japanese' syndrome. *The Japan Times.*

Goffman, E. (1981). *Forms of talk.* Philadelphia: University of Pennsylvania.

Goodman, R. (1990). *Japan's 'international youth.'* New York: Clarendon Press.

Grabe, W. (1987). Contrastive rhetoric and text-type research. In U. Connor & R. B. Kaplan (Eds.), *Writing across languages: Analysis of L2 text.* Reading, MA: Addison-Wesley.

Gray, M. (1990). *A dictionary of literary terms* (6th printing). Harlow, Essex, England: Longman York Press.

GRE 1992-93 registration and information bulletin. (1992). Educational Testing Service. Princeton, NJ

Gudykunst, W. B., & Kim, Y. Y. (1992). *Communicating with strangers.* (2nd ed.). New York: McGraw-Hill.

Gudykunst, W. B., & Nishida, T. (1994). *Bridging Japanese/North American differences.* Thousand Oaks, CA: Sage.

Gudykunst, W. B., Ting-Toomey, S., & with Chua, E. (1988). *Culture and interpersonal communication.* Newbury Park, CA: Sage.

Gundersen, E. (1990, May 25). Japanese pop star eyes west. *USA Today* (International ed.), p. 9A.

Gunji, T. (1987). *Japanese phrase structure grammar.* The Netherlands: D Reidel.

Hall, E. T. (1966). *The hidden dimension.* Garden City, NY: Doubleday.

Halverson, J. (1991). Olson on literacy. *Language in society,* 20, 619-640.

Hamabata, M. M. (1990). *Crested kimono.* Ithaca, NY: Cornell University Press.

Hammond, P. (Ed.). (1997a). *Cultural difference, media memories: Anglo-American images of Japan.* London: Cassell.

Hammond, P. (1997b). Introduction: Questioning cultural difference. In P. Hammond (Ed.), *Cultural difference, media memories: Anglo-American images of Japan*. London: Cassell.

Hammond, P., & Stirner, P. (1997). Fear and loathing in the British press. In P. Hammond (Ed.), *Cultural difference, media memories: Anglo-American images of Japan.* London: Cassell.

Haneda, S., & Shima, H. (1982). Japanese communicative behavior as reflected in letter writing. *Journal of Business Communication,* 19, 19-32.

Harris, P. R., & Moran, R. T. (1991/1987/1979). *Managing cultural differences.* Houston: Gulf Publishing.

Haruhara, A. (1985). The development of Japanese newspapers. In Japan Newspaper Publishers and Editors Association (Ed.), *The Japanese press* (Vol. 1985). Tokyo: Newspaper Publishers and Editors Association.

Hashin, S. (1994, November 14). Interviewed on *MacNeill/Lehrer News Hour.* PBS.

Hatano, G., Kuhara, K., & Akiyama, M. (1997). Kanji help readers of Japanese infer the meaning of unfamiliar words. In M. Cole, Y. Engeström, & O. Vasquez (Eds.), *Mind, culture and activity.* New York: Cambridge University Press.

Hendry, J. (1993). *Wrapping culture: Politeness, presentation and power in Japan and other societies.* Oxford: Clarendon Press.

Hiatt, F. (1989, June 23). Hidden wall: A native son battles Japan's trade barriers. *Washington Post,* pp. G1, G10.

Higa, M. (1975). The use of loanwords in Hawaiian Japanese. In F. C. C. Peng (Ed.), *Language in Japanese Society.* Tokyo: University of Tokyo Press.

Hill, C., & Larsen, E. (1983). What reading tests call for and what children do (ERIC Document Reproduction Service No ED 238 904). Washington, DC: National Institute of Education.

Hill, J. H. (1988). Language, culture, and worldview. In F. J. Newmeyer (Ed.), *Language: The sociocultural context* (Vol. 4 *Linguistics: The Cambridge survey*). Cambridge: Cambridge University Press.

Hinds, J. (1980). Japanese expository prose. *Papers in Linguistics,* 13, 117-158.

Hinds, J. (1981). Paragraph structure in Japanese expository prose. In

S. Makino (Ed.), *Papers from the Middlebury Symposium on Japanese Discourse Analysis.* Urbana: University of Illinois.

Hinds, J. (1983a). Linguistics and written discourse in English and Japanese A contrastive study 1978—1982. In R. B. Kaplan (Ed.), *Annual Review of Applied Linguistics.* Rowley, MA: Newbury House. [This article bears different titles between the actual article and that in the table of contents. The title here is from the actual article.].

Hinds, J. (1983b). Contrastive rhetoric: Japanese and English. *Text,* 3, 183-195.

Hinds, J. (1983c, March). Retention of information using a Japanese style of presentation [Audio tape]. Presented at the 17th Annual TESOL Convention, Toronto, Canada. Distributed by Audio Archives of Canada, Toronto. [This paper is listed in Hinds (1987a) as appearing in *Studies in Linguistics* but that is erroneous. In absence of the printed version, reliance has been made on this audio tape version.]

Hinds, J. (1984). Japanese. In W. S. Chisholm Jr (Ed.), *Interrogativity.* Amsterdam and Philadelphia: John Benjamins.

Hinds, J. (1985). Misinterpretations and common knowledge in Japanese. *Journal of Pragmatics,* 9, 7-19.

Hinds, J. (1986a). *Japanese* [in Croom Helm Descriptive Grammars Series]. London and New York: Routledge.

Hinds, J. (1986b). *Situation vs. Person Focus.* Tokyo: Kuroshio.

Hinds, J. (1986c). The mysterious language of Japan. *Gamut,* 17, 67-71.

Hinds, J. (1987a). Reader versus writer responsibility: A new typology. In U. Connor & R. B. Kaplan (Eds.), *Writing across languages: Analysis of L2 text.* Reading, MA: Addison-Wesley.

Hinds, J. (1987b). Thematization, assumed familiarity, staging, and syntactic binding in Japanese. In J. Hinds, S. K. Maynard, & S. Iwasaki (Eds.), *Perspectives on topicalization: The case of Japanese* wa. Amsterdam and Philadelphia: John Benjamins.

Hinds, J. (1990). Inductive, deductive, quasi-inductive: Expository writing in Japanese, Korean, Chinese, and Thai. In U. Connor & A. M. Johns (Eds.), *Coherence in writing*. Alexandria, VA: TESOL.

Hinds, J., & Iwasaki, S. (1995). *An introduction to intercultural communication.* Tokyo: Nan'undo.

Hirano, S. (1994, January 3). It's time Japan sought a new image. *Asahi Evening News,* p. 8.

Hobbs, J. (1979). Metaphor, metaphor schemata, and selective inferencing. Menlo Park, CA: SRI International.

Hoey, M. (1983). *On the surface of discourse.* London: George Allen and Unwin.

Hoey, M. (1991). *Patterns of lexis in text.* Oxford: Oxford University Press.

Hofstede, G. (1980). *Culture's consequences: International differences in work-related values.* Beverly Hills, CA: Sage.

Hofstede, G. (1991). *Cultures and organizations: Software of the mind.* New York: McGraw-Hill.

Holden, N. (1983). The Japanese language: A partial view from the inside. *Multilingua,* 2-3, 157-166.

Holman, C. H. (1978). *A handbook to literature.* Indianapolis: Odyssey Press.

Honna, N., & Hoffer, B. (Eds.). (1989). *An English dictionary of Japanese ways of thinking.* Tokyo: Yuhikaku.

Hori, M. (1995). Subjectlessness and honorifics in Japanese: A case of textual construal. In R. Hasan & P. H. Fries (Eds.), *On subject and theme: A discourse functional perspective.* Amsterdam and Philadelphia: John Benjamins.

Horioka, C. Y. (1998). Do the Japanese live better than Americans? In J. Mak, S. Sunder, S. Abe, & K. Igawa (Eds.), *Japan—Why it works, why it doesn't: Economics in everyday life.* Honolulu: University of Hawaii Press.

Horowitz, R. (1987). Rhetorical structure in discourse processing. In R. Horowitz & S. J. Samuels (Eds.), *Comprehending oral and written language.* New York: Academic Press.

Hoshi, S. (n.d.; approx. 1980). The secretary on the shoulder (trans., Robert Matthew). *Occasional Papers,* No. 9 (Dept. of Japanese, Univ. of Queensland, (Brisbane, Australia). Orig. pub., 1971, as Kata no ue no hisha in *Sekai S.F. Zenshu* 28, 193-6, Tokyo: Hayakawa Shobo.

Hsu, F. L. K. (1985). The self in cross-cultural perspective. In A. J. Marsella, G. DeVos, & F. L. K. Hsu (Eds.), *Culture and self: Asian and western perspectives.* New York & London: Tavistock.

Hume, N. G. (Ed.). (1995). *Japanese aesthetics and culture.* Albany: State University of New York Press.

Hunt, S. (1998, March 3). Great country inns [TV program from The Learning Channel, USA and broadcasted in Japan as *Yookoso kantorii hoteru e (II)* by NHK].

Husband, C. (Ed.). (1982). *'Race' in Britain.* London: Hutchinson.

Ichijo, Y. (1997, May). Wasabi. *Biggu Komikku Supirittsu,* v. 25, 121-124.

Iino, Y. (1991, October 15). From 150 data sheets to a fast divorce, one man tells of his arranged marriage. *The Japan Times,* p. 3.

Imahori, T., & Cupach, W. (1991). A cross-cultural comparison of the interpretation and management of face. Paper presented at the Conference on Communication in Japan and in the United States,

California State University, Fullerton.

Inamoto, N. (1982). *Nihonjin tai Amerikajin.* Tokyo: Waseda University Press.

Inglehart, R. (1990). *Culture shift in advanced industrial society.* Princeton, NJ: Princeton University Press.

Irmscher, W. F. (1979). *Teaching expository writing.* New York: Holt, Rhinehart and Winston.

Ishii, S. (1984). Enryo-sasshi communication: A key to understanding Japanese interpersonal relations. *Cross Currents,* XI, 49-58.

Ishii, S., & Bruneau, T. (1988). Silence and silences in cross-cultural perspective: Japan and the United States. In L. A. Samovar & R. E. Porter (Eds.), *Intercultural communication: A reader* [fifth ed.]. Belmont, CA: Wadsworth.

Isshiki, K. I. (1981). Some aspects of the Japanese language as a reflection of its culture. MA thesis, University of Southern California.

Jaeger, M. E., & Rosnow, R. L. (1988). Contextualism and its implications for psychological inquiry. *British Journal of Psychology,* 79, 63-75.

Japan 1998: An international comparison. (1998). Tokyo: Keizai Koho Center.

Jenkins, M. (1993). *Japan*. London: Cassell.

Jenkins, S., & Hinds, J. (1987). Business letter writing: English, French, and Japanese. *TESOL Quarterly,* 21, 327-349.

Jeremy, M., & Robinson, M. E. (1989). *Ceremony and symbolism in the Japanese home.* Manchester: Manchester University Press.

Johnson, H. (1997, January 20). Interviewed on *The News Hour* [TV broadcast]. PBS.

Johnson, S. K. (1988). *The Japanese through American eyes.* Stanford, CA: Stanford University Press.

Jordan, M. P. (1984). *Rhetoric of everyday English texts.* London: George Allen and Unwin.

Kabashima, T. (1980). *Bunshoo kosei-hoo.* Tokyo: Kodansha.

Kaneko, A. (1990). *Japanese for all occasions.* Rutland, VT: Charles E. Tuttle Company.

Kaplan, R. B. (1972). *The anatomy of rhetoric: Prolegomena to a functional theory of rhetoric*. Philadelphia Center for Curriculum Development.

Kaplan, R. B. (1987). Cultural thought patterns revisited. In U. Connor & R. B. Kaplan (Eds.), *Writing across languages: Analysis of L2 text.* Reading, MA: Addison-Wesley.

Kaplan, R. B. (1988). Cultural thought patterns in inter-cultural education. In J. S. Wurzel (Ed.), *Toward multiculturalism*. Yarmouth, ME: Intercultural Press. Orig. pub., 1966, in *Language*

Learning, 16, 1-20.

Karatsu, H. (1992, March 23). Never as easy as it sounds. *The Japan Times*, p. 24.

Kasahara, Y. (1974). Fear of eye-to-eye confrontation among neurotic patients in Japan. In T. S. Lebra & W. P. Lebra (Eds.), *Japanese culture and behavior*. Honolulu: The University Press of Hawaii.

Kato, N. (1988). Nihonjin no seiritsu. *Kokusaigaku kenkyuu* 2 (March).

Katz, P. A. (Ed.). (1976). *Towards the elimination of racism*. New York: Pergamon.

Keene, D. (1982). *The distinctiveness of the Japanese*. Tokyo: Asahi Press.

Kelley, L. (1981, October 6). Japanese management and cultural determinism. Paper presented at the Japan-America Business Conference, Lincoln, NB.

Kenkyusha's new collegiate dictionary. (1987). Tokyo: Kenkyusha.

Kennedy, R. (1997, March 27). Tax hike is confiscation of public resources. *The Chubu Weekly* [Japan], p. 7.

Kerbo, H. R., & McKinstry, J. A. (1995). *Who rules Japan?* Westport, CT: Praeger.

Kerr, A. (1996). *Lost Japan*. Melbourne: Lonely Planet.

Kikuchi, Y. (1993). Interviewed in *Japan: Behind the mask* [Video]. Northbrook, IL: Coronet/MTI.

Kitano, H. H. L. (1993). Japanese American values and communication patterns. In W. B. Gudykunst (Ed.), *Communication in Japan and the United States*. Albany, NY: State University of New York Press.

Knapp, M. L. (1978). *Nonverbal communication in human interaction*. New York: Holt, Rhinehart and Winston.

Knight, J. (1997). Japanese war memories. In P. Hammond (Ed.), *Cultural difference, media memories: Anglo-American images of Japan*. London: Cassell.

Kobayakawa, M. (1994). America, a dream country. In K. Shirai, K. Komatsu, & K. M. Shimoda (Eds.), *To our friends and neighbors: Messages from Japanese women living in New York*. Scarsdale, NY: Editors.

Kobayashi, H. (1984). Rhetorical patterns in English and Japanese. Unpublished doctoral dissertation, Teachers College, Columbia University, New York.

Kodansha encyclopedia of Japan. (1983). Tokyo: Kodansha.

Kokuritsu Kokugo Kenkyuujo National Language Research Institute. (1970-1974). *Denkikeisanki ni yoru shimbun no goi choosa* (Vol. 1-4). Tokyo Shuppan. [Citation by Stanlaw (1992).].

Kolker, A., & Alvarez, L. (1991). *The Japanese version* [Film]. New York: Center for New American Media.

Kondo, D. K. (1990). *Crafting selves*. Chicago: University of Chicago

Press.

Koppel, T. (1994, February). Interview on *Nightline* [TV broadcast]. ABC News.

Koyama, S. (1985). An island country. In T. Umesao (Ed.), *Seventy-seven keys to the civilization of Japan.* Tokyo: Sogensha.

Koyama, T. (1992). *Japan: A handbook in intercultural communication.* Sydney, Australia: National Centre for English Language Teaching and Research, Macquarie University.

Krauss, E. S. (1996). The mass media and Japanese politics: Effects and consequences. In S. J. Pharr & E. S. Krauss (Eds.), *Media and politics in Japan.* Honolulu: University of Hawaii Press.

Kristof, N. D. (1997, September 14). Japan, Korea and 1597: A year that lives in infamy. *New York Times.*

Kubota, R. (1992). Contrastive rhetoric of Japanese and English: A critical approach. Unpublished doctoral dissertation, University of Toronto.

Kuno, S. (1972). Functional sentence perspective: A case study from Japanese and English. *Linguistic Inquiry,* 3, 269-320.

Kuno, S. (1986). The Japanese language. In H. Stevenson, H. Azuma, & K. Hakuta (Eds.), *Child development and education in Japan.* New York: W. H. Freeman.

Kurita, I. (1987a). *Setsu getsu ka no kokoro/Japanese identity.* Tokyo: Shootensha.

Kurita, I. (1987b). The Japanese *zuihitsu*. In Public Relations Dept., Nippon Steel Corp (Ed.), *Essays on Japan from Japan.* Tokyo: Maruzen.

Kurokawa, S. A. (1987). *Common misunderstandings in Japanese-American communication.* Tokyo: Kinseido.

Kushida, N. (1993). 'Discrimination,' a report in the course, Multicultural Education. University of Virginia, Charlottesville.

Lakoff, G., & Johnson, M. (1980). *Metaphors we live by.* Chicago: The University of Chicago Press.

Lanham, R. A. (1968). *A handlist of rhetorical terms.* Berkeley: University of California Press.

Larson, R. L. (1984). Classifying discourse: Limitations and alternatives. In R. J. Connors, L. S. Ede, & A. A. Lunsford (Eds.), *Essays on classical rhetoric and modern discourse.* Carbondale: Southern Illinois University Press.

Lebra, T. (1976). *Japanese patterns of behavior.* Honolulu: University of Hawaii Press.

Lee, O. (1982). *Smaller is better.* Tokyo & New York: Kodansha International.

Lehner, U. C. (1996). Is Japan polite or rude? It depends who you ask. In U. C. Lehner (Ed.), *Let's talk turkey (about Japanese turkeys) and other tales from the* Asian Wall Street Journal. Tokyo: Charles E. Tuttle.

Leki, I. (1991). Twenty-five years of contrastive rhetoric: Text analysis and writing pedagogies. *TESOL Quarterly,* 25, 123-143.

Lemert, J. B. (1989). *Criticizing the media.* Newbury Park, CA: Sage.

Levey, J. S., & Greenhall, A. (Eds.). (1983). *The concise Columbia encyclopedia.* New York: Avon.

Levine, R. (1998). Measuring the silent language of time. In T. M. Singelis (Ed.), *Teaching about culture, ethnicity, and diversity.* Thousand Oaks, CA: Sage.

Levine, R., & Norenzayan, A. (1996). The pace of life in 31 countries. Unpublished manuscript.

Lewis, E. H. (1894). *The history of the English paragraph.* Chicago: The University of Chicago Press.

Lipset, S. M. (1994). Binary comparisons: American exceptionalism—Japanese uniqueness. In M. Dogan & A. Kazancigil (Eds.), *Comparing nations.* Oxford: Basil Blackwell.

Loveday, L. (1986). *Explorations in Japanese sociolinguistics.* Amsterdam and Philadelphia: John Benjamins.

Ludden, D. (1994). Ten myths about the Japanese language. *The Language Teacher* 18:12, pp. 10, 11, 32.

Ma, K. (1996). *The modern Madame Butterfly.* Rutland, VT: Charles E. Tuttle.

MacDonald, R. K. (1988). *Dr Seuss.* Boston: Twayne Publishers.

Magnusson, D. (Ed.). (1988). *Individual development from an interactional perspective.* Hillsdale, NJ: Lawrence Erlbaum.

Major, R. (1993). Sociolinguistic factors in loss and acquisition of phonology. In K. Hyltenstam & A Viberg (Eds.), *Progression and regression in language.* Cambridge: Cambridge University Press.

Makino, S. (1978). *Kotoba to kuukan.* Tokyo: Tokai University Press.

Makino, S. (1993, April). An interface between language and culture: A case study of Japanese *uchi* and *soto*. Lecture presented at the University of Virginia, Charlottesville.

Makino, S., & Tsutsui, M. (1986). *A dictionary of basic Japanese grammar.* Tokyo: The Japan Times.

Maraini, F. (1973). In R. Bell (Ed.), *The Japan experience.* New York: Weatherhill.

Markels, R. B. (1984). *A new perspective on cohesion in expository paragraphs.* Carbondale: Southern Illinois Press.

Marsella, A. J., DeVos, G., & Hsu, F. L. K. (Eds.). (1985). *Culture and self: Asian and western perspectives.* New York and London: Tavistock.

Martin, S. (1975). *A reference grammar of Japanese.* New Haven: Yale University Press.

Mason, A., & Ogawa, N. (1998). Why avoid the altar? In J. Mak, S. Sunder, S. Abe, & K. Igawa (Eds.), *Japan—Why it works, why it doesn't: Economics in everyday life.* Honolulu: University of Hawaii Press.

Matsumoto, D. (1996). *Unmasking Japan.* Stanford, CA: Stanford University Press.

Matthew, R. (1989). *Japanese science fiction: A view of a changing society.* London and New York: Routledge.

Mayes, T., & Rowling, M. (1997). The image makers: British journalists on Japan. In P. Hammond (Ed.), *Cultural differences, media memories: Anglo-American images of Japan.* London: Cassell.

Maynard, S. K. (1989). *Japanese conversation.* Norwood, NJ: Ablex.

Maynard, S. K. (1997). *Japanese communication: Language and thought in context.* Honolulu: University of Hawaii Press.

Mazuka, R., & Nagai, N. (Eds.). (1995). *Japanese sentence processing.* Hillsdale, NJ: Lawrence Erlbaum Associates.

McBride, J. (1992). *Frank Capra: The catastrophe of success.* New York: Simon and Schuster.

McCormack, G. (1996a). Introduction. In D. Denoon, M. Hudson, G. McCormack, & T. Morris-Suzuki (Eds.), *Multicultural Japan.* Cambridge: Cambridge University Press.

McCormack, G. (1996b). Kokusaika: Impediments in Japan's deep structure. In D. Denoon, M. Hudson, G. McCormack, & T. Morris-Suzuki (Eds.), *Multicultural Japan.* Cambridge: Cambridge University Press.

Memmott, M. (1990, May 9). Drucker belittles Japan's surplus. *USA Today* (International ed.), p. 9B.

Meo, L. D. (1968). *Japan's radio war on Australia 1941—1945.* Carlton, Victoria: Melbourne University Press.

Miller, A. G. (1982). Historical and contemporary perspectives on stereotyping. In A. G. Miller (Ed.), *In the eye of the beholder.* New York: Praeger.

Miller, L. (1988). Interethnic communication in Japan: Interactions between Japanese and American co-workers. Unpublished doctoral dissertation, University of California, Los Angeles.

Miller, R. A. (1967). *The Japanese language.* Chicago: University of Chicago Press.

Miller, R. A. (1977). *The Japanese language in contemporary Japan.* Washington, DC: American Enterprise Institute for Public Policy Research.

Miller, R. A. (1986). Nihongo: *In defense of Japanese.* London: Athlone.

Miyoshi, M. (1991). *Off center: Power and culture relations between*

Japan and the United States. Cambridge, MA: Harvard University Press.

Moeran, B. (1988). Japanese language and society: An anthropological approach. *Journal of Pragmatics,* 12, 427-443.

Moeran, B. (1990a). *British images of Japan.* Tokyo: Kinseido.

Moeran, B. (1990b). Introduction: Rapt discourses, Anthropology, Japanism, and Japan. In E. Ben-Ari, B. Moeran, & J. Valentine (Eds.), *Unwrapping Japan.* Manchester: Manchester University Press.

Monane, T. A. (1976). The interplay of language and cultural perceptions: Universals and specifics. In *Proceedings of the First HATJ-UH Conference on Japanese Language and Linguistics.* Honolulu: University of Hawaii Press.

Monane, T., & Rogers, L. (1977). Cognitive features of Japanese language and culture and their implications for language teaching. In J. Hinds (Ed.), *Proceedings of the UH—HATJ Conference on Japanese Language and Linguistics.* Honolulu: University of Hawaii.

Montgomery, M. (1986). *An introduction to language and society.* London and New York: Methuen.

Moriya, T. (1985). Osaka. In T. Umesao (Ed.), *Seventy-seven keys to the civilization of Japan.* Tokyo: Sogensha.

Morris, E. K. (1988). Contextualism: The world view of behavior analysis. *Journal of Experimental Child Psychology,* 46, 289-323.

Mouer, R., & Sugimoto, Y. (1986). *Images of Japanese society.* London: Routledge and Kegan Paul.

Mourdoukoutas, P. (1993). *Japan's turn.* Lanham, MD: University Press of America.

Murphy, C. (1988). In Japan a place that is forever England. *Far East.*

Myers, D. G. (1994). *Exploring social psychology* (International ed.). New York: McGraw-Hill.

Nakada, T. (1992, March 24). Sorry seems to be the hardest word. *The Japan Times,* p. 15.

Nakamura, J., & Shimbo, H. (1988 March 3). The market, human capital formation, and economic development in Tokugawa Japan. Unpublished paper for University Seminar on Economic History, Columbia University.

Nakane, C., & Ooishi, S. (Eds.). (1990). *Tokugawa Japan: The social and economic antecedents of modern Japan.* Tokyo: University of Tokyo Press.

Narasaki, K. (1997, September 9). Interviewed on *The News Hour* [TV broadcast]. PBS.

National Conference. (1994). Taking America's pulse: The full report of the National Conference Survey on inter-group relations. New

York: National Conference.

'Naze?' o renpatsu Amerika no kodomotachi. (1992, May 3). *Chunichi Shimbun.*

Neustupný, J. V. (1978). *Post-structural approaches to language*. Tokyo: University of Tokyo Press.

Neustupný, J. V. (1987). *Communicating with the Japanese.* Tokyo: The Japan Times.

Nida, E. (1976). A framework for the analysis and evaluation of theories of translation. In R. W. Brislin (Ed.), *Translation: Applications and research.* New York: Gardner Press.

Nida, E. A. (1984). Rhetoric and styles: A taxonomy of structures and functions. *Language Sciences,* 6, 287-305.

Nunan, D. (1993). *Introducing discourse analysis.* London: Penguin.

Oda, T. (1992, February 17). Media errors fuel misunderstanding. *Asahi Evening News,* p. 8.

Odell, L. (1981). Defining and assessing competence in writing. In C. R. Cooper (Ed.), *The nature and measurement of competency in English.* Urbana, IL: NCTE.

Odlin, T. (1989). *Language transfer.* New York: Cambridge University Press.

Ogawa, D. M. (1973). *Jan ken po: The world of Hawaii's Japanese Americans* (2nd ed.). Honolulu: The University Press of Hawaii.

Ohmae, K. (1988). *Beyond national borders.* Tokyo: Kodansha International.

Ohnuki-Tierney, E. (1984). *Illness and culture in contemporary Japan.* Cambridge: Cambridge University Press.

Okabe, R. (1983). Cultural assumptions of east and west: Japan and the United States. In W. Gudykunst (Ed.), *Intercultural communication theory*. Beverly Hills, CA: Sage.

Okabe, R. (1991, July 28). Aite no kutsu no naka ni wagami o okemasu ka? *Chunichi Shimbun,* p. 17.

Okazaki, S. (1993). Stating opinions in Japanese: Listener-dependent strategies. In J. E. Alatis (Ed.), *Georgetown University roundtable on languages and linguistics 1993.* Washington, DC: Georgetown University Press.

Okuaki, Y. (1988, September 20). Interviewed in 'The trouble with *anata* (you) is that there are no alternatives.' *The Japan Times,* p. 23.

Oppenheim, P. (1992). *Japan without blinders.* Tokyo and New York: Kodansha International.

Oshima, H. (1998). Is Japan an egalitarian society? In J. Mak, S. Sunder, S. Abe, & K. Igawa (Eds.), *Japan—Why it works, why it doesn't: Economics in everyday life.* Honolulu: University of Hawaii Press.

O'Sullivan, T., Hartley, J., Saunders, D., Montgomery, M., & Fiske, J. (1994). *Key concepts in communication and cultural studies* (2nd. ed.). London and New York: Routledge.

Owens, G. (1997). The making of the yellow peril: Pre-war western views of Japan. In P. Hammond (Ed.), *Cultural difference, media memories: Anglo-American images of Japan.* London: Cassell.

Perrin, N. (1988). *Giving up the gun.* Boston: David R Godine.

Pfeiffer, J. (1988, January). How not to lose the trade wars by cultural gaffes. *Smithsonian,* pp. 145-156.

Picturesque Expressions. (1985). Detroit, MI: Gale Research Co.

Price, W. F., & Crapo, R. H. (1992). *Cross-cultural in introductory psychology*. Eagan, MN: West.

Prosser, M. H. (1989). *The cultural dialogue An introduction to intercultural communication.* Washington, DC: SIETAR International. [Orig. pub. by Houghton Mifflin, 1978].

Prosser, M. H. (1992, September). Lecture on intercultural communication, Department of Rhetoric and Communication, University of Virginia, Charlottesville.

Pulvers, R. (1982). *The Japanese inside out.* Tokyo: Japan Translator Training Center.

Putting a stop to trade. (1995, May 27). *The Economist,* pp. 16-18.

Quirk, R., Greenbaum, S., Leech, G., & Svartvik, J. (1985). *A comprehensive grammar of the English language.* London & New York: Longman.

Random House Webster's college dictionary. (1991). New York: Random House.

Reagan, J. (1992, November). Giving a paper, Presented at the Teaching Resource Center, University of Virginia, Charlottesville.

Reischauer, E. O. (1977). *The Japanese.* Tokyo: Charles E. Tuttle.

Reischauer, E. O. (1981). *Japan: The story of a nation* [3rd ed.]. New York: Knopf.

Reischauer, E. O. (1988). *The Japanese today.* Cambridge, MA: Harvard University Press.

Reischauer, E. O. (1989, May 6). Interviewed on Taidan 21 Seiki [TV broadcast]. Chukyo Television, Japan.

Riccomini, D. R., & Rosenzweig, P. M. (1985). *Unexpected Japan.* New York: Walker.

Rodgers, P. C., Jr. (1966). A discourse-centered rhetoric of the paragraph. *College Composition and Communication,* 17, 2-11.

Roget's international thesaurus [4th ed.]. (1977). New York: Harper-Collins.

Ronen, S., & Shenkar, O. (1985). Clustering countries on attitudinal dimensions: A review and synthesis. *Academy of Management Review,* 10(3), 435-454.

Rosnow, R. L., & Georgoudi, M. (1986). *Contextualism and understanding in behavioral science: Implications for research and theory.* New York: Praeger.

Ross, L. (1977). The intuitive psychologist and his shortcomings: Distortion in the attribution process. In L. Berkowitz (Ed.), *Advances in experimental social psychology* (Vol. 10). New York: Academic Press.

Ross, L., & Nisbett, R. E. (1991). *The Person and the situation.* Philadelphia: Temple University Press.

Rubin, J. (1992). *Gone Fishin': New Angles on Perennial Problems* [Power Japanese language series]. Tokyo: Kodansha International.

Ruch, W. V. (1984). *Corporate communications: A comparison of Japanese and American practices.* Westport, CT: Quorum Books.

Ryan, E. B. (1979). Why do low-prestige language varieties persist? In H. Giles & R. H. St. Clair (Eds.), *Language and social psychology.* Oxford: Basil Blackwell.

Sabato, L. (1994). Interviewed by Jim Lehrer on *The MacNeill/Lehrer News Hour* [TV broadcast]. PBS.

Saeki, T. (1991, September 23). Square-peg labor: Japan no easy fit for migrant workers of Japanese descent. *Asahi Evening News.*

Samovar, L. A., & Porter, R. E. (1995). *Communication between cultures* (2nd. ed.). Belmont, CA: Wadsworth.

Samovar, L. A., Porter, R. E., & Jain, N. C. (1981). *Understanding intercultural communication.* Belmont, CA: Wadsworth.

Sanford, A. J., & Garrod, S. C. (1981). *Understanding written language.* Chichester: John Wiley.

Sato, N. (1995). *The magical power of* suru*: Japanese verbs made easy.* Tokyo: Charles E. Tuttle.

Sautman, B. (1995). Theories of East Asian superiority. In R. Jacoby & N. Glauberman (Eds.), *The bell curve debate.* New York: Times Books.

Scarcella, R. C. (1984). How writers orient their readers in expository essays: A comparative study of native and non-native English writers. *TESOL Quarterly,* 18, 671-688.

Scharfstein, B. (1989). *The dilemma of context.* New York: New York University Press.

Scheflen, A. E. (1973). *How behavior means.* New York: Gordon and Breach Science Publishers.

Schiffrin, D. (1994). *Approaches to discourse.* Oxford, UK & Cambridge, USA: Blackwell.

Schoppa, L. J. (1997). *Bargaining with Japan.* New York: Columbia University Press.

Scollon, R., & Scollon, S. W. (1995). *Intercultural communication: A discourse approach.* Oxford, UK & Cambridge, USA: Blackwell.

Scribner, S. (1979). Modes of thinking and ways of speaking: Culture and logic reconsidered. In R. O. Freedle (Ed.), *New directions in discourse processing.* Norwood, NJ: Ablex.

Sebastian, R. J., & Ryan, E. B. (1985). Speech cues and social evaluation: Markers of ethnicity, social class, and age. In H. Giles & R. N. St. Clair (Eds.), *Recent advances in language, communication, and social psychology.* London: Lawrence Erlbaum.

Segall, M. H., Campbell, D. T., & Herskovits, M. J. (1966). *The influence of culture on visual perception.* Indianapolis, IN: Bobbs-Merrill.

Seward, J. (1968/1976). *Japanese in action.* New York: Weatherhill.

Shaner, D. E., & Duval, R. S. (1990). *Shinshin tooitsu aikidoo* as a means to personal growth. In M. Kiyota & H. Kinoshita (Eds.), *Japanese martial arts and American sports.* Tokyo: Nihon University.

Shibatani, M. (1990a). *The languages of Japan.* Cambridge: Cambridge University Press.

Shibatani, M. (1990b). Japanese. In B. Comrie (Ed.), *The major languages of East and South-East Asia.* London: Routledge.

Shishin, A. (1985). Rhetorical patterns in letters to the editor. *Bulletin of Aichi Institute of Technology,* 20(A), 17-28.

Simon, P. (1980). *The tongue-tied American: Confronting the foreign language crisis.* New York: Continuum.

Sirevåg, T. (1991). *American patterns.* Tokyo: Seibido.

Sitaram, K. S. (1995). Culture and communication: A world view. New York: McGraw-Hill.

Smith, D. L. (1978). Mirror images in Japanese and English. *Language,* 54, 78-122.

Smith, P. B., & Bond, M. H. (1993). *Social psychology across cultures.* London: Harvester Wheatsheaf.

Soares, D. C. (1996). Mutual attraction and mixed messages in Japanese-western romantic relationships. *Communiqué* [SIETAR newsletter], 3 & 4: p. 3.

Sonoda, H. (1985). Posts and telecommunications. In T. Umesao (Ed.), *Seventy-seven keys to the civilization of Japan.* Tokyo: Sogensha.

Sowell, T. (1994). *Race and culture: A world view.* New York: Basic Books.

Spradley, J. P., & Phillips, M. (1972). Culture and stress: A quantitative analysis. *American Anthropologist,* 74, 518-529.

Stanlaw, J. (1992). 'For beautiful human life' The use of English in Japan. In J. J. Tobin (Ed.), *Re-made in Japan.* New Haven: Yale University Press.

Statler, O. (1984). Introduction. In L Dalby et al. (Eds.), *All Japan: The catalogue of everything Japanese.* Kent, England: Columbus

Books.

Steinberg, D. D. (1982). *Psycholinguistics: Language, mind and world.* London & New York: Longman.

Stephens, L. F. (1991). The world's media systems: An overview. In J. C. Merrill (Ed.), *Global journalism.* New York and London: Longman.

Stern, H. H. (1983). *Fundamental concepts of language teaching.* Oxford: Oxford University Press.

Sternberg, R. J. (1997). *Thinking styles.* Cambridge: Cambridge University Press.

Stewart, E. C. (1976). Cultural sensitivities in counseling. In P. Pedersen, W. J. Lonner, & J. G. Draguns (Eds.), *Counseling across cultures.* Honolulu: University Press of Hawaii.

Stokes, B. (1994, November 14). Interviewed on *The MacNeill/Lehrer news hour* [TV broadcast]. PBS.

Stronach, B. (1989). Japanese television. In R. G. Power & H. Kato (Eds.), *Handbook of Japanese popular culture.* Westport, CT: Greenwood Press.

Sugimoto, Y. (1997). *An Introduction to Japanese society.* Cambridge: Cambridge University Press.

Suzuki, T. (1975). *Tozasareta gengo: Nihongo no sekai.* Tokyo: Shinchoosha.

Suzuki, T. (1980). Gengo seikatsu. In H. Minami (Ed.), *Nihon no ningen kankei jiten*. Tokyo: Kodansha.

Takemata, K. (1976). *Genkoo shippitsu nyuumon.* Tokyo: Natsumesha.

Tannen, D. (1982). The oral/literate continuum in discourse. In D. Tannen (Ed.), *Spoken and written language.* Norwood, NJ: Ablex.

Tannen, D. (1990). *You just don't understand.* New York: Ballantine Books.

Tannen, D. (1994). *Gender and discourse.* New York: Oxford University Press.

Teikoku's complete atlas of Japan [8th ed.]. (1985). Tokyo: Teikokoku-Shoin.

Thian, H. (1988). *Setting up and operating a business in Japan: A handbook for the foreign businessman.* Vermont & Tokyo: Charles E. Tuttle.

Tobin, J. J. (1983). Strange foreigners: American reactions to living in Japan. Unpublished doctoral dissertation, University of Chicago.

Today's Japan [TV broadcast]. (1995, January 5). NHK.

Tonedachi, M. (1992, September 15, 1992.). Shimei bikkurikaesu Nipponjin no fushigi. *Asahi Shimbun Weekly Aera.* [Citation by Ma (1996)].

Toner, R. (1992, July 16). Choice is affirmed: Differences in ideology smoothed as party embraces nominee. *New York Times*, p. A1.

Top leaders criticize US for yen's rise [article #8509]. (1993, June 1). *Clarinet Electronic Newspaper*.

Triandis, H. C. (1990). Theoretical concepts that are applicable to the analysis of ethnocentrism. In R. Brislin (Ed.), *Applied cross-cultural psychology*. Newbury Park, CA: Sage.

Triandis, H. C., Brislin, R., & Hui, C. H. (1988). Cross-cultural training across the individualism-collectivism divide. *International Journal of Intercultural Relations,* 12, 269-289.

Trudgill, P. (1983). *Sociolinguistics* (Rev. ed.). London: Penguin.

Tsuda, A. (1984). *Sales talk in Japan and the United States.* Washington, DC: Georgetown University Press.

Tsujimura, N. (1996). *An introduction to Japanese linguistics.* Oxford: Blackwell.

Tsujimura, T. (1977). Nihongo no keigo no kozo to tokushoku. In S. Ono & T. Shibata (Eds.), *Nihongo 4: Keigo.* Tokyo: Iwanami Shoten.

Tsunoda, T. (1978). *Nihonjin no noo.* Tokyo: Taishuukan Shoten.

Ueno, T. (1994). The other and the machine. In M. N. Abé & Y. Fukushima (Eds.), *The Japan/America film wars: World War II propaganda and its cultural contexts.* Chur, Switzerland and Langhorne, PA: Harwood Academic.

Umesao, T. (1990). *The Roots of contemporary Japan.* E.B. Mikals-Adachi, trans. Tokyo: The Japan Forum.

United States Army Pictorial Service. (1945). *Your Job in Germany* [Film]. Washington, DC: The Service.

United States Army Pictorial Service. (1946). *Our Job in Japan* [Film]. Washington, DC: The Service.

US-Japan 'bashing' likely to get worse. (1991, May-June). *East-West Center Views,* 1,2: p. 1.

Uzawa, K., & Cumming, A. (1989). Writing strategies in Japanese as a foreign language: Lowering or keeping up the standards. *The Canadian Modern Language Review,* 46, 178-194.

van den Berghe, P. L. (1967). *Race and racism.* New York: Wiley.

van Dijk, T. A. (1984). *Prejudice in discourse.* Amsterdam & Philadelphia: John Benjamins Publishing Co.

van Dijk, T. A. (1985). Structures of news in the press. In T. A. van Dijk (Ed.), *Discourse and communication.* Berlin: Walter de Gruyter.

van Dijk, T. A. (1987). *Communicating racism.* Newbury Park, CA: Sage.

van Dijk, T. A. (1991). *Racism and the press.* London and New York: Routledge.

van Wolferen, K. (1989). *The enigma of Japanese power.* London: Macmillan.

Vaughn, C. (1988). Cognitive independence, social independence, and achievement orientation: A comparison of Japanese and US students. Unpublished doctoral dissertation, University of California, Berkeley.

We will never stop looking for you. (1990, October 23). *USA Today* [International ed.], p. 2A.

Weiner, M. (1997). Introduction. In M. Weiner (Ed.), *Japan's minorities: The illusion of homogeneity.* London and New York: Routledge.

Weiss, P. A. (1971). Life, order, and understanding. *The Graduate Journal* [Supplement to Volume 8]. University of Texas Press, Austin.

Wenger, J. (1984). Variation and change in Japanese honorific forms. In S. Miyagawa & C. Kitagawa (Eds.), *Studies in Japanese language use.* Edmonton, Canada: Linguistic Research, Inc.

White, M. (1993). *The material child: Coming of age in Japan and America*. New York: The Free Press.

White, S. (1989). Backchannels across cultures: A study of Americans and Japanese. *Language in Society,* 18, 59-76.

White, T. H. (1985, July 28). The danger from Japan. *The New York Times Magazine.*

Widdowson, H. G. (1983). *Learning purpose and language use.* Oxford: Oxford University Press.

Wilkinson, E. (1981). *Misunderstanding: Europe versus Japan.* Tokyo: Chuokoron-Sha.

Wilkinson, E. (1983). *Japan versus Europe: A History of Misunderstanding.* Harmondsworth, Middlesex UK: Penguin.

Williams, D. (1996). *Japan and the enemies of open political science.* London & New York: Routledge.

World Almanac. (1991). Mahway, NJ: World Almanac.

Yagasaki, J. (1990). Emotionally becoming 'Japanese'?: A study of cultural identity of Americans living in Japan. Unpublished doctoral dissertation, University of California, Los Angeles.

Yamada, H. (1992). *American and Japanese business discourse: A comparison of interactional styles.* Norwood, NJ: Ablex.

Yamada, H. (1997). *Different games, different rules: Why Americans and Japanese misunderstand each other.* New York: Oxford University Press.

Yamada, K. (1990). Intercultural communication and understanding: Myth and reality. In Y. Sugiyama (Ed.), *Between understanding and misunderstanding.* Westport, CT: Greenwood Press.

Yamaguchi, M. (1967). Shuji ni tsuite. In K. Morita, M. Nagano, H. Miyaji, & T. Ichikawa (Eds.), *Sakubun kooza* (Vol. 2). Tokyo: Meiji Shoin.

Yamamoto, A. Y. (1984). Presuppositional culture spaces: Language use in everyday life. In S. Miyagawa & C. Kitagawa (Eds.), *Studies in Japanese language use.* Carbondale & Edmonton: Linguistic Research Inc.

Yellow Monkey: Rock on my mind, The [TV broadcast]. (1997, April). NHK.

Yoshida, M. (1986). *The People's Culture from Kyoto to Edo* (L. E. Riggs, trans.). Hiroshima: Mazda Motor Company.

Yoshida, M., Tanaka, I., & Sesoko, T. (Eds.). (1984). *The hybrid culture.* Hiroshima: Mazda.

Yoshida, Y. (1978). Sources and causes of Japanese emigration. In D. M. Ogawa (Ed.), *Kodomo no tame ni for the sake of the children.* Honolulu: The University Press of Hawaii. [Originally published in 1909 in *The Annals of American Academy of Political and Social Science* 34, 157-167].

Yoshino, K. (1992). *Cultural nationalism in contemporary Japan.* London and New York: Routledge.

Yoshino, K. (1997). The discourse on blood and racial identity in contemporary Japan. In F. Dikötter (Ed.), *The construction of racial identities in China and Japan.* St. Leonards, Australia: Allen & Unwin.

Young, L. W. L. (1982). Inscrutability revisited. In J. J. Gumperz (Ed.), *Language and social identity.* Cambridge: Cambridge University Press.

Young, R., & Sullivan, P. (1984). Why write? A reconsideration. In R. J. Connors, L. S. Ede, & A. A. Lunsford (Eds.), *Essays on classical rhetoric and modern discourse.* Carbondale: Southern Illinois University Press.

Yutani, Y. (1976). Newspapers in English: Basic editing rules 'at ebb'. *Kenkyuu Ronsoo* [Kyoto Gaikokugo University], 17, 12-27.

Yutani, Y. (1977). Current English: Translation of news articles and 'non-sequence' of tenses. *Kenkyuu Ronsoo* [Kyoto Gaikokugo University], 18, 52-63.

Zimbardo, P. G. (1977). *Shyness.* Reading, MA: Addison-Wesley.

Index

A

Accommodation, social, 23, 162, 183
Age, 44, 46, 131, 133, 135, 138, 142, 145, 152-153, 154, 171-172, 174, 183, 194
Ainu, 39, 42, 105-106
Aisoo warai, 287
Aizuchi, see Back-channeling
Amae, see Interdependence
Amnesia about war atrocities, 109
Analytical thought, 206-209
Anata, 140, 144
Ancestor worship, 172
Antipodes, 72, 325n.8
Apology, 131
Arguing, 217, 312
"Asia," concept of, 201-202
Attribution
- vs. description, 96-97
- fundamental error of, 54-55, 75-77, 84

B

Back-channeling (*aizuchi*), 126, 146-147, 149-150, 154
Back-translation, 248-249, 251
Bargaining, 176, 185, 198
Baseball as *bushido,* 169
Baseline theme, see Discourse
Bunke, 32
Burakumin, 39, 42, 106
Bushido, 169

Business letters, 213, 339n.38

C

Chinese, 3, 11, 14-24, 29-33, 110, 113-116, 155, 175;
  language, 113, 116, 136, 200-202, 263
  minority in Japan, 39, 106, 113-116
Chotto muzukashii ("no"), 185, 198
Christianity, 179, 180
Circumlocution, 212
Clannishness, 30, 32, 195
Collectivism, 4, 11-13, 29, 31-32, 34, 36, 203
Communication style, 7, 82 119-120, 124-126, 134, 146, 152, 154, 161, 216
Conformity, 4, 18, 115-116, 153
Confucianism, 30-31, 155
Contextualism, 53, 67, 240
Contrastive rhetoric, 7, 199, 204, 223-224, 240-243, 247, 263-264, 270-272, 276, 278-279
Corporal punishment, 28
Cowboy metaphor used by Americans, 26
Critical communication, 64
Cross-cultural comparison, considerations about, 58, 67, 211-212, 234-235, 239, 249, 268, 276-277
Cubist approach to Japanese culture, 42-43
Cultural identity 57, 101, 103, 163, 262
Cultural logics, def. 8; 220, 240, 274-275
Cultural metaphors 284, 295-296, 299, see also Cowboy, Iemoto, Samurai
Cultural superiority, 31, 58

D

Deduction, see Discourse
Delay of purpose, see Discourse
Depth of description, see Discourse
Discourse
  circular style, 224-225, 243, 267
  deduction, 210, 278
  depth of description, 228-231
  headline or title as a discourse element, 239, 245, 255, 290-298
  informational focus, 278
  Japanese patterns (proposed)
    baseline theme, Chap. 8
    business letters, 213-214
    delay of purpose, 278
    dot-like ("connect-the-dots"), 204-205
    induction, 210-211, 219, 278
    ki-shoo-ten-ketsu, 242, 247-249, 337n.3; 339n.38
      classical, 256-261
      modern, 256-261
    tempura style, 243, 245, 247
    zuihitsu, 255-256
    zuisoo, 255-256
  newspaper writing
    inverted pyramid style, 244, 246-247

Discourse (continued)
summary lead, 244-247
spatio-temporal relations, 231-234
SPRE, 258-260
structure, 225
Diversity, 33, 35-37
Dot-like pattern, see Discourse
Double standards, 7, 53-55, 58-59, 64, 67
intercultural, 55-57
international, 57-63
interpersonal, 54-55
Drinking, social, 150-151

E
Education, 19, 34, 47, 105, 113, 209, 212
Ellipsis, 162, 165, 167, 170, 180, 183, 186, 264
Emotions
and culture/language study, 5
and interpersonal synchrony, 5-6, 98
negative, 28, 74, 132, 150, 153-154
tolerance for unexpressed, 154
Empathy
model of, 65-66
vs. sympathy (Japanese), 185, 265-266
Enculturation, 72, 83
English, commercial use by Japanese 2, 176-177
Enryo, 23, 100
Ethnocentrism, 15, 31, 54, 57-58, 284, 286, 299-300, 304
Eurocentrism, 59
Executive thinking style (Sternberg's), 209
Eye contact, 265-267

F
Fairness, 307
Family, 5, 8, 12, 16-17, 19, 23, 32-33, 35, 45, 82, 88, 110-111, 114, 122-123, 129, 133, 136-140. 163, 171-172, 175, 187-189, 217, 221, 236-237; as social model, 139-140
Form vs. content, 100
Frankness, 44
Full-moon illusion, 112
Functional perspective, 225

G
Gaijin, 40, 95, 106, 235, 269
henna gaijin, 269
Gakureki shakai, 27
Gender, 120-124, 126, 132, 133-134, 137-138, 154, 173-175, 181-184, 186-189, 236, 336n.35
Generalizations, 23, 67, 90-92, 94-95
reasonable, 94
Group model, 4
Guessing culture (*sasshi no bunka*), 195, 215-218

H
Hawaii, 12, 25, 226-235
Health
care, 35

Health (continued)
  and gender, 174
  hospital stays, length of, 35
Hierarchy, social, 22, 26-27, 30, 32, 41, 46, 134-143, 152, 153, 199, 217, 235, 237
High-context culture, 14
Hiroshima, 109
Homogeneity, 4, 18, 39-42, 103-105, 111-112
Honne/tatemae, 100
Honorifics, 126, 134-136, 143-146, 154, 205, 267-268
Huang, Ming Shi, essay by, 113-116
Human rights, 105, 110
Humor across cultures, 5-6; 166-167, 184
  ethnic jokes, 91; Chap. 10

I

Icons, American, 316-317
Iemoto, 26-28, 32-33
Income earnings for
  CEOs vs. workers, 13
  families with students at
    Tokyo University vs.
      national average, 105
  women, 173
Independent thought, 199-200
Indexing, sociocultural, 83
Indirectness, 44, 164, 167, 193-196, 198, 211, 214, 218, 220-221, 258, 264
Individualism, 11-12, 36, 61, 68, 126, 203, 218
Induction, see Discourse
Inferiority complex, 21-23, 264
Informational focus, see Discourse
Informational mode, 122
Infrastructure, 27, 38
Innuendo, 166-167
Inscrutability, 69, 72, 77, 83, 130, 242
  as complex of concepts, 201-202
Intelligence
  vs. age, 152
  underestimating the Other's, 56-57, 78, 91, 99, 276-277, 296-298
Interdependence, 126-128
Inverted pyramid style, see Discourse

J

Japanese Americans, 80, 83, 226-228, 232, 235, 240, 312-313
Japanese language
  discourse, see Discourse
  ellipsis, 162, 165, 167, 170, 180, 183, 186, 264
  foreign loanwords, 201
  images of, 132, 161
  utterance length, 149
  vocabulary, 273
  word order, 162-165
Japanese Nobel prize winner, 24, 100
Japanism, 268-269
Judicial thinking style (Sternberg's), 209
"Just Do," 170, 172

K

Keigo, see Honorifics
Keiretsu, 32
Kinship, 32, 46, 128
Ki-shoo-ten-ketsu, see Discourse
Korea(ns), 2, 15-16, 21, 23, 34, 39, 42, 77, 91, 105, 108-109, 116, 201, 305
Kotodama, 166
Kpelle, 94, 277-278

L

language loss, 313
Lexical differences, 273-274
Life force, 168-170
Linguistic crossover, 134
Linguistic determinism, 343-344n.159
Longevity, 174
Love of nature, 168, 170, 202 205
Low-context culture, 170

M

Marriage, 12, 127 135, 170-171, 174, 189, 235
Masculinity, 131-132, 137
Mask, 81-83, 299
Mass consumerism, 189, 209
Matthew, Robert, translation by 155-158
Media (North American), Chaps. 3, 10, 11
Meishi, 237
Mindsets, 97, 99-100
Minorities, 39, 81, 103-106, 108-110, 113-116, 297-298
Money is "dirty" belief, 176
Mr. Q., case of, 151-153
Myth about Japan's size, 102
Mysteriousness, 69, 71-74, 77-78, 201, 213

N

Native identity, 2, 57, 309
Negotiation, see Bargaining
Nihonjinron, 100, 268, see also Uniqueness myth
Nonverbal communication, 119

O

Okinawa, 8, 42
Okuda, Audrey, essay by, 186-189
Omiai, 27, 135
Other-directedness, 126, 184-186, 214
Our Job in Japan, 75, 77, 81, 88, 268

P

Pace of life, 34-36
Paradox, cultural, 3, 20, 35
Personal pronouns, 138-144
Phobia, eye-contact, 265
Poetic prose, 239,256
Politeness, 24-25, 44, 46, 134, 136, 142, 145-146, 159, 164, 218
Population density, 34, 36, 235
Pragmatism, 30-33
Productivity, labor 153; 331-332n.70

Propaganda
in Japanese wartime media, 84-85
Public manners, 129
Purity, 110, 176, 237

R

"Race," 42, 76, 88, 101, 104-108, 110-111
Racial epithets, 98; Chap. 3
Racism, 7, 56, 85, 89, 105-108, 110
Receiver responsibility, 33, 256
Reductionism, 67-68
Redundancy 166
Regional differences, 37-39
Relational identity, 138
Respect
for other cultures, 33, 44, 48, 87, 92,
social (Japanese), 14, 19, 27, 28, 48, 83, 126-131, 135-143, 152, 154, 218, 237, 267
Rhetorical patterns or styles, see Discourse
Riggs, David, essay by, 16-21
Rituals, 37, 178, 216

S

Sales talk 195
Saleem, Hamid, essay by, 44-49
Samurai, 3, 25-26, 28, 30-31, 132, 176, 177
Sasshi no bunka, see Guessing culture
Schema
mysterious Orient(al), 71-73, 81, 84
schema theory, 72
cognitive, 72, 344n.159
social (group), 72-73, 83
schema transfer, 73, 298
Scientific laboratory, Japanese 44-45
Secretary on the Shoulder, The 155
Setting focus, 179-180
Sexism, 175
Shimaguni, 102
Shinto, 78, 100, 175, 178
Shyness, 28-30, 194, 265
Silence, 6, 30, 147-149, 173, 182, 215, 217, 265-266, 287
Smiles, 287, 290, 299
aisoo warai, 287
Social mode, 150
Sociotypes, 94-95
Sophistication, consumer, 19, 58, 274
Soto, 129
Spatio-temporal relations, see Discourse
Speech and writing, 193, 199, 202, 214, 267
Speech levels, 143, 145, 152
Spirituality, 168-169, 172, 202
SPRE, 258
Stereotypes, 6, 7, 15, 53, 63, 73, 84, 90-95, 124, 213, 284, 298, 299, 302, 308, 309, 315
Strangers in society 30, 62, 115, 119, 139-140, 150, 218, 237
Structuralism, linguistic 224-

Structuralism (continued)
225, 239, 270-272
structural paragraph, 270
Sukinshippu, 150
Superiority
complex, superiority/inferiority 21-23
cultural, attitude of, 5, 21-23, 31, 57-58, 85, 101-103, 105, 238, 261, 297-298

T
Target group, 90-91
Tempura style, see Discourse
Thinking style, 209
Three-way force, cultural imaging 268
TOEFL, 116
Tokugawa era, 24-25
Trade barriers, 303-304, 307, 309-310, 319
Trade deficit, 303, 309
Tsukiai, 151

U
Uchi, 129
Uniqueness myth, 101-104 108, 111-112, 115-116, 162-163, 261-270
Urbanization, 35

V
Visitors
foreign visitors, 39, 189
Japanese abroad, 23, 35, 235
Japanese at home, 128-129, 142, 144

W
Wholistic thought, 206-210
Whorfian hypothesis, 278; 343-344n.159
Why-questions, 208-209, 216
Wilson, Michiko Niikuni, essay by, 215-218
Women's language, 133-134
Word order, 162-164

Y
Your Job in Germany, 75, 87

Z
Zuihitsu, 255-256
Zuisoo, 255-256

About the Author

Ray T. Donahue (PhD, University of Virginia) is a professor of intercultural communication in the Institute for Japanese Studies and in the Faculty of Foreign Studies at Nagoya Gakuin University in Japan. With credentials also in applied linguistics and in counseling, he brings a rich background in racial relations and cross-cultural counseling to the field of communication studies. He has taught at universities in Japan, the United States, and China. His previous publications include two books, *Japanese Non-Linear Discourse Style* and *Diplomatic Discourse: International Conflict at the United Nations* (with Michael H. Prosser), as well as articles on discourse analysis, cross-cultural images, perception, and intercultural training.